Mastering Framework II

Mastering Framework II™

Douglas Hergert
and
Jonathan Kamin

San Francisco • Paris • Düsseldorf • London

Cover design by Thomas Ingalls + Associates
Cover photography by Casey Cartwright
Book design by Lorrie Fink Graphic Design

ACKNOWLEDGMENTS

This book reflects the work of many people. We wish to thank them all for their contributions. We owe a great debt to Barbara Gordon, who edited the previous version of this book, *Mastering Framework;* Tanya Kucak, who edited the present version; David Kolodney, who managed the project; and Jeremy Elliott and Nick Wolfinger, who did a conscientious technical review of the manuscript.

Many people at the Forefront Corporation, developers of Framework II for Ashton-Tate, contributed in ways too numerous to mention. Suffice it to say that the present work would not exist without the help of Steve Aubrey, David Greene, Chris Kirkpatrick, Marilyn McMahon, Hal Schectman, Rich Strauss, and Dave Welch, who gave unstintingly of their time and expertise. Thanks also to Kent Irwin of Ashton-Tate, Rosemary Morrissey of IBM, and Joe Campbell, who gave us the benefit of his considerable knowledge of telecommunications.

Dr. R. S. Langer got the project started and Karl Ray took care of the squeaky wheels.

In addition, the following people contributed their skills and talents: Olivia Shinomoto and Dave Clark, word processing; Lorrie Fink, design and art; Brenda Walker, typesetting; Aidan Wylde and Gwenyth Swain, proofreading; Elizabeth Wilcox, production coordinator; Bret Rohmer, production manager. Our thanks to all.

TABLE OF CONTENTS

Introduction   xii

1 A First Look at Framework II   1

Overview   1
  Introduction   1
  The Elements of Framework II   7
  Framework II Components   28
  Saving Frames   42
  Printing Frames   45

Examples   45
  An Employee Database   46
  A Costing Spreadsheet   47
  A Promotional Flier   49

Exploring Further   49
  A DOS Frame   49
  The Library   52

Summary   54

2 Outlining   57

Overview   57
  Introduction   57
  Creating an Outline   58
  Changing the Outline   69
  Entering the Outline Frames   84
  Building an Outline from an Empty Frame   86
  Creating a Table of Contents   87
  Saving Outlines—Using the Disk Menu   88

Printing Outlines—Using the Print Menu 91

Examples 93
    Outlining the Promotional Flier 94
    Organizing Expense Spreadsheets into an Outline 95

Exploring Further 98
    Multi-Line Frame Labels 98
    Dragging and Sizing Frames 100
    Other Ways of Labeling Outline Components 101
    Displaying Disk Subdirectories in an Outline Form 103

Summary 104

3 Spreadsheets 107

Overview 107
    Introduction 107
    Creating a Spreadsheet 110
    Changing the Spreadsheet's Appearance 131
    Using the Spreadsheet 140
    Saving and Printing Spreadsheets 159
    Creating Graphs from a Spreadsheet 162

Examples 170
    Sales Comparisons by Activity 170
    A Table of Loan Payments 172
    Expense Spreadsheets, with a Summary 177

Exploring Further 183
    The Date Functions 183
    Sorting 184
    The Goto Command 185

Summary 186

4 Word Processing   189

Overview   189
   Introduction   189
   Creating a Word Frame   190
   Formatting Your Document   198
   Using a Word Frame   205
   Checking Your Spelling   214
   Saving Your Work   218
   Printing the Document   218

Examples   228
   Outlining an Invoice Form   228
   Printing and Saving the Invoice and Survey Outline   232

Exploring Further   235
   Storing Templates in the Library   235
   Page Breaks   236
   Printing Parts of Frames   238
   Special Effects in Headers and Footers   239
   Page Layout   241
   Printing a Frame to Disk   243
   Counting Your Words   244

Summary   244

5 Databases   249

Overview   249
   Introduction   249
   Creating a Database   253
   Using the Database   262
   Filtering the Database   277

Examples   285
   Creating an Inventory Database   285

Printing the Inventory Database   290
Filtering to Determine Inventory Reorder Times   291

Exploring Further   292
Using the Forms View of a Database   293
MailMerge Printing   297
Printing Mailing Labels   300
Using the dBASE View of a Database   301
Linking Spreadsheets with Database Frames   301

Summary   304

6 **Telecommunications**   307

Overview   307
Introduction   307
Telecommunications Basics   307
Basic Telecommunications Modes   310
Creating a Telecommunications Frame   313
Preparing Framework II for Telecommunications   315
Logging onto a Network   320
Transferring Files   327

Examples   334
Receiving a File through a Protocol Transfer   336
Logging onto a Bulletin Board   338
Using Answer Mode   340
Logging onto CompuServe   341

Exploring Further   342
Automatic Phone Dialing   343
Terminal Emulation   344
Hardwire Transfers   346

Summary   346

7 An Introduction to FRED Programming   349

Overview   349
    Introduction   349
    The Uses of the Library   354
    FRED Programming Functions   370
    Getting Help   376

Examples   378
    Computing "Attractive" Retail Prices   379

Exploring Further   381
    The Letters Program   381
    Creating a User-Defined Function   400

Summary   405

8 Working with Other Programs   409

Overview   409
    Introduction   409
    Converting Files   410
    More about DOS Access Frames   418
    Adding Applications to the Apps Menu   420

Examples   428
    Integrating the VisiCalc DIF File   430

Exploring Further   432
    Integrating a Columnar ASCII File into a Spreadsheet
      or Database   433
    Special Techniques for Comma-Delimited Files   434
    Exporting Columnar Data to a Word Processing Program   437
    Special Considerations in Exporting to Word Processors   437

Summary   438

Appendix A   Installing and Customizing Framework II   441

    Installing Framework II for the First Time   441

    Tailoring Framework II to Your Hardware   442

    Customizing the Desktop   447

    Installing Telecommunications Setups   448

    Miscellaneous Features   448

    Using RAM-Resident Software with Framework II   449

Appendix B   FRED Functions   451

    Introduction   451

    The Functions   454

Appendix C   Tables of ASCII Characters   493

    MS-DOS ASCII Displayable Characters   494

    MS-DOS ASCII Control Codes and Their Effects   498

    Index   500

INTRODUCTION

Framework II is an *integrated software package* that offers all of the most important personal computer applications in one coherent program.

With Framework II you can use your computer to perform all of the following tasks:

- Building spreadsheets of numbers

- Creating word processed documents

- Assembling and working with databases

- Producing graphs

- Communicating directly with other computers via modem and telephone lines

- Sharing data with other software packages

To tie these diverse elements together, Framework II supplies you with a tool called *outlining*. An outline can serve either of two essential functions in your work: you can use outlining to combine several different applications that you have already developed, creating a single integrated document from them; or you can use outlining as a way of planning and organizing a task that you have not yet begun.

On your computer's display screen Framework II provides you with a visual "desktop" on which all of your work will take place. You will create "frames" on the desktop to contain each different task that you undertake. Just as on a real desktop, you might find yourself working with many different documents at once in Framework II—spreadsheets, word processed texts, databases, and graphs.

To create and work with these documents, Framework II gives you a number of essential tools, all of which are easy to find and easy to use. Framework II is primarily a menu-driven program, which means that its main operations are displayed on the screen for you to examine and select. Choosing a menu option seldom requires more than two or three keystrokes.

But in addition to the menus, Framework II also supplies a set of ten frequently used operations that you access through the ten function keys on your keyboard. These function keys, along with the menu operations, give you complete control over the size, shape, and contents of the document frames that you place on the desktop.

One of the great advantages of Framework II is that all these menu and function-key operations work consistently throughout the program. Learn to use them for one kind of application, and you will almost instinctively be able to apply your knowledge to all the other kinds of Framework II documents.

Finally, Framework II includes a complete programming language, called FRED—a language designed to operate exclusively within the Framework II environment. FRED includes all the features and facilities of most other PC programming languages, like BASIC or Pascal. Yet FRED is in many ways even more powerful than these traditional languages, because it is designed to work along with all the tools included in Framework II itself. The powers of FRED programming can be exploited at many levels; new computer users and seasoned programmers alike will find themselves using aspects of FRED to increase the versatility of Framework II documents.

This book is designed to introduce you to both the mechanical details of operating Framework II and the kinds of business tasks you will be able to perform with the program. Chapter 1 gives you a broad look at all that Framework II can do; thereafter, each chapter of the book is devoted to one of Framework II's major functional applications: outlining, spreadsheet programming and graphing, word processing, database management, telecommunications, FRED programming, and working with other programs.

In this book you will learn about Framework II by studying examples of the program in action. Each of the many examples in this book is designed specifically to illustrate one or more of Framework II's features. The best place to read this book, then, is in front of your own computer, with Framework II running; the examples are presented as hands-on tutorials, for you to work through, step by step, on your computer.

Each chapter in this book is divided into four main sections: an overview, describing the details and the conceptual background of a given application area; a set of practical examples, demonstrating how the application might actually be put to work in a business environment; a section called "Exploring Further," which will help you expand and deepen your understanding of Framework II; and finally a summary.

The chapters are meant to be read in sequence, as each one builds upon the material of its predecessors. Following is a brief description of what you will find in each chapter.

Chapter 1: A First Look at Framework II. This chapter supplies a general introduction to the operational elements and the functional components of Framework II. You'll learn how Framework II makes use of your computer system's hardware, including the display screen, the keyboard, the disk drives, the printer, and the computer's internal memory, RAM. You'll also start to explore the practical significance of each of Framework II's major components: outlining, spreadsheet programming, graphing, word processing, database management, and telecommunications.

Chapter 2: Outlining. Here you will begin learning about outlining as an application and as a tool for integrating other applications. You'll find out how to create, expand, and modify an outline. You'll also discover how outlining can be used both for planning new projects or for pulling together a set of documents that you have already developed. Outlining never strays far from the center of our attention throughout this book.

Chapter 3: Spreadsheet Programming. In this chapter you'll learn how to create and work with tables of numbers within Spreadsheet frames. You'll find out how a spreadsheet is organized and how you can control its appearance and format. You'll learn how to write formulas to produce calculated values for spreadsheets, and then you'll learn how to *copy* formulas across rows and down columns of a spreadsheet. You'll also begin using FRED functions in this chapter; FRED will take on increasing importance from this point forward in the book. Finally, you'll discover how a spreadsheet can be used as a tool for exploring "what-if" scenarios.

Chapter 4: Word Processing. Framework II's word processing capabilities are elegantly simple to use, yet as powerful as many standalone word processing programs. This chapter will show you how to create, format, style, edit, save, and print a word processed document. In particular, you'll learn how to exploit the options of the Words menu, how to check your spelling, and how to print your documents in just the format you require. You'll also continue working with Framework II's outlining facility to combine Word frames with other kinds of frames, producing integrated documents.

Chapter 5: Databases. Database management is a carefully designed component of Framework II, not just an extra feature tacked onto a spreadsheet program. In this chapter you'll learn what a database is and how you can design and create your own databases in Framework II. You'll work through the essential database management operations: sorting, searching, replacing, appending records and fields, writing formulas to calculate field values, and "filtering" the database to display a selected subset of your data. You'll also discover Framework II's "Forms view" and "dBASE view" for databases, and you'll learn how these alternative views of the database can be used. Finally, you'll continue to expand your understanding of *integration;* here, you'll learn how to link a database with a spreadsheet, to increase the power of both, and how to link a database with a word processed document to create a form letter, or "mailmerge."

Chapter 6: Telecommunications. This chapter introduces Framework II's telecommunications component. It begins by explaining some of the terms and requirements of telecommunications. You'll learn how to use telecommunications to interact with a remote computer through a terminal, to send files from your disks or the desktop, to receive files directly on your disks, and to send and receive files using routines that test for accuracy in transmission. You'll also learn how to use the conveniences of Framework II's Telecommunications menu, to write files that store the information you need to link up with a particular remote computer, and to send files directly to another computer without the use of a modem.

Chapter 7: An Introduction to FRED Programming. This chapter describes the features of the FRED programming language, and offers some significant programming examples for you to examine and study. Even if you have never written a computer program before, this chapter will be worth your attention. You will learn about the features of Framework II's desktop Library, which allows you to write several kinds of programs that appeal even to beginners: macro programs, abbreviations, and assumptions. You'll also glimpse the expanded power that is available to you should you choose to become a FRED programmer. If you have already learned to program in some other language, this chapter will help you to translate your programming skills into practice with FRED. In particular, you'll want to focus on the complex programming examples at the end of the chapter.

Chapter 8: Working with Other Programs. This chapter explains the various ways to run other programs while using Framework II. You'll learn how to write a program to call another software package and how to install your program on Framework II's menu. You'll also learn about the other file formats that Framework II can read and write, and how to use them.

This book ends with several appendices. **Appendix A, Installing and Customizing Framework II**, will show you how to make Framework II run smoothly and efficiently on your particular computer system, and point you toward the many ways you can customize Framework II for your particular style of working. **Appendix B, FRED Functions**, provides a listing and brief explanation of all the FRED programming functions, with their syntax forms. **Appendix C, Tables of ASCII Characters**, lists the MS-DOS displayable characters and their ASCII codes, as well as the standard ASCII control codes.

If you are just getting started in Framework II, you may want to take a look at Appendix A, on configuring the program for your own computer system. However, on IBM PC equipment with two floppy disk drives, Framework II is essentially ready to run; you need not worry about working through complex configuration tasks. If you have a hard disk system, you will want to install Framework II on your hard disk before you use it. Appendix A will guide you. When you start Framework II on a hard disk system, you will see the screen shown in Figure I.1. Press the Return key, and you will soon find yourself looking at the Framework II desktop.

Although this book assumes a hard disk system, you can easily run Framework II on a computer with two floppy disk drives. Two of the seven disks supplied in the Framework II package are required to get Framework II running on your computer. To start Framework II on a system with two floppy drives, follow these steps:

1. Turn on your computer with your DOS disk in drive A, and set the correct date and time. Remove the DOS disk.

2. Place System Disk 1 in drive A, and a disk for your data files in drive B.

3. At the DOS prompt "A>" enter the command

   fw

4. After the program is loaded into your computer from System Disk 1, the screen shown in Figure I.1 will appear, with the additional message

   Please insert SYSTEM DISK 2 in DRIVE A:

   Remove System Disk 1 and place System Disk 2 in drive A.

5. Press the Return key, and the Framework II desktop will appear on your screen.

You are now ready to begin reading Chapter 1.

```
                    Framework II  Version 1.1

                    This Software is Licensed to:
                 Douglas Hergert, Jonathan Kamin
                       SYBEX Computer Books


       Copyright (c) Ashton-Tate 1984, 1985, 1986. All Rights Reserved.
        Framework II and FRED are trademarks and dBASE II, dBASE III
              and Framework are reg. trademarks of Ashton-Tate.

       You may use the software  and printed  materials in  the  Framework II
       package under the terms of the Software License Agreement; please read
       it.  In summary,  Ashton-Tate grants you a paid-up,  non-transferable,
       personal license to use Framework II on one computer work station. You
       do not become the owner of the  package nor  do you have  the right to
       copy (except permitted backups of  the software) or alter the  software
       or printed materials. You are legally accountable for any violation of
       the License Agreement and copyright, trademark, or trade secret law.


                    Press RETURN to assent to the License Agreement
                           and begin Framework II
```

Figure I.1: *The Opening Framework II Screen*

CHAPTER ONE

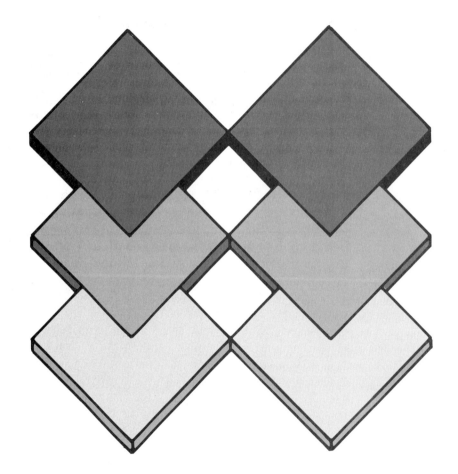

A FIRST LOOK AT

FRAMEWORK II

INTRODUCTION

Framework II is a multi-functioned, multi-layered personal computer program for business use. Within a single software environment, the program offers you tools for performing and organizing your work under some of the most important general categories of personal computer activity:

- ☐ Working with numbers
- ☐ Working with words
- ☐ Working with records of information
- ☐ Working with graphs
- ☐ Communicating with other computers

We refer to these activities as *spreadsheet programming, word processing, database management, business graphing,* and *telecommunications,* respectively.

Framework II is rich and complex enough to handle elaborate business tasks in all of these categories. At the same time, Framework II's design is simple, consistent, and intuitive. As a result, when you use Framework II, you will be able to concentrate on the business tasks at hand rather than on the intricacies of operating your computer.

This first chapter will introduce you to Framework II. Later chapters will present a sequenced, hands-on approach to learning the details of Framework II. In this first chapter you should not try to memorize anything, but rather acquire a general sense of Framework II's characteristics. You'll learn what the program can do for you and how you can best approach accomplishing jobs with it.

You'll also begin to see how Framework II operates on your computer. You'll examine the important features of the keyboard and the display screen, the functions of the disk drives and your printer, and the requirements Framework II imposes on your computer's internal memory (RAM).

Finally, you'll get a preview of the skills you'll develop and the capabilities you'll add to your computer repertoire as you master Framework II. We'll be looking at examples of each of the program's major capabilities. Here, briefly, are the activities we'll be studying:

1. *Working with numbers: spreadsheet programming.* A spreadsheet is a table of numbers and headings, organized in rows and columns. Framework II will help you create spreadsheets and work easily and flexibly with the numeric information that spreadsheets contain. You can perform simple arithmetic on that information, calculating totals and averages from the rows and columns of numbers. Or you can perform more complex tasks, choosing among the large set of statistical and financial functions that Framework II offers. If you change a number somewhere in the middle of a spreadsheet, Framework II automatically redoes all your arithmetic for you.

2. *Working with words: word processing.* You can use Framework II to prepare and store any kind of written documents, from short memos and letters to book-length projects. Framework II's word processing features give you flexible ways to create, edit, and revise your document, and then print it out on paper in just the format you choose.

3. *Working with records of information: database management.* Framework II will help you organize your personal or business record-keeping jobs. A list of addresses, a collection of information about your business clients, a personnel file, an inventory of parts or supplies—all of these are candidates for Framework II's data-handling facilities. You'll be able to create such records and then place them in any order. You can also revise records, delete records, add new records, and locate any record or group of records instantly.

4. *Working with graphs: business graphing.* Given a set of numbers that you have been working with—either in a spreadsheet or a database—Framework II can quickly create elaborate business graphs from those numbers. You can look at these graphs on your display screen, or you can print them on paper.

5. *Communicating with other computers: telecommunications.* Framework II includes a powerful, easy-to-use telecommunications function. If you have the necessary peripheral equipment, you can use it to send information from your computer to other computer users via telephone lines, receive information in a similar manner, gain access to information services and computerized bulletin boards, and communicate directly with mainframe computers.

(In addition, Framework II includes facilities to convert its files to the formats used by five popular programs—Lotus 1-2-3, WordStar, MultiMate, and the dBASE programs—as well as to two other widely used formats, and to convert its own files to any of these seven formats. Therefore, even if you work in an environment where your co-workers use other programs, you can be assured that you can share your files with many of them. See Chapter 8 for details.)

Framework II is called an *integrated software package* because it gives you tools for all of these activities, along with consistent ways of using and managing the program itself. Framework II also helps you to *combine* and *organize* these different elements of your computer work.

This is one of the advantages of an integrated package over stand-alone, single-function programs. Real-life jobs are seldom as clear-cut and distinct as words versus numbers or data versus graphs. More often we are required to combine different elements of our work, producing creatively integrated results.

For example, consider these typical business tasks:

- Inserting a spreadsheet table of sales statistics into a word processed memo you are writing to your regional sales managers.

- Finding the total current value from your inventory database, and moving that value to a financial spreadsheet you are preparing.

- Writing a word processed form letter and creating a personalized copy for each of the people listed in your database of business clients.

- Preparing a presentation-quality bar graph to summarize the financial data contained in a spreadsheet, and then incorporating both the spreadsheet and the graph into a word processed document you are preparing.

- Using an on-line information service to look up the recent performance of a stock on the New York Stock Exchange and graphing the statistics in a form that shows high, low, and closing prices.

Each of these jobs involves sharing information and mixing functions in ways that could be complex, time consuming, or just plain messy without the benefit of a good integrated software package. With Framework II you'll learn to manage all these jobs efficiently, letting your computer work out the mechanical details while you concentrate on the more creative and interesting parts of your work.

Finally, along with its major productivity components—spreadsheet programming, word processing, database management, business graphing, and telecommunications—Framework II also gives you a special tool to organize all of the work that you accomplish under its auspices. This tool takes the form of another of Framework II's working components: *outlining*. We'll explore outlining in detail in Chapter 2, but in fact the outlining facility is so essential to the character of Framework II that we'll see examples of its use throughout this book. As we set out to look specifically at the elements of Framework II, we should begin by discussing the significance of outlining.

DIVIDING YOUR WORK INTO PARTS . . .
AND PUTTING IT BACK TOGETHER

A simple but essential piece of practical philosophy lies behind the design of the Framework II program:

> People work most effectively when they can divide
> large jobs into smaller, interrelated tasks, which they
> can then accomplish one at a time.

Whether you are working with words, numbers, data, graphs, or some combination of these elements, Framework II encourages you to work in small, manageable components. After all the components are complete, you can go back and organize them into a coherent whole.

Two essential elements of the Framework II program—frames and outlines—will lead you naturally toward this approach:

1. *Frames.* For every job you perform in Framework II—whether it involves spreadsheet programming, word processing, database management, business graphing, or telecommunications—you will always begin by creating a *frame* for the job. A frame is simply an area on your display screen that represents, and contains, a specific kind of work. You may find yourself with many frames on the screen at once, but generally you will work with just one frame at a time.

2. *Outlines.* Whenever you need to establish a relationship among several frames you have created, you can put those frames in an outline. An outline imposes a hierarchy on the diverse elements of a large job, and it also gives you a practical way of handling many frames at once.

Let's consider a short example that illustrates this approach. At the end of a given tax year, you decide that you need to gather data about your financial activities over the year, so that you can estimate your tax liability. On the surface you think the job should be simple: Determine your total income for the year, subtract business expenses and deductions, and look up the tax you owe on the remainder. But upon closer examination, you see that the picture is more complex. Several kinds of income, expenses, and deductions come into play, each of which will have to be tallied up on its own.

You begin creating spreadsheets for a number of different calculations. These spreadsheets include the following elements:

> Business income
> Interest income
> Business expenses
> Depreciation expenses
> Interest deductions
> Charitable contributions
> Deductible professional fees
> Deductions for state and local taxes

Each of these spreadsheets covers a single aspect of your financial picture for the year; you work on each of them individually, producing a "bottom-line" total in each category. Finally, you need some way to bring all this information together to come up with a figure for your actual taxable income.

In Framework II, each of these small spreadsheets would be contained within its own individual frame. To bring the frames together, you could create an outline like the following:

> Taxes—1984
> > Income
> > > Business
> > > Interest
> > Expenses
> > > Business
> > > Depreciation
> > Itemized Deductions
> > > Interest
> > > Charitable Contributions
> > > Professional Fees
> > Taxable Income

The lowest-level headings in this outline all represent the spreadsheets that contain your financial information. The final spreadsheet,

"Taxable Income," will take bottom-line information from all the other spreadsheets to show you your taxable income.

Framework II actually allows you to use outlining in two different ways:

- You can begin by creating an assortment of spreadsheets, word processed texts, databases, and graphs, each contained within its own frame. When you are ready to organize these diverse elements of your work, you can create an Outline frame and move the work frames into the outline.

- Or you can begin by creating an outline of your work, and then filling in the details in individual frames beneath your outline headings.

In the tax example we chose the first approach, beginning with a series of spreadsheets and then using an outline to impose an order on them. Let's look at an example of the other approach.

As the sales executive of a national retail firm, it is your job to keep in touch with the regional sales managers. At the end of the current quarter, you are planning to write a memo to the regional managers to let them know how the company is doing and how each region is doing. Your memo will be a combination of text, spreadsheets, and graphs. Before you begin writing the memo, you decide to create an outline of all the information it will contain:

```
Memo to Regional Managers
    The Big Picture
        The Company's Sales this Quarter (text)
        Quarterly Sales (spreadsheet)
        Illustration of Quarterly Sales (graph)
    The Regional Picture
        From the Best to the Worst (text)
        Comparative Quarterly Sales (spreadsheet)
        Illustrated by Region (graph)
    The Sales People
        The Best (text)
        Bonus Calculations (spreadsheet)
        Illustrated by Sales Person (graph)
```

When you create an outline like this one in Framework II, each low-level heading in the outline (that is, each heading that does not contain subheadings of its own) represents a frame for you to work in. And, as we have seen, each working frame can contain any one of the following:

- Word processed text
- A spreadsheet

    □ A database

    □ A graph

    □ An outline

In summary, outlining is a special element that helps you organize all the work you do in Framework II. An outline consists of headings and subheadings, each of which can in turn represent a frame for part of the work you are actually performing—work in any one of the functional categories that Framework II offers you. Now let's begin looking at Framework II on your computer.

THE ELEMENTS OF FRAMEWORK II

Like all computer programs, Framework II has its own distinctive appearance on your display screen. The program also makes use of your keyboard for its own special purposes; its keyboard functions are different from those of any other program you may be familiar with. Fortunately, though, the display screen and keyboard are designed to work consistently throughout all the Framework II components. Once you have become familiar with the way the program presents itself to you on the screen—and with the way you control the program's functions from the keyboard—you will learn to rely on the program's logical consistency as you move from one kind of work to another.

This consistency is another one of the advantages of working with an integrated software package like Framework II. You can do all your work in one unified software environment, without having to deal with the different syntax and command structure of differently designed programs.

In this section we'll study how Framework II uses your IBM Personal Computer. (If you use one of the IBM PC compatibles, you may find some minor differences between the details we discuss here and the actual workings of your computer.) Starting with the display screen and the keyboard and then moving on to the other components of your computer, we'll examine the way Framework II makes use of the resources of your computer hardware.

THE DISPLAY SCREEN

Figure 1.1 shows how Framework II appears when you first begin running the program on your computer. The screen consists of a number of distinct areas. Framework II uses these areas for displaying your current work or for displaying certain messages to you during your work. Each of these areas has a name that describes its function in Framework II:

□ The desktop

□ The menu line

□ The clock

□ The status panel

□ The message area

You don't need to remember the names of these areas, but after a little experience in running Framework II you'll get used to looking in certain areas of the screen for the particular information you need.

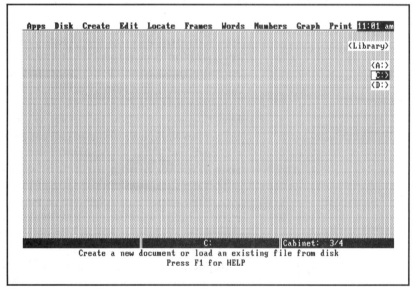

Figure 1.1: *The Opening Framework II Screen*

► **THE DESKTOP**

The *desktop* takes up the bulk of the display screen. On a monochrome screen the desktop has a background of light vertical stripes; on a color screen the desktop has a textured background. The desktop is where most of your work in Framework II will take place. Whenever you create a frame or retrieve a frame from disk, it will appear on the desktop, where you can examine its contents and work with it. You will learn that this metaphoric desktop gives you the same kind of flexibility that your real-life desktop does for arranging your work in just the way that suits you:

- You can increase or decrease the number of frames that are on the desktop at a given time.
- You can put frames aside in "trays" on the desktop, where they'll still be available to you but out of the way of your other work.
- You can "drag" frames around to different areas of the desktop, so that you can look at more than one frame at once.
- You can increase or decrease the size of a frame, so that you can see more or less of the frame's contents.
- You can move your work frames into an Outline frame so that you can establish a relationship between different elements of your work.

We'll be looking at the keyboard functions that allow you to perform all of these desktop feats. Meanwhile, for a preview of what a working desktop might look like, Figure 1.2 shows you three different frames—a Word frame, a Spreadsheet frame, and a Graph frame—all arranged on the desktop for viewing at once. You can see that these frames overlap and have been set at different sizes. Figure 1.3 shows the same three frames placed in their respective "trays" at the lower-right corner of the desktop. We say that a frame is *closed* when it is put away in its tray and *open* when it is displayed on the desktop. Shifting a frame between the desktop and its tray requires only a single keystroke from you.

Near the upper-right corner of the desktop reside the trays of some very special frames, which you will be using constantly. These frames are called *file cabinets*. There are two types. Each cabinet of the first type is devoted to a single disk drive, so you have as many cabinets of this type as you have drives. The second type is actually a unique cabinet called the *Library cabinet*. The disk drive cabinets display the names of the disk drives. In Figure 1.3, they display the names

<A:>
<C:>

and

<D:>

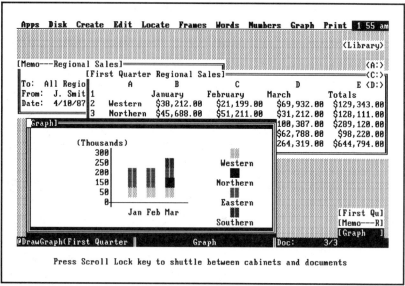

Figure 1.2: *Three Frames on the Desktop*

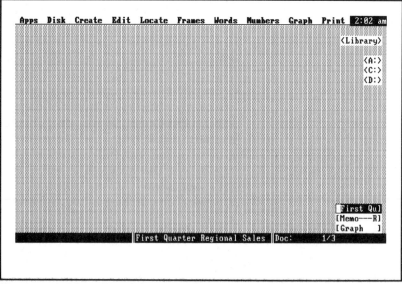

Figure 1.3: *Three Closed Frames in Their Trays*

but the names will vary depending on the number and kind of drives your computer has.

Although Framework II can be used on a computer with two floppy disk drives, its large size—it uses four program disks, plus a fifth for special files to tailor Framework II to your computer—makes it cumbersome to use without a hard disk. If you do use two floppy disk drives, the one on the left (or the top) is named A and the one on the right (or the bottom) is B. (Disk drive names are usually followed by a colon, as shown in the illustration.) In a system with two floppy disk drives, you'll usually keep one of the Framework II program disks in drive A, and you'll use drive B to save the information you create.

If you use a hard disk, it is probably named C. To keep track of your Framework II program files, you should create a special *subdirectory* for the program. You may also want to create subdirectories for those files you originate using Framework II, as well as for any other programs you use. If you use a hard disk and you are not familiar with subdirectories, consult your DOS manual.

Any other disk drives you may use—external hard drives, hard disk cards, or RAM disks—will also have their own file cabinets. The system represented in Figure 1.3 has a single floppy disk drive called A, a hard disk drive called C, and a RAM disk called D. When you save a frame on the desktop to a disk, it becomes a *file*. You can save a frame onto disk or read a file from the disk at any time.

When you open one of the disk drive cabinets, the frame will show a directory of the disk. If you use subdirectories, the directory displayed will be the current subdirectory. You can see a sample disk directory of drive C in Figure 1.4. We'll discuss disks, drives, and directories more later in this chapter.

The Library cabinet is a place to store various types of files that you always want to have available for immediate use. It is designed to make using Framework II speedy and effortless. We'll look into the Library cabinet later in this chapter as well.

► **THE MENU LINE**

Just above the desktop, on the top line of your display screen, appear a series of ten words:

Apps Disk Create Edit Locate Frames Words Numbers Graph Print

These words represent Framework II's main *menu*. Just like a menu in a restaurant, a program menu gives you a series of options. Framework II's menu has ten main options, represented by the ten words in the menu

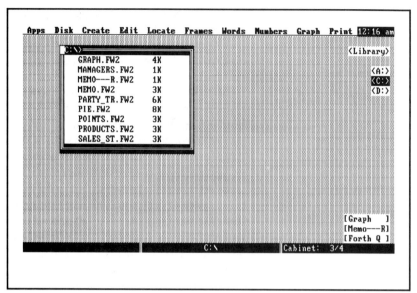

Figure 1.4: *A Disk Directory Frame*

line. These options allow you to control, modify, and work with the frames you create.

We'll postpone looking at these options until we know a little more about Framework II; but if you think you can guess what most of the options do, you're probably right. Framework II's intuitive design often allows you to accomplish tasks with a minimum of previous knowledge about how the program works.

► THE CLOCK

Just to the right of the menu is Framework II's clock. The display on this clock changes every minute, and the colon between the numbers blinks every second. Framework II takes the time from the computer's system clock and displays it on the screen for you. From time to time the clock may stop—for example, when you are performing disk operations (saving frames on disk or reading files from disk). But when the operation is complete, the clock will start up again at the correct time.

Of course, the time displayed on the Framework II clock depends on your setting the time correctly when you first turn on your computer. If you fail to set the time, or if you set it incorrectly, Framework II's clock will not display the right time. If your system does not have a clock that sets the time for you automatically, you should get in the habit of setting the correct time each time you turn on your computer to use Framework II.

► **THE STATUS PANEL**

Directing your attention down the display screen, you can see that there are two areas of information located below the desktop. The single reverse-video line directly below the desktop is called the *status panel.* This line is divided into three parts, and it always displays certain information about the frame you have selected for your current work. You can see in Figure 1.1 that the disk drive cabinet, C, is the current frame selection. The name of the frame is displayed in the center section of the status panel. The section on the right tells you that C is the third of four cabinets:

Cabinet: 3/4

When we look in more detail at the structure of a frame, we'll find out more about this status panel.

► **THE MESSAGE AREA**

Below the status panel is the message area. This area of your display screen has two lines: the *edit line* and the *message line.*

When you enter a value into a frame or choose to edit a value that is already in a frame, the value will first appear on the edit line. As you enter keystrokes to change the value itself, the changes will occur on the edit line, and will also be reflected in the original location.

Below the edit line, on the bottom line of your display screen, is Framework II's message line. Framework II reserves this area to display special information. The information in the message line is always relevant to your current activity in Framework II. The message may concern something you are about to do, something you have just done, or some action that is available to you at a given turn in the program.

For example, as you prepare to select activities from Framework II's menu, the message line will explain briefly what action a given menu choice will perform. Or, if you hit one or more keystrokes that Framework II doesn't know what to do with at a given point, the message line will display some sort of *error message.* Often Framework II will also beep when an error occurs, so you will know to check the message line to see what has happened.

Your understanding of Framework II's display screen organization will increase as you begin using the program. There is very little about the display screen that you need to memorize; most of the time you will simply get into the habit of looking in a certain area of the screen for the information you want.

We have already seen some frames displayed on the desktop; before we begin mastering the Framework II keyboard, we should pause to examine the structure of a frame.

WORK FRAMES

You know by now that Framework II lets you create frames for any of six types of activities:

1. Spreadsheet frames, for working with numbers
2. Word frames, for word processing
3. Database frames, for database management
4. Graph frames, for displaying graphs
5. Telecommunications frames, for sharing data with other computers
6. Outline frames, for organizing your work and grouping other frames together

Even though frames for different activities look quite different on the screen, all of the frames you create in Framework II have certain elements in common. Every frame has four distinct parts:

- A border
- A label (or name)
- A contents area
- A programming area behind the frame

Figure 1.5 shows a Spreadsheet frame that has just been created. The spreadsheet is empty: it doesn't yet have any values entered into its rows and columns. We'll use this figure to discuss the four structural parts of a frame.

► THE BORDER

The border of a frame is represented by the thin double lines that surround the rectangular frame area. When you *select* a frame for your current work, the border is filled in with a thick reverse-video rectangle.

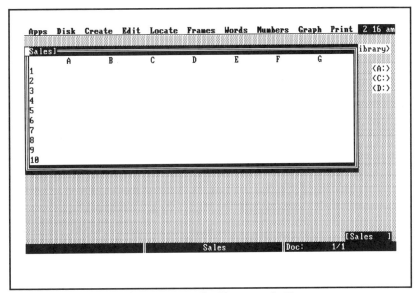

Figure 1.5: *A Spreadsheet Frame—The Elements of a Frame*

This is called the *highlight.* You can see that the frame in Figure 1.5 has been selected for some activity.

Another visual indicator that Framework II gives you to let you know where you are currently working on the screen is the *cursor.* The cursor is a small rectangle that takes up the space of one character on the screen. In Figure 1.5 you can see the cursor at the upper-left corner of the Spreadsheet frame's border.

What you can't see on a printed page—but will notice right away on the screen—is that the cursor constantly flashes on and off. This makes it easy for you to find your current location on a crowded desktop. When the cursor and the highlight are located on the border of a frame that you have selected, you can perform any Framework II action that affects the frame as a whole. For example, you can drag the frame to a new location on the desktop, move the frame into an outline, change the display size of the frame, or save the frame as a disk file.

► **THE LABEL**

At the upper-left corner of every frame's border is a space, enclosed in square brackets, which is reserved for a frame label. A label is simply a name that you supply for a frame you have created. In Figure 1.5, you can see that the name "Sales" has been given to this Spreadsheet frame.

Notice that the same name also appears in the frame's tray at the lower-right corner of the desktop. (The central portion of the status panel also displays the label of the currently selected frame.)

Frame labels are important for a number of reasons. First, they allow you to identify, with names that you yourself assign, each frame that you create and work with. Second, when you save a frame onto disk, the disk file in which you save your work will take the name that you have assigned to the desktop frame. For this reason, you cannot save a frame until you have given it a name.

Finally, as you advance in your knowledge of Framework II, you'll discover all sorts of activities that link different frames together or establish relationships between frames. These activities often depend on the ability to refer to a frame by name.

► **THE CONTENTS AREA**

The visible area *inside* a frame is, of course, reserved for the frame's contents—that is, the main work that you have created the frame for. The contents of frames will be at the center of our attention throughout this book. Each type of frame—Spreadsheet, Word, Database, Graph, Telecommunications, and Outline—has its own distinctive inner organization, designed specifically to meet the requirements of a specific kind of work. You can see, for example, that the contents of the three frames in Figure 1.2 are organized in quite different ways. You'll quickly learn to recognize the different frame types by their appearance.

► **THE PROGRAMMING AREA**

Every frame has yet another area that is normally out of view. This area, which we say is located *behind* the frame, is reserved for special programming activities. In accomplishing most tasks in Framework II your use of this area is completely optional; still, you should be aware that the area exists. Behind every frame is an area reserved for you to write a formula or a program.

For advanced users, Framework II includes a complete programming language that can control and expand the capabilities of the Framework II program. If you have ever worked in BASIC on your computer, you know that a programming language consists of a large set of commands that your computer can perform. You can write and store a series of such commands—called a *program*—that will perform a planned sequence of actions on the computer.

Framework II's programming language is called FRED (an acronym for Frames Editor). We'll be dealing with FRED from time to time, on a rather casual basis, throughout this book. When these occasions arise, you'll be reminded about the programming area behind frames. Chapter 7 will also give you a quick introduction to the rules and capabilities of FRED. For now, simply remember that a FRED program can reside behind any frame.

In summary, the visible and most active elements of a frame are its border, its label, and its contents. In order to work with frames, you have to learn to use the keys on your keyboard that control the movement of Framework II's cursor and highlight from one point to another. (Remember, the cursor and the highlight indicate the location of your current work on the desktop.) You can move the cursor and the highlight in a number of different ways, to select frames and to select a working location inside a frame. In the next section we'll discuss the keys that allow you to move from one place to another on the desktop. Throughout the remainder of this chapter, we'll use the terms *cursor* and *highlight* more or less synonymously. Just remember that both of these visual markers show you where you are working on the display screen. Starting with Chapter 2, we'll begin to distinguish more carefully between their respective functions.

THE FRAMEWORK II KEYBOARD

If you've used other programs on your PC, you know that your keyboard is divided roughly into three areas. The largest area, in the center, works pretty much like the keyboard of a typewriter. The letters, the digits, and an assortment of punctuation marks are all located where you would expect to find them on a typewriter.

At the right side of the keyboard is a number pad, which also serves as the *cursor-control area.* And at the left side of the keyboard are two columns of *function keys,* labeled F1 to F10. (As you move from one program to another on your PC, these function keys tend to be the most elusive of all, because they are usually designed to offer completely different functions in each program you use.)

The cursor-control keys and the ten function keys, along with several other important keys located on either side of the alphabetic keys, are all essential to the design of Framework II. They give you a rich array of functions you cannot do without. They also make Framework II easier to use than many other programs of equal complexity. If you compare Framework II to other integrated packages, you will find that Framework II's menu—represented by the ten words above the desktop—is remarkably concise and simple. One of the reasons for this is that Framework II has moved so many control functions directly to the keyboard.

► **THE CURSOR-MOVEMENT KEYS**

The number pad at the right side of the keyboard works in two different ways. It can give you an alternative way of entering numbers into your computer, or it can give you ways of controlling the movement of the cursor on the display screen. The key that shifts the number pad between these two modes of operation is labeled "NumLock."

We call NumLock a *toggle key* because it toggles a part of the keyboard back and forth between two different modes. When you press NumLock in Framework II, you will see a small message appear at the far right side of the status panel:

NUM

This means that the right side of the keyboard has been shifted into its number-pad mode. You can use it for ten-key numeric data entry. Press the NumLock key again, and the NUM message disappears from the screen. Now the right side of the keyboard is available for cursor-movement functions.

Usually you will use the right side of the keyboard for cursor movement in Framework II. Whenever Framework II does not respond to the keyboard in the way you were expecting, always check to see if you have inadvertently pressed the NumLock key, toggling the keyboard into the wrong mode.

Table 1.1 summarizes the basic cursor-movement keys. (To use them, make sure the NUM message is *not* showing on your screen.) Framework II gives its own special names to these keys. To help you remember the names and functions of these keys, the Framework II package includes two plastic templates that you can place on your keyboard. One of the templates fits over the function keys (at the left side of the keyboard), reminding you what the F1 to F10 keys do in Framework II. The other template can be glued onto the flat area at the top of your keyboard, just above the number pad. This second template describes the cursor- and highlight-movement keys.

Keyboard Name	Framework II Name	Description
–	Up Level	Moves the cursor and the highlight from the contents area of a frame to the border of the same frame.
+	Down Level	Moves the cursor and the highlight from the border of a selected frame to the contents area of the frame.
⏎	Return	Opens a frame that is in its tray, or puts an open frame back in its tray.
Scroll Lock	Shuttle	Moves the cursor between the desktop frames and the disk drive cabinets.
Ins	Instruct	Selects the Framework II menu, allowing you to select one of the menu's activities.
Del	Delete	Deletes frames from the desktop, files from the disk directory, or words, numbers, or data from the contents of a frame.
NumLock	NumLock	Toggles the keyboard between number-pad mode and cursor-movement mode.
The arrow keys (↑, ↓, ←, →)		On the desktop, these keys move your selection from one frame to another.

Table 1.1: The Cursor- and Highlight-Movement Keys

As you study Table 1.1, notice the different kinds of cursor and high-light movement that are possible:

□ Between a frame's border and its contents (the Up Level [–] and Down Level [+] keys)

□ Between desktop work frames and the disk drive cabinets (the Shuttle [Scroll Lock] key)

□ Between one frame and another on the desktop (the arrow keys)

□ From the desktop to the menu (the Instruct key)

In addition, the Ctrl key, when used in conjunction with the cursor-movement keys, can amplify the cursor movements. We'll talk about these extended effects as they become relevant in different types of frames.

Also note the role of the Return key in handling frames. The Return key opens and closes a frame. If a frame is in its tray, at the side of the desktop, you can select the tray and press the Return key to open the frame onto the desktop. Likewise, you can close a frame—returning it to its tray—by positioning the cursor on the frame's border and pressing the Return key again. In this sense, Return is a toggle key for opening and closing frames.

Be prepared to learn about other uses for the Return key in Framework II. In different contexts, this important key does different things.

The keys at the right side of your keyboard are used so frequently in Framework II that they will quickly become second nature to you. You'll practice using them in exercises throughout this book.

► THE FUNCTION KEYS

The function keys, F1 to F10, help you work with frames in some important ways. We'll be studying their use as we need them. If you want a preview of what they do, Table 1.2 provides a summary.

One function key that you should learn about right away is the Help key, F1. You can press the Help key at any point during your work, and Framework II will quickly put you into its "on-line help" facility. This facility consists of an extensive series of help screens that describe in detail the entire Framework II program. When you press the Help key, Framework II first determines the nature of your current work. Then it places you at exactly the help screen that applies to the activity you are involved in. (In the words of the Framework II documentation, help is "context sensitive." This means that Framework II determines what kind of help you need from the context of your current activity.) If you are in

Keyboard Name	Framework II Name	Description
F1	Help	Supplies you with a help screen that describes your current Framework II activity.
F2	Edit	Allows you to create or edit a formula or program that resides behind a frame.
F3	Drag	Lets you move a frame from one place to another on the desktop.
F4	Size	Lets you increase or decrease the visible portion of a frame on the desktop.
F5	Recalc	Recalculates a frame or the formula behind a frame.
F6	Extend Select	Allows you to select a group of frames or data as the object of a subsequent action.
F7	Move	Allows you to move frames or data from one place to another.
F8	Copy	Allows you to copy frames or data from one place to another.
F9	Zoom	Enlarges your view of a selected frame to take up the entire display screen.
F10	View	Toggles between Outline view and Frames view.

Table 1.2: The Framework II Function Keys

the menu and you press the Help key (F1), Framework II will show you a help screen that describes the menu option you were about to select.

The Escape key (labeled Esc, at the upper-left corner of your keyboard) gets you out of the help facility and back to your work on the desktop. You should get into the habit of pressing the Help key (F1) whenever you have a question about Framework II.

Like the function keys, the full power of Framework II's menu comes into focus only after you have begun creating frames in each working category. We'll investigate the menu in a preliminary way now, filling in many of the details in subsequent chapters.

FRAMEWORK II'S MENU

As we have already seen, the menu is displayed as a group of ten words at the top of your screen. Each of these words represents a set of options you can select for working with frames or the contents of frames. When you select one of the ten words, you are presented with a *submenu* of still more selections. Through this hierarchy of menu selections, Framework II presents you with an elaborate yet simple-to-use set of options for accessing the program's control functions.

Table 1.3 summarizes, in general terms, some of the most elementary menu operations. This summary is by no means a complete description of the menu; each submenu option has several operations that you'll probably find yourself using all the time, and others that you'll use only rarely.

As we have seen, the key that puts you into the menu is the Instruct key, labeled Ins on your keyboard. (You press this key to "instruct" Framework II what to do next. Most programs call Ins the *Insert* key.) When you press the Ins key, Framework II immediately displays the submenu for one of the ten menu options at the top of the screen. For example, Figure 1.6 shows the submenu for the Create option.

Once you have pressed the Instruct key to select the menu, you can use the ← and → keys to move from one menu option to the next. Each time you press an arrow key, a new submenu will be displayed on the screen, below the corresponding menu option.

When you have reached the menu option that you wish to work from, you can use the ↑ and ↓ keys to move within the submenu. The cursor and highlight will show you the current selection in the submenu. To choose an option in a submenu, you position the cursor appropriately and press the Return key. This tells Framework II to act on your selection.

Let's look at an example of using the menu, keystroke by keystroke. Say you want to create a new Spreadsheet frame, like the one shown in

Menu Option	Description
Apps	Controls telecommunications and spelling check. Also allows you to run other programs directly from the desktop.
Disk	Reads files from disk and stores frames onto disk. Gives you access to submenus through which you can read files created by other programs into Framework II, or convert Framework II files into formats that other programs can read. Also provides a way to quit Framework II and return to DOS.
Create	Creates new Outline, Word, Spreadsheet, or Database frames. Allows you to specify the dimensions of a Spreadsheet or Database frame before you create it. Also allows you to add new rows or columns to a current Spreadsheet frame, or new records or fields to a current Database frame. In addition, permits you to record a series of keystrokes as a *keyboard macro*, which you assign to a specific key to be pressed in combination with the Alt key, to be played back at any time, or to which you give an abbreviation, which Framework II will replace with your keystrokes.
Edit	Potentially undoes the most recent Framework II action (for example, an inadvertent deletion). Deletes columns or rows from a Spreadsheet frame, records or fields from a Database frame. Allows you to protect selected frames or contents from editing.
Locate	Provides three important functions for all types of frames: sorting (i.e., arranging data in alphabetical or numeric order), searching (i.e., looking for a certain sequence of data within a frame), and search and replace (i.e., replacing instances of a certain value with a new value, either selectively or throughout a frame).

Table 1.3: A Summary of the Framework II Menu

Menu Option	Description
Frames	Works on the appearance of frames on the desktop; particularly valuable for setting the format of an Outline frame.
Words	Controls the style and format of text in Word frames and other frames. Boldface and italics are examples of styles. Right justification and centering are examples of formatting.
Numbers	Offers you a range of number styles for Spreadsheet and Database frames—for example, currency, percent, scientific.
Graph	Allows you to create a graph from a selected set of numbers in a Spreadsheet or Database frame. Offers an assortment of bar, pie, line, and point graphs, plus options for determining how they will be created.
Print	Sends a selected frame to the printer to produce a hard copy. Determines the layout of the printed page.

Table 1.3 (continued): A Summary of the Framework II Menu

Figure 1.5. Here is the sequence of keystrokes you will follow:

Instruct	(to get into the menu)
→	(to move to the Create option)
↓	(to position the cursor over the Spreadsheet option)
Return	(to select the Spreadsheet option)

In response to this sequence, Framework II will create a new Spreadsheet frame for you and place it on the desktop.

You may have to press each of the arrow keys more than once to move the highlight to the correct options. When you enter the menu for the very first time during a given session with Framework II, the Instruct key places you in the second submenu, the Disk option. But subsequently, each time you press the Instruct key to go to the menu, Framework II will return you to the menu option that you chose during your *previous* menu

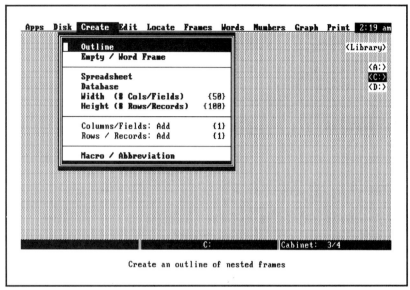

Figure 1.6: *The Create Submenu*

activity. You can always use the → and ← keys to move to a new menu option, and the ↑ and ↓ keys to move to a specific submenu option.

Once you get used to the menu and learn about the most commonly used options inside each submenu, you'll be able to use a faster technique for making menu selections, one that bypasses both the menus and the cursor-movement keys. The technique is to use the Ctrl key (called the *Control* key) along with the first letter of the option you wish to select. The Ctrl key works just like the shift keys on a typewriter. You have to hold it down along with a second key for it to have any special effect.

To indicate that you have to press the Ctrl key and another key concurrently, we often use a special hyphenated notation in print. For example, the following notation means, "Hold down the Ctrl key and press the C key":

Ctrl-C

Let's say that you want to create a new Spreadsheet frame, this time using the faster keyboard technique. Here are the keystrokes necessary for the operation:

Ctrl-C   (to open the Create submenu)

S   (to select the Spreadsheet option)

That's all. The Spreadsheet frame will be created for you, just as before. You don't even need to pause to look at the Create submenu when it comes onto the screen. The operation will be accomplished as soon as you press the S key.

You may not want to use this faster technique at the beginning. Sometimes it can be more reassuring to examine the menu carefully before you select an option. But as you become more adept with Framework II, keep in mind that this technique is available.

Before reading further, you should look through the entire Framework II menu on your own screen and compare the menu options with the summarized descriptions in Table 1.3. You can see that some of the options will interest us primarily in the context of one specific type of frame, while other options have a more general applicability.

Conveniently, Framework II has a way of telling you at any point in your work precisely which menu options can be used. The options in a given submenu that are applicable to your current work will always appear in a high-intensity text on the display screen, while the options that do not apply—and which you cannot choose—will appear in normal intensity. (On a color monitor the options that are applicable to your current work appear in normal type, while the options that do not apply are italicized.)

Now that we have discussed the features of Framework II's desktop, the elements consistent to each working frame, the cursor-movement and function keys, and the Framework II menu, we need to take a brief look at Framework II's use of your computer's hardware.

HARDWARE CONSIDERATIONS

There are many ways in which you can put together a complete computer system around the PC. Here are just a few of the variables:

- ☐ The amount of internal memory (RAM) in your computer
- ☐ The kind of display device attached
- ☐ The kind of printer you have
- ☐ The kind and number of disk drives you have

In general, Framework II does a good job of adjusting itself to whatever hardware configuration it finds itself in. But if you are preparing to do extensive work with Framework II, or if you are planning to buy a computer system specifically for running Framework II, there are a few considerations you should keep in mind.

► **MEMORY**

One of the most important hardware resources for running Framework II is memory. As PCs with large amounts of memory have become commonplace, a new generation of software products, including Framework II, have appeared that require such memory. The minimum recommended memory for Framework II is 512K; however, it operates more efficiently with 640K. Moreover, if you have a Personal Computer AT with expanded memory (more than 640K), or an extended memory board that meets the Lotus-Intel-Microsoft standard, Framework II can be customized so that it uses this type of memory as well.

We have discussed ways in which you might establish relationships between frames in Framework II. This includes exchanging data between frames, creating graphs from Spreadsheet and Database frames, and grouping several frames together under one outline. In order to perform any of these feats, all of the frames involved have to be present on the desktop, not just stored on disk. Because each frame on the desktop takes up some of your computer's RAM, you can see that the more elaborate a system of frames you plan to create, the more memory you will need.

► **DISPLAY SCREEN**

For your display screen, you can choose either a monochrome or a color monitor for Framework II, and with either one you can be assured of enjoying the full range of the program's capabilities. Framework II can create business graphs on either kind of screen, using any of the major IBM or non-IBM display adapter cards. (Some other major integrated packages can display graphs only in a high-resolution graphics environment. Graphs in these programs are not available on a monochrome monitor that is controlled by an IBM monochrome display card.)

On a color monitor, Framework II will give you high-resolution, color graphs, just as you would expect. On a monochrome monitor, Framework II creates graphs out of the special graphics characters that are available in the high range of the IBM PC's character set. Each of these graphics characters takes up the space of one normal character on the screen, but they can be used in groups to build interesting graphics effects. This works just fine for bar graphs and point graphs. A pie chart is a bit more of a problem, but even so, Framework II makes a valiant attempt.

► **PRINTER**

When you get ready to send text, numbers, and graphs to your printer, Framework II is once again ready to adjust as necessary to the hardware you own. Graphics will be printed to the extent of the resolution possible on your printer. (On a daisywheel printer, Framework II selects convenient characters to build graphs with. For example, the H character may be used to build bar graphs.)

Most printers use special sets of control codes to switch into particular printing modes (condensed print, for example). When you give Framework II the information that it needs about your printer, the program lets you select most of these printing modes from a menu. In addition, there is a function that will allow you to send any printing codes that do not appear on the menu, so that you can make full use of your printer. We will discuss printing in Chapter 4, "Word Processing."

In summary, Framework II's flexibility extends not only to your work on the desktop, but also to the hardware devices you have attached to your computer.

So far we have concentrated on the appearance and the characteristics of Framework II rather than on the actual kinds of work you can accomplish with the program. Let's now explore in a more concrete way the meaning of the major Framework II components: outlining, spreadsheet programming, graphing, word processing, database management, and telecommunications.

FRAMEWORK II COMPONENTS

In this section we'll see what the different types of frames look like, and we'll explore some of the specific features that Framework II offers in each of its functional categories.

OUTLINING

As we have already discussed, outlining can serve two quite different roles in your work with frames:

1. You can create a complete outline of a project before you actually begin doing any of the work.

2. You can create a series of frames, work on their contents, and then establish a logical relationship among the frames by placing them all in an outline.

To accommodate these two different approaches to outlining, Framework II's menu gives you two ways to establish an Outline frame.

The first way is to choose the Outline option in the Create submenu. In response, Framework II creates a frame that looks like the one in Figure 1.7. This frame contains a kind of template for an outline. The template has room for three major outline headings, numbered 1 to 3. Each heading in turn has three subheadings, numbered 1.1, 1.2, 1.3, and so on.

```
1
    1.1
    1.2
    1.3
```

These are all Empty frames. An Empty frame is available to you for word processing. This means that each of these three subheadings contains three Word frames that you can work with.

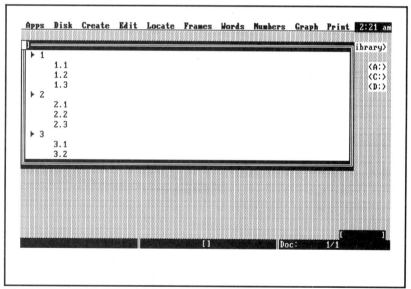

Figure 1.7: An Outline Frame

How can you use this Outline template? Let's say you are planning to write a long memorandum to your sales people describing a new product that your company is getting ready to put onto the market. You want first to focus on the product itself, then describe the marketing approach for the product, and finally discuss your competition.

You can use Framework II's Outline template to plan your memo. Your first step will be to enter headings and subheadings into the outline itself. Let's look at a possible outline for the Product Memo.

    1   The Product
        1.1   general description
        1.2   technical aspects
        1.3   pricing
    2   The Market
        2.1   who will buy
        2.2   distribution
        2.3   advertising
    3   The Competition
        3.1   other products
        3.2   other marketing strategies
        3.3   where we stand

Once you have created your outline, you can use each of the Empty frames for word processing. In other words, you will write your memo into the outline itself.

Of course, you have to open up the Empty frames before you can work in them. To open frames that reside in an outline, Framework II gives you two function keys, which work in quite different ways:

□ The Zoom key (F9) opens an individual frame (or a group of frames) in the outline and devotes the entire screen to its contents. You will use the Zoom key whenever you want to focus your attention on one or more frames. Figure 1.8 shows the effect of Zoom on the first subheading of the Product Memo outline. Notice that the name of the subheading appears in the status panel, below the desktop. Pressing the Zoom key a second time will return you to the original format of the outline.

□ The View key (F10) shifts your outline between *Outline view* and *Frames view*. Figure 1.9 shows part of the Product Memo outline in Frames view. You can see that each of the subheadings consists of an Empty frame. Pressing the View key again will return you to the original Outline view.

You have a great deal of flexibility in working with Outline frames. Outlines would not be very useful if you were always required to work within three sets of three subheadings. Framework II allows you to change the size, organization, and contents of your outline in any way that meets your requirements:

□ You can add new major headings and give them new subheadings of their own.

```
  Apps  Disk  Create  Edit  Locate  Frames  Words  Numbers  Graph  Print  2:36 am
  ▌



















                                    ║ Product.general description ║Char:      1/1
```

Figure 1.8: *The Effect of the Zoom Key*

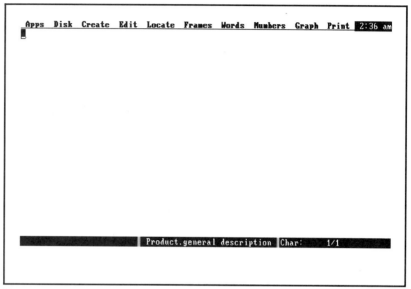

```
  Apps  Disk  Create  Edit  Locate  Frames  Words  Numbers  Graph  Print  2:12 pm
                                                                    <Library>
 ⌐Memo]═══════════════════════════════════════════════════════
 [1  The Product]─────────────────────────────────────          <A:>
 [1.1  general description]───────────────                       <C:>
                                                                 <D:>




 [2  The Market]──────────────────────────
 [2.1  who will buy]──────────────



                                                            mo    ]
                                      Memo          ║Doc:      1/1
```

Figure 1.9: *Frames View of an Outline*

□ You can create new logical levels, producing an outline that contains frames that are many levels deep.

□ You can delete headings or subheadings.

□ You can move headings or subheadings to a new location in the outline. Framework II will automatically renumber the outline to reflect the new sequence of headings.

□ You can number your outline sections in either traditional or technical style.

□ Finally, you can insert Spreadsheet, Database, and Graph frames into the outline, so that your outline will not be restricted to Word (or Empty) frames only.

The second way you can create an outline is to begin with an Empty frame. Notice the second option in the Create submenu in Figure 1.6:

Empty / Word Frame

Choose this option and Framework II will create an Empty frame for you, as shown in Figure 1.10. You can always use an Empty frame for word processing. You can also use an Empty frame to contain other frames in an outline form. If you have already created some other work frames that you want to place in an outline, you can simply move them into an Empty frame.

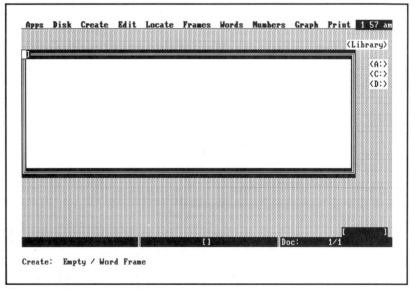

Figure 1.10: An Empty Frame

At the beginning of this chapter we discussed an outlining example involving tax forms. To organize these forms you would first create an Empty frame. Then you would move the various tax spreadsheets into the frame to create your outline. Framework II's Move key, F7, is your tool for moving frames from the desktop into an outline.

In summary, outlining in Framework II is a way for you to plan ahead, to organize your thoughts before you begin working. Outlining is also a way to bring together pieces of work that you have already completed. In Chapter 2 you'll learn exactly how all this can be done.

SPREADSHEET PROGRAMMING

Tables of numbers are an inescapable part of our lives. Tax tables, mortgage tables, test scores, sales figures, population statistics, discount rates, insurance payments—all these, and more, are the kinds of numeric data that pass daily across our desks and demand attention.

Such tables typically have a row of headings at the top, to explain the significance of the columns, and a column of labels at the left, to describe the rows. Figure 1.11 shows a small example: sales statistics for three products—X, Y, and Z—over a six-month period. Notice that the last column on the right shows the total sales for each month, and the last row (at the bottom of the spreadsheet) shows the total sales for each product.

Producing tables like this one by hand is no fun, as anyone who has worn out the erasers on a collection of stubby pencils can attest. Just as you finish totaling up all the columns and rows, and you finally come up with a grand total at the lower-right corner of your spreadsheet, you look at your original data and discover an incorrectly entered figure. Typically, the way these things go, the error will be located right in the middle of the table, like the figure for Product Y sales in the month of March. Correcting your mistake means redoing a lot of arithmetic—retotaling rows and columns, and finding a new grand total.

Electronic spreadsheets like Framework II's were made for situations like this one. Spreadsheet programming simply means setting up a table of numbers and letting the computer do all the associated arithmetic for you. In Framework II, the painful task described above would be reduced to the following simple steps:

1. Create a Spreadsheet frame big enough to hold your table.

2. Enter the column and row headings into the first row and first column.

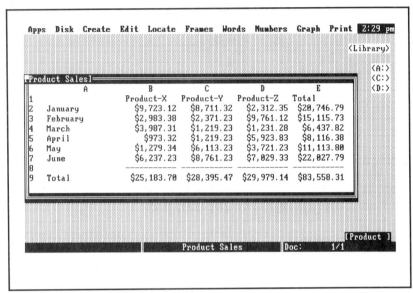

Figure 1.11: *A Spreadsheet Example*

3. Enter all the numbers.

4. Write *formulas* for the row and column totals, and *copy* those formulas across and down the spreadsheet.

5. To correct an error—for example, the figure for Product Y in March—simply type a new number in the correct location. Framework II will automatically recalculate all your totals for you.

Look for a moment at the way a Framework II spreadsheet is organized. The columns are all identified by letters and the rows by numbers. At each intersection of a row and column, you can enter (by typing at the keyboard) a number or a label. These intersections are called *cells*, and you can refer to each cell in a spreadsheet by its *address*. An address is made up of a column letter and a row number. For example, the sales figure for Product Y in March is at cell address C4, as you can see in Figure 1.11.

Because each cell has a name, you can write arithmetic formulas that refer to cells, or rather to the *contents* of cells. Adding the contents of three cells and putting the total into a fourth cell is as simple as entering a formula like this one:

+B2 + C2 +

This is the formula that yields the total sales for January. Once you've written a formula like this, you can copy it to apply it to other rows in your spreadsheet.

Chapter 3, on spreadsheet programming, will show you how to do all this and much more. For now, simply remember that an electronic spreadsheet is a table of numbers that is designed to respond to change. You might hear people talking about "what-if's" when they discuss the power of a spreadsheet. What if you decide to change the estimated tax rate? What if you revise your bonus plan? What if the price of Product X increases again? Or what if you simply make a mistake in data entry? A Spreadsheet frame can respond instantly to numeric changes like these—it gives you newly calculated results before you can get up to sharpen your pencil.

GRAPHING

We have long been taught that a picture is worth a thousand words. In the business environment, one picture is worth a thousand numbers. Busy people would often rather spot trends off a graph than pore over the numeric data that lies behind the graph.

Framework II's graph-drawing ability is related directly to its components that deal with numbers: spreadsheets and databases. Any time you create a table of numbers, you can also make a graph from those numbers. Amazingly, creating a graph in Framework II seldom requires more than half-a-dozen keystrokes from you.

Figures 1.12, 1.13, and 1.14 show three different graphs that Framework II created from the Sales spreadsheet we've been looking at. Examine these graphs, and notice the details that Framework II automatically works out in each case:

- □ The scale of the graphs
- □ The labels on the horizontal axes
- □ The numbers on the vertical axes
- □ The keys that explain the different elements of the graphs
- □ The choice of visual textures to distinguish among the elements represented on the graphs

Framework II offers seven different graph types in all: bar, stacked bar, pie, line, marked points, high-low-close (for analyzing stock quotations), and x-y. We'll look at examples of these graphs and explore the use of Framework II's Graph submenu in Chapter 3. One important point to

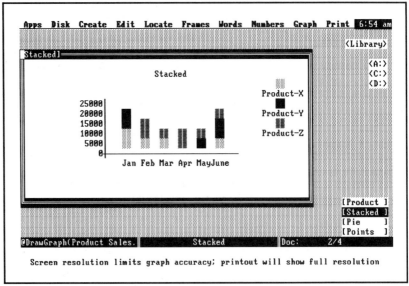

Figure 1.12: *A Stacked Bar Graph Example*

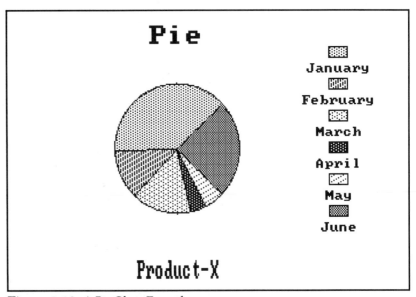

Figure 1.13: *A Pie Chart Example*

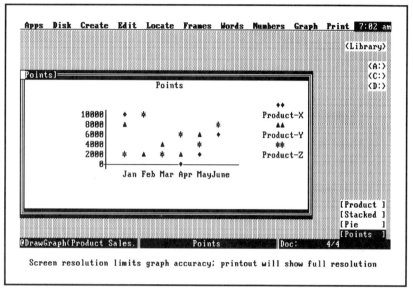

Figure 1.14: *A Marked Points Graph*

keep in mind is this: When you create a graph from a Spreadsheet frame, the graph, like the spreadsheet itself, can respond to changes in your numeric data. Change a number on the spreadsheet, and Framework II can quickly redraw the graph to reflect your new data.

WORD PROCESSING

People who love to write and people who hate to write often have one characteristic in common: a remarkable fondness for editing, revising, and rewriting. Whatever the genre—from business documents to personal correspondence to the Great American Novel—writers love to experiment with variations in their own writing: trying out new words, inserting sentences, changing the order of paragraphs, deleting the unnecessary adjective, until every word sounds and looks just right.

Clearly, this kind of attention to literate and literary detail is good. But no one enjoys typing someone else's words—or even one's own words—several times in a row. What secretary has not at some point pondered the life-threatening effects of a typewriter speeding through the air, upon hearing the familiar request, "Could you just make these few corrections, and switch those two paragraphs around—and have it ready before lunch?"

Small wonder that computerized word processing has produced a stir in the business world. Now all the variations of text editing, including inserting, deleting, changing, correcting, and, yes, switching things around, can be done electronically, within your computer's memory, before a single word ever appears on paper.

In Framework II Word frames, you can create documents and accomplish all kinds of editing tasks with a minimum of effort. Seldom has word processing been so easy to learn. Chapter 4 will get you started; we'll also examine special effects such as boldface, underlining, italics, right justification, headers, footers, and so on. The special effects—underlining, boldface, and italic type—will show up not only in your printed documents, but right on the screen. (If you customize your system to use a color monitor in certain ways, the special effects will appear as different colors of text. See Appendix A for details.) Some of these effects are illustrated in the Word frame shown in Figure 1.15.

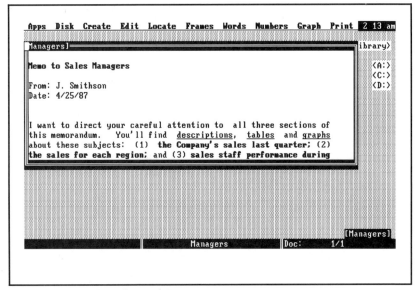

Figure 1.15: *A Sample Word Frame*

DATABASE MANAGEMENT

A database is simply a collection of related information. A personal or business address book is a database. So are the records you keep for periodic activities such as banking and paying bills. The card catalog at your local library is a rather large database, arranged in several different ways for the convenience of locating books. The telephone book is yet another database that we all use daily.

The main practical differences between a paper database and an electronic database are ease of handling and ease of use. When you create a database in Framework II, you can expect all of the following activities to be easy to perform:

- ☐ Sorting (i.e., arranging the information in some order)
- ☐ Searching (i.e., locating just the information you want)
- ☐ Adding new records
- ☐ Deleting old records
- ☐ Performing arithmetic calculations on the database
- ☐ Creating printed reports from the database

Database terminology uses the words *record* and *field* to describe categories of information. A record is one complete unit of information in a database. Consider a list of names, addresses, and phone numbers. A single record in such a list consists of all the information about one person. For example, a record might include the following information:

First name
Last name
Address
City
State
Zip code
Home phone
Work phone

We can expect that each record in the database will contain all of these items of information about someone. These items are called fields. In the case of this address book, a record consists of eight fields of information. Every record in a single database will contain the same number and type of fields.

Typically, a database is arranged in columns and rows, in a way that is similar to a spreadsheet. But the structure of a database is more consistent than a spreadsheet needs to be. Each row of a database is guaranteed to contain one record. Each of the fields of the database resides in a separate column. The column headings are therefore called *field names* in a database.

Figure 1.16 shows a Database frame. It contains the sales records of a group of ten sales people. These are the field names of this database:

Last (name)
First (name)
Region
Sales
Bonus

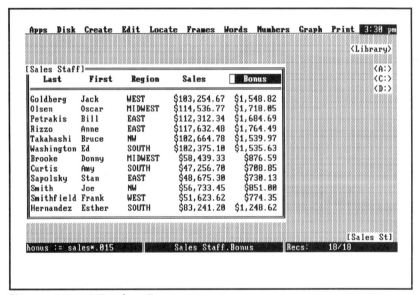

Figure 1.16: *A Database Frame*

This database illustrates several of the most important features Framework II offers for managing data:

- The data is *sorted* by last name. We could select some other order if we wished—placing the people in order by region; or in ascending or descending order of total sales.

- The bonus amount for each sales person was calculated by Framework II from a formula that was entered in the bonus column. (Each person receives a bonus of 1.5 percent of total sales.) This bonus amount can be changed simply by changing the formula.

- We can *filter* this database, instructing Framework II to select and display only certain records that match *criteria* that we establish. In such a small database, this would just be a learning exercise, but you can imagine the importance of filtering if your database had hundreds of records. You might want to look at all the sales people who work in the Midwestern region, or all the people who had total sales greater than $50,000.

Chapter 5 will show you how to create and manage a database in Framework II.

TELECOMMUNICATIONS

The Framework II package includes one final part: a telecommunications component that will help you hook up your own computer, via telephone lines, with other computers. To use it, you must install a device called a *modem* in your computer. A modem *mo*dulates outgoing computer data into audio signals that can be sent over telephone lines, and it *dem*odulates incoming audio signals into data that your computer system can work with.

For both business and recreational uses, the field of telecommunications continues to increase in importance. Some working people use modems to hook up with office computers from their home computers. Many banks offer home computer banking services, which allow you to use your PC to pay bills and transfer money from one account to another.

But probably the most widespread use of personal computer telecommunications involves *information services,* such as The Source, CompuServe, and Dow Jones News/Retrieval. These are all special-interest information sources, updated daily, that you can access only with your computer. They offer business news, current events, computer recreation, and so on.

To use any of these services—or to use any of the free bulletin boards, or simply to send data directly to another computer—you need software to handle the technical details involved in making the connection. Framework II's telecommunications component is designed for the purpose. With the telecommunications component you can send a file that you have already prepared directly from your disk (which is called *uploading*). You can also *download* files, which means receiving them via your modem and storing them immediately on disk. Moreover, the telecommunications component will run "in the background." This means that once you have these tasks under way in a Telecommunications frame, you can safely close the frame and work in another frame on the desktop. You need only return to the Telecommunications frame when it is time to perform a different task, or to end the session. Framework II will even warn you when there is no more activity in the Telecommunications frame, so you can hang up the phone. You'll learn about the telecommunications component in Chapter 6.

As you begin creating frames for your own work, you'll want to learn about saving frames on disk and printing them on paper. These are the subjects of the next two sections.

SAVING FRAMES

The file cabinets for your disk drives are always available to you on the desktop. They are there for two purposes: to allow you to examine, at any time, the contents of your disks; and to provide you with a convenient means of reading files from the disks and saving files to the disks.

We have seen that Framework II's Shuttle key (marked ScrollLock on your keyboard) moves the highlight from your work frames to the disk cabinets. Here is the complete sequence of keystrokes you will use to read a file from your data disk:

Shuttle (Scroll Lock)	(to move the highlight to the disk frames)
An arrow	(to select the correct disk)
Return	(to open the frame)
Down Level (+)	(to move the highlight into the frame)
↑ or ↓	(to select a file)
Return	(to move the file to the desktop)

The extension name ".FW2" identifies Framework II files on your disk; these files become frames when you move them onto the desktop. The file name you see on the disk directory may be only part of the frame's complete label. This is because DOS file names are limited to up to eight characters, plus an extension name that can be up to three characters long. Framework II frame labels may be practically any length (up to 32,000 characters).

When Framework II saves a frame on disk, it takes the first eight characters of the frame's label as the file name. For this reason you have to write labels carefully: the first eight characters of each frame label must be distinct from other frames that you intend to save on a given disk.

DOS imposes certain restrictions on file names. Some characters, such as commas, periods, and the space character, are not allowed. Framework II labels, however, can contain any character except the square brackets, *[* and *]*. Frame labels that contain illegal DOS file name characters will be transformed automatically when you save a frame on disk. Illegal DOS characters will be changed to an underscore character (_). So, for example, a frame called Sales Memo will be saved on disk under the file name

    SALES_ME.FW2

We have seen how to get a file by shuttling into the disk drive cabinet. A second way you can move a file to the desktop from a disk is via the Disk submenu's Get File by Name option:

    Ctrl-D   (to select the Disk submenu)

    G   (to invoke the Get option)

Framework II will ask you for the name of the file you wish to bring to the desktop. You must specify the entire file name, although you need not include the extension if the file is a Framework II file. (You'll learn in Chapter 8 how to bring other types of files to the desktop.) You can also indicate a disk drive—for example:

    A:TAXES.FW

If you do not specify a disk drive, Framework II always assumes that you want to read from or write to the *default* drive. The default drive is B in a system that has two floppy disk drives and C in a system that has a hard disk. (You can change the default disk drive by selecting another disk drive cabinet and pressing Ctrl-Return. This new cabinet will be your default drive until you exit Framework II or change the default again.)

Framework II gives you several ways to save a file on disk. One important procedure is called "Save and Continue." You use this procedure whenever you want to save a frame that you are in the process of completing. Save and Continue saves a copy of the frame in its current condition, and then it leaves the frame on the desktop so you can continue working with it.

You can perform a Save and Continue operation in one of two ways. First, if there is more than one frame on the desktop, you have to make sure that you have selected the frame you want to save. The highlight can be either on the border of the frame or inside in the contents of the frame. Then you can select the Disk submenu's Save and Continue option:

Ctrl-D	(to select the Disk submenu)
S	(to invoke the Save and Continue option)

If the frame you are saving is an outline, all of the frames contained in the outline will be saved in the one file you are writing to disk.

An even more convenient way to perform a Save and Continue operation is with the following keystrokes:

Ctrl-Return	(Save and Continue)

Pressing these two keys will automatically save to disk any frame that you are currently working on.

The Save and Continue operation is a good way for you to secure the safety of your current work. People who use personal computers have to learn, sometimes through painful experience, the importance of regularly creating *backups* of computer-generated documents and information. You never know when some minor mishap will result in a loss of data—someone accidentally unplugging your computer, a power failure in your neighborhood, or an inadvertent sequence of keystrokes. If you have recently saved your work, you will be confident that you can lose only what you have done since the last save operation.

Yet another way to save a frame is to use the Disk submenu's Put Away option:

Ctrl-D	(to select the Disk submenu)
P	(to invoke the Put Away option)

This operation saves the currently selected frame on disk and then deletes the frame from the desktop.

By the way, if you get a file from disk, change the frame in some way on the desktop, and then save the frame back to disk, Framework II will remember the directory the frame originally came from, and it will send it back to the same place.

You can always delete a frame from the desktop *without* first saving it to disk if you really want to. Simply select the frame and press the Delete key (labeled Del on your keyboard). Happily, Framework II can bring back a deletion if you have second thoughts. The Edit submenu has an Undo option that will undo the last operation you performed. To invoke this handy operation, press these keys:

Ctrl-E	(to select the Edit submenu)
U	(to invoke the Undo option)

If you delete a file from a disk cabinet, however, you cannot bring the file back. For this reason, Framework II asks you to confirm that you truly want to delete a file from your disk. To delete a file, select the correct file name in the disk cabinet and press the Delete key.

You can get a fuller view of a disk directory—complete with dates and times—by pressing the View key (F10) while the disk's cabinet is selected.

PRINTING FRAMES

We'll be discussing Framework II's printing options several times, in the context of each different type of frame. There will be variations to learn for printing in each Framework II component. However, the essential Print submenu is easy to use. You select the frame or frames you want to print, make sure your printer is turned on, and press

Ctrl-P   (to select the Print submenu)

B   (to begin printing)

When you print an Outline frame, you have to decide between printing just the outline or the contents of each frame in the outline. The View key (F10) controls this option: Outline view prints only the outline itself; Frames view prints the contents. (Look back at Figures 1.7 and 1.9 to review the difference between Outline view and Frames view.)

EXAMPLES

In each chapter of this book, after looking at selected elements of Framework II in detail, we'll complete our study with realistic examples. We'll be looking in on The Sophisticated Palate, Inc., a fictitious company that uses Framework II for a variety of computer applications, and we'll nose around a bit in the company's books and documents, to see how Framework II's resources might be used in a business situation.

The Sophisticated Palate is, as you might expect, a fancy food company. It produces a variety of gourmet pastries, international breads, salads, pâtés, fresh pastas, and other delicatessen and international food items, which it distributes to retail outlets and uses in its catering service. In addition, it distributes fancy imported foods such as cheeses, cookies and crackers, and jams and jellies.

The company was started as a partnership eight years ago by Eileen Wilcox and George Farley strictly as a catering service. However, demand for their products was so great that they have since incorporated and branched out into the wholesale arena. Although Eileen and George started out by preparing all the foods themselves, they now have a staff of nine cooks, five order clerks, four drivers, eighteen part-time waiters and waitresses (for the catering service), a bookkeeper, and an administrative assistant. They bought a PC with a hard disk drive two years ago, and started out using the original version of Framework for their clerical and record-keeping chores. They have since expanded the machine's memory to 640K and upgraded to Framework II, which they use almost exclusively for all their computer work. Before the PC, these tasks used to take a great deal of pleasure out of running the company.

Since this chapter's overview has taken us casually through the whole range of Framework II's capabilities, we'll try to find a few documents from The Sophisticated Palate's business office that illustrate what we've studied. We'll look at a database, a rather imaginative spreadsheet, and an outline-based integrated document.

AN EMPLOYEE DATABASE

George handles the company's personnel matters. Since the work is low-keyed and pleasant, the business is successful, and there is a great deal of camaraderie among the workers, there has been little employee turnover: most of the current group of workers have been with the company over three years.

George meets with each employee individually for an informal evaluation every six months or so. He listens to complaints, makes suggestions, handles any scheduling problems that Ariana Katz, the administrative assistant, cannot resolve, and usually offers small salary increases during these meetings.

Figure 1.17 shows a printout of a database that George has developed in Framework II to keep track of his employees' work histories and evaluation dates. He has discovered that Framework II databases can work effectively with dates. Framework has functions that allow you to enter dates into a table and then perform certain kinds of date arithmetic operations, such as finding the number of days between two dates. George's database contains the following fields of information about each employee:

> Last name
> First name
> Date hired
> Position
> Months with the company
> Last evaluation date
> Months elapsed since last evaluation
> Starting hourly wage
> Current hourly wage

The field names of the database are of course abbreviated, so that all the information can appear on the screen at once. Given the date an employee was hired, a Framework II formula that George has written calculates the number of months that the employee has worked for The Sophisticated Palate. A similar formula calculates the number of months since the last evaluation. George keeps the database sorted by this months-elapsed figure, in descending order. He can glance at the list and immediately find the employees who are coming due for an evaluation, their salary history, and their length of employment with the company.

A COSTING SPREADSHEET

Eileen has been developing a line of special-order party trays, which are available both as retail items and through the catering service. She has used a Spreadsheet frame to help her keep track of costs and pricing. She generally offers a combination of five delicatessen items in each tray. The trays are available in sizes for 10, 20, 50, or 80 people. To calculate the company's costs for these trays, she must include the cost of supplies and labor for each item on the tray.

She has come up with spreadsheet formulas for determining costs and retail prices for three different party trays. A printout of the spreadsheet she used for costing one of the trays is shown in Figure 1.18. The cost of supplies is directly proportional to the number of people the tray will serve. Labor costs also increase for the larger trays, but not as quickly. After determining the cost of a tray, she calculates a 40 percent markup to obtain the retail price.

Last	First	Hired	Job	M/w.Co	LastEval	Elapsed	StSal	CurSal
Munter	Cookie	Feb 13, 1986	Cook	13	Aug 20, 1986	7	$7.50	$7.85
Dexter	Gordon	Sep 18, 1985	Clerk	18	Oct 2, 1986	6	$7.00	$7.00
Greene	Jane	Aug 31, 1984	Waitr/s	31	Oct 2, 1986	6	$2.70	$3.75
Estevez	Ray	Oct 19, 1983	Waitr/s	42	Oct 2, 1986	6	$2.20	$3.75
Lopez	Rick	Oct 3, 1985	Waitr/s	18	Oct 3, 1986	6	$3.75	$3.75
Poulos	Costas	Sep 11, 1984	Cook	31	Oct 13, 1986	5	$5.90	$7.85
Mayer	Oscar	Sep 3, 1984	Waitr/s	31	Oct 13, 1986	5	$2.70	$3.75
Costanza	Dom	Mar 15, 1984	Waitr/s	37	Oct 13, 1986	5	$2.70	$3.75
Hardy	Felicia	Apr 1, 1986	Waitr/s	12	Oct 28, 1986	5	$3.75	$3.75
Castillo	Dolores	Oct 26, 1985	Cook	17	Oct 28, 1986	5	$7.25	$7.85
Shapiro	Ernie	Mar 29, 1985	Driver	24	Nov 8, 1986	4	$6.00	$6.75
Birnbaum	Sue	Nov 6, 1984	Waitr/s	29	Nov 8, 1986	4	$2.70	$3.75
Leung	Sharon	May 12, 1983	Clerk	47	Nov 8, 1986	4	$5.50	$7.00
Whitfield	Julian	Nov 8, 1981	Clerk	65	Nov 8, 1986	4	$4.50	$7.25
Kyle	Selina	Oct 31, 1983	Waitr/s	41	Nov 17, 1986	4	$2.20	$3.75
Gillespie	Joan	Nov 17, 1986	Cook	4	Nov 23, 1986	4	$7.85	$7.85
Osawa	Frank	Nov 14, 1984	Bookkpr	29	Nov 23, 1986	4	$10.75	$12.10
Satdeva	Krishna	Nov 8, 1984	Cook	29	Nov 23, 1986	4	$5.90	$7.85
Jaron	Howard	Nov 20, 1979	Cook	89	Nov 23, 1986	4	$5.50	$8.25
Tate	Howard	Jun 4, 1982	Driver	58	Nov 17, 1986	4	$5.00	$7.00
Freund	Bobbie	May 22, 1985	Driver	22	Dec 1, 1986	4	$6.00	$6.25
Khoury	Jamil	May 15, 1985	Waitr/s	23	Dec 1, 1986	4	$2.80	$3.75
Goldstein	Bert	Dec 4, 1984	Waitr/s	28	Dec 1, 1986	4	$2.80	$3.75
Yee	Tony	Dec 2, 1984	Waitr/s	28	Dec 1, 1986	4	$2.80	$3.75
Jones	Kate	Dec 1, 1984	Clerk	28	Dec 1, 1986	4	$6.25	$7.50
Ortega	Maya	Jun 27, 1986	Waitr/s	9	Jan 8, 1987	3	$3.75	$3.75
Parker	Charlene	Jul 8, 1986	Waitr/s	9	Jan 8, 1987	2	$3.75	$3.75
Stavros	Sandra	Jan 23, 1987	Waitr/s	2	Jan 23, 1987	2	$3.75	$3.75
Powell	Earl	Jun 22, 1983	Waitr/s	46	Jan 23, 1987	2	$2.20	$3.75
Carroll	Nancy	Jun 20, 1983	Cook	46	Jan 23, 1987	2	$5.80	$8.25
Jordan	Alex	Jul 13, 1984	Driver	33	Feb 14, 1987	1	$5.50	$6.75
Katz	Ariana	Feb 2, 1984	Adm.Ast	38	Feb 14, 1987	1	$11.25	$13.50
Rollins	Ted	Feb 14, 1987	Waitr/s	1	Feb 14, 1987	0	$3.75	$3.75
Shimozu	Lana	Aug 15, 1985	Cook	19	Feb 23, 1987	0	$7.50	$7.85
Bromberg	Dan	Jul 12, 1985	Clerk	21	Feb 23, 1987	0	$7.00	$7.00
Nasir	Abdul	Jul 7, 1985	Waitr/s	21	Feb 23, 1987	0	$3.75	$3.75
Charles	Otis	Feb 25, 1984	Waitr/s	37	Mar 4, 1987	0	$2.70	$3.75
Silvestri	Maria	Feb 6, 1984	Cook	38	Mar 4, 1987	0	$5.90	$7.85

Figure 1.17: *The Sophisticated Palate—An Employee Database*

```
*****  BUFFET TRAY  *****
# People        10               20               50               80
            Supplies  Labor   Supplies  Labor   Supplies  Labor   Supplies  Labor
Beaucaire     $8.75   $6.25    $17.50  $12.50    $21.88  $31.25    $70.00  $50.00
Mousse       $10.80   $4.10    $21.60   $5.13    $27.00   $6.87    $86.40   $8.20
Shrimp/Av    $12.00   $6.00    $24.00   $6.20    $30.00   $6.50    $96.00   $6.80
Turkey        $9.20   $8.00    $18.40   $8.00    $23.00   $8.00    $73.60   $8.00
Primavera     $7.00   $3.20    $14.00   $3.70    $17.50   $4.45    $56.00   $7.70

Total        $47.75  $27.55    $95.50  $35.53   $119.38  $57.07   $382.00  $80.70
Supp+Labor           $75.30           $131.03           $176.44           $462.70
Markup (40%)        $105.42           $183.44           $247.02           $647.78
Rounded Price       $105.00           $183.00           $247.00           $648.00
```

Figure 1.18: *The Sophisticated Palate—A Costing Spreadsheet*

A PROMOTIONAL FLIER

The costing spreadsheets are, of course, for her own use only. But Eileen has found that an easy way to promote the party tray line is to announce, early in the month, what will be available for that month. Moreover, taking orders early in the week makes it easier for her to be prepared for the weekend. For this reason, she has developed a one-page promotional flier describing the month's trays. She word processes the flier, which she then duplicates for distribution to customers.

Figure 1.19 shows the printed flier. Eileen writes a short description of each tray, followed by a spreadsheet table of prices. To produce the flier, she combines these diverse elements—Word frames and a Spreadsheet frame—in an Outline frame, which she then prints.

These are three of the smallest tasks that Eileen and George perform with Framework II. We'll see the solutions they find for more significant business record-keeping problems in subsequent chapters.

EXPLORING FURTHER

Before ending this chapter, let's examine some of the advanced features available to you in Framework II. We'll look at a way for you to access DOS programs without quitting the Framework II program and we'll discuss the Library.

A DOS FRAME

From time to time it is convenient to be able to leave an applications program temporarily to perform an operation in the disk operating system. When you finish in DOS, you would like to return to your uninterrupted work in the applications program. Framework II allows you to do this by creating a frame that is temporarily devoted to DOS. These are the keys you press to use this feature:

Ctrl-D	(to select the Disk submenu)
D	(to invoke the DOS Access option)

```
Party Trays for this Weekend

Cocktail Tray I

Two cocktail sandwiches are featured on this tray: Nova Scotia
smoked salmon on a dill rye and the English Classic, cucumber
sandwiches.  In addition, the tray features California figs
wrapped in prosciutto, Belgian endive leaves onto which a Greek-
style red caviar spread is piped in attractive rosettes, and
miniature artichoke-heart quiches.

Prices

# of People        10         20         50         80
Price            $35        $65       $150       $220


Cocktail Tray II

Marinating in a special mixture of lemon grass, cilantro, and
other exotic spices and using a mesquite grill results in an
exotic barbecued chicken that's ours alone.  Jumbo shrimp are
served with a spicy Louisiana Creole dip.  The tray also includes
new potatoes filled with sour cream and caviar; a selection of
fresh raw vegetables and dips; and cream-cheese, black-olive, and
pimento canapés.

Prices

# of People        10         20         50         80
Price            $50        $85       $185       $240


Buffet Tray

Start with the buffet tray, add one of our fresh-baked desserts,
and you have a complete dinner for your guests. Salade Beaucaire,
served on the luxury liner The France, combines Belgian endive,
celery root, ham, apples, and potatoes in a seasoned mayonnaise
dressing made with crème fraîche. The Vitello Tomato Mousse is
the classic Italian dish transformed into a light mousse of veal
subtly flavored with lemon, tuna, and capers. Shrimp and Avocado
Spread is blended from the freshest ingredients, in a cream
cheese base, and lightly seasoned with a blend of old-world
spices, topped with a fine layer of chopped egg and Hungarian
paprika. A boned turkey, filled with a mixture of veal and pork,
layered with truffles and pistachios, is rolled into a sausage
shape for our Galantine of Turkey. It is sliced and served cold
with a sherry-scented aspic. Spring's first harvest is the basis
of Salad Primavera. Asparagus, red peppers, new peas, and sweet
corn are tossed with pasta in a light citrus dressing.

Prices

# of People        10         20         50         80
Price           $105       $183       $247       $648
```

Figure 1.19: The Sophisticated Palate—A Promotional Flier

In order to access DOS, Framework II must go by way of a frame. If
your currently selected frame is empty, it will use that frame. If the current frame is a Word frame, it will open the frame, and display the

following message:

Delete all contents (y/n)?

If you press N, or if your current selection on the desktop is not a Word frame or an Empty frame, Framework II will create a new frame for DOS access, and label it

Dos Access Frame

If a Word frame is selected, and you respond to the prompt by pressing Y, the contents will be deleted, and that frame will be used for DOS access, although it will retain its label. Figure 1.20 shows a typical DOS Access frame.

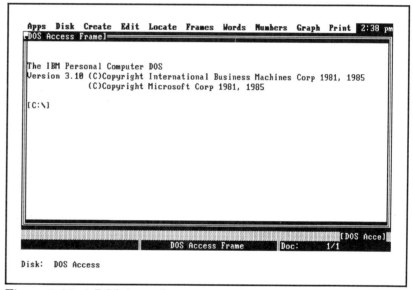

Figure 1.20: A DOS Access frame

Ordinarily when you exit from a DOS Access frame, it retains whatever characters appeared on the screen while you were using DOS. However, if you have the ANSI.SYS device driver installed, or use certain "background" programs such as SuperKey, DOS access works somewhat differently. In a short time, the desktop will disappear, and you will have a blank screen with a DOS prompt. If your Framework II subdirectory is called FRAMEWK, the screen will display

C:\FRAMEWK>

While you are in the DOS frame, you can perform any of the DOS internal or external commands, or any program that runs on DOS. To return to Framework II from DOS or any other program, you simply enter the DOS command

EXIT

This command will put you back in the Framework II desktop, with any frames that you were working on still intact.

Using the DOS Access frame can be convenient in a variety of situations; for example:

□   You can use it to perform some advanced disk operation that is not available while you are in Framework II.

□   You can run a BASIC program that you have written yourself.

□   You can temporarily work in some other applications package, without disturbing your desktop work in Framework II.

After any of these activities, you can return to Framework II and continue whatever you were doing before you entered the DOS frame. You'll learn more about DOS Access frames in Chapter 8.

THE LIBRARY

The Library is a unique part of the desktop. It is always loaded automatically. Therefore, it is a good place to store any pieces of information that you need frequently.

The Library is a file cabinet, not a frame (although it behaves like a frame in many ways). Therefore, if the highlight is on a frame, you must press the Shuttle key (Scroll Lock) to look at it. To view the contents of the Library, press the following keys:

Shuttle (Scroll Lock)	(to move to the file cabinets)
↑ or ↓	(to select the Library cabinet)
Recalc (F5)	(to get a full-screen view of the Library cabinet's contents)

The Library is in outline form, containing the major headings

Macros
Abbreviations

Printing Templates
User-defined functions
Phone book

One important feature of Framework II is that when it searches for a frame, it always looks in the Library, as well as on the desktop. Moreover, it will search the entire Library, so it will find anything in the Library no matter how deeply it is nested within a subheading of an outline. This feature makes the Library an extremely powerful tool for customizing the way Framework II behaves. You can add any number of special frames that you use frequently, and Framework II will always find them.

FEATURES OF THE LIBRARY

Let's take a brief look at the types of items that are supplied with the Library. These are only some of the sorts of things that you might want to include in your own library.

▶ PREDEFINED MACROS AND ABBREVIATIONS

The Library includes ten predefined macros and several abbreviations. A *macro* is a series of keystrokes (which can include both text and Framework II commands) that can be played back when you press an Alt-key combination. An *abbreviation* is a series of keystrokes that, when properly treated, will be replaced by a longer series of keystrokes. Abbreviations are more appropriate than macros when you want to insert a large body of text. Both macros and abbreviations are created by way of the Create submenu. The macros are all combinations of the Alt key and a function key. Although they are intended as samples for you to study, you will find most of them quite useful. The abbreviations are self-explanatory. We'll learn how to create macros and abbreviations in Chapter 7, "An Introduction to FRED Programming," and we'll use some of the predefined macros in Chapter 6, "Telecommunications."

▶ PRINTING TEMPLATES

Whenever you print a document, you are given the option of specifying a printing template to use. Printing templates contain all the printer settings for a specific type of document—the ones in the library are just samples for you to look at. We'll explore printing templates in Chapter 4, "Word Processing."

► **USER-DEFINED FUNCTIONS**

You can use the FRED language to create new functions to perform various tasks for you automatically. If you store them in the library, you can call them by name just as if they were a native part of the FRED language. We'll create a user-defined function in Chapter 7, "An Introduction to FRED Programming."

► **PHONE BOOK**

If you have a modem, Framework II can dial phone numbers for you. If you include your phone directory in the Library, a single keystroke-combination will display it for you. Then all you need to do is use the search function to find the name of the party you want to call, and use another keystroke-combination to dial the phone automatically. We'll explore these capabilities further in Chapter 6, "Telecommunications."

SUMMARY

Framework II is an integrated package that you can use for spreadsheet programming, word processing, database management, business graphing, and telecommunications. Outlining is a sixth essential component of the package that allows you to tie together your work in the other components. In addition, Framework II provides an easy way of sharing files with other application programs, and of running other application programs from within Framework II.

You create a separate frame for each component of your work in Framework II. Each frame has a border, a label, a contents area, and a background programming area.

Framework II encourages you to divide your work into small, easily handled modules. The elements of Framework II that help you work with the frames you create are the menu, the function keys at the left side of the keyboard, and an important set of cursor-movement keys at the right side of the keyboard.

All your work in Framework II takes place on the desktop. In addition to work frames, in which you create business documents, the file cabinets for the disk drives and the Library are always available on the desktop. Files that you read from disk become frames on the desktop; likewise, a frame that you save from the desktop becomes a disk file, with the DOS extension name ".FW2". The Library is a place to store any frames that you use frequently. Framework II's Print submenu supplies you with an easy way to send any frame to the printer.

With Chapter 2 we'll begin our detailed study of the Framework II components, starting with outlining.

CHAPTER TWO

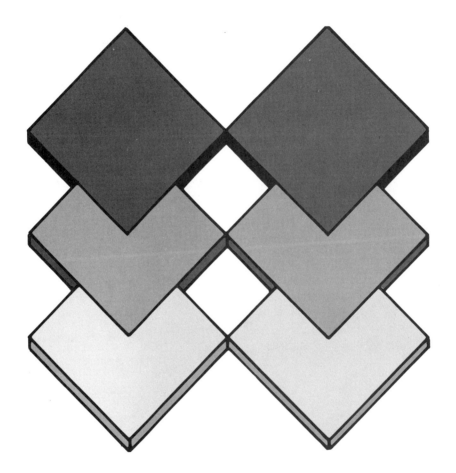

OUTLINING

INTRODUCTION

In Chapter 1 we discussed the two reasons for outlining in Framework II. On the one hand, you can think of outlining as a productivity component in its own right. No matter what kind of project you are planning, you can use the outlining feature to organize your thoughts, to anticipate the order and logic of the work ahead of you, and to establish a successful approach for accomplishing your goals. All this can occur before you begin concentrating on the *content* of your work.

On the other hand, you can also think of outlining simply as a useful tool that improves your productivity with Word, Spreadsheet, Database, Graph, and Telecommunications frames. With outlining you can group documents together in meaningful ways and establish links among the various elements of your work.

In this chapter we'll practice using Framework II's outlining functions. The first step will be to learn the mechanical details: using the keyboard and the Framework II menus to create, modify, and expand outlines. You'll recall that you can begin outlining with either an Outline frame or an Empty frame. We'll examine both of these approaches.

We'll begin working with several of the Framework II function keys that manipulate frames and outlines: the Move (F7) and Copy (F8) keys, which move frames from one place to another inside an outline or from the desktop to the inside of an outline; the Zoom (F9) and View (F10) keys, which look at outlines and frames in different kinds of detail; and the extremely important Extend Select key (F6), which makes it possible to work with several frames or elements at once.

We'll also master several of the menu options that work with frames and outlines; the Frames menu offers several interesting options for creative use of outlines. In addition, we'll be looking at the Create, Disk, and Print menus.

This is a lot of detail to learn all at once. Fortunately, the function keys and the menus work in similar ways in other Framework II contexts. Once you learn to use these function keys and menus for outlining, you will find that you can almost automatically apply the same tools to all your other work, whether in spreadsheet programming, word processing, database management, or telecommunications.

Let's begin, then, with Outline frames.

CREATING AN OUTLINE

As you can see in Figure 2.1, Outline is the first of the options in the Create menu. Let's review the two approaches you can use to create an outline:

- □ Use the Instruct key to open the menu, then use the ← or → key (if necessary) to choose the Create option.

- □ Or press Ctrl-C, for a shortcut into the Create submenu.

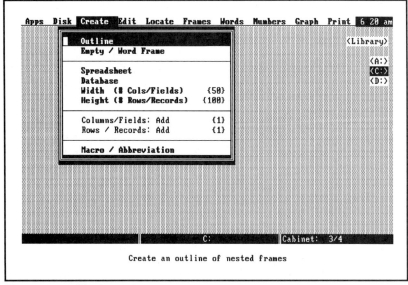

Figure 2.1: *The Create Menu*

With the Create menu displayed on the screen, you have three ways of choosing the Outline option:

- □ Use the ↑ or ↓ key, if necessary, to position the highlight over the word Outline, and press Return.

- □ Press the Home key (to get to the top of the menu), and press Return.

- □ Or simply press the O key.

In summary, here are two sequences of keystrokes you can use to create an outline:

Instruct	(to open the menu)
→ or ←	(to select Create)
↑ or ↓ or Home	(to select Outline)
Return	(to invoke the option)

or

Ctrl-C	(to select the Create submenu)
O	(to invoke the Outline option)

Figure 2.2 shows the Outline frame that is placed on the desktop as a result of only of these keystroke sequences. You'll recall that this outline begins with room for three major headings, with each major heading allowing room for three subheadings. Your next step is to enter a frame label. Then you can begin entering outline headings.

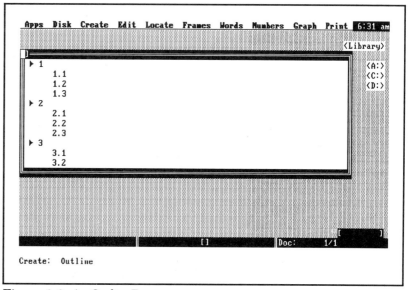

Figure 2.2: *An Outline Frame*

ENTERING FRAME LABELS

The first thing you'll normally want to do when you create any frame is to assign the frame a label. You should write labels that will serve to identify the contents of the frames you create. Imagine that you have created a couple dozen frames with Framework II, and you've stored them all as files on a floppy disk. You're going to want to be able to examine the disk directory and recall more or less what each of your files contains. Hence you should be guided by two criteria in writing good frame labels:

1. The whole label should function as a descriptive title for a frame on your desktop.

2. The first eight characters of the label must serve as a unique identifier for the file that will ultimately store your frame on disk.

You enter a frame label when the highlight is located on the frame's border, as shown in Figure 2.2.

Let's imagine a situation in which you are likely to create an outline to help you plan ahead. You have been assigned the responsibility of preparing a 30-minute talk to present at an upcoming business meeting. Your proposed topic is the effective use of personal computers in the business environment. You decide that the best way to organize your thoughts on the subject is to start with an outline. Let's call your Outline frame "Computer Talk"; we'll use this exercise to illustrate the whole range of outlining techniques in Framework II.

Begin entering the frame label simply by typing the characters themselves. As soon as you press the uppercase C, the first letter of your label, some interesting action will take place on the display screen. Several things will happen below the desktop—on the edit line, in the status panel, and on the message line:

1. The characters you type will appear on the edit line. As you type, the edit cursor will lead one space ahead of each character.

2. The third section of the status panel, in the lower-right corner of your display screen, will give you information about the length of the frame label you are creating.

3. The message line will tell you exactly what activity you are involved in, and what you should do to complete the activity:

Label editing; RETURN finishes

Figure 2.3 shows the appearance of the screen after you have typed the first ten characters of the label. Notice the status panel's message:

Char: 11/1

This message tells you that the cursor is currently located at the eleventh character position of the first line of your label. (We will discover later that labels can consist of more than one line of text.)

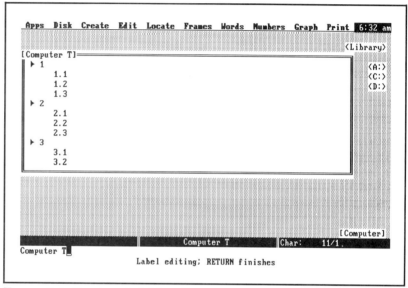

Figure 2.3: Entering a Label for a Frame

Also note that the label that you are entering is actually appearing at four different locations on the screen. Each of these locations ultimately serves a different function in Framework II's screen presentation:

1. The edit line—this is where you are actually entering (and changing, if necessary) the label.

2. The central section of the status panel—this section always tells you the name of the currently selected frame on the desktop.

3. The label area on the border of the frame itself—this area identifies the frame while it is on the desktop.

4. The tray, at the lower-right corner of the desktop—with room for only eight characters, the tray tells you what the name of this frame will be when you save it as a file on disk.

▶ **USING THE CURSOR-MOVEMENT KEYS**

While you are using the edit line to enter information in Framework II, you can use several cursor-movement keys to help you complete your data entry correctly. You will use the edit line and the corresponding cursor-movement keys for many kinds of data entry in Framework II, not just for entering frame labels. Here are the special keys you can use:

□ *The Backspace key.* This key, located on the top row of the keyboard, just to the left of the NumLock key, *erases* the last character you entered on the edit line; it also moves the edit cursor one space backward.

□ *The ← and → keys.* These keys move the cursor backward and forward on the edit line *without* erasing the characters you have already typed. You might want to use these keys to reposition the cursor so that you can insert some new characters inside the line you have already begun to enter.

□ *The Home and End keys.* The Home key moves the cursor to the beginning of the edit line, and the End key moves it to the space beyond the last character you've entered on the edit line. You can use these keys to move quickly back and forth within the data you are entering.

□ *The Delete key.* This key deletes the character at the current cursor location and moves the characters located after the cursor to the left, to take up the empty space.

□ *The Return key.* This key completes your data entry and returns the cursor to its original location on the desktop—in this case, the frame label area. (The edit cursor does not have to be located at the end of the edit line before you press Return.)

You can see that the edit line gives you complete control over the process of entering a frame label—or entering any other information into some element of the desktop. You can move the cursor, delete characters, and insert characters before you press the Return key to complete the entry.

▶ **THE CURSOR AND THE HIGHLIGHT**

In Chapter 1 we saw that the *cursor* and the *highlight* are two visual markers that Framework II uses to show you where you are currently working on the display screen. In much of your work, the cursor and the highlight will be located together. For example, when you select a frame, the cursor is located on the border of the frame, and the high-light simply extends and emphasizes the visual effect of the cursor.

However, when you are entering information on the edit line, the cursor shows your position on the line, character by character. From now on, we'll think of the *highlight* as the marker for the currently selected frame or element, and the *cursor* as the marker for character-by-character text entry on the edit line.

The edit cursor does not look exactly the same as the cursor you saw on the frame's border. On a frame's border, the cursor is a small, dark, flashing rectangle, taking up one character space. On the edit line, the cursor is a reverse-video space that displays the current letter or digit. Beneath the letter or digit is a flashing underscore character.

In summary, the *general* role of the cursor and the highlight together is to show you where you are currently working on the display screen. The highlight (along with the cursor) marks a frame or several frames that you have selected for some specific activity. The cursor alone marks your place in a line of text that you are entering or editing.

► EDITING A LABEL

We have seen that the edit line allows you to make changes in your data entry before you press the Return key. But what if you still make a mistake in the entry of a label? For example, let's imagine you acciden-tally left out a letter of the name you intended to give to the frame. After you press the Return key, you see that your frame label is

Comuter Talk

There are two ways you can correct your work. The simplest way is to return the label to the edit line for further editing. The key that does this for you is the Space bar. Press the Space bar once, while the frame's border is highlighted, and you will find the cursor back on the edit line, located at the beginning of the current version of the frame's label. To correct your mistake, then, you would press the following keys:

Space bar	(to go to the edit line)
→, three times	(to position the edit cursor)
p	(to insert the missing character)
Return	(to complete the correction)

The other way you can correct an error is simply to retype the whole label. As soon as you enter the first character (C), the original version of the frame label will disappear, and the cursor will be positioned in the edit line, ready for you to enter a new sequence of characters.

ENTERING OUTLINE HEADINGS

Once you have given your Outline frame an appropriate name, you'll be ready to go inside the frame and begin typing the headings of the outline itself. The data entry technique is identical: the process occurs on the edit line, and you can use the same cursor-movement keys to modify your work as you go along.

The first step, however, is to position the cursor inside the Outline frame. To do this, you'll recall, you use the Down Level key, located at the lower-right corner of the keyboard. (This key is labeled with a plus sign on the keyboard itself.) When you press this key, the highlight will be positioned over the first line of your outline, as shown in Figure 2.4.

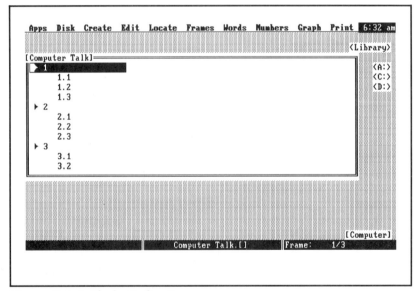

Figure 2.4: *Inside the Outline Frame*

Now that you are ready to work with the outline itself, you should examine the symbols and characters that Framework II uses to designate the structure of the outline. In Chapter 1 we discussed the numbering system of an outline. The main headings are numbered sequentially, 1, 2, 3. The numbers of subheadings have two parts; the first part identifies the subheading's location in the entire outline, and the second part indicates the sequential order inside a given section of the outline.

For example, consider the subheading number 2.3. The number tells you that this is the third subheading beneath the second major heading. However complex your outlines ultimately become, you will always be able to identify a subheading's location and logical order simply by examining its number.

As we talk about headings and subheadings, keep in mind that the outline actually represents a hierarchy of frames. Each major heading is a *containing* frame; each subheading, a subframe. Framework II supplies symbols within the outline that tell you what type of frame each heading represents. Notice that each major heading in the outline is preceded by a pointer, a small triangle that points toward the heading number. Framework II uses the pointer to tell you that this heading represents a *containing frame*—that is, a frame that contains other frames. Headings that do not contain other frames are preceded by a minus sign.

An Empty frame can serve your outlining requirements in one of two ways: You can perform word processing tasks inside the frame, in which case the frame becomes a Word frame. Or you can put other frames inside the frame, creating a new level in the hierarchy of your outline. In this case, the subframe itself becomes a containing frame.

You'll recall that each of the subheadings in an outline represents an Empty frame. Let's try a little experiment. Press the following keys:

Ctrl-F   (to select Frames)
R   (to invoke the Reveal Type option)

You'll notice, in Figure 2.5, that now each subheading has

(E)

following its numerical designation. This stands for Empty. When you choose the Reveal Type option, each type of frame is labeled with a letter—E for Empty frames, W for Word frames (which is what Empty frames become once you have entered text in them) and Telecommunications frames (which will also contain text once they have been used), S for Spreadsheet frames, and D for Database frames. Outline frames—or any frames that contain other frames—never have an identifier of this type.

Although Framework II doesn't normally display the indicator that tells you what types of frames are contained in an outline, we will continue with the Reveal Type option selected for the rest of this exercise, so that you can see what happens when you make changes to your outline.

But for the moment let's not worry about the *contents* of the frames in our outline. In fact, let's go back to thinking of the outline as a set of

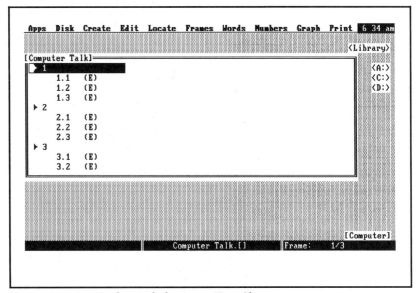

Figure 2.5: *An Outline with the Frame Type Shown*

headings and subheadings that you are using to organize your upcoming computer talk. We were about to begin entering labels into the outline to describe the sequence of this talk.

With the highlight positioned at the first major heading of the outline, as shown in Figure 2.4, notice the messages supplied in the status panel below the desktop. The central section of the panel gives you the *full name* of the current selection:

Computer Talk.[]

A full name is a sequence of labels, separated by periods, indicating the hierarchy of the outline. The first label shows the name of the outline frame itself: "Computer Talk". This name is followed by a period; then the empty brackets show that you have not yet entered a label for this first outline heading.

The right-hand section of the status panel shows the following message:

Frame: 1/3

This tells you that you are located at the first of the three major headings in your outline. You can see that Framework II has many overlapping ways of telling you exactly where you are working in an outline.

The messages and symbols that supply this information are often deliberately redundant: you are free to make use of the display screen's resources in whatever way makes sense to you.

Let's see what happens as you begin entering a label at this first heading position in the outline. The first part of your upcoming talk is going to be a general introduction to business computing. So you want to enter the word "Introduction" at heading 1. Begin typing the letters and watch the display screen. Figure 2.6 shows the screen as you're entering the word. Once again the cursor moves down to the edit line, where you can enter and modify your label. The status panel shows the new full name of the outline heading and the character-by-character progress of the edit cursor. When you finish typing the label, press the Return key. The cursor will move back up into the outline.

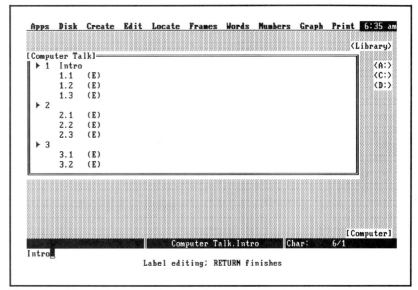

Figure 2.6: Entering an Outline Heading

So we see that the process of entering labels into the outline is the same as the process of entering a frame label. Let's enter the other labels into the major heading positions of the outline. You decide that the second part of your talk is going to be about word processing, and the third will cover spreadsheet programming. So you want to reposition the highlight and enter the following headings:

    2   Word Processing
    3   Spreadsheets

From the position of major heading 1, you can use the ↓ key to move the highlight down the outline. There are two ways to proceed. You can move one step at a time, subheading by subheading, until you reach your destination. Or, for a quicker way to move from one *major* heading to the next, you can press two keys at once:

    Ctrl-↓   (to move to the next major heading)

Likewise, the ↑ key moves you back up the outline, and Ctrl-↑ moves you up to the previous major heading.

After you have entered labels for the three major headings of your outline, you are going to enter subheadings. Figure 2.7 shows the entire outline, including subheadings for the three sections of your talk. Before you read on, practice entering labels by creating this outline on your desktop.

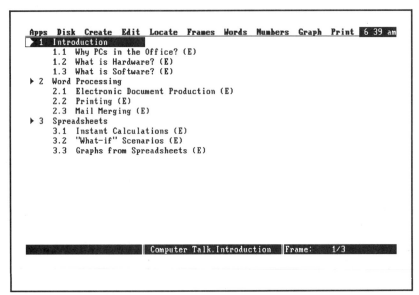

Figure 2.7: *An Outline with Subheadings*

Now that we have the beginnings of an outline, let's see what techniques are available for working with it.

CHANGING THE OUTLINE

First, you may have noticed that Figure 2.7 devotes the entire screen to the outline rather than just the space inside the frame on the desktop. The Outline frame itself, as shown in Figure 2.6, was not big enough for you to see the entire outline at once. When you move the highlight down to the subheading numbered 3.3, the outline *scrolls* one line up the screen. In other words, to make room to display the bottom line of the outline, Framework II has to push the top line temporarily out of view.

Scrolling is a common phenomenon in all kinds of computer work, because your display screen has only enough room for showing a certain number of contiguous lines at once. You can scroll either up or down with the cursor keys. Lines that are out of view are still part of the document; they are just temporarily off the screen. You can reach them again by scrolling back to their location.

ENLARGING YOUR VIEW OF THE OUTLINE

Framework II gives you a couple of ways to devote more than the normal frame area to a given document. One way is to use the Zoom key (the function key labeled F9). In order to zoom in on a frame, you place the cursor on the frame's border and press the Zoom key.

To reach the border of the Outline frame from inside the outline, you use the Up Level key (the key labeled with a minus sign, on the far right of your keyboard). Each time you press Up Level, the highlight moves one level higher in the outline, until it reaches the border of the frame itself. For example, from subheading level 3.3, you would have to press Up Level twice to reach the border: first to reach the heading level 3, then to move to the border of the frame.

Alternatively, you can press two keys at once, Ctrl-Up Level, to reach an Outline frame's border from any location inside the outline. So to zoom in on the entire outline, producing a display like the one in Figure 2.7, here are the keys you will press:

Ctrl-Up Level(−)   (to move the highlight to the border)
Zoom (F9)   (to zoom in on the frame)

Now you can see the entire outline at once, without scrolling. Of course, if you add new sections to the outline, as we are going to do next, the outline may once again be too large to fit on the screen. In this case, scrolling will still take place when you move from one part of the outline to another.

FOCUSING ON PARTICULAR SECTIONS

There is another simple technique for changing the amount of information shown on the screen. Occasionally you may want to concentrate on one particular section of your outline. You may find it convenient to have a temporary way of hiding the details of other sections. With one keystroke, Framework II allows you to *close* an entire section of your outline, so that you see only the main heading of that section. Closing a section of an outline is equivalent to closing a frame by putting it in its tray. The frame—or the outline section—is still available to you when you need it. You have simply put it out of view for the moment.

For example, let's say you have temporarily finished working on the Introduction section of your talk, and you want to concentrate on the other two sections. You can close this section by moving the highlight to the first major heading and pressing the Return key. The result is shown in Figure 2.8—the subheadings of the Introduction section are no longer visible.

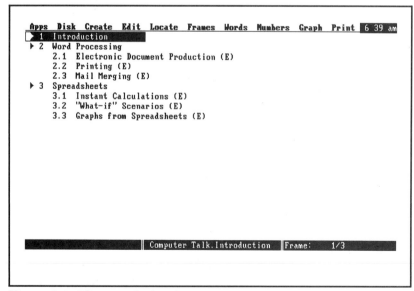

Figure 2.8: *Closing an Outline Section*

To reopen the Introduction section, press Return again while the highlight is positioned over the same heading. When you do so, the subheadings will reappear on the screen. You can use this technique to open or close any section of your outline.

In the following paragraphs, we'll explore a number of ways in which you can change the size and organization of your outline, including the following:

- Adding new headings

- Deleting headings

- Adding new levels to the structure of the outline

- Moving and copying sections of the outline

- Moving frames from the desktop to the outline

- Changing your view of the outline

To illustrate all these functions, we'll continue making plans for your upcoming computer talk.

ADDING NEW HEADINGS

There are several techniques for adding or inserting new headings to your outline. The technique you choose will depend on the type of frame you want to insert. It will also depend on whether you want to insert a new, Empty frame, or one that you have already developed somewhere else on the desktop. In this section we'll look at two ways to add frames to your outline.

Let's say you have decided to add a new subheading to the section of your talk that deals with spreadsheets. Between sections 3.1 and 3.2 you want to place an actual example of a spreadsheet. Recall that headings 3.1 and 3.2 are both Empty frames, potentially available for word processing. The new frame that you place between them will be a Spreadsheet frame, the contents of which you will develop after you have completed your outline.

You will need to use the Create option of Framework II's menu to add this new frame—or, rather, to add this new *outline subheading*, since we are still thinking of our work as an outline rather than a group of frames. To add a subheading at a specific point in your outline, you must be careful to position the highlight properly. Here is the rule for doing so:

Place the highlight at the heading immediately *above* but *at the same level* as the position where you want the new heading to appear.

In other words, if you want a new subheading to appear between 3.1 and 3.2, you will move the selection highlight to heading position 3.1 in the outline.

Once you have put the highlight in the correct place, you simply invoke the appropriate option of the Create menu to create the new heading. In this case, to create a Spreadsheet frame, you will press the following keys:

Ctrl-C   (to open the Create menu)
S   (to create a Spreadsheet frame)

Figure 2.9 shows what the outline will look like after you press these keys. A number of interesting things have happened. First of all, the new subheading has been given the number 3.2. Furthermore, the subheadings located farther down in this section have been automatically incremented. The former headings 3.2 and 3.3 have become 3.3 and 3.4, respectively.

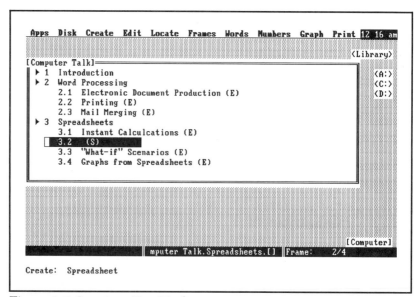

Figure 2.9: *Inserting a New Heading*

Because we have selected the Reveal Type option, the new subheading's frame type has also appeared on the screen:

3.2   (S)

We can see that the frame represented by this position in the outline will be available to us for spreadsheet programming. The next step you should take is to give this new subheading a name. Call it "Example":

   3.2 Example (S)

At this point you decide that your talk should have a fourth major section, covering database management. Like the other major sections, this one will have several subheadings of its own. You need to find a convenient way to add a new group of headings to your outline.

Again, you have several techniques to choose from to expand your outline. Perhaps the simplest way in this case is to use the Outline option of the Create submenu. Just as when we created the original outline, this option will add three major headings, each with three subheadings. Since we want only one new major heading, we'll then have to delete the other two.

You must carefully determine the correct position for the highlight before adding the new headings. Since you are adding major headings to your outline, you need to position the highlight at the major heading you want the new headings to follow. In short, place the highlight at heading 3, the one labeled "Spreadsheets." Then press the following keys to create the new headings:

   Ctrl-C   (to open the Create menu)
   O   (to create new headings)

You can see the new sections in Figure 2.10.

DELETING OUTLINE HEADINGS

Since you need only one additional section in your outline, instead of the three that you now have, you have to find some way to get rid of the rest. The Delete key will do the trick. You can delete either entire sections or just subheadings. Simply position the highlight over the part of the outline you want to delete and press the Delete key.

In this case, you want to delete sections 5 and 6. But just to experiment, place the highlight over heading 4 instead. Press Delete once. You'll see that when you delete 4, the old sections 5 and 6 are renumbered as 4 and 5. Press Delete again. Now the old section 5 has become section 4, leaving you with precisely the outline length you want.

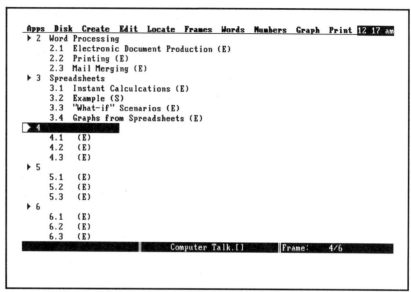

Figure 2.10: *Adding New Sections*

Deletions in Framework II are just easy enough to be dangerous. One of the major reasons for loss of valuable data on a computer is simple human error, leading to inadvertent deletions.

Fortunately, Framework II has a helpful way of bringing back accidental deletions. You may recall from Chapter 1 that the Edit menu has an Undo option. The keys you press to invoke this option are

      Ctrl-E   (to open the Edit menu)
      U   (to undo the last operation)

You may want to practice using this option now, so you'll know how to take advantage of it when you need it. You may find this option especially useful with frame labels. Recall that you can correct an error in a label simply by retyping the label. This means that you can also erase a label by pressing a key while a label is highlighted. To get back the old label, press the Escape or Return key before pressing Ctrl-E U.

After practicing the Undo option, make sure your outline has exactly four sections. Section 4 is to have only two subheadings, as follows:

    4   Database Management
       4.1   Definitions (E)
       4.2   Practical Applications (E)

Enter these headings into your outline. Then delete the third subheading from section 4. Use the same process: place the highlight over the unwanted subheading and press the Delete key.

ADDING NEW LEVELS TO THE OUTLINE

Up to now, all but one of the subheadings in your outline have represented Empty frames, potentially available to you for word processing. The outline has only two *levels*: the major headings, 1, 2, 3, and 4; and the subheadings 1.1, 1.2, and so on.

In many outlines two levels are not adequate to express the logical organization of a given task. So the next thing to learn is how to add more levels to your outline.

The discussion of database management in your talk is currently divided into two sections: Definitions and Practical Applications. You decide that the Definitions section needs more detail—that is, more subdividing. You want to specify the database definitions that you will be presenting. In the context of databases, you are planning to discuss three terms that you think your audience will want to learn about: files, records, and fields. You would like your outline to look like this:

> Database Management
>   Definitions
>   Files
>   Records
>   Fields
>   Practical Applications

Follow these steps to create a new level in your outline:

1. Place the highlight at the heading below which you want to create a new level.

2. Press two keys simultaneously: Ctrl and Down Level.

Let's try it. First move the highlight to subheading 4.1, with the label "Definitions." Then press

> Ctrl-Down Level (+)   (to create a new level of outlining)

Here is what you will see in your outline:

> 4 Database Management
>   4.1 Definitions
>   4.1.1   (E)

Notice that subheading 4.1 is no longer an Empty frame. It has lost its (E) designation, and on the screen you can see that it has a pointer, to show you that it is a containing frame. The new subheading (or sub-subheading, if you like), numbered 4.1.1, is an Empty frame.

Now you need to add two more subheadings at this new, third level of your outline. Place the highlight at subheading 4.1.1 and press

Ctrl-C	(to open the Create menu)
E	(to create heading 4.1.2)
Ctrl-C	(to open the Create menu again)
E	(to create heading 4.1.3)

Make sure you understand the difference between adding a new heading at an already established outline level and adding a new, deeper level. The former action uses the Create menu; the latter, the Ctrl-Down Level keystrokes.

Now type headings for the three new sublevels, 4.1.1, 4.1.2, and 4.1.3. Recall that the headings will be "Files", "Records", and "Fields". Figure 2.11 shows the current organization of your outline.

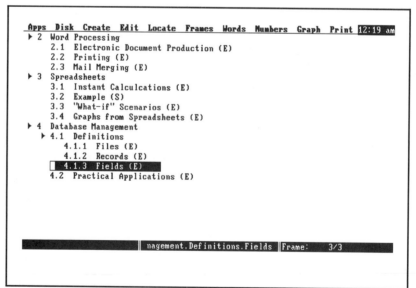

Figure 2.11: Adding a New Level

As you examine your work up to now and consider the material you'll be presenting to your audience, you suddenly realize that you've made a mistake in organizing your talk. Your audience will be a group of managers, and their primary interest will be in spreadsheet programming. For this reason, you decide that you might risk losing their attention if you discuss word processing near the beginning of your presentation. A better approach would be to begin with spreadsheets.

This kind of change is, of course, a common occurrence in the thought process represented by an outline. When you look at the whole outline, you will often decide that you would like to rearrange some of the sections. Let's see how this can be done in a Framework II outline.

MOVING PORTIONS OF THE OUTLINE

The Move key (function key F7) and its companion the Copy key (F8) have important applications in every Framework II component. They are both involved in transferring desktop information from one place to another. The keys' names clearly indicate the difference between their respective functions:

- The Move key (F7) actually displaces information. After a move, the information will no longer be found in its original location; instead, it will be at the target location.

- The Copy key (F8) leaves the information intact at its source *and* produces a new, identical copy of the information at the target location. (Perhaps the most important use of Copy is in spreadsheet programming, where the word "identical" does not always apply to the copy or copies that are produced. We'll see why in Chapter 3.)

At this point in our outlining work, we require the services of the Move key. Before the end of this chapter, we'll also see examples of the Copy operation in an outline.

Your goal at this point is to rearrange the Computer Talk outline in this new order:

1   Introduction
2   Spreadsheets
3   Word Processing
4   Database Management

Here are the steps you will take to accomplish this change:

1. Place the highlight on the third major heading, labeled "Spreadsheets".

2. Press the Move key (F7).

3. Move the highlight up to the first major heading, "Introduction".

4. Press the Return key.

To generalize the steps of a Move operation: you begin at the *source* location (i.e., the location of the information you want to move), press the Move key, move the highlight to the *destination* location, and press the Return key to complete the operation.

In an outline, you indicate the destination of a move by placing the highlight on the heading immediately *above* the target location.

Figure 2.12 shows what your outline will look like after the move. The Spreadsheets section of the outline has become the second major heading. All of its subheadings have been renumbered correctly. The Word Processing section has become the third major heading; its subheadings have also been renumbered.

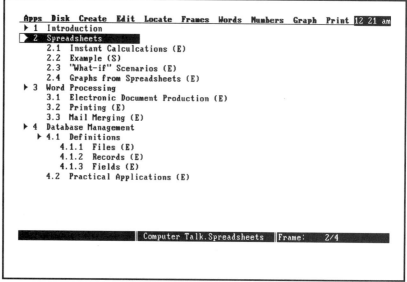

Figure 2.12: Rearranging the Outline

We've seen how easy it is to rearrange the order of your outline using the Move key. Now we'll use the same key to move frames from the desktop to the outline.

INCORPORATING OTHER FRAMES INTO THE OUTLINE

Once again you decide to make some changes in the way your outline is organized. As you examine the section on Spreadsheets, you realize that you need to have at least two examples to show your audience: a Spreadsheet frame and a Graph frame. You decide to eliminate the current Spreadsheet frame, 2.2, and to create a fourth subheading, numbered 2.4, to contain the two examples you want to show.

You move the highlight to subheading 2.2 and press the Delete key. Then you move down to 2.3 and create a new subheading below it by pressing the sequence

Ctrl-C   (to open the Create menu)
E   (to create an Empty frame)

You label this new subheading "Examples". Here is the new order of the Spreadsheets section:

    2   Spreadsheets
        2.1   Instant Calculations (E)
        2.2   "What-if" Scenarios (E)
        2.3   Graphs from Spreadsheets (E)
        2.4   Examples (E)

For a moment, let's assume that you have been working with Framework II for a couple of months. Looking through the Framework II files that you have stored on disk, you find a Spreadsheet file and a Graph file that you have already developed. These will serve as good examples for your presentation, and they will save you the trouble of creating new ones. You bring the two files onto the desktop and rename them Spreadsheet and Graph, respectively.

Your task now is to move these two frames from their trays at the side of the desktop to the outline, a level below subheading 2.4. This is how you want the outline to look after the move:

    2.4   Examples
        2.4.1   Spreadsheet (S)
        2.4.2   Graph (G)

Completing this operation is a little tricky. The problem is that you must create the new outline level, beneath heading 2.4, before you can move the two examples into it. There is no way to move frames into an outline level that doesn't exist yet. So you'll have to perform this operation in three steps: first create an Empty frame at the new level; then move the two example frames to locations below the Empty frame; and finally delete the unused Empty frame.

The first step, then, is to move the highlight to subheading 2.4 and press Ctrl-Down Level to create the Empty frame at the new level. Here is what you'll see:

> **2.4   Examples**
>   **2.4.1   (E)**

The second step involves learning how to use a new function key—the Extend Select key (F6). You are planning to move *two* frames from the desktop into the outline. It would be a waste of time to have to move them one at a time. Fortunately, whenever you want to perform an identical operation with more than one frame (and the frames you want to select are adjacent), Framework II gives you a special way to *extend* the frame highlight over all the frames you want to work with. Let's see how this is done.

Figure 2.13 shows your current desktop. In the open Outline frame, you can see the new Examples subheading, with its own subheading, numbered 2.4.1. In the tray area of the desktop, you can see the Spreadsheet and Graph frames that you want to move into the outline. Here are the keys you press to get out of the open Outline frame and to move the highlight to the closed tray frames:

Ctrl-Up Level (-n-)	(to move to the border of the Outline frame)
↓	(to move to the first of the trays)

Now you need to select *both* frames, so that they can both be moved together into the outline. To do so, you press the Extend Select key (F6). Extend Select is certainly one of the most powerful of the ten Framework II function keys. We'll be using it in many different ways as we examine spreadsheets, word processing, and database management. When you press this key, Framework II displays the following instructions on the message line:

> **SELECT: extend selection with cursor keys; RETURN finishes**

In this case, you want to select both the Spreadsheet and the Graph trays. The highlight is already positioned on the Spreadsheet tray. After pressing Extend Select, you simply press the ↓ key to extend the highlight over the second of the two trays.

You can begin to see the significance of Framework II's highlight feature. Up to now we have used the highlight to select individual frames

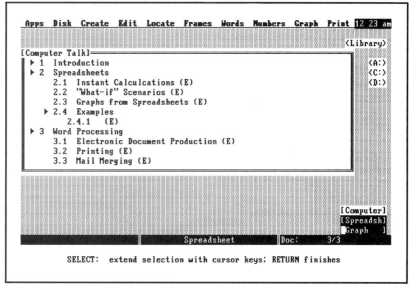

Figure 2.13: Using Extend Select

or headings in the outline. Now you can see that the highlight can be enlarged, or extended, to select many frames or headings at once.

To complete the Extend Select operation, you press the Return key (following the instructions displayed on the message line). This leaves the two trays selected for the next step of our move procedure.

Next, press the Move key (F7). Again you'll see instructions on the message line:

MOVE: cursor to the move destination; RETURN finishes

To complete the move operation you must now move the highlight back into the Outline frame and position it at the correct destination for the two frames you have selected. The following sequence of keystrokes will accomplish the move:

↑	(to move to the Outline frame)
Down Level (+)	(to move into the frame)
↓, several times	(to highlight subheading 2.4.1)
Return	(to complete the move)

As soon as you press the Return key, the two trays on the desktop are instantly moved into the outline. All during the move operation, Framework II remembers which two frames you selected for the move.

(Note that the original trays will *not* remain on the desktop; we are moving, not copying.) Something odd has happened, though; the two new outline subheadings do not look like the rest of the outline. They don't have numbers or type indicators:

2.4   Examples
  2.4.1   (E)
  Spreadsheet
  Graph

▶ NUMBERING AND INCLUDING THE TYPE INDICATORS

This situation is typical of a move from the desktop to an outline. Frames that you move into the outline do not start out with outline numbers or type indicators. If you want to add this information to the outline, you must invoke two options from the Frames menu.

Figure 2.14 shows the Frames menu. The two options that we want to use at this point are

  -- Number Labels
  -- Reveal Type

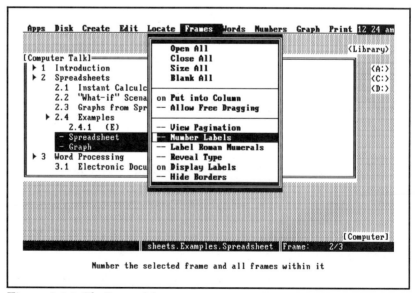

Figure 2.14: The Frames Menu

You can switch any of these options on by selecting the option. A Framework II menu option is in effect when you see the word "on" in the menu; for example:

on Number Labels

The option is off when you see two hyphens before the option.

These options work on whatever parts of the outline are currently selected for activity. At this point, both the Spreadsheet and Graph headings are still highlighted; the Extend Select operation is still in effect. Thus, as we invoke these two Frames options, they will work on both of the headings. Here are the keystrokes:

Ctrl-F	(to open the Frames menu)
N	(to number the selected frames)
Ctrl-F	(to open the Frames menu)
R	(to reveal the types of the frames)

Finally, Figure 2.15 shows your outline after all these operations are complete. Only one detail remains: you must still delete the Empty frame numbered 2.4.1.

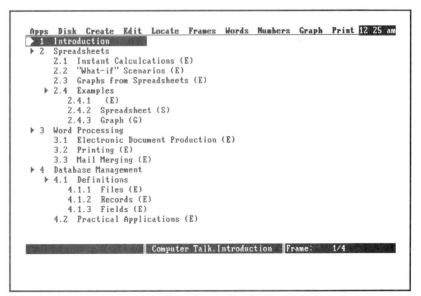

Figure 2.15: Moving Frames from the Desktop to the Outline

At this point you are satisfied with your outline, and you are ready to begin using it as a template for preparing the contents of your presentation. Up to now, we have been completely preoccupied with organizing the outline itself, and we have never once concerned ourselves with the contents of the frames in the outline. In the next section we'll discuss two ways that you can use to move inside the Empty frames.

ENTERING THE OUTLINE FRAMES

We have already seen how the Zoom key can be used to devote the entire screen to the contents of the Outline frame. When you get ready to enter information into any of the Empty frames in the outline, you can also use the Zoom key.

For example, let's say you want to start writing some notes for the very first topic of your presentation: the first subheading in the Introduction section. If you open the Introduction section again (by placing the highlight over the first major heading and pressing Return), you can review this part of the outline:

    1   Introduction
       1.1   Why PCs in the Office? (E)
       1.2   What is Hardware? (E)
       1.3   What is Software? (E)

Now you want to open the Empty frame represented by subheading 1.1, so you can begin typing some notes. Move the highlight to 1.1 and press the Zoom key (F9). As a result, the entire screen will be given over to this one Empty frame, as shown in Figure 2.16. You can begin writing whatever information you want directly into this frame.

As soon as you start typing, this Empty frame will become a Word frame, for word processing. When you finish your work on this first section and you want to return to the outline, simply press Zoom (F9) again. The Zoom key is actually a toggle; it switches you into and out of full-screen mode for a given frame.

When you return to the outline, you shouldn't be too surprised to find that the type indicator of the first subheading has changed:

       1.1   Why PCs in the Office? (W)

The W, for Word, shows that this frame is no longer empty. We'll be discussing the details of word processing in Chapter 4; but meanwhile, you

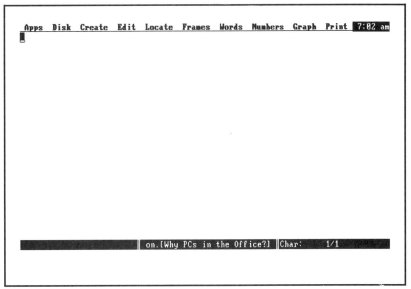

Apps Disk Create Edit Locate Frames Words Numbers Graph Print 7:02 am

on.[Why PCs in the Office?] Char: 1/1

Figure 2.16: *Zooming into an Empty Frame*

shouldn't hesitate to experiment with entering words and sentences into the Empty frames of your outline.

The View key is also a toggle; it switches an outline between "Outline view" and "Frames view." We've been working in Outline view throughout this chapter. Frames view transforms the display of each heading in the outline into an individual frame on the display screen. When you are working in Frames view in a large outline like the one we have developed, you will have to scroll from one frame to the next; generally only two or three frames can be seen on the screen at a time in this mode.

Figure 2.17 shows a Frames view of the Introduction section of the outline. To produce this screen, place the highlight on the first major heading and press the View key (F10). Then, to devote the entire screen to the Frames view, press the Zoom key. (You can also produce this screen by simply pressing the Zoom key with the highlight on the first major heading.) Notice that you can see all three subframes of the Introduction section at once. To move inside any one of the frames, select the frame's border and press the Down Level key (+). To return to the Outline view, press the View key again.

NOTE: If you want to return all the way to a frame's outer border, you can do so by pressing Ctrl-Up Level from any point in an outline, even if you have used the Zoom key to get a full-screen view of a small portion of your outline.

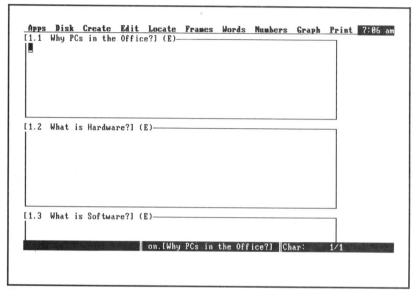

Figure 2.17: *Frames View*

We've seen all the ways that you can use an Outline frame to organize your thoughts for a given task. To summarize, Framework II gives you simple techniques for adding headings and levels to the outline, for deleting headings or entire levels, for rearranging the order of selected sections in the outline, for bringing in frames from the desktop, and for viewing the outline as a group of frames that you can enter information into.

BUILDING AN OUTLINE FROM AN EMPTY FRAME

You can also use an Empty frame as the starting point for an outline. You might decide to do so if the major purpose of your outline is to organize a set of work frames that you have already created. Building such an outline involves the same techniques that we discussed above. You can take advantage of a number of Framework II tools.

□   The Move key, to begin moving desktop frames into your outline

□   The Create menu, to incorporate new frames (of any type) into the outline

□   The Ctrl-Down Level keystroke combination, to create new levels in your outline

□   The Frames menu, to control the appearance of the outline, including the appearance of numbering and type designators

□   The Move and Copy keys, to rearrange the order of frames in the outline

□   The Zoom and View keys, to examine and work in the contents areas of the frames

CREATING A TABLE OF CONTENTS

The Frames submenu has other interesting options that can be used on Outline frames or on outlines that you have built in Empty frames. Among these options is one that transforms an outline into a table of contents that includes page numbers. This option is called

-- View Pagination

Let's say you complete the preparation for your talk on business uses of personal computers, and the day comes for you to present the talk to your audience. Everyone is favorably impressed with the clarity of your ideas and the organization of your talk. Several people ask if you can produce a written version of your presentation, turning your notes and examples into a report that can be distributed to the managers who didn't make it to the meeting.

You agree to print out what you have written. The report turns out to be a number of pages long, so you decide to include the original outline as a table of contents. The pages of the report are numbered, and you would like to find an easy way to incorporate these page numbers into the table of contents. Here's how to do it:

Ctrl-Up Level (–)	(to select the frame's border)
Ctrl-F	(to select the Frame menu)
V	(to view page numbers)

Figure 2.18 shows what you get; you can see that the entire report covers eight pages of documents. Your table of contents will help readers
zero in on just the information they need. Note that when Reveal Type
is on, /p appears after the frame type, if a frame has ever been formatted
for printing, as shown in the figure.

```
 Apps  Disk  Create  Edit  Locate  Frames  Words  Numbers  Graph  Print  2:57 am
▶ 1  Introduction /p . . . . . . . . . . . . . . . . . .   1
     1.1  Why PCs in the Office? (W) . . . . . . . . . .   1
     1.2  What is Hardware? (W)  . . . . . . . . . . .    1
     1.3  What is Software? (W) . . . . . . . . . . . .   2
▶ 2  Spreadsheets  . . . . . . . . . . . . . . . . . .   2
     2.1  Instant Calculations (W) . . . . . . . . . .   2
     2.2  "What-if" Scenarios (W) . . . . . . . . . .    3
     2.3  Graphs from Spreadsheets (W) . . . . . . . .   3
   ▶ 2.4  Examples  . . . . . . . . . . . . . . . . .    3
        2.4.1  Spreadsheet (S) . . . . . . . . . . . .   3
        2.4.2  Graph (G) . . . . . . . . . . . . . . .   4
▶ 3  Word Processing  . . . . . . . . . . . . . . . .    4
     3.1  Electronic Document Production (W) . . . . .   4
     3.2  Printing (W) . . . . . . . . . . . . . . . .   5
     3.3  Mail Merging (W) . . . . . . . . . . . . . .   5
▶ 4  Database Management  . . . . . . . . . . . . . .    6
   ▶ 4.1  Definitions . . . . . . . . . . . . . . . .    6
        4.1.1  Files (W) . . . . . . . . . . . . . . .   6
        4.1.2  Records (W) . . . . . . . . . . . . . .   6
        4.1.3  Fields (W) . . . . . . . . . . . . . .    7
     4.2  Practical Applications (W) . . . . . . . . .   7
                    Computer Talk.Introduction  Frame:   1/4
```

Figure 2.18: *Creating a Table of Contents*

SAVING OUTLINES—USING THE DISK MENU

The Disk menu, shown in Figure 2.19, saves entire Outline files on
disk. Here is a brief description of the two relevant options of the menu.

Save and Continue. This option saves a copy of your current outlining
work and then lets you continue where you left off on the desktop. You
can invoke this option from any position inside an outline; the highlight does not need to be located on the outside border of the outline.
Recall that there are two ways to perform a Save and Continue operation. If you go through the Disk menu you press these keys:

Ctrl-D   (to open the Disk menu)
S   (to Save and Continue)

You can also use a shorter alternative that does not go through the menu; all you press is

    Ctrl-Return   (Save and Continue)

Put Away. This option saves the current Outline frame on disk and then removes it from the desktop. Once again, you can perform this operation either from inside the outline or from the border of the Outline frame.

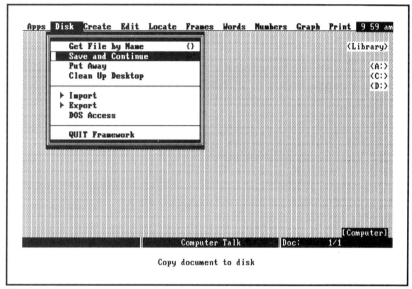

Figure 2.19: *The Disk Menu*

Both of these operations save your entire Outline frame on disk, with all of the frames it contains. The Outline frame will be stored as a single file, under the name determined by the Outline frame's label.

Sometimes you may want to save as individual files one or more of the frames located *inside* an Outline frame. For example, look at the Computer Talk outline in Figure 2.20. Let's say you've decided to save the three Word frames located in the Database Management section of your outline under the Definitions subheading. You want these three Word frames each to become individual files on the disk, so you can work with each of them separately later on. Unfortunately, neither the Save and Continue nor the Put Away options of the Disk menu will help you with this operation. These Disk options work only with your entire Outline frame.

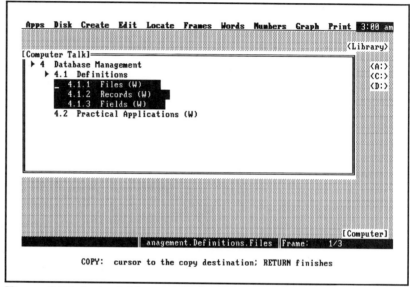

Figure 2.20: *Saving Subframes to Disk*

To save the three Word frames individually, you'll use either the Move key or the Copy key. Here are the steps you'll follow:

1. Use the Extend Select key to highlight the three Word frames (you can see in Figure 2.20 that this has already been done). Position the highlight over heading 4.1.1 and press the following keys:

Extend Select (F6)	(to extend the highlight)
↓	(to include 4.1.2)
↓	(to include 4.1.3)
Return	(to complete the selection)

2. Press the Move key (F7) or the Copy key (F8); we'll discuss in a moment the difference between these two operations in this case.

3. Move the highlight to the inside of the disk drive cabinet B, and complete the Move or Copy operation. Here is how to do it:

Shuttle (Scroll Lock)	(to select the disk drive cabinet)
Down Level (+)	(to move into the drive cabinet)
Return	(to complete the move)

(Recall that the Shuttle key always moves you to the disk drive cabinets.)

When you press Return, the three Word frames will be saved one at a time on your disk, as three different files. You'll be able to see them the next time you look at the disk directory.

There is an important difference between using the Copy key and the Move key for this operation. If you use the Move key (F7), the headings will disappear from your outline. They will literally be displaced—moved into the disk directory. If you use the Copy key (F8), however, the headings will be *copied* to the disk cabinet, and the originals will remain in your outline.

Near the end of this chapter we'll come back to our discussion of the disk drive cabinets to see how Framework II handles your disk if you have divided it into DOS subdirectories.

PRINTING OUTLINES—USING THE PRINT MENU

When you set out to print an Outline frame on paper, you have to decide which part of the frame to send to the printer:

- □ Outline headings only
- □ Contents of the subframes only
- □ Both the headings and the contents

The View key (F10) will help you carry out your decision. Recall that View toggles an Outline frame between Frames view (where you see the contents of the frames in the outline) and Outline view (where you see only the headings of the outline). The Print operation will conform to the current View setting.

If you want to print an outline or a table of contents, print the Outline frame while it is displayed in Outline view.

If you want to print the contents of the Word, Spreadsheet, Database, or Graph frames that are contained inside your Outline frame, print the frame while it is displayed in Frames view.

The Print menu appears in Figure 2.21. To print a frame, place the highlight on the frame's border, select the view of your choice, and then press

Ctrl-P   (to open the Print menu)

B   (to begin printing)

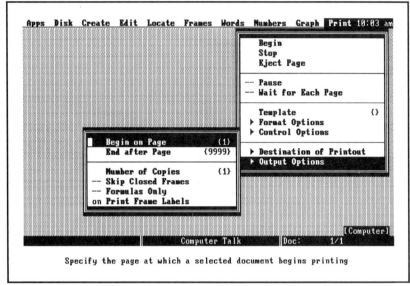

Figure 2.21: The Print Menu

Don't be surprised if you see your disk drive lights go on before the printer begins to print. Framework II goes through an efficient process called "spooling" while it is getting ready to print your frame. It first stores an image of the printed frame as a file on your disk, and then it transfers that file to the printer. While this is happening, Framework II displays

PREPARING TO PRINT

in the message area at the bottom of the screen. The advantage to this process is that you can work on the desktop while Framework II is printing your document. (When the printing process is complete, Framework II erases the print file from the disk.)

You can see in Figure 2.21 that the Print menu has several submenus of its own. The one you see in the center of the desktop is the submenu for Output Options. You can look at this submenu on your own screen by pressing

Ctrl-P	(to open the Print menu)
O	(to select Output Options)

The Output Options submenu gives you three important options for controlling the way an outline is printed. You can switch any of these options on simply by selecting the option on the submenu.

The Skip Closed Frames option tells Framework II not to print any sections of your outline that are closed. (Remember how we closed the Introduction section of the Computer Talk outline by pressing the Return key with the highlight over the first outline heading.) If you want to print parts of your outline selectively, this is the option to work with.

The Print Frame Labels option, which is on by default but can be toggled off and on, tells Framework II to print the outline headings (that is, the frame labels, if you think of your outline as a collection of frames) along with the contents of the outline.

Finally, an advanced feature: the Formulas Only option. We have seen that each frame on the desktop can hold a formula or a program; formulas reside *behind* frames. It turns out that an Outline frame is often a convenient structure for building a FRED program—a collection of formulas stored behind a hierarchy of frames. If you write such a program and you want to print it out on paper, the Formulas Only option tells Framework II to print the program behind the outline rather than the outline itself. We'll talk more about this in Chapter 7, which discusses FRED programming.

We've discussed in detail the techniques you can use for creating Outline frames and changing them to match your own thought processes. We've also seen how to save and print outlines. Now it's time to check back with Eileen Wilcox and George Farley at The Sophisticated Palate.

EXAMPLES

In Chapter 1 we examined an outline that Eileen developed to create an advertising flier for her party trays. Let's look at exactly how she created this flier.

You'll remember that her flier contains three party tray descriptions, with a small spreadsheet below each description. The spreadsheets display a range of prices for each tray, depending on the number of people the tray is to serve.

OUTLINING THE PROMOTIONAL FLIER

To develop this document, Eileen began with an Outline frame. She deleted the subheadings in each of the original three outline sections and entered labels for the three remaining headings:

1   Cocktail Tray I
2   Cocktail Tray II
3   Buffet Tray

Her next step was to develop a template for the small spreadsheet that follows each major heading. She used the Create menu to insert a Spreadsheet frame between the first and second headings of her outline:

1   Cocktail Tray I
2
3   Cocktail Tray II
4   Buffet Tray

Then she pressed the View key (F10) so she could work on the contents of her frames. She developed the necessary two-line spreadsheet, with column headings for the number of people and a row for the prices of each tray. She left the prices out for the moment. You can see her work up to this point in Figure 2.22.

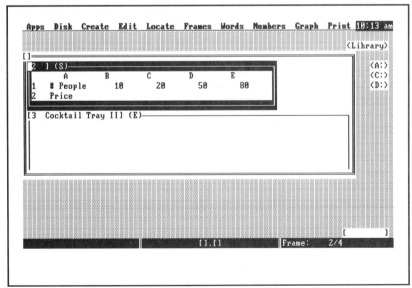

Figure 2.22: *Developing the Party Tray Flier*

Returning the frame to Outline view, she gave her Spreadsheet frame a name—Prices—and copied it twice, placing copies beneath each of the other two tray descriptions. Placing the highlight over the Spreadsheet label, she performed the following keystrokes to produce the copies:

Copy (F8)	(to begin the copy operation)
↓	(to move the highlight to heading 3)
Return	(to produce the copy)
Copy	(to copy again)
↓	(to position the highlight)
Return	(to produce the third copy)

Here is the resulting outline:

1   Cocktail Tray I
2   Prices
3   Cocktail Tray II
4   Prices
5   Buffet Tray
6   Prices

At this point, before entering any specific data into the frames of the outline, Eileen decided to save a copy of this outline onto disk. She realized that she would be able to use this empty outline to produce quick advertising fliers for other party trays she offers in future weeks. She called the copy TRAYTEMP for "tray template."

Finally, she typed the text describing this week's trays into each of the Empty frames (which then became Word frames), and entered the appropriate prices for each tray into the three spreadsheets. She moved the highlight to the border of the Outline frame and pressed the View key to put the outline in Frames view. Just before printing out the flier, she used an option in the Frames menu to get rid of the outline numbers. Then she used the Print menu to begin printing. You can look back at her work in Figure 1.19.

ORGANIZING EXPENSE SPREADSHEETS INTO AN OUTLINE

George has also begun to use outlining, as a way to keep track of the company's monthly expenses. He has asked Frank Osawa, the bookkeeper, to maintain a series of expense spreadsheets for each month, to record the cost of running the company. Here are the names of Frank's spreadsheets:

> Advertising Expenses
> Cost of Goods Sold
> Equipment Loan Payments
> Equipment Maintenance
> Insurance
> Rent
> Utilities
> Wages

We'll examine some of these spreadsheets in Chapter 3. For now, simply imagine the rows and columns of numbers that might be involved in each kind of expense. The bottom line on each spreadsheet will represent the total expense, in a given category, for the month.

Over time George finds himself asking for more and more new spreadsheets for specific expense categories. As the number of spreadsheets increases, George realizes that he needs some way to organize all these documents and pull them together for a given month's expense accounting. An Outline frame seems to be what he needs.

He creates an Outline frame and calls it Monthly Expenses. The frame begins with just two headings:

> 1 Fixed Expenses
> 2 Variable Expenses

To fill in the outline, he brings all of the various expense spreadsheet files from disk to the desktop. Figure 2.23 shows his desktop with the spreadsheet files in trays. He realizes that he will ultimately use the Move key (F7) to move the desktop frames into the outline. But before he can do this, he has to create new sublevels beneath each of the current headings. Consulting with Eileen, he learns that the correct keystroke combination is

> Ctrl-Down Level (+)   (to create a new outline level)

He presses these keys twice, with the highlight positioned over each of the major headings. Here is what he gets:

> 1 Fixed Expenses
>   1.1
> 2 Variable Expenses
>   2.1

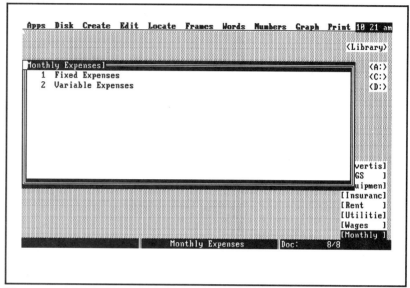

Figure 2.23: Developing an Outline of Expense Spreadsheets

Now he can move each of the Spreadsheet frames from the desktop into the appropriate outline sections. He begins by moving the Cost of Goods Sold spreadsheet, his only variable expense. He returns to the frame border and uses the Frames menu to add numbers and a type indicator to his new outline:

   1   Fixed Expenses
      1.1   (E)
   2   Variable Expenses
      2.1   (E)
      2.2 COGS (S)

Finally, he uses the Extend Select key (F6) to extend the highlight over all of the other spreadsheets on the desktop, so he can move them all at once into the Fixed Expenses category. He quickly deletes the two extraneous Empty frames, and smiles at a job well done:

   1   Fixed Expenses
      1.1   Advertising (S)
      1.2   Equipment Loans (S)
      1.3   Equipment Maintenance (S)
      1.4   Insurance (S)
      1.5   Rent (S)

1.6   Utilities (S)
1.7   Wages (S)
2   Variable Expenses
2.1   COGS (S)

SHARING DATA AMONG THE SPREADSHEETS

Eileen looks over his shoulder on the way to the kitchen and asks him what he's doing. He's delighted to have the chance to show her how he's been able to use Framework II's outlining capabilities.

But Eileen points out that he's forgotten the most important part. Outlining is, of course, a great way to bring together groups of related documents—to organize them, to save them on disk together, and to print them out in a single printing operation. But in spreadsheet work the most useful function of all is Framework II's ability to link different spreadsheets together for exchanging data—and, in this case, to produce a complete summary of all the various expense categories.

Eileen leans over George's shoulder to add one final frame to the outline:

3 Summary of Expenses (S)

She tells him that this summary spreadsheet can be organized to take bottom-line data from each of the other spreadsheets in the outline and produce a total expense figure for the month. If he then made changes in the detail spreadsheets, the summary would automatically be updated.

We'll have to wait until Chapter 3 to pursue Eileen's idea about spreadsheets. In the meantime, let's take a quick look at a few more features of Framework II.

EXPLORING FURTHER

MULTI-LINE FRAME LABELS

At the beginning of this chapter we learned how to enter a label onto the border of a frame. We learned that a frame label serves to identify the frame on the desktop and to supply a file name when you store the frame on disk.

Actually, frame labels may consist of many lines of information, even though only the first line is displayed on the frame's border. From time to time you may find it useful to enter several lines of notes into the label of a frame, simply as comments—to remind yourself of the information that the frame contains.

For example, let's add a few sentences to the label of George's Monthly Expenses outline. To move the current label back to the edit line, you simply press the Space bar, as we learned earlier. Now, to expand the label into more lines, you press the Zoom key (F9). Framework II devotes the entire screen to the frame label and gives you the chance to enter any information there that you want to save along with the frame itself.

Figure 2.24 shows some notes we might want to keep in the label of the Monthly Expenses Outline frame. Once they are stored there, these notes are available for reading at any time. All you have to do is place the cursor on the frame border and press

| Space bar | (to move the label to the edit line) |
| Zoom (F9) | (to give the whole screen to the label) |

Press the Zoom key again to return to the normal view of the desktop.

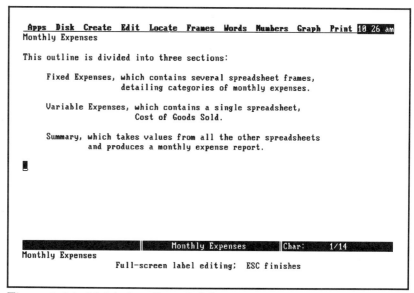

Figure 2.24: A Multi-Line Frame Label

DRAGGING AND SIZING FRAMES

Two function keys that we haven't discussed yet are Drag and Size. These keys allow you to slide a frame into a new position and change the size of a frame on the desktop. Their respective actions are both amusing and useful.

To use the Drag key, place the highlight on the border of the frame you want to move. Press the Drag key, F3. Then use the ↑, ↓, →, and ← keys to move the frame to any new location on the desktop. Press the Return key to complete the move.

The Size key has applications throughout Framework II. To use it with a frame, make sure the highlight is on the border and then press Size (F4). The → key increases the horizontal length of the frame's area on the desktop; the ↓ key increases the vertical height. Likewise, the ← and ↑ keys *decrease* the size of the frame.

Both sizing and dragging operations can be amplified by pressing the Ctrl key at the same time as an arrow key. When you've pressed the Size key (F4), the Ctrl key, in conjunction with an arrow key, increases or decreases the size of a frame by several screen rows or text columns. You can use the Ctrl-arrow keys to quickly make major adustments, and then use an arrow key alone to fine-tune the size of your frame. In addition, pressing the Size key twice will expand the selected frame so that it fills the entire desktop.

When you've selected Drag (F3), the Ctrl key amplifies the movements of the selected frame so that it jumps across the screen at larger intervals. If you make a mistake and want to return your frame to its original size or position, press Escape instead of Return, and your desktop will be restored as though you had never performed the operation.

Create several experimental frames, and play with the Size and Drag keys. You'll be amused with the results. You can switch from one of these functions to the other without pressing Return first. Pressing the Escape key returns the frame to its original size and position.

These keys can also be used with frames contained in an Outline frame. Normally, frames in an outline are arranged in a column, but you can use an option in the Frames menu to allow you to move frames horizontally in an outline. The option is

-- Allow Free Dragging

You can turn this option on for a given frame by pressing

Ctrl-F   (to open the Frames menu)

A   (to allow free dragging)

Dragging and sizing frames in an outline can be very useful when you want to arrange—and print—information in parallel columns. Figure 2.25 shows an example of this—an alternative way of presenting Eileen's party tray flier. This display was produced by reducing the size of the Word frame, on the left, and dragging the Spreadsheet frame up to the side of the Word frame. Of course, you must do this sort of work in Frames view rather than in Outline view.

Just as on the desktop, Framework II allows you to correct your mistakes easily if dragging frames inside a containing frame produces unintended results. An additional option on the Frames menu, labeled

-- -- Put into Column

will restore your frames to their original arrangement, lined up in a column against the left side of the containing frame.

The flexibility that the Drag and Size keys give you will also be useful when you want to display several independent frames (frames that are not within an outline) on the desktop at once.

OTHER WAYS OF LABELING OUTLINE COMPONENTS

In addition to the number labels discussed earlier in this chapter, Framework II gives you the option of labeling your outline headings and subheadings in the traditional—rather than the technical—style, which you probably learned in elementary school. To select this option, choose

-- -- Label Roman Numerals

from the Frames menu. Figure 2.26 shows an outline with several levels of nesting, with traditional style heading numbers.

Moreover, you can mix traditional, technical, and unnumbered sections in the same outline if it suits your purposes to do so. Remember that Framework II's menu commands operate only on what is selected. Thus, you can use different numbering systems for different parts of your outline by selecting the major heading of the section you want to change and toggling the Label Roman Numerals and Number Labels options on and off. Try experimenting with these options before you use them in a frame you intend to keep, because the results can be confusing if you're not careful.

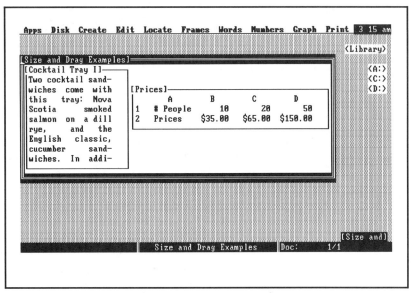

Figure 2.25: *Dragging and Sizing Frames in an Outline*

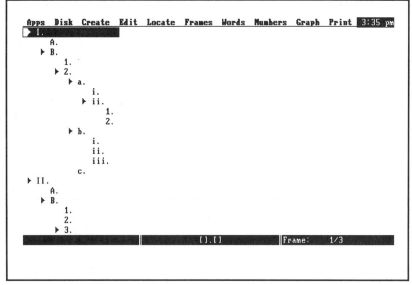

Figure 2.26: *Outline with Traditional Numbering*

DISPLAYING DISK SUBDIRECTORIES
IN AN OUTLINE FORM

Finally, Framework II has incorporated its outlining capability in its display of disk subdirectories. Recent versions of the PC disk operating system, PC-DOS (or MS-DOS on compatibles), have allowed the creation of subdivisions of storage areas on a disk. This feature is primarily designed for organizing the relatively large area on a hard disk, but it can also be used with floppy disks.

PC-DOS gives you ways to create subdirectories and to store files in them as though these subdirectories were separate disks. When you have more files than can fit on a single screen directory listing, you may find it helpful to organize the files under several subdirectories. Framework II, in turn, supports the use of subdirectories. If you use a data disk in Framework II that contains subdirectories, the disk frame will display those directories in an outline form when you open them.

Figure 2.27 shows an example of a subdirectory outline. Only one of the subdirectories in this outline is open, revealing the names of the files it contains. Many of the keystrokes that we learned for controlling outlines also apply to the use of subdirectories in Framework II. For

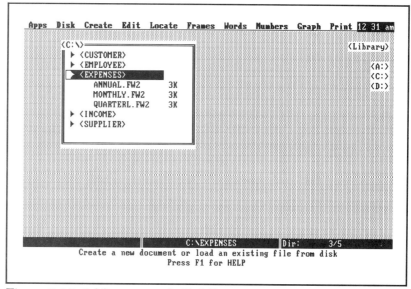

Figure 2.27: *Subdirectories in the Disk Frame*

example, you can *open* a subdirectory by placing the highlight over its name in the disk drive cabinet and pressing the Return key.

Once a subdirectory is open, you can load frames onto the desktop in the normal way. Place the highlight over the file or files you want to read, and press Return.

You can designate a given subdirectory as the *current* directory, for default disk operations, in the following way: Place the highlight over the directory and press

Ctrl-Return   (to designate a default directory)

SUMMARY

Framework II gives you complete control over the creation of outlines, whether you are using the outlining process to record your extemporaneous thought processes or to organize a group of important business documents. You can start an outline with either an Outline or an Empty frame. You can add new headings, delete headings, create new sublevels, rearrange portions of the outline, zoom in on details of the outline, view the frames of an outline, change the sizes of frames, and drag the frames horizontally and vertically—an impressive array of powers.

Outlining is a general, almost abstract kind of task that can apply in specific ways to everything you do in Framework II. We'll be returning to outlining as we move on to Framework II's productivity components: spreadsheet programming, word processing, database management, and telecommunications.

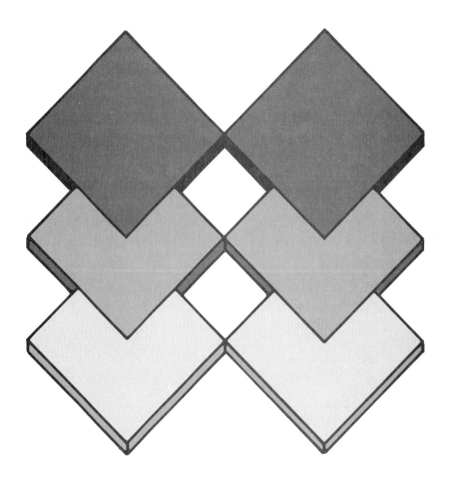

CHAPTER THREE

SPREADSHEETS

INTRODUCTION

Spreadsheet programming means designing tables of numbers that allow Framework II to do all the necessary arithmetic to summarize, evaluate, and explore the meaning of those numbers. A skillfully designed spreadsheet table will always respond arithmetically to your requirements, even when those requirements change over time. In Chapter 1 we discussed some of the advantages you will enjoy in using Framework II spreadsheets:

- You can minimize the tedium of performing repetitive arithmetic operations on groups of numbers.

- You can easily explore "what-if" scenarios; that is, you can find out how specific calculated values will change in response to changes in the raw data those calculations are based upon.

- You can instantly produce a variety of presentation-quality graphs from any table of numbers.

In this chapter we will study examples of all these activities. The screen in Figure 3.1 shows an empty Spreadsheet frame. Let's briefly review how Framework II organizes the rows and columns of a spreadsheet.

Notice first that Framework II identifies each column with a letter of the alphabet, starting with A, and each row with a number, starting with 1. The intersection of a row and a column is called a *cell;* in each cell you can store a single data item. The *address* of a cell is the name by which you can refer to the value the cell contains. An address consists of a cell's column letter and row number. For example, the cell at the intersection of column C and row 4 is called C4.

In each cell of a spreadsheet you can enter data in one of three forms:

1. *Labels,* which you might create to explain the significance of the rows and columns of numbers (labels can consist of combinations of letters, symbols, and numbers)

2. *Numbers,* upon which you can ultimately expect to perform various arithmetic operations

3. *Formulas,* which perform the arithmetic calculations of your spreadsheet

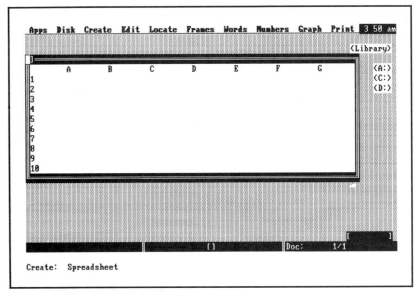

Figure 3.1: *An Empty Spreadsheet*

One of the most important things you will learn in this chapter is how to write formulas to perform arithmetic on the numbers in your spread-sheets. Most formulas you'll write for a given cell will contain *references* to the values in other cells. For example, the following formula contains references to the values stored in three different cells, and it results in a single number that is calculated from these cells:

+A2 + B2 – C2

In words, this formula instructs Framework II as follows: "Start with the value stored in cell A2, add the value stored in cell B2, and then sub-tract the value stored in cell C2." The numeric *result* of this formula will be stored in whichever cell you enter the formula itself.

We'll be studying exactly how to enter a formula into a cell, how to edit that formula if necessary, and—most importantly—how to *copy* the formula into other cells, to produce new calculated values in your spreadsheet.

To make formula writing even more powerful and versatile, Frame-work II supplies you with a large set of special-purpose tools that you can work with; these tools are called *functions*. We'll be introducing sev-eral categories of functions in this chapter, including those on the fol-lowing page.

□ *Statistical functions*, which are used to find a variety of statistical values—sums and averages, the largest and smallest values in a group of numbers, and even complex statistics such as the variance and standard deviation of a group of numbers

□ *Numeric functions*, which are used to round off values, take square roots, and work in higher mathematical realms such as trigonometry and exponentials

□ *Financial functions*, which can be used to compute a surprising range of simple and difficult financial values: for example, mortgage payments, the present value of an investment, or the internal rate of return of a business project

□ *Date functions*, which allow you to incorporate dates into your spreadsheets and perform *date arithmetic*—such as finding the number of days between two dates

Framework II also gives you many important ways to control the appearance and organization of your spreadsheet; for example:

□ You can change the width of columns, to accommodate more or fewer characters per cell.

□ You can move values or blocks of values from one place to another in your spreadsheet.

□ You can insert or delete entire rows or columns.

□ You can determine the *style* in which numbers will be presented on your spreadsheet—dollars and cents, percentages, scientific notation, and so on.

Exercising this control involves learning to use Framework II's menus and function keys. As promised, the use of these menus and keys will already seem familiar to you after your work with Outline frames.

Finally, as you work on spreadsheets, you should keep in mind the essential philosophy behind the design of Framework II: the best way to approach a large, complex project is to divide it into small, relatively simple tasks.

Other spreadsheet programs give you just one large spreadsheet area to work in. If you want to divide your current work into sections, you must set aside different blocks of cells inside that single spreadsheet to perform the various tasks—this can lead to confusion.

In Framework II, you can have many Spreadsheet frames on the desktop at once, with each one just the right size for the task it performs. Since you can give each frame a name, you can always locate the specific spreadsheet you want to examine or work with. Furthermore, a given spreadsheet on the desktop can contain references to one or more values contained in another spreadsheet; thus, you can *link* spreadsheets together by sharing values among them.

We'll explore all of these features in this chapter. Let's begin by finding out how to create a Spreadsheet frame and enter data into it.

CREATING A SPREADSHEET

Like any other type of frame, a new Spreadsheet frame is placed on the desktop through the Create menu. Three different options on the Create menu are involved in the process of making a spreadsheet; you can study these options in Figure 3.2.

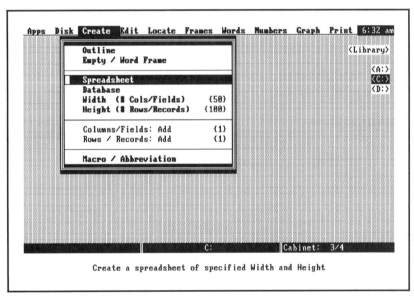

Figure 3.2: *The Create Menu*

The central section of the Create menu begins with the Spreadsheet option. Selecting this option results in the appearance of a new Spreadsheet frame on the desktop. The sequence of keystrokes that create a spreadsheet is

Ctrl-C   (to open the Create menu)

S   (to create a Spreadsheet frame)

But before you begin any new spreadsheet job, you will want to think about the dimensions of the spreadsheet you'll be working in.

HOW MANY ROWS? HOW MANY COLUMNS?

How many rows and columns will be required in your new spreadsheet? Exactly how big is the table of numbers you are planning to work with? Different numeric tasks call for differently organized spreadsheets; it is up to you to plan specifically for a given table of numbers before you begin your work. Framework II allows you to plan Spreadsheet frames that will exactly fit the job for which they were created.

Consider a few examples. Figures 3.3 to 3.5 show three tables of numbers, dealing with three very different subjects. All three include combinations of numeric input data and arithmetically calculated values, so they would all be good candidates for Spreadsheet frames. One of the tables is oriented vertically, one horizontally, and the third has more of a two-dimensional appearance. Let's think about how we would go about planning to create these tables in Spreadsheet frames.

Names	Scores
Alcott, Susan	92.3
Bobs, John	59.3
Carlson, Daniel	72.0
Duncan, Rober	78.9
Everet, Elinore	82.4
Fineman, Jack	80.2
Himes, Liz	95.0
Jackson, Don	66.4
Katz, May	62.9
Mann, April	55.0
Nesbit, Jerry	93.0
Ralston, Pat	71.0
Smithson, Billy	70.2
Stern, Mary	80.1
Wu, Tim	85.0
Average Score------------------	76.2
Best Score--------------------	95.0
Worst Score-------------------	55.0

Figure 3.3: A Table of Test Scores

The table in Figure 3.3 is a list of students' test scores; it records the scores and then analyzes them in a brief set of statistics at the bottom of the table. The table contains only two columns—one for the students' names and a second for the scores themselves. There are 15 students,

```
F   32  47  62  77  92  107 122 137 152 167 182 197 212
C    0   8  17  25  33   42  50  58  67  75  83  92 100
```

Figure 3.4: *A Temperature Conversion Table*

```
               Consulting and Speaking Activities
                   Quarterly Income Statement

                 Quarter-1   Quarter-2   Quarter-3   Quarter-4

      Earnings  $2,367.82   $7,513.87  $12,875.44   $6,321.87
      Expenses    $546.92     $832.88   $2,145.72   $1,287.22
           Net  $1,820.90   $6,680.99  $10,729.72   $5,034.65
      Est.Tax
           31%    $564.48   $2,071.11   $3,326.21   $1,560.74
     After Tax  $1,256.42   $4,609.88   $7,403.51   $3,473.91
```

Figure 3.5: *Quarterly Income Statement*

but the table contains 19 rows in all—with the extra 4 rows containing the headings for the columns and the statistics at the bottom of the table.

In contrast, Figure 3.4 shows a horizontally oriented table, containing 2 rows and 14 columns. The table contains conversions between degrees centigrade and degrees Fahrenheit, over a range from freezing to boiling. The first column has labels identifying the two rows of figures. Each subsequent column juxtaposes a Fahrenheit temperature with its equivalent in centigrade.

Finally, Figure 3.5 contains a table of numbers representing quarterly income calculations for a small business. This table has five columns and seven rows. Notice that the first row is devoted to column headings—identifying the four quarterly periods—and the first column describes the various elements of each quarter's activity.

Each of these three tables has different dimensions. So before you create a Spreadsheet frame for any of these tables, you would want to specify the precise size of the spreadsheet required. As you can see in Figure 3.2, the Create menu has two options that allow you to do this:

Width (# Cols/Fields)   {50}
Height (# Rows/Records)   {100}

The numbers in braces after each of these options show you the *default* values Framework II uses for the dimensions of a spreadsheet. Unless you specify otherwise, Framework II will create a spreadsheet that is 50 columns wide by 100 rows high. Depending on the task you have in mind, these dimensions may be too large or too small.

If you want to change these specifications, you must do so *before* you invoke the Spreadsheet option of the Create menu. To change the dimensions, choose the Width and Height options in turn; for example:

Ctrl-C	(to open the Create menu)
W	(to invoke the Width option)

At this point, the *current width value* will appear on the edit line, below the desktop, along with a message informing you that you are about to edit a value on the menu itself:

50

Menu editing; RETURN finishes

To change the spreadsheet width setting, you simply enter the number of columns you want your new spreadsheet to contain and press the Return key. The new value will then be displayed on the Create menu. For example, if you change the width setting to five columns, the Width option will appear as

Width (# Cols/Fields)   {5}

Likewise, to change the height setting, you invoke the Height option on the Create menu and enter (on the edit line) the number of rows you want your spreadsheet to contain.

Here is an example of the entire process. Let's create a frame for the income table shown in Figure 3.5. The keys you should press are as follows:

Ctrl-C	(to open the Create menu)
W	(to invoke the Width option)
5	(to specify the number of columns)
Return	(to record the new width setting)
H	(to invoke the Height option)
7	(to specify the number of rows)
Return	(to record the new height setting)
S	(to create the spreadsheet)

Notice that the final step is to create the actual spreadsheet, by invoking the Spreadsheet option. This step results in your Spreadsheet frame appearing on the desktop.

The next time you open the Create menu (during the same session with Framework II), you will see the new settings you have just entered: 5 columns, 7 rows. To change these settings again for another new Spreadsheet frame, you go through the same process.

What happens if you discover, halfway through your work with a Spreadsheet frame, that you have not given it the correct dimensions? If your frame has too few—or too many—rows or columns, Framework II allows you to insert new elements or delete parts of the spreadsheet at any time. The Create menu has options for adding rows and columns:

    Columns/Fields: Add   {1}
    Rows/Records: Add   {1}

And the Edit menu has options for deleting rows and columns:

    Columns/Fields: Remove
    Rows/Records: Remove

We'll see how to use these options as we begin working with spreadsheets.

In summary, Framework II encourages you to create Spreadsheet frames whose dimensions are tailored to the tasks they are to perform. But as you work with spreadsheets, you can always increase or decrease the number of rows or columns if you find that your plans have changed.

Once your spreadsheet is on the desktop, you are ready to give the frame a label and then move inside to begin your work. To illustrate the material in the coming sections of this chapter, we are going to develop and work with the quarterly income statement shown in Figure 3.5. Imagine yourself in the following situation, explaining the need for this spreadsheet. You are a consultant and sometime lecturer, specializing in the use of personal computers in the office environment. You run this small business out of your home, where you have set up an office for yourself in the den. Your expenses are simple—they include supplies, transportation, and telephone costs. Because your office is in your home, you can also count a portion of your rent and utilities as a business expense.

It is now the end of your business year, and you wish to summarize the year's activities—partly to estimate your tax liability and partly to investigate the year's progress. Following the instructions outlined above, you have created an empty Spreadsheet frame, containing five columns, from A to E, and seven rows, 1 to 7.

With the highlight positioned on the frame's border, you enter the following label for the frame:

    Quarterly Income

Now let's move inside the frame and begin working with spreadsheets.

MOVING AROUND THE SPREADSHEET

Several important keyboard functions work the same way with spreadsheets as with other frames. The Down Level key (labeled "+") moves the Framework II highlight into the spreadsheet itself. Likewise, the Up Level key (labeled "–") moves you back up to the frame's border. Try moving back and forth a few times, and notice the changes that occur on the display screen as you move into the spreadsheet.

The highlight (which, you'll remember, always marks your current working place on the desktop) initially lands in cell A1, and it fills the entire cell with a reverse-video rectangle. Additional information about your location is supplied in the status panel. The central section of the panel tells you the current cell's full name:

Quarterly Income.A1

You can see that the full name consists of two elements separated by a period: the name of the Spreadsheet frame and the address of the cell you are in. While we are working inside the Spreadsheet frame, we can safely abbreviate this name to the cell address, A1.

The right side of the status panel supplies the current cell's location in a different form:

SS: 1/1

The letters SS stand for spreadsheet, and the numbers inform you that the highlight is located at the first column of the first row in the spreadsheet. As you move the highlight to new locations in the spreadsheet, you will see the messages in the status panel change in response.

As we have already noted, different areas of the desktop often give you the same information in different forms. This duplication is not superfluous: depending on the situation, you may find one kind of message more helpful than another.

Inside the spreadsheet, the most essential keys for moving the highlight from one cell to another are the four arrow keys: ←, →, ↑, and ↓. Recall that these keys act as direction keys only if the NumLock key is toggled correctly. If you see the NUM message at the lower-right corner of the screen, you are in the wrong mode. Press NumLock to shift the direction keys into their cursor-movement mode.

Pressing one of the four arrow keys moves the highlight one cell in the direction indicated. These keys *autorepeat*, like the rest of the IBM PC keyboard: holding a key down for a few seconds is equivalent to pressing the key several times. If you hold an arrow key down, the highlight will be moved a number of columns or rows in the expected direction. (If you find the highlight—or the cursor—getting away from you, press Ctrl-Break to make it stop.)

But there are other, more controllable, ways to move the highlight several cells at a time. The Home and End keys, the PgUp and PgDn keys, and the Ctrl key, used in association with any one of the cursor-movement keys, are all special tools for moving the highlight more efficiently around the spreadsheet. Table 3.1 describes all these keys and key combinations. You should spend some time practicing them before you read on. Some of the keys will make more sense once you have begun entering data into the spreadsheet; we will continue discussing them as we create our Quarterly Income spreadsheet.

There is one final characteristic to notice about moving the highlight. If the highlight is already located at one of the spreadsheet's boundaries—that is, at the first or last row or the first or last column—and you try to move the highlight outside the frame, the computer will beep gently at you, to let you know that you cannot move outside of the defined dimensions of the spreadsheet.

The Zoom key (F9) also works with Spreadsheet frames. Our current spreadsheet is so small that we can see all of it within the frame on the desktop. But later, when we work with larger spreadsheets, it will be convenient to be able to devote the entire display screen to the rows and columns of data. Press the Zoom key once and the usual elements of the desktop will disappear, giving way to a full-screen spreadsheet. Press Zoom again to redisplay the frame on the desktop.

Finally, a large spreadsheet will be *scrolled,* horizontally or vertically, as you move the highlight from place to place. Or, to mix metaphors a bit, the screen will become a *window* onto the spreadsheet, showing you a portion of the spreadsheet at a time. This will happen whenever you create a spreadsheet that has too many rows and columns to be displayed at once. When you move the highlight beyond the borders of the current display (not the actual borders of the spreadsheet), the window will move to show you new columns and rows. This is another effect we will explore later.

ENTERING DATA INTO THE SPREADSHEET

As we begin entering data into the spreadsheet, you'll discover that the data-entry techniques will vary, depending on whether you are

Keys	Action
←, →, ↑, ↓	Moves the highlight one cell in the direction indicated.
Home	Moves the highlight to the first cell in the current row of cells.
End	Moves the highlight to the last cell in the current row of cells.
PgUp	Scrolls one entire frame up; or, in a spreadsheet that occupies less space than the frame, moves the highlight to the top row.
PgDn	Scrolls one entire frame down; or, in a spreadsheet that occupies less space than the frame, moves the highlight to the bottom row.
Ctrl-←, Ctrl-→, Ctrl-↑, Ctrl-↓	Moves the highlight to the beginning of the next block of data or the end of the current block of data.
Ctrl-Home	Moves the highlight to cell A1.
Ctrl-End	Moves the highlight to the cell at the lower-right corner of the spreadsheet.
Ctrl-PgUp	Moves the highlight to the top row in the current column of cells.
Ctrl-PgDn	Moves the highlight to the bottom row in the current column of cells.
Return	Enters data, or moves the highlight one cell down.
Tab	Enters data and/or moves the highlight one cell to the right.
Shift-Tab	Enters data and/or moves the highlight one cell to the left.

Table 3.1: Keys for Moving the Spreadsheet Highlight

entering labels, numbers, or formulas. Let's first enter the labels at the left of our Quarterly Income spreadsheet.

► **LABELS**

Look again at Figure 3.5, and examine the five labels in the first column. They read as follows:

Earnings

Expenses

Net

Est. Tax

After Tax

(Notice that 31%, although it also appears in this column, is not a label but a number.) Since these labels begin in the second row of the table, the first one, "Earnings", will go into cell A2. If your spreadsheet highlight is positioned at A1, press the ↓ key once to move to A2. (If you have moved to some other location in the spreadsheet, Ctrl-Home will move the highlight to cell A1.)

Enter the uppercase E of the first label. As soon as you do so, Framework II recognizes that you are entering a label—not a number or a formula—into this cell of the spreadsheet. The characters you enter into the label will appear on the edit line, above the following message:

Text editing; RETURN finishes

This message is important and is always worth noting when you begin entering a data item. It tells you what *type* of data Framework II is accepting from your input; in this case, the word "text" in the message confirms that this is a label.

If it is necessary to edit your work, you can use the arrow keys to move the edit cursor backward or forward, and the Backspace and Delete keys to delete characters, as we discussed in Chapter 2.

The Return key completes the data entry. After you press Return, the label you've entered will appear in the spreadsheet, at cell location A2. Now you are ready to move to cell A3 to enter the next label.

You have two choices for moving the highlight down the spreadsheet. The more obvious choice is the ↓ key. But if you are entering a long column of labels or numbers quickly, there is a more convenient key for moving down the column: the Return key. You have just hit the Return key once to complete the data entry; now simply hit it again to move down to the next cell. Touch typists will particularly appreciate this

Framework II keyboard feature; you don't have to search around for the ↓ key between entering one columnar data item and the next.

Practice entering data into a column by typing the rest of the labels into column A:

Expenses	(the label)
Return	(to complete the data entry)
Return	(to move down one cell)
Net	(the label)
Return	(to complete the data entry)
Return	(to move down one cell)

and so on. For the moment, leave row 6, between "Est.Tax" and "After Tax", blank.

We'll enter one more label before we begin placing numeric data in the spreadsheet: the column heading "Quarter-1". From the highlight's current location, A7, there are a number of ways to move up to cell B1. One very fast way is to press

Tab	(to move one cell to the right)
Ctrl-PgUp	(to move to the top of the spreadsheet)

The Tab key is an alternative to the → and ← keys. Pressing Tab by itself moves the highlight one cell to the right. Shift-Tab moves the highlight to the left.

You can also use Tab for data entry when you are entering adjacent values into a single row. Normally you would have to press two keys between one entry and the next:

Return	(to complete the data entry)
→	(to move to the next cell to the right)

The Tab key takes the place of both of these keystrokes, entering the previous value and moving the highlight one cell over.

Once the Tab key has moved the highlight into cell B7, Ctrl-↑ will move it to the top of the spreadsheet. In Table 3.1 you can read about the use of the Ctrl key with the arrow keys. These key combinations can be used for moving the highlight to the beginning of the next block of data, or to the end of the current block of data in your spreadsheet. At this point in our Quarterly Income spreadsheet, column B does not yet have any data in it. So Ctrl-↑ simply moves you up to row 1.

With the highlight at B1 enter the label

Quarter-1

Then press Return twice, once to complete the data entry and once to move down one cell. Now we're in a position to begin entering the numbers.

▶ **NUMERIC VALUES**

Your consulting business showed earnings of $2,367.82 during the first quarter of the year. For the moment, enter this value as

2367.82

As soon as you press the key representing the first digit of this number, your data entry will appear on the edit line, below the desktop. You will also see the following message:

Formula/number editing; RETURN finishes

Because you began your data entry with a digit, Framework II immediately recognizes that you are entering a numeric value. As we proceed in this chapter, we'll discover other initial characters that will indicate to Framework II that you are entering a number—or a formula that will result in a number—into a cell.

Once again, you can edit the data before you press the Return key. When you complete the data entry, the number will appear in cell B2 as expected.

Press the Return key again to move the highlight down to cell B3. The expenses for the same quarter were $546.92, so enter that value (without the dollar sign) and press Return. When you do, the first four rows of your spreadsheet will appear as follows:

Quarter-1
Earnings   2367.82
Expenses   546.92
Net

Studying this data carefully, you can learn a good deal about the way Framework II normally displays data on the screen. Unless you specify otherwise, here are the rules Framework II follows:

- Labels are left justified within the space of their respective cells; this means that the first character of the label appears in the very first, or left-most, space of the cell.

- Numbers are right justified within the space of their respective cells; however, Framework II always leaves one blank space after a number in a cell.

These are the *default* rules for data display; later in this chapter we'll learn how you can change the way Framework II displays data to suit your own requirements.

With the first-quarter earnings and expenses stored in the spreadsheet, the next step is to find the net income for the company during the quarter—obviously a simple matter of subtracting expenses from earnings. We'll use this simple calculation to examine the different techniques Framework II allows for entering formulas into the spreadsheet.

► **FORMULAS**

Up to now, we have alternately used the words *name* or *address* to describe a cell indicator like B2. Both of these terms, though perhaps informal, are correct: B2 is at once the name by which we can identify a certain cell and the column-row address at which we can find that cell. Now, however, it is time to introduce yet another, almost synonymous term: a cell *reference*.

A cell address that appears as part of a formula is called a reference. The distinction is simple but important: a cell reference stands for the *value that is contained in a certain cell,* while a cell address represents a location in the spreadsheet. In an arithmetic formula, a cell reference represents some actual numeric value that is currently stored somewhere in the spreadsheet. Now let's begin entering formulas.

Move the highlight down to cell B4, where the net income should appear. Knowing that a formula consists of arithmetic operations and cell references, your first inclination might be to enter the formula into B4 as follows:

    B2 – B3

After all, B2 contains the earnings and B3 the expenses; what more can be required than to subtract one from the other? But if you were to enter the first character, B, of this formula as shown above, you would receive a surprising message at the bottom of the screen:

    Text editing; RETURN finishes

Clearly, something is wrong; you do not mean this to be a text—or label—entry at all. How do you make Framework II understand that this is a formula—that B2 is a cell reference, representing a numeric value?

We have learned already that Framework II determines the *type* of any data entry from the first character of that entry. If the first character is a letter of the alphabet, Framework II assumes you are entering a *label* into the spreadsheet. If the first character is a digit, Framework II assumes numeric data entry. So we have to find an initial character that will flag this data entry as an arithmetic formula rather than as text.

One solution is this: We can use the plus sign (+) as the initial character of a formula. Framework II reads this sign as the beginning of numeric or formula entry. (Notice that the plus sign is located on the same key as the equal sign on your keyboard, above and to the right of the P. Be careful to distinguish between this key and the Down Level key, which is also labeled with a plus sign but is shaded gray.)

What do you do if you somehow get started in the wrong type of data entry? For example, what if you mistakenly begin your formula with a B rather than a +? Two keys, Escape and Delete, will get you out of the error:

Escape   (to move out of the edit line)

Delete   (to delete the contents of the current cell)

After pressing these two keys, you can start your formula entry over again in an empty cell.

Looking back at the Quarterly Income spreadsheet, the highlight should still be positioned at cell B4. Begin the formula entry with the plus sign, and continue as follows:

+ B2 – B3

As soon as you enter the plus sign, Framework II displays the message you are looking for:

Formula/number editing; RETURN finishes

When you complete the formula and hit the Return key, the *result* of the formula is instantly displayed in cell B4:

1820.90

In summary, to write effective formulas you have to keep three things in mind:

1. You must choose an appropriate initial character for the data entry, so that Framework II will know that you are typing a formula, not a label. (Besides +, you can use –, *, /, @, or a number.)

2. You must create an arithmetic expression that, when evaluated, will result in the correct calculation.

3. You must find the right cell references to put into the formula.

When you enter such a formula into a cell, Framework II displays the numeric result of the formula in the cell. If you want to reexamine the formula itself, you will find it displayed in the first section of the status panel.

Typing cell references into a formula is only one of the ways you can enter a formula into a spreadsheet. Another, often simpler way is to use *pointing*. Framework II allows you to indicate the cells that go into a formula by moving the spreadsheet highlight to those cells.

Let's reenter the formula for the net income, this time using the pointing technique. Delete the current contents of cell B4 by pressing the Delete key while the highlight is positioned over the cell.

As before, you should first type a plus sign, to begin the formula entry. The plus sign will appear on the edit line, followed by the edit cursor. The highlight temporarily disappears from the spreadsheet. From the edit line, the ↑ (or ↓) key initiates pointing in Framework II. As soon as you press ↑, several changes occur on the screen:

1. The highlight returns to the spreadsheet, to cell B4.

2. You will see the following message appear below the desktop:

   CURSOR POINTING; RETURN finishes

3. The formula on the edit line will suddenly expand to

   + B4

When you point to a cell in the spreadsheet, that cell automatically becomes a reference in the formula you are building. Pointing thus provides you with a visual way of telling Framework II exactly which references you want included in a formula.

But B4 is not the reference you want in this formula, so now you must use the arrow keys to move the spreadsheet highlight to the cell you do want to appear in the formula. In this case the cell is B2, representing first-quarter earnings. When you move the highlight up to this cell, your formula on the edit line will change to

   + B2

The next element of the formula is a minus sign, to subtract the expenses from the earnings. Press the minus key, and the cursor returns again to the edit line; your formula has become

   + B2 –

Now you can use pointing again to produce the second reference in your formula. Press the ↑ key. The highlight returns to the cell that you pointed to previously, and your formula on the edit line becomes

   + B2 – B2

To point at the correct cell on the spreadsheet, press the ↓ key to move the highlight down one cell and then press Return to complete the pointing. You will finally see the correct formula on the edit line:

+ B2 − B3

Press Return once more to complete the formula entry. The result is the same as before; the net income for the quarter appears in cell B4 as

1820.90

The formula for the cell appears in the first section of the status panel.

To summarize, here is the correct sequence of keystrokes for entering the net income formula in cell B4, using the pointing technique:

+	(to begin formula entry)
↑	(to initiate pointing)
↑, twice	(to move the highlight to the earnings cell)
−	(to continue the formula)
↑	(to initiate pointing again)
↓	(to move to the expenses cell)
Return	(to complete the pointing)
Return	(to enter the formula)

Two more calculations remain to complete the first quarter of the Quarterly Income spreadsheet—the estimated taxes and the after-tax income. These two values go into cells B6 and B7, respectively. But before we can perform these calculations, we have to enter a value for the estimated tax rate into cell A6.

Move the highlight to A6. Let's say that, based on last year's taxes, you are estimating a tax rate of 31 percent. Into cell A6, enter the value

.31

Now, you know that the estimated taxes will be calculated as

net income × estimated tax rate

and the after-tax income will be

net income − estimated taxes

Let's use the pointing technique to translate these two calculations into spreadsheet formulas with appropriate cell references.

Position the highlight at cell B6 to enter the formula that will calculate your estimated tax. Here are the keystrokes you will use to enter the formula by pointing:

+	(to begin the formula)
↑	(to initiate pointing)
←	(to point at cell A6)
*	(to multiply)
↑	(to initiate pointing again)
→	(to move into column B)
↑, twice	(to point at cell B4)
Return	(to complete the pointing)
Return	(to complete the formula)

These keystrokes result in the formula

+ A6 * B4

Notice that the asterisk character represents *multiplication* on your computer. (You can type this symbol either by pressing Shift-8 or by pressing the asterisk key directly to the right of the right-hand Shift key, next to the cursor keypad.) The result of this formula, your estimated tax liability for the quarter, is displayed in cell B6 as

564.48

You will be able to complete the final formula on your own, using pointing. Just remember these things:

- Begin your formula with a + character, so Framework II will know that this is a formula, not a label.
- Use the ↑ key to move the cursor from the edit line to the spreadsheet, initiating the pointing process.
- Use the arrow keys to point to the correct cells.
- Press Return twice—once to complete the pointing and a second time to complete the formula entry.

The formula that goes into cell B7 is

+ B4 − B6

And the value that results is

1256.42

Figure 3.6 shows how your spreadsheet should look at this point. You can review the three formulas you have written into the spreadsheet by moving the highlight over cells B4, B6, and B7; while the spreadsheet cell shows you the *result* of the formula, the first section of the status panel shows you the formula itself. As you examine the three formulas, remember the two techniques you used to create them:

1. Typing them character by character onto the edit line

2. Using the *pointing* method to indicate the references in the formulas

There is no difference in the actual formulas you create using either of these techniques; the only difference is in the convenience of creating the formula.

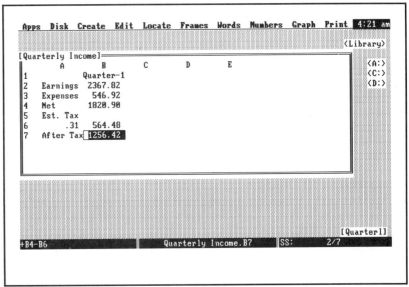

Figure 3.6: *Quarterly Income Spreadsheet, First Quarter*

With these three formulas written into the spreadsheet, you now can begin to experiment with Framework II's ability to respond to changes in the original data. For example, what if you find that you've entered the wrong number for the quarter's expenses? Or what if you want to modify your estimate for the tax rate? If you make changes like these, Framework II automatically recalculates any formulas that are dependent on the values you change.

Give it a try. Move the highlight to cell B3 and enter a new expense figure—say, 653.82. As soon as you enter the new amount, all the values below B3 in the column will be recalculated. This is because all of the spreadsheet's formulas are directly or indirectly related to the expense amount.

Now move the highlight to cell A6 and enter a new tax rate—.27, for example. Once again, the formulas that are dependent on the tax rate will be recalculated, and new values will appear in the appropriate cells.

These experiments begin to give you an idea of the real value of a spreadsheet. Change the original data, and Framework II automatically recalculates all formulas that depend on that data.

Before you continue, go back and reenter the original values for the expenses (546.92) and the tax rate (.31). In the next section, we'll discover ways of *editing* the data that is currently stored in a spreadsheet cell.

EDITING DATA IN THE SPREADSHEET

You can change the data stored in a cell whenever you want in Framework II. You have just seen one simple way to do so: simply move the highlight to the cell you want to change and enter a new value. When you begin the new data entry, the previous value disappears from the cell and the cursor moves down to the edit line, where you can type and edit the replacement.

In many instances, however, you might prefer to revise the current value of a cell rather than replace it with a new value. Framework II conveniently allows you to move the current value of a cell down to the edit line, where you can revise that value. You press one of two keys, depending on the type of data you are planning to edit:

□ *The Space bar*—to edit labels

□ *The Edit key (F2)*—to edit numbers or formulas

In either case, the current value of the cell appears on the edit line, where you can use the usual keys to edit it: the arrow keys, to move the edit cursor to a specific location in the value; the End key, to move the cursor to the end of the value, or the Home key, to move back to the beginning; the Delete or Backspace keys, to delete characters, and the digit or character keys, to *insert* new characters into the value.

When you have made the necessary changes, press the Return key to complete the editing session. The new version of the data will return to its original cell in the spreadsheet.

Let's try editing some data in the Quarterly Income spreadsheet. Begin by moving the highlight to cell A6, where the estimated tax rate is located. Because this is a number, you will press the Edit key (F2) to change it. When you do so, you will see the number appear on the edit line, with the following message below it:

.31
                Formula/Number editing; RETURN finishes

The edit cursor is positioned over the first character of the value, the decimal point. Let's say you want to change the value to .33. Press the following sequence of keys:

End	(to move the cursor to the end of the value)
Backspace	(to erase the last digit)
3	(to insert a new digit)
Return	(to complete the edit)

When you press the Return key, several things will happen in the spreadsheet. First, the new value will appear in cell A6; then, because two formulas in the spreadsheet depend on the value, the values produced by those formulas will automatically be recalculated.

You can try a similar experiment on a label on the spreadsheet. Position the highlight over a cell that contains a label, and press the Space bar. The label will appear on the edit line above this message:

    Text editing; RETURN finishes

After you have tried editing the spreadsheet, restore its original values so that your version once again looks like Figure 3.6.

These particular editing experiments may seem insignificant because the values and formulas are so short. But ultimately you will be entering longer and more complex labels, values, and formulas into the cells of your spreadsheet, and the ability to edit them will become very convenient.

The Edit key (F2) and the Space bar are also useful in another situation. Sometimes when you begin a new data entry, you will want a way to specify, in advance, the type of data you are planning: label, number, or formula. The Edit key or the Space bar will move the cursor down to the edit line even when the current cell is empty.

Think of an example—imagine for a moment that you are creating a spreadsheet that records and totals a set of invoices. You have set aside one column for the invoice numbers and another column for the invoice amounts. Your invoice numbers each consist of three digits, a hyphen, and three letters; for example:

312-ABC

Now even though *you* call this value a number, Framework II will consider it a label. Framework II has no way to deal numerically with a value that contains nonnumeric characters like ABC. It will not accept your invoice numbers unless you enter them as text labels.

But the problem is this: as soon as you begin the data entry with a digit, Framework II puts you into the numeric data entry mode:

Formula/number editing; RETURN finishes

You need to tell Framework II that this is not a number but rather a label entry.

The solution is simply to press the Space bar before you begin the data entry. When you do so, you will see the correct entry message:

Label editing; RETURN finishes

Then you can enter the invoice number, beginning with a digit, and Framework II will accept it as a text label rather than a number.

Returning once again to our Quarterly Income spreadsheet, let's discover an alternative way of looking at cell references.

ENGLISH NAME REFERENCES

Position the highlight on cell B2 of the spreadsheet. In the central section of the status panel, you should now see the following name:

Quarterly Income.B2

This tells you that the highlight is on cell B2 of the Quarterly Income spreadsheet.

Framework II actually gives you two different ways to look at cell references in a spreadsheet. The first way, as we have seen throughout this chapter, uses a cell's column and row location, such as B2. The second way, called *English name references*, depends on the labels that you enter into the first column and first row of your spreadsheet. Because we have labels in column A and row 1, we can examine some English name references in our Quarterly Income spreadsheet.

Any time the highlight is inside the spreadsheet, you can shift between normal address references and English name references by typing an exclamation point. Do so now, with the highlight positioned at cell B2, and you will see the following message in the central section of the status panel:

Income.[Quarter-1].Earnings

The *full* English-language name of this cell—even though there is not room in the status panel to display the whole name—is

Quarterly Income.[Quarter-1].Earnings

In this name, you can see that the column heading, Quarter-1, has taken the place of the column letter, B; and the row label, Earnings, has taken the place of the row number, 2. You will also notice some unfamiliar punctuation. The normal cell reference, B2, contains no punctuation at all. The English name reference contains a period between the two elements of the name, and the first part of the name, Quarter-1, is surrounded by square brackets.

You can see additional English name references by moving the highlight down column B. For example, the English names of cells B3 and B4 are

[Quarter-1].Expenses

and

[Quarter-1].Net

respectively. You will see these names displayed in the central section of the status panel.

What is the advantage of using English name references rather than the simpler address references? English names—which you supply yourself in the form of labels on your spreadsheet—are more descriptive and meaningful than the rather abstract address references. It's not hard to see which of the following two expressions is intuitively clearer; the English name reference formula:

[Quarter-1].Earnings + [Quarter-2].Earnings

or the address reference formula:

+B2+C2

On the other hand, the design of a spreadsheet may not always lend itself to the use of English name references. Sometimes it is not convenient to devote the first column and the first row of the spreadsheet to descriptive labels—which is a requirement if you want to use English name references. Or, depending largely on personal preference, address references may just seem simpler. On a small spreadsheet, such as the Quarterly Income spreadsheet, you may have no trouble at all remembering that cell B2 contains the business earnings for the first quarter of the year.

Whichever system of references you use, always remember that they represent the same thing. The two formats

[Quarter-1].Earnings

and

B2

both refer to the value contained in the cell itself.

We need one final word of explanation about the use of brackets in English name references. To avoid any ambiguity, Framework II uses square brackets whenever a label in an English name happens to contain a character that has a special arithmetic meaning. For example, the hyphen in "Quarter-1" might be mistaken for a minus sign in a formula. Putting brackets around Quarter-1 is Framework II's way of separating the reference from any other elements of a formula.

Framework II will supply these brackets as soon as you shift your spreadsheet into English name reference mode. Therefore, you should always avoid including square brackets of your own as part of a Framework II label.

To shift back into address references, simply type another exclamation point. Once again, when you move the highlight back up to B2, you will see the familiar reference to the current cell:

Quarterly Income.B2

We will now begin exploring some ways in which you may want to change the appearance of the spreadsheet, without changing the actual values that the spreadsheet contains.

CHANGING THE SPREADSHEET'S APPEARANCE

Framework II gives you a number of tools that help you control the way spreadsheet data are displayed on the screen. Data items can be right or left justified or centered within their cells. Numbers can be displayed in a variety of styles. Special effects such as boldfacing and underlining can also be used in spreadsheets.

Another important spreadsheet characteristic that you can control is the width of the columns. When Framework II first creates a spreadsheet, each column is by default nine characters wide. Sometimes this width may be too large or too small to suit the data you want to display. Framework II allows you to change the width of one or more columns in the spreadsheet, so that each individual column is just right for the data it contains.

We will study all these possible changes in this section. As you start working with these tools, keep in mind the distinction between editing a value and changing its appearance. Changing the style in which a number is displayed has no effect on the numeric value itself. Formulas that depend on the numeric value will not need to be recalculated after a style change.

Looking back at the original quarterly income table in Figure 3.5, you can see a number of display changes that we might want to make to improve the appearance of our Framework II spreadsheet. The most obvious is the display of the currency values. They should all be shown as dollars and cents, including the dollar sign and commas where necessary.

Furthermore, the tax rate should be expressed as a percent, not a decimal. And finally, the labels in column A look better when they are right justified, that is, aligned on the right rather than the left. They also stand out more in boldface. Let's begin working on these changes. Along the way, we'll also see how to use the Extend Select key in a spreadsheet, to perform a spreadsheet operation on several cells at once.

CHANGING NUMBER STYLES

The Numbers menu appears in Figure 3.7; the first section of this menu offers a list of styles in which you can display numbers on your spreadsheet. Table 3.2 gives you a summary and some examples of each of these styles.

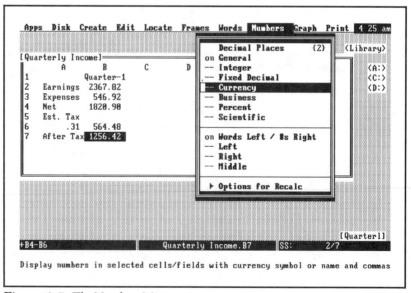

Figure 3.7: The Numbers Menu

Option	Style
General	Following the style of the data entry itself: 6328.96
Integer	Rounded to the nearest integer: 6329
Fixed Decimal	Displaying a fixed number of digits after the decimal point, specified by the Decimal Places option: 6328.96
Currency	Including a dollar sign and commas: $6,328.96
Business	Including commas but no dollar sign: 6,328.96
Percent	Followed by a percent sign, with the decimal point moved two digits to the right (for display purposes only): 632896.00%
Scientific	In "exponent" form, where the symbol E represents the exponent: 6.33E+3 (read this as 6.33×10^3)

NOTE: In all styles except Integer, the number of digits displayed after the decimal point is determined by the setting of the Decimal Places option.

Table 3.2: Summary of the Numbers Menu: Styles

When you first begin working with a spreadsheet, Framework II displays numbers in General style. Essentially, this means that numbers are displayed pretty much in the way you enter them.

In the Quarterly Income spreadsheet, we want to change the numbers in column B to Currency style. The way to change the style of a number is this:

1. Place the highlight over the value you want to change.

2. Then open the Numbers menu and choose the appropriate style option.

You can start out by trying these steps on a single value. Place the high-light over the expenses value in cell B3. Press these keys:

Ctrl-N   (to open the Numbers menu)

C   (to choose Currency style)

The expenses value will be displayed as

$546.92

Of course, it would be more convenient to be able to style a whole group of values in the spreadsheet at once. This is where the Extend Select key (F6) becomes important. You may recall that we used the Extend Select key in Chapter 2 to select and work with several frames at a time. Likewise, we can use this function key to work with several spreadsheet cells at a time.

Place the highlight over the first number in column B, at cell B2, and press the following keys:

Extend Select (F6)   (to extend the highlight)

Ctrl-↓   (to move the highlight down, to the end of the column)

Return   (to complete the extend operation)

As soon as you press the Extend Select key, the following message appears below the desktop:

SELECT: extend selection with cursor keys; RETURN finishes

Notice the use of the Ctrl key with the ↓ key. Rather than extend the high-light by only one cell at a time, the Ctrl key, along with an arrow key, moves the highlight by entire blocks of data, as described in Table 3.1.

You can see the result of this operation in Figure 3.8. For the first time in our spreadsheet, the highlight covers not just a single cell but an entire *range* of cells. The significance of this is that you can now per-form spreadsheet operations—such as changing the numeric display style—on the entire range you have selected, rather than on a single cell at a time.

Now let's make all the numbers we have selected appear in Currency style:

Ctrl-N   (to open the Numbers menu)

C   (to select the Currency option)

The results are a bit alarming and not at all what we were expecting. Somehow, we have lost several of the numbers in the column. Here's

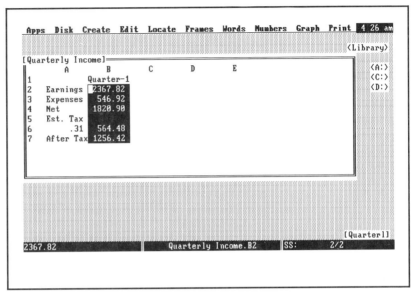

Figure 3.8: *Result of Extend Select*

what the column looks like now:

```
* * * * * * * * *
    $546.92
* * * * * * * * *

    $564.48
* * * * * * * * *
```

The problem, as you may have guessed, is that the column is no longer wide enough to display the larger numbers. Recall that Framework II's default column width is nine characters. With the dollar signs and commas, the larger numbers in the column are now exactly nine characters long. But Framework II also puts an extra space after a number in a cell, as we learned at the beginning of this chapter. For this reason, the column needs to be at least ten characters wide to display these numbers.

As you can see, Framework II replaces the numbers it can't display with a string of asterisks to indicate that the column is too narrow. To correct the problem, we'll use the Size function key (F4) to increase the column width.

CHANGING COLUMN WIDTHS

In a spreadsheet, the Size key works on the column or columns that are currently selected by the highlight. Press the Size key (F4), and you'll see the following message appear below the desktop:

SIZE: stretch frame size with cursor keys; RETURN finishes

The Size key works as well with spreadsheet columns as it does with frames. Let's increase the width of column B by two spaces. Press the → key twice, and then press Return. With the column thus enlarged, the row of numbers will appear as follows:

$2,367.82
$546.92
$1,820.90

$564.48
$1,256.42

Now there is room to display all the numbers in Currency style.

We have seen, then, that Framework II will not display numbers successfully in a column that is too narrow. The width of the column must be at least one space larger than the length of the number you want to display. Interestingly enough, Framework II does not impose the same rule on labels. You can enter labels of any length into a cell. If there are empty cells to the right of the current cell, Framework II will allow the display of a label to extend across the boundaries of cells. We'll experiment with this effect a little later when we add a title to our spreadsheet. (If the cells to the right of the current cell are occupied, the label will be truncated where it crosses the cell's boundary.)

We can now use the Numbers menu again, this time to change the style of the estimated tax rate in cell A6. Move the highlight to A6. (When you first press the ↓ key, the extended highlight will once again become a single-cell highlight; then you can use the ← and ↑ keys to move to A6.) Next, go into the Numbers menu:

Ctrl-N   (to open the Numbers menu)

P   (to select the Percent option)

In response to this operation, the tax rate is now displayed as

31.00%

This is not quite what we want. In this case, there is no need to display the two digits after the decimal point. Once again we can turn to the

Numbers menu to correct the situation:

Ctrl-N   (to open the Numbers menu)

D   (to select the Decimal Places option)

The default value for the Decimal Places option is 2, as you can see on the menu. When you select this option, its current value drops down to the edit line, where you can change it. You'll also see the message

Menu editing; RETURN finishes

Enter the value 0, because we want no digits after the decimal point in this case. Press the Return key, and the tax rate will now appear as

31%

Examine the first section of the status panel to see what is actually stored in this cell. You will see the number

.31

This shows us once again that changing the display style of a number has no effect on the value of the number itself.

Next we'll work on column A, the labels that describe the information contained in the Quarterly Income spreadsheet.

CHANGING THE DISPLAY OF LABELS

We have two changes to make on the column of labels—first, we want them to be right justified inside the width of the column, and second, we want them to appear in boldface.

In addition to numeric styles, the Numbers menu deals with the horizontal alignment of values in the spreadsheet. Looking back at Figure 3.7, you can see that the second section of the menu has four alignment options:

Words Left / #s Right

Left

Right

Middle

The first of these options is the default condition; labels are normally left justified in a cell, and numbers are normally right justified. You can change the alignment of any value, however, by selecting the appropriate cell and invoking the Left, Right, or Middle option. These options stand for left justification, right justification, or centering, respectively.

To right justify the labels in column A, we should begin by selecting the range of cells that will be involved in the operation. Move the highlight to cell A2 and press the following sequence of keys:

Extend Select (F6)	(to extend the highlight)
Ctrl-↓	(to extend down through the entire block of data)
Return	(to complete the extend operation)
Ctrl-N	(to open the Numbers menu)
R	(to select the Right option)

Now, while the highlight is still extended over the entire column of labels, we can also use the Words menu to select boldfacing:

Ctrl-W	(to open the Words menu)
B	(to select the Bold option)

Now press the ↑ key to move the highlight to cell A1, and examine the column of labels. On your screen, they will appear in a high-intensity or boldfaced display. When we eventually print this spreadsheet onto paper, they will be boldfaced.

The Words menu contains several other options that deal with special display and printing effects. We'll examine this menu in more detail when we discuss word processing in Chapter 4.

To continue working with the Quarterly Income spreadsheet, the next step will be to begin entering your consulting business's income and expense values for the other three quarters of the year. Before doing so, however, we have already learned that we have to increase the width of the remaining columns, to make them wide enough to display the numbers involved. Previously, we used the Size key to extend the width of a single column. We can also use it, along with the Extend Select key, to enlarge more than one column at a time. Let's see how.

Move the highlight to cell C1, and press the following keys:

Extend Select (F6)	(to extend the highlight)
Ctrl-→	(to extend to the right side of the spreadsheet)
Size (F4)	(to enlarge the columns . . .)
→, twice	(. . . by two spaces)
Return	(to complete the operation)

Now each of these columns, C, D, and E, is 11 spaces wide; there will be plenty of room to enter all the new numbers for the three final quarters.

It might also be convenient to specify a style for these columns before we begin entering the numeric values. Up to now, we have seen how to specify a style for a specific cell or block of cells within the spreadsheet. Framework II also gives you a way to assign a numeric style *globally,* to the entire spreadsheet. We'll examine this technique in the next section.

GLOBAL SPREADSHEET STYLING

In the Quarterly Income spreadsheet most of the numbers represent dollars and cents. The only exception is the estimated tax rate. In spreadsheets like this, it is convenient to work with a global style, dealing with exceptions separately.

It turns out that if you specify a style while the highlight is on the *border* of the frame, the style you have chosen will be applied globally, to all numeric values inside the spreadsheet.

Let's try using this technique. We'll have to begin by moving the highlight to the border:

Up Level (–)	(to move to the border of the frame)
Ctrl-N	(to open the Numbers menu)
C	(to choose the Currency option)
Down Level (+)	(to move back into the spreadsheet)

Now move the highlight to cell C2, and enter the earnings for the second quarter:

7513.87

The figure will be displayed as

$7,513.87

Spend a few moments entering the remaining data for the final three quarters. You will find that each numeric value will be displayed in Currency style:

Quarter-2	Quarter-3	Quarter-4
$7,513.87	$12,875.44	$6,321.87
$832.88	$2,145.72	$1,287.22

What has happened to the estimated tax rate, now that the style has been set globally? Nothing—it still appears as a percentage:

31%

Whenever you set or reset a style *locally*, for an individual cell or block of cells inside the spreadsheet, those cells will not be affected by the global style.

Our next step, to complete this stage of the Income Statement spreadsheet, is to provide formulas for net income, estimated tax, and after-tax income for the three remaining quarters of the business year. We have learned how to create formulas, either by typing both the arithmetic operations and cell references onto the edit line or by typing the arithmetic operations and pointing to the cell references. One way to perform the remaining calculations would be simply to repeat this process for each quarter.

But Framework II has an easier and much more elegant way to apply these similar formulas to the entire table. We'll find out how in the next section.

USING THE SPREADSHEET

Up to now, we have concentrated on the mechanical details of entering data and controlling the appearance of the spreadsheet. Now it is time to discover some of the essential characteristics of spreadsheet programming. The first subject at hand is learning how to copy a formula, so we can complete the calculations in the Quarterly Income spreadsheet.

COPYING FORMULAS

Each calculation in row 4 of the spreadsheet will be based on the same formula:

net income = earnings − expenses

We have already developed this formula in cell B4; in spreadsheet terms, the formula was translated into

+ B2 − B3

In copying this formula across row 4, we will want to maintain the formula's exact format, but we will have to change the column references. For example, the correct formula for the net income of the second quarter, in column C, will be

+ C2 − C3

Likewise, the third and fourth quarters, in columns D and E, will require the following formulas:

+D2 – – D3
+E2 – E3

Framework II automatically copies this formula in a *relative* way. This means that as the formula is copied across row 4, the arithmetic operations of the formula and the *row references* will remain identical in each copy of the formula; but the *column references* will automatically be changed to represent the appropriate values in each column.

The Copy key (F8) performs the task of copying formulas in Spreadsheet frames. To produce a successful copy operation, you need to supply Framework II with two pieces of information:

1. The source location of the information that you want to copy

2. The destination of the information

You use cell pointing to specify both the source and the destination of the copy. Framework II assumes the source to be the location of the highlight at the time you press the Copy key. A message below the desktop prompts you to point to the destination.

Let's try it. Place the highlight at cell B4, which contains the net income formula that we want to copy into cells C4 to E4. Press Copy (F8); when you do, this message appears on the screen:

Copy: cursor to copy destination; RETURN finishes

If this message does not seem very specific, it is because the Copy key can be used in many different ways in Framework II, depending on the kind of frame you are working with. In a *spreadsheet* copy operation, we need to extend the highlight over the entire range of cells that we want to copy our formula to. We'll use the Extend Select key in this process. Here is the sequence of keystrokes to complete this operation:

→	(to move the highlight to C4)
Extend Select (F6)	(to stretch the highlight)
Ctrl-→	(to extend to cell E4)
Return	(to complete the extend operation)
Return	(to complete the copy operation)

When you complete these keystrokes, Framework II copies the formula instantly, and the three new calculated values appear on the screen—the net income figures for the final three quarters of the year.

Move the highlight over the cells that contain the three new values, C4, D4, and E4. As you do so, watch the formulas that are displayed in the first section of the status panel. You can see that Framework II has precisely met the requirement of producing *relative* copies of the formula. Each new formula applies itself specifically to the data in its own column.

This first example of formula copying was simple: it involved one formula, copied over only a few cells. But relative copying works just as successfully with complex formulas, copied over large ranges of data. The steps are the same:

1. Position the highlight at the location of the formula you want to copy.

2. Press the Copy key (F8).

3. Use the Extend Select key (F6) to stretch the highlight over the entire destination range of the copy.

4. Press the Return key twice, first to complete the Extend Select operation, then to complete the copy operation.

Sometimes spreadsheets will contain values that serve as arithmetic constants. If you copy formulas that refer to such a constant, relative copying is no longer appropriate. We'll look at an example of such a situation in the next section, and we'll see Framework II's solution to the problem.

► **ABSOLUTE VERSUS RELATIVE COPYING**

The next formula down in our Quarterly Income spreadsheet calculates the estimated tax:

estimated tax = tax rate × net income

The current implementation of this formula, in cell B6, is

+A6*B4

Once again, we would like to copy this formula through all of row 6.

But there is something a little different here. One of the references in this formula, the tax rate at A6, should not be copied in a relative manner. The tax rate is shown in only one location on the spreadsheet, and it must be applied uniformly to each quarter's income. In other words, its cell reference should not be revised while the copy operation is performed over the columns of the destination range. This situation calls for what we call *absolute* copying.

To perform absolute copying, we need some way to let Framework II know that the cell that contains the tax rate, A6, should be considered a fixed reference. After the copy operation, each new formula must contain a relative reference to the net income value in its own column and an absolute reference to the tax rate in A6:

+A6*C4

+A6*D4

+A6*E4

Framework II's way of specifying an absolute cell reference is to place dollar signs in the cell reference, preceding the column letter and the row number. For example, to express A6 as an absolute reference, we would call it

$A$6

Actually, some copy operations call for *mixed* references, where only the column or the row is to be considered as absolute, and the other element is taken as a relative reference for copying purposes:

$A6

A$6

But the simplest and most common case is a full absolute reference like $A$6.

Keep in mind that the notation for absolute references only has meaning in a copy operation. Generally, when you write a formula for a given cell in the spreadsheet, you will *anticipate* whether ultimately you are going to copy that formula into other cells. If you plan to copy the formula, you will have to decide which of the formula's references will be copied in a relative manner and which, if any, will be copied in an absolute manner.

In creating a new formula, there are two ways to introduce an absolute reference—either by typing the $ symbols directly into the reference or by using a special extension of the pointing technique.

At the moment, we already have a formula in our Quarterly Income spreadsheet for the estimated tax. So before we try to copy this formula, we have to modify it to make the tax rate an absolute reference. Typing the $ symbols from the keyboard will be the easier technique in this case. But we will nonetheless try both techniques before we copy the formula.

Begin by positioning the highlight over the value in cell B6. Press the Edit key (F2) to edit the formula that is behind the value. The formula will appear on the edit line:

+A6*B4

Here is an instance where the ability to edit a current value on the spreadsheet turns out to be very convenient. To transform A6 into an absolute reference, we only need to insert $ symbols. These are the keystrokes you use to edit this formula:

→	(to move the edit cursor one space to the right)
$	(to insert the "absolute" symbol)
→	(to move the edit cursor again)
$	(to insert the second symbol)
Return	(to complete the edit operation)

When you press the Return key, you will see that the new formula for cell B6 is now

+ $A$6 * B4

Notice that there is no change in the calculated value shown in the cell itself. The absolute reference has no new effect on the calculation; it is there only because we anticipate making copies of the formula.

Now let's look at the second technique for producing an absolute reference, the pointing method. We'll have to start with an empty cell, so begin by deleting the current contents of cell B6 with the Delete key.

The pointing begins in the normal way:

+	(to begin the formula)
↑	(to initiate pointing)
←	(to point at cell A6)

At this point the edit line will contain the beginning of the formula:

+ A6

Now, while we are still in the pointing mode, we can simply type the $ symbol once from the keyboard, and Framework II will automatically create an absolute reference. The edit line now displays the beginning of the formula as

+ $A$6

Complete the formula just as we did originally, by supplying the multiplication symbol and pointing to the cell that contains the net income, B4:

*	(to multiply)
↑	(to initiate pointing again)
→	
Ctrl-↑	(to point to B4)

Return (to complete the pointing operation)

Return (to enter the formula)

The formula will appear as

 + $A$6*B4

To summarize, the pointing technique allows you to create absolute references in three simple steps:

1. Press the ↑ key to start the pointing.

2. Use the arrow keys to point to the correct reference on the spreadsheet.

3. Type the $ symbol to make the reference absolute.

Interestingly enough, the pointing technique also allows you to create *mixed* references. To do so, you repeatedly type the $ symbol until you see the exact reference you want. Framework II steps you through all the possible combinations of references, absolute, mixed, or relative, one at a time:

 + $A$6

 + A$6

 + $A6

 + A6

 + $A$6

You'll see each version appear on the edit line, and if you keep typing $, the original version will reappear.

You are now ready to copy the estimated tax formula into the rest of row 6. But before doing so, take another look at the Quarterly Income spreadsheet. To complete the spreadsheet at this stage, we actually still have *two* formulas left to copy—the one we've been working with, in cell B6, and the one that calculates the after-tax income, in cell B7. It would be convenient to be able to copy both formulas at once.

Framework II allows us to do that with the Extend Select key. Here are the steps:

1. First use Extend Select (F6) to stretch the highlight over the *source range*—i.e., the formulas you want to copy.

2. Press the Copy key (F8) to begin the operation.

3. Use Extend Select again, to stretch the highlight over the *destination range*—the cells to which you want to copy the original formulas.

This is the process we'll follow to copy both the estimated tax and the after-tax income formulas. Beginning with the highlight positioned at cell B6, follow this sequence of keystrokes:

Extend Select (F6)	(to stretch the highlight over the source range)
↓	(to include B7 in the source range)
Copy (F8)	(to begin the copy operation)
→	(to position the highlight at the beginning of the destination range)
Extend Select	(to stretch the highlight)
Ctrl-→	(to indicate the entire destination range)
Return	(to complete the extend operation)
Return	(to complete the copy operation)

As a result of these keyboard commands, you will see two new rows of values appear instantly on the spreadsheet, the estimated taxes and the after-tax income for the second, third, and fourth quarters of the business year.

Move the highlight through this block of cells to examine the formulas that have been copied into it, and watch the display in the first section of the status panel. You will see all of the following formulas as you move from cell to cell:

	Quarter-2	Quarter-3	Quarter-4
31%	+$A$6*C4	+$A$6*D4	+$A$6*E4
After Tax	+C4−C6	+D4−D6	+E4−E6

The formulas were all copied correctly; in particular, the absolute reference to $A$6 was carried forward unchanged, as a spreadsheet constant, to each cell in row 6.

This completes the initial stage of the Quarterly Income spreadsheet for your consulting and speaking business. In the following section we'll continue adding some new elements.

ADDING ROWS AND COLUMNS

The entire five-column by seven-row spreadsheet is now completely filled with the information we planned for it. Often at this point in your work with a spreadsheet, you'll decide to expand your original plans.

You'll think of new ways in which your spreadsheet might become even more valuable if additional information were included. In the case of the Quarterly Income spreadsheet, for example, you may want to add a title, a column of totals, and a few columns of simple statistics that will help you analyze the business year.

Before you can add any information, though, you clearly have to expand the dimensions of the spreadsheet. We saw at the beginning of this chapter that the Create menu contains two options that will do this for you:

> Columns/Fields: Add
>
> Rows/Records: Add

To use either of these Create options, you must follow these three steps:

1. Place the highlight inside the spreadsheet, at a cell located immediately *before* the position you want the new columns or rows to appear.

2. Open the Create menu and choose either the Columns or the Rows option.

3. Specify the number of columns or rows you want to add, and press the Return key to complete the operation.

The new columns or rows will appear at the position you have specified, and the organization of the spreadsheet will be expanded appropriately. New column letters or row numbers will appear. Even more significantly, any formulas that you have already entered into your spreadsheet will automatically be revised, if necessary, to allow for the changes in the spreadsheet.

The process of adding rows or columns presents one small problem. There is no immediate way to insert new rows at the top of the spreadsheet or new columns at the left side of the spreadsheet. You can see why if you think about the first step of the process:

□ To add rows, the highlight must be placed at the row immediately above where the new rows are to appear.

□ To add columns, the highlight must be placed at the column immediately to the left of where the new columns are to appear.

But there is no way for you to place the highlight above row 1 or to the left of column A.

To solve this problem in a spreadsheet that already contains data, we have to add an extra step to the process. We'll insert the rows or columns at some point below or to the right of where we actually want them. Then we'll *move* the current data into the new empty cells, creating empty rows at the top of the spreadsheet, or empty columns at the left side of the spreadsheet.

Let's look at an example. Now that you have completed your Quarterly Income spreadsheet, you decide that you would like to place a title at the top of it. The title will contain two lines and will look like this:

Consulting and Speaking Activities
Quarterly Income Statement

You would also like to see a blank line between the title and the data itself. In all, you have to add three rows to the spreadsheet.

We'll add the three rows at the bottom of the spreadsheet and then move the current block of data down by three rows. The Move key (F7) moves data to new locations in a spreadsheet. Here are the keystrokes that will add the three rows:

Ctrl-End	(to move the highlight to the lower-right corner of the spreadsheet)
Ctrl-C	(to open the Create menu)
R	(to choose the Rows option)
3	(to specify the number of rows you want to add)
Return	(to add the rows)

To add rows below row 7, you can place the highlight in *any* cell in row 7. Using Ctrl-End is simply the most convenient way to move the highlight quickly to the bottom of the spreadsheet. When you complete these keystrokes, you will see three new rows inserted below row 7. Now the spreadsheet contains ten rows, numbered 1 to 10.

To move the current block of data down into the new rows, we'll use the Move key. Here are the steps that a move requires:

1. Expand the highlight over the entire block of data you want to move.

2. Press the Move key (F7).

3. Move the highlight to the destination of the move operation, and press Return to finish.

When you press the Move key, you will see the following message:

MOVE: Cursor to move destination; Return finishes

If you are moving a two-dimensional block of cells, as in the Quarterly Income spreadsheet, you can specify the destination of the move by placing the highlight at the upper-left corner of the area to which you want the block of data moved. In this case, the new upper-left corner of the data will be cell A4, since we want to empty rows 1 to 3.

Here are the keystrokes to perform the move:

Ctrl-Home	(to move the highlight to the upper-left corner of the spreadsheet)
Extend Select (F6)	(to expand the highlight)
↓	
Ctrl-↓	
Ctrl-→	(to select the entire block of data)
Move (F7)	(to move the selected data)
Ctrl-Home ↓, three times	(to move the highlight to the upper-left corner of the destination)
Return	(to complete the move)

Press Ctrl-Home again to move the highlight back up to the top. Your spreadsheet should look like Figure 3.9. We now have room to place a title above the data.

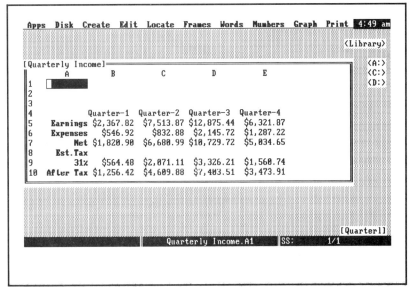

Figure 3.9: *Adding Rows and Moving the Data*

We have already discussed the way Framework II handles the display of long labels: text is allowed to cross the borders between cells. Conveniently, we'll be able to enter the two lines of the title into cells B1 and B2 respectively. Move the highlight to B1 and type the first line of the title:

Consulting and Speaking Activities

As you type the text into the edit line, you'll see the characters also appear in the spreadsheet. Press Return to complete the data entry. This entire label is contained in cell B1, even though its display takes up the space of more than three cells.

Enter the second line of the title into cell B2:

Quarterly Income Statement

To center the second line below the first, you'll need to begin the text with four blank spaces. First press the Space bar once to begin the edit mode; then press it four more times for the blank spaces. Enter the text and include four trailing spaces after the word "Statement"; finally, press Return.

Now use the Words menu to change the display of the two title lines. The first line should be in boldface, and the second should be underlined. (Use the Words menu options B and U, respectively.) The underlining extends over the blank spaces in the second title line, as you can see in Figure 3.10.

In the next section we'll be studying ways to add totals, averages, and other statistics to your spreadsheet. We'll be placing all this new information in columns to the right of the current income table. To prepare, you should insert four new columns into the spreadsheet, beyond column E:

Ctrl-End	(to move the highlight to the last column)
Ctrl-C	(to open the Create menu)
C	(to choose the Columns option)
4	(to specify the number of new columns)
Return	(to complete the operation)

These keystrokes will add columns F through I to the spreadsheet. There are now too many columns to see in Frames view, so you should press the Zoom key (F9) to expand the display of the spreadsheet over the full screen. Even in full screen, however, you will discover that only seven complete columns can appear on the screen at once. As you move the highlight horizontally back and forth across the length of the

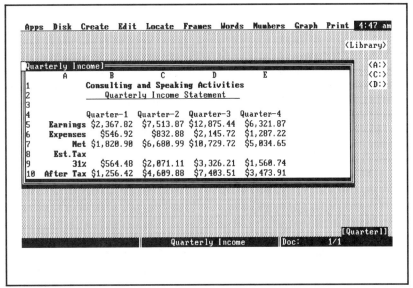

Figure 3.10: *Adding a Title*

spreadsheet, the columns at the beginning and end will *scroll* in and out of view. Or, to put it another way, your window onto the spreadsheet will move to the right or to the left.

Take the following steps to further prepare the four new columns for the work ahead:

1. Use the Extend Select key (F6) and Ctrl-→ to select all four columns.

2. Using the Size key (F4), increase the size of the columns to 11 spaces.

3. Add the following labels into cells F4, G4, H4, and I4, respectively:

   Totals   Average   Most   Least

4. Open the Edit menu and select the Lock option:

   Lock First Column/Row

This final step changes the way Framework II scrolls your spreadsheet; when you toggle the Lock option into its *on* state, column A and row 1 will always stay in view, no matter how you scroll the spreadsheet. This is a convenience when viewing a large spreadsheet that contains identifying labels in column A or row 1.

Notice that the new columns are formatted in Currency format; the global setting also applies to columns or rows that you add later.

From the labels we added in columns F, G, H, and I, you can see that the formulas we will be writing in these columns will require different arithmetic than simple addition, subtraction, multiplication, or division. In the next section we'll begin looking at a category of tools Framework II provides for building special spreadsheet formulas. These tools are called *functions*.

USING SPREADSHEET FUNCTIONS

Functions in Framework II can serve many different purposes. In fact, whenever you use a function or write a formula, you are actually working with the resources of FRED, the programming language that is built into Framework II. We'll have more to say about FRED in Chapter 7; for now, just keep in mind that the language consists of a large and versatile collection of functions that give you extended powers over the work you perform in Framework II. One of these extended powers is the use of functions in spreadsheet formulas.

Framework II's spreadsheet functions give you shortcuts for working with values and ranges of values. They can save you the trouble of having to write complex formulas to derive certain kinds of results.

Consider a quick example. Let's say you have entered three numbers into column A of a spreadsheet:

	A
1	476
2	529
3	764

You decide that you want to find the average of these three numbers. Of course, one way to do so would be to write a formula that adds up the numbers and divides the sum by 3:

$$(A1 + A2 + A3)/3$$

You may not object to having to write this short formula; but what if the column of numbers were 30 elements long instead of only three? To write a formula to find the average of 30 numbers would be a long and tedious task.

This is why Framework II supplies functions: to give you short, easy ways to write what might otherwise be long or complex formulas. In this particular case, you would select the function that automatically computes the average of a series of numbers. But as we will soon see, Framework II supplies functions that provide many kinds of values—not just averages—for your spreadsheets.

Framework II functions have three essential characteristics:

1. Every function has a name. To use a function in your spreadsheet, you simply refer to the function by name. Without exception, every function's name begins with a special character—the "at" symbol, "@". Following this symbol, the function's name usually indicates fairly clearly what the function does. For example, the function that finds averages is called @AVG.

2. Most functions require one or more *parameters*. A parameter is simply an expression of the specific value or values that you want the function to work on. When you use a function, you enter the parameters, between parentheses, immediately after the name of the function. For example, to compute the average of the values stored in cells A1 to A3, you would write the formula as

   @AVG(A1:A3)

   We'll see that different functions require different formats for the parameter expression.

3. All functions return a value or produce some programmed result. (Just like the results of other formulas, the result of a spreadsheet function is displayed in the cell in which you enter the function. For example, if you were to enter the above @AVG formula into cell A4, the average of the three cells, A1 to A3, would be displayed in A4.)

Table 3.3 describes the four categories of functions you might find yourself using most often in spreadsheets: statistical, numeric, financial, and date. We'll see working examples of many of these functions before the end of this chapter. (You will find a list of all the Framework II functions in Appendix B.) Remember that functions are available to you throughout your work in Framework II, not just in Spreadsheet frames.

Let's begin now with the statistical functions, which we'll use to create columns of statistical values in the Quarterly Income spreadsheet.

Statistical Functions

Parameters for each of the following statistical functions:

A range or list of numbers or numeric expressions

@SUM returns the sum of all the numbers in the parameter list.

@AVG returns the average of all the numbers in the parameter list.

@MIN returns the smallest number in the parameter list.

@MAX returns the largest number in the parameter list.

@STD returns the standard deviation of the numbers in the parameter list.

Numeric Functions

Parameter for each of the following numeric functions:

A number, a numeric expression, or a reference to a number

@SQRT returns the square root of the number. (Parameter cannot be negative.)

@LOG returns the logarithm, base 10. (Parameter must be positive.)

@LN returns the logarithm, base *e*. (Parameter must be positive.)

@EXP returns the value of *e* to the *n*, where *n* is the parameter.

Parameter for each of the following three trigonometric functions:

An angle, expressed in radians

(The function **@PI** is available to help you express an angle in radians. @PI requires no parameter, and it yields a value of pi correct to 15 digits.)

@SIN returns the sine of the angle.

@COS returns the cosine of the angle.

@TAN returns the tangent of the angle.

Table 3.3: A Selection of Framework II Functions

Numeric Functions *(continued)*

@ROUND(n,d) results in the value of *n*, rounded off to *d* decimal places.

@MOD(a,b) results in the value of *a modulus b* (i.e., the *remainder* from the division of *a/b*). The value of *b* cannot be zero.

@RAND yields a random number between 0 and 1, inclusive. (Requires no parameter.)

Financial Functions

@PMT(principal,rate,periods) computes the payment per *period* required on a *principal* loan at a specified interest *rate* per period.

@PV(amount,rate,periods) computes the present value of a series of equal income or payment *amounts* for a specified number of *periods*, given the discount *rate*.

@NPV(rate,list) computes the net present value of a *list* of periodic inflows or outflows of cash, given the discount *rate*.

@IRR(estimate,list) computes the internal rate of return of a *list* of period cash flows, given a first *estimate* of the rate.

Date Functions

@DATE(yyyy,mm,dd) displays the date in the current cell and results in a date value that can be sorted or used in the date arithmetic functions, @DIFFDATE and @SUMDATE.

@TODAY displays today's date in the current cell. (Requires no parameters.)

Both of the following date functions perform arithmetic on Framework II date values.

@DIFFDATE(date1,date2) finds the number of days between *date1* and *date2*.

@SUMDATE(date,days) adds the specified number of *days* to *date* and yields the resulting date.

Table 3.3: *A Selection of Framework II Functions (continued)*

► **WORKING WITH STATISTICAL FUNCTIONS**

The four columns that we added in the Quarterly Income spreadsheet—labeled Totals, Average, Most, and Least—are reserved for computing the statistical values that will help us analyze the four income periods. To compute all these values, we'll use the @SUM, @AVG, @MAX, and @MIN functions, respectively.

Our approach will be as follows: we'll write all four of the statistical functions in the first row of the table, row 5 (Earnings). Then we'll simply copy the formulas into the remainder of the spreadsheet.

You can see in Table 3.3 that all four of the functions we'll be using take *list* or *range* parameters. In the Quarterly Income spreadsheet, we'll want each function to work on a range of values located in columns B to E. For example, to find the total earnings for all four quarters, we'll enter the function

>   @SUM(B5:E5)

Notice how the colon character is used to express a range of references. This function tells Framework II to find the sum of all the numeric values in row 5, from column B to column E.

Begin by moving the highlight to cell F5; this is where we'll enter the formula for calculating the total earnings for the four quarters. Press the @ character. When you do, you'll notice that Framework II recognizes this character as the beginning of a formula; you'll see this familiar message appear below the desktop:

>   Formula/number editing; RETURN finishes

Continue entering the name of the function and the opening parenthesis:

>   @SUM(

Case is not important in function names; you can enter letters in all uppercase, all lowercase, or any combination.

Now is the moment to enter the range parameter for this @SUM function. We'll do so by pointing and extending the highlight over the range. Here are the keystrokes:

↑	(to initiate pointing)
Home	(to position the cursor . . .)
→	(. . . over cell B5)
Extend Select (F6)	(to extend the highlight)
Ctrl-→	(to specify the range, from B5 to E5)
Return	(to finish the pointing)

When you press the ↑ key to begin the pointing and then move the highlight to B5, the formula on the edit line will be expanded to

@SUM(B5)

Pressing the Extend Select key and extending the highlight will result in the formula

@SUM(B5:E5)

The correct range notation is supplied automatically as you extend the highlight; you don't have to enter the colon character from the keyboard.

The final character required to complete the function is a closing parenthesis. Enter the character now, and press the Return key to complete the formula entry. You will see the result of the @SUM function in cell F5:

$29,079.00

This figure represents the total earnings of your business over the four quarters.

Now enter the other three functions, @AVG, @MAX, and @MIN, into cells G5, H5, and I5, respectively. Use the same sequence of steps we followed for the @SUM function:

1. Enter the name of the function, starting with the @ character, along with an open parenthesis.

2. Begin pointing (press ↑), and move the highlight to cell B5.

3. Press Extend Select (F6), and extend the highlight to cell E5.

4. Enter a closing parenthesis, and press Return to complete the formula entry.

Notice that after you extend the highlight over the range, you can avoid a keystroke by simply entering the closing parenthesis. Pressing the Return key to complete the Extend Select process is not required.

Here are the values that the three new functions will display in their respective spreadsheet cells:

Average	Most	Least
$7,269.75	$12,875.44	$2,367.82

You may note that the average earnings for the four quarters falls about halfway between the best and worst quarters' earnings.

Now we can copy the four new formulas down into the remaining rows of the Quarterly Income table. Position the highlight at F5, and proceed as follows:

Extend Select (F6)	(to extend the highlight)
Ctrl-→	(to specify the range to be copied: F5 to I5)
Copy (F8)	(to copy the range)
↓	(to specify the beginning of the destination range: row 6)
Extend Select (F6)	(to extend the highlight)
Ctrl-↓	(to specify the entire destination range: rows 6 to 10)
Return	(to complete the Extend Select operation)
Return	(to complete the copying)

Figure 3.11 shows the result of the copy operation. All four statistical values have been successfully calculated in each row of the table. If you move the cursor down a given column of the spreadsheet, you'll find that this was, indeed, a *relative* copy operation. The row numbers in the range references were automatically incremented for each row down the table. For example, here are the formulas you will see in column F:

```
@SUM(B5:E5)
@SUM(B6:E6)
@SUM(B7:E7)
@SUM(B8:E8)
@SUM(B9:E9)
@SUM(B10:E10)
```

There is an interesting set of displays in row 8. Since this row has no data in it between columns B and E, the functions we copied have nothing to work with. For @AVG, @MAX, and @MIN, this creates an error situation. Framework II displays the following message in the cells that contain these functions:

```
#N/A!
```

This tells us that the values for these cells are *not available*. If you position the highlight over one of these cells, you'll see an additional message below the desktop:

Function requires at least one numeric value

When you create a spreadsheet formula that cannot be calculated, Framework II does its best to tell you what is wrong. You can simply

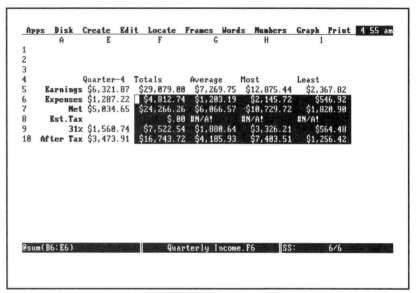

Figure 3.11: *Using Statistical Functions*

delete the contents of row 8, from columns F to I, by using Extend Select (F6) and the cursor keys to select the row, and then using the Delete key.

The Quarterly Income spreadsheet is now complete. Once again, you may want to try out some "what-if" scenarios on this spreadsheet. For example, change the estimated tax rate or one of the quarterly earnings figures. Each time you change a numeric value on the spreadsheet, all of the formulas will be recalculated, including, of course, the statistical formulas in columns F to I. For example, you can easily find out what happens to the average quarterly after-tax income (in cell G10) as a result of a change in the tax rate.

After all this work, you'll probably be interested in learning about two Framework II operations that will help you keep permanent records of your spreadsheet: saving and printing. We'll look briefly at these operations in the next section.

SAVING AND PRINTING SPREADSHEETS

In Chapter 2, we discussed the Save and Continue operation. This operation lets you save a frame in its current condition and then continue your work with the same frame. All you have to do to execute this operation is press Ctrl-Return. You can perform the Save and

Continue operation with the highlight positioned either on the Spread-sheet frame's border or inside the spreadsheet. In either case, Framework II will save a copy of the spreadsheet on the current disk and then return you to the desktop.

Alternatively, you can use the Disk menu's Put Away option to save a file. This option stores the currently selected frame on disk and then removes the frame from the desktop.

To print your spreadsheet, use the Print menu. In many cases, all you will have to do is enter a few keystrokes to print out an entire spreadsheet:

Ctrl-P   (to open the Print menu)

B   (to begin printing)

Again, it doesn't matter where the highlight is located when the printing operation begins; the highlight can be either on the frame's border or inside the spreadsheet.

When a spreadsheet contains more columns than can be printed with the currently established line length (more on that in Chapter 4), Framework II will print as many columns as possible in one block and then proceed with subsequent columns in a second block. If you have toggled the Lock First Column/Row option (from the Edit menu) into its *on* condition, Framework II will repeat the first column in each block of the printout.

Figure 3.12 shows a printout of the Quarterly Income spreadsheet. You can see that columns A through F were printed in the first block of the printout. The second block repeats column A and then continues with columns G through I.

```
              Consulting and Speaking Activities
                 Quarterly Income Statement

              Quarter-1  Quarter-2  Quarter-3  Quarter-4  Totals

    Earnings $2,367.82  $7,513.87 $12,875.44  $6,321.87 $29,079.00
    Expenses   $546.92    $832.88  $2,145.72  $1,287.22  $4,812.74
         Net $1,820.90  $6,680.99 $10,729.72  $5,034.65 $24,266.26
    Est.Tax
         31%   $564.48  $2,071.11  $3,326.21  $1,560.74  $7,522.54
   After Tax $1,256.42  $4,609.88  $7,403.51  $3,473.91 $16,743.72


              Average      Most       Least
    Earnings $7,269.75 $12,875.44  $2,367.82
    Expenses $1,203.19  $2,145.72    $546.92
         Net $6,066.57 $10,729.72  $1,820.90
    Est.Tax
         31% $1,880.64  $3,326.21    $564.48
   After Tax $4,185.93  $7,403.51  $1,256.42
```

Figure 3.12: The Printed Spreadsheet

You can also print a selected portion of a spreadsheet. To do so, first select the portion you want to print with Extend Select (F6). Then, just as you did for printing the entire spreadsheet, press

Ctrl-P   (to open the Print menu)

B   (to begin printing)

If you have locked the first row and column, as we have done in our exercise, they will be printed along with the selected cells. Figure 3.13 shows a printout of a selected portion of the spreadsheet—the part containing all the summary figures (cells F4 through I10). Notice that the row labels from column A appear at the left. However, since the only column label—Consulting and Speaking Activities—is in row 1, it is not printed.

	Totals	Average	Most	Least
Earnings	$29,079.00	$7,269.75	$12,875.44	$2,367.82
Expenses	$4,812.74	$1,203.19	$2,145.72	$546.92
Net	$24,266.26	$6,066.57	$10,729.72	$1,820.90
Est.Tax				
31%	$7,522.54	$1,880.64	$3,326.21	$564.48
After Tax	$16,743.72	$4,185.93	$7,403.51	$1,256.42

Figure 3.13: *Printing a Portion of a Spreadsheet*

If you want to see how your printout is going to look before you actually send it to paper, you can begin by storing the output as a print file on disk. The Print menu has a submenu that allows you to specify where the printout will be sent:

Destination of Printout

Select this submenu, and then choose the DOS File option inside the submenu:

Ctrl-P   (to open the Print menu)

D   (to open the Destination submenu)

D   (to select the DOS File option)

Up Level (–)   (to return to the main Print menu)

B   (to begin "printing" to disk)

When you "print" the frame, Framework II will send the copy to a file on disk, with the extension name ".PRT". To examine this print file, simply load it onto the desktop from the disk.

As a final step in your work with the Quarterly Income spreadsheet, you might want to create some graphs. We'll see how easily this can be done in the next section.

CREATING GRAPHS FROM A SPREADSHEET

Figure 3.14 shows the Graph menu. Using this menu to create graphs from a Framework II spreadsheet is a concise and efficient process.

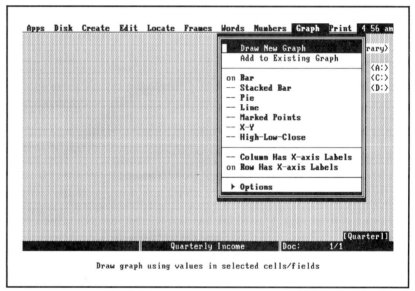

Figure 3.14: *The Graph Menu*

The steps are simple:

1. Extend the highlight over the block of spreadsheet numbers that you want to graph.

2. Open the Graph menu and select the graph type you want to create.

3. Set options, if necessary, for your graph; for example, specify titles for the x- and y-axes (that is, the horizontal and vertical axes of your graph).

4. Select the appropriate Graph menu option to draw the graph.

5. When you are prompted, tell Framework II where you would like the graph to appear.

Several important aspects of designing the graph are automatically taken over by Framework II; for example:

☐ The graph is scaled appropriately.

☐ Labels to identify scaled values along the x- and y-axes of the graph are taken from row 1 and column A of the spreadsheet.

☐ The title for the graph is copied from the label that you give to the Graph frame.

Framework II also automatically determines the nature of the hardware environment it is working in. Framework II can draw graphs on either a monochrome monitor (controlled by a monochrome display card installed inside your computer) or a color graphics monitor (controlled by a color display card).

To create monochrome graphs, Framework II makes use of the special "text graphics" characters that are provided at the high end of the ASCII character code used by MS-DOS. (ASCII, an acronym for American Standard Code for Information Interchange, is simply a code that assigns a fixed number, from 0 to 255, to every character that the computer uses or displays on the screen.) You can see the text graphics characters in Appendix C, which displays the entire ASCII code. These characters are just fine for drawing graphs that are by nature horizontally or vertically oriented, such as bar graphs and marked-points graphs. Framework II can create attractive graphs of these types on the monochrome screen. Some other types of graphs, such as the pie graph, will be drawn a little clumsily with text graphics characters.

On a color graphics monitor, Framework II enjoys the advantages of color and high-resolution graphics. On this equipment Framework II can therefore produce graphs that are more accurate and precise—and often more attractive—than those created on a monochrome monitor. In addition, Framework II can display the graphs in color.

One of Framework II's advantages over other integrated spreadsheet packages is that it works successfully with whatever display hardware you have installed on your computer. Some other spreadsheet and graphing programs will display graphs only on a color graphics monitor.

Once you have highlighted the spreadsheet range that you want to graph and selected a graph type, Framework II gives you two options for creating the display itself. These options are identified at the top of the Graph menu:

> **Draw New Graph**
> **Add to Existing Graph**

If you select the Draw New Graph option, you must then specify the destination of the graph:

☐ You can put the new graph in an Empty frame that already exists on the desktop; this frame becomes a Graph frame.

☐ You can let Framework II create a new Graph frame for you.

The other graphing option, Add to Existing Graph, allows you to lay one graph over another inside the same Graph frame. An overlay is restricted to specific types of graphs—you can overlay a line or marked-points graph over another line, marked-points, or bar graph that you have already created.

We'll create two graph examples from the Quarterly Income spreadsheet: a pie graph representing the earnings of the four quarters, each quarter as a wedge of the pie, and a combination bar and marked-points graph, posing quarterly expenses against quarterly after-tax income.

To create these graphs we'll want to begin by making some changes in the format of the spreadsheet. We've already mentioned that Framework II takes the labels for the graph from column A and row 1 of the spreadsheet. For this reason, we'll want to start with a version of the spreadsheet that begins with the four quarter headings in row 1. (In other words, we'll go back to the version of the Quarterly Income spreadsheet as it appeared before we added the three rows for a spreadsheet title.)

Furthermore, there will not be room on the graph for long labels such as Quarter-1. We'll have to revise these labels to the following abbreviations:

> Q1   Q2   Q3   Q4

You may often find yourself going through this process of making small revisions in a spreadsheet before you create graphs. The goal is to make the spreadsheet's format conform as closely as possible to the simple requirements of Framework II's graphing options. You can easily keep two versions of your spreadsheet: one finished version for viewing and printing and another, simplified version for creating graphs.

Make sure you have saved to disk our current version of the Quarterly Income spreadsheet, with the spreadsheet title displayed in rows 1 and

2. Then revise the spreadsheet on the desktop, following these steps:

1. Use the Edit menu to delete the first three rows of the spreadsheet. Extend the highlight over these three rows, open the Edit menu, and select the option

   Rows/Records: Remove

   This deletion cannot be undone, so Framework II will ask you to confirm that you really want to go through with it.

2. Change the quarter headings, now in row 1, to the two-character abbreviations Q1, Q2, Q3, and Q4.

3. Select column A with the Extend Select key (F6), and use the Words menu to change the style of the text from bold to normal. To do so, press

Ctrl-W	(to open the Words menu)
N	(to select normal text)

Now let's create our graphs. Begin by extending the highlight over the four numbers representing quarterly earnings, in row 2 of the current spreadsheet. We'll create a pie graph of these values. Here are the necessary keystrokes:

Ctrl-G	(to open the Graph menu)
P	(to select the Pie option)
D	(to draw the new graph)

At this point Framework II will display the following message below the desktop:

Press RETURN to draw graph here, or select desired frame
   and press RETURN

We haven't bothered to set aside an Empty frame for the graph, so we'll let Framework II create the frame for us. Simply press the Return key, and the new Graph frame will appear on the desktop.

The Zoom key is an important tool for viewing Framework II's graphs. You'll find that detail will be superior when you view a graph in full-screen mode rather than inside a frame on the desktop. Press Zoom (F9) to look at the pie graph in full-screen mode. Figure 3.15 shows the graph.

A pie graph provides a clear way to compare a few values that make up a whole. In this case the "whole" is the total earnings for the year,

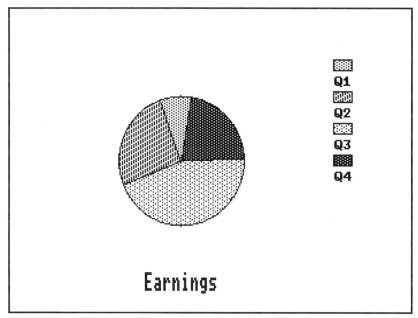

Figure 3.15: *A Pie Graph of Quarterly Earnings*

the wedges that make up the pie represent the quarterly earnings. You can see at a glance in which quarters you earned the most and the least.

Now let's try creating a Graph frame that contains two graphs: an original and an overlay. This time let's begin by creating an Empty frame for our work:

Zoom (F9)	(to return to the desktop view)
Ctrl-C	(to open the Create menu)
E	(to create an Empty frame)

Enter the following label into the frame's border:

Income vs. Expenses

Press the Return key to close the frame, putting it aside temporarily in its tray at the corner of the desktop.

Inside the revised Quarterly Income spreadsheet, highlight the four quarterly after-tax income figures in the last row. Then press the following keys:

Ctrl-G   (to open the Graph menu)

| B | (to select the Bar option) |
| O | (to select the Options submenu) |

Figure 3.16 shows the Options submenu of the Graph menu. This submenu gives you ways of manually specifying some graph characteristics that Framework II would otherwise determine automatically. It also allows you to enter titles for the x- and y-axes using the following options:

| X-axis Title | {} |
| Y-axis Title | {} |

With the Options submenu open on the desktop, type the following commands and data:

X	(to choose the X-axis option)
Quarters	(the title for the x-axis)
Return	(to enter the title into the menu)
Y	(to choose the Y-axis option)
Amount in $	(the title for the y-axis)
Return	(to enter the title into the menu)
Up Level (–)	(to return to the main Graph menu)
D	(to draw the graph)

At this point, you will have to select the frame in which you want the graph to appear. Using the ↑ or ↓ key, move the highlight to the frame we have created for this graph. It is in its tray and looks like this:

[Income   v]

Press the Return key to complete the graphing operation.

Before we even look at the graph, let's create the overlay. Return the highlight to the inside of the spreadsheet, and extend the highlight over the four values representing quarterly expenses. Press the following keys:

Ctrl-G	(to open the Graph menu)
M	(to select Marked-points)
A	(to select the Add to Existing Graph option)

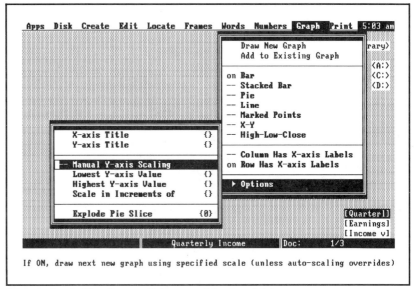

Figure 3.16: *The Options Submenu of the Graph Menu*

↑ or ↓   (to select the Income vs. Expenses Graph frame on the desktop)

Return   (to draw the graph overlay)

Now select the Graph frame again and press the Zoom key (F9). Figure 3.17 shows the graph you have created. The after-tax income figures are represented by bars, and the quarterly expenses by "marked points" inside each bar. The titles that you entered into the Options submenu are displayed below and to the side of the x- and y-axes. Also notice that Framework II has automatically created a legend at the upper-right corner of the graph, to identify the various elements.

For exploring "what-if" scenarios, graphs may be as valuable as the spreadsheets they are based on. Framework II will redraw Graph frames in response to changes you make in the numeric data of the original spreadsheet. However, because the graph resides in a different frame than the spreadsheet, the revision of the graph does not occur automatically. If you make changes in the spreadsheet, you must then move the highlight to the Graph frame and press the Recalc key (F5). Recalc makes Framework II redraw the graph according to the new data in the spreadsheet.

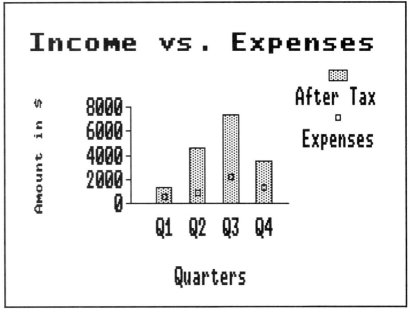

Figure 3.17: *A Composite Graph: After-Tax Income vs. Expenses*

Later in this chapter we'll learn more about using the Recalc key. We'll also discover a way to link two frames explicitly, so that changes in one frame will automatically result in changes in the other frame.

Using a graph that's been saved to disk presents a special problem. To work successfully with a graph, Framework II relies on the presence, on the desktop, of the spreadsheet from which the graph was originally created. If you save a graph and later bring it back to the desktop without its corresponding spreadsheet, Framework II will have no way of redrawing the graph.

For this reason, it is a good idea to create an Empty frame to store a spreadsheet together with all of the graphs that you create from that spreadsheet as an outline. Save this Outline frame on disk under a different name than the original spreadsheet (Quarterly Income); then, when you load the frame back onto the desktop, you can be assured that the Graph frames will have access to the appropriate Spreadsheet frame.

Framework II will print a graph on any printer. The resolution of the paper copy will depend on the graphics capabilities of your printer and on whether you are using a monochrome display card or a color display card. If you have a daisywheel printer, which prints only characters,

Framework II will use appropriate letters and symbols to build the graph on paper.

We have examined a broad range of Framework II activities, from building Spreadsheet frames to creating Graph frames. Now let's make another visit to The Sophisticated Palate to see how all these features might be put to use.

EXAMPLES

In addition to simple record-keeping tasks, Eileen Wilcox and George Farley use spreadsheets to analyze past business events and project future transactions. In this section we'll look at three spreadsheets and spreadsheet systems that they have put together for analyzing, projecting, and recording various financial aspects of their business:

1. A spreadsheet and graph that help the principals compare and analyze sales revenues over time from the three major activities of their business

2. A spreadsheet that they have devised to help them make decisions regarding an upcoming real estate investment

3. The outline of expense spreadsheets that we began investigating in Chapter 2

SALES COMPARISONS BY ACTIVITY

George Farley has recently started keeping separate monthly sales records for the three parts of The Sophisticated Palate's business: the catering service, the imported items for which they act as wholesale distributors, and the prepared foods that they distribute wholesale. He wants to begin developing semiannual comparative summaries of these three activities to track their relative growth rates.

Figure 3.18 shows a spreadsheet he has created for the first six months of the year. He has typed in the dollar sales for each of the three activity categories—Catering, Wholesale Imports, and Wholesale Prepared

Foods—for each of the months. Then, using the @SUM function, he computed the total sales for January and the total sales for the grocery across the entire six-month period. Finally, he used the Copy key (F8) to copy the monthly total formulas across from January, and the activity-total formulas down from the Deli total.

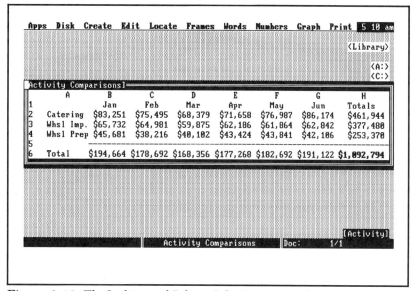

Figure 3.18: The Sophisticated Palate—Sales Comparisons by Activity

At this point, he decided he would like to create a graph that would give him a picture of comparative sales for each month. The Stacked Bar option of the Graph menu turned out to be just what he wanted. Figure 3.19 shows the graph that this option produced for him from his spreadsheet data. Each bar of the graph, representing a month of sales, is a composite of three different textural shades, representing the three business activities.

To create the graph, he began by extending the highlight over all of the numeric "raw" data of the spreadsheet: the rectangular block containing the sales figures for all three business activities, over the six-month period. Then he opened the Graph menu and selected first the Stacked Bar option, then the Draw New Graph option. Finally he pressed the Return key to instruct Framework II to create a new frame for this graph.

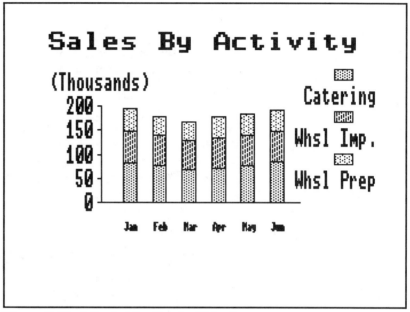

Figure 3.19: *A Stacked-Bar Graph of Sales Revenues*

To add a title to the graph, he entered the following label into the border of the Graph frame:

Sales by Activity

He had to press the Recalc key (F5) to make Framework II redraw the graph including the new title he had supplied.

He plans to create a graph like this every six months, to keep a continual comparison of sales revenues from the three parts of the business.

A TABLE OF LOAN PAYMENTS

The Sophisticated Palate has been doing extremely well in recent years. In fact, it has experienced increasing demand for its services from neighboring cities. However, since both the wholesale prepared foods and the catering trays must be prepared fresh daily, meeting the demand will require some form of expansion. One possibility is to increase the size of its fleet of trucks and expand the kitchen. However, it seems more sensible to obtain a new building in a neighboring city. This alternative would allow the business to maintain the quality and freshness of its products. While it would still have to expand the fleet of trucks, the smaller distances they would have to cover would result in lower overall transportation costs.

George and Eileen have found a suitable building in an ideal location. However, it is for sale, rather than for lease, at a price of $320,000. They would like to buy the building, hoping to pay 20 percent down and cover the rest by means of a loan. Adding three new trucks will cost an additional $27,000. They have been negotiating for a business loan, while Ariana Katz, the administrative assistant, has been handling dealings with a real estate agent who believes the price is negotiable. In the meantime, Eileen has asked Frank, the bookkeeper, to calculate the probable rate of payment, based on the various factors that might affect it.

Framework II has a function, @PMT, that calculates a monthly payment based on three parameters:

1. The principal amount of the loan
2. The annual interest rate
3. The number of months in the term of the loan

Based on the worst-case assumption that they pay the asking price for the building, Frank calculates that they will pay $69,400 down on the building and borrow the remaining $347,000. He has created a small spreadsheet to find the resulting monthly payment:

	A	B
1	principal:	277600
2	rate:	7
3	yrs to pay:	15
4		
5	payment:	2495.15

Cells B1 to B3 contain the raw data: the principal, the annual interest rate, and the term of the loan in years. In cell B5, Frank entered the following formula:

@PMT(B1,B2/1200,B3*12)

As you can see from Table 3.3, the @PMT function computes the payment per period (defined by B3*12) required on a principal loan (B1) at a specified interest rate per period (B2/1200). Frank used the pointing technique to develop the formula. The expression B2/1200 represents the *monthly* interest rate in decimal form. The expression B3*12 represents the number of months in the term of the loan.

Eileen has discovered that she can change the raw data in this spreadsheet to produce an instantly recalculated figure for the payment. For example, if she wants to find out the payment on the same loan over a 30-year term, she can simply move the highlight to cell B3 and enter the number 30.

Finally, she realizes that she could easily use the @PMT function to create an entire two-dimensional table of loan payments, given a range of principals and a range of interest rates. This exactly suits her needs, since neither the principal nor the rate are determined yet. She asks Frank to complete this spreadsheet.

Figure 3.20 shows the spreadsheet he creates. In the upper-left corner of the spreadsheet are the input values required for the payment calculation. But now the value in cell B1 represents the starting principal in the table, that is, the first of a range of possible principals. Likewise, the value in cell B2 is the first of a range of possible interest rates. These two values are carried forward to cells A6 and B5, respectively. Row 5 contains a series of interest rates, each incremented by a quarter of a percent. Column A, from cells A6 to A18, contains a range of principals, decremented by $1,000. These rates and principals are used to generate a table of loan payments.

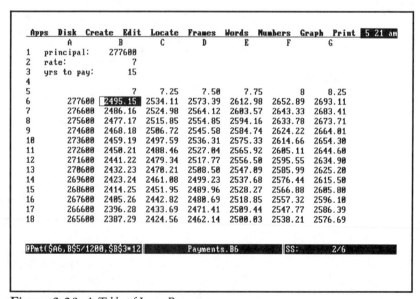

Figure 3.20: A Table of Loan Payments

Here are the steps Frank followed to formulate this table:

1. *To create the column of principals:* He entered the following reference into cell A6:

   + B1

   and the following formula into cell A7:

   + A6 – 1000

   He then used the Copy key (F8) to copy this decrementing formula down column A into cells A8 to A18.

2. *To create the row of loan rates:* He entered the following reference into cell B5:

   + B2

   and the following formula into cell C5:

   + B2 + .25

   He then copied this formula across row 5 into cells D5 to G5.

3. *To create the payment table:* Using the pointing technique, he entered the following formula into cell B6:

   @PMT($A6,B$5/1200,$B$3 * 12)

   Replicating this formula required two separate copy operations: first copying the single formula across row 6; then copying all the @PMT formulas of row 6 down into rows 7 to 18.

For the copy operations to be successful, Frank had to distinguish carefully between relative and absolute references in the @PMT formula. In the reference to the principal amounts ($A6), the column, A, is fixed, but the rows, 6 to 18, are relative. In contrast, the interest rate (B$5) has a relative column reference but an absolute row reference. Finally, the "years to pay" ($B$3) is an absolute reference both for the column and the row. No other combination of references would have yielded the desired table.

Because this spreadsheet required something of an effort to prepare, Eileen wanted to protect Frank's work. Looking at the spreadsheet, she realized that the only cells that she would ever want to change would be the three input cells, B1, B2, and B3. Accidental deletions or changes in the values or formulas of any of the other cells would be undesirable and would require some effort to repair.

Conveniently, Framework II offers a way to protect selected cells in a spreadsheet from any accidental changes. This option is controlled from the Edit menu and is called

Protect from Editing

This option protects the current contents of the spreadsheet cells that you have selected from being accidentally revised or deleted. The Edit menu also has an option that removes this protection if you decide to go back and modify a protected cell:

Allow editing

To protect the spreadsheet, then, Eileen extended the highlight over all the values in rows 5 to 18 and pressed the following keys:

Ctrl-E   (to open the Edit menu)

P   (to select the Protect option)

Placing the table in protected mode does not, of course, change the spreadsheet's responsiveness to changes in the input data. A change in any one of the three input values—the starting principal, the starting interest rate, or the term of the loan—results in an immediate recalculation of the entire table.

Unfortunately, the recalculation process is rather slow in this table; Framework II takes a long time to perform so many @PMT functions. This becomes a problem when Eileen wants to change two input values at once. For example, let's say she wants to change the starting principal to $265,000 and the loan term to 30 years. In its current settings, Framework II recalculates the entire table after *each* of these new entries, even though Eileen is interested only in the *final* result, after both entries have been changed. She finds it annoying to have to wait for the recalculation to occur twice.

The Options submenu of the Numbers menu (shown in Figure 3.21) presents a solution to this problem. When you first create a new Spreadsheet frame, Framework II by default goes into Automatic recalculation *mode*, and the default *order* in which it recalculates is called Natural. This means that the spreadsheet will be recalculated whenever you enter a new numeric value that will have an effect on some other value. Using the Options submenu, you can change the recalculation mode to Manual. In this mode, Framework II recalculates the spreadsheet only when you explicitly command it to do so by pressing the Recalc key, F5. (A change in the recalculation mode applies only to the current spreadsheet.)

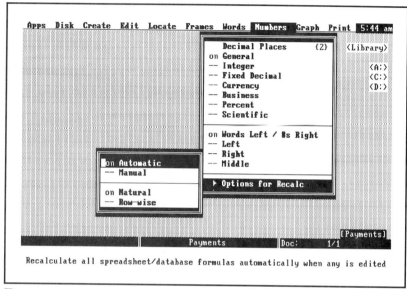

Figure 3.21: *The Options Submenu of the Numbers Menu*

Eileen pressed the following keys to change Frank's payment spreadsheet to Manual recalculation:

Ctrl-N   (to open the Numbers menu)

O   (to select the Options submenu)

M   (to switch to Manual recalculation mode)

Now she can change as many of the input values as she wants; when she is ready for the table to be recalculated, she presses Recalc (F5).

We'll discuss the other recalculation options, which define the *order* of recalculation, in the next section, as we examine George's business expense Outline frame.

EXPENSE SPREADSHEETS, WITH A SUMMARY

At the end of Chapter 2 we left George organizing a monthly summary of the business's expenses. Figure 3.22 shows the Outline frame he has prepared. The outline holds nine different spreadsheets: seven for the various categories of fixed expenses, one for Cost of Goods Sold, and finally the Summary of Expenses spreadsheet at the bottom of the outline.

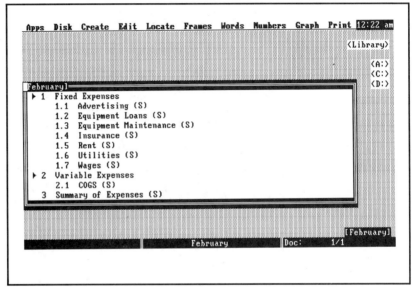

Figure 3.22: *The Sophisticated Palate—Grocery Expense Outline*

George has organized this outline so that it can be reused each month for two purposes: to record fixed and variable expenses in a series of categories and to yield a summary spreadsheet of all those expenses. Let's examine George's work.

Figure 3.23 shows the Summary spreadsheet located at the very end of George's outline. This spreadsheet takes one value from each of the other spreadsheets in the outline. These values represent the bottom-line, total expenses in each of the expense categories. The values are transferred from the expense spreadsheets to the Summary spreadsheet through references that George has typed into the summary.

For example, you can see that The Sophisticated Palate spent $3,420 on advertising this month. Figure 3.24 shows the Advertising spreadsheet. It has four columns of data: the date of each expense, a description, the amount of each item, and a total for all the advertising expenses. George computed this total using the @SUM function.

The total amount is in cell D14 of the Advertising spreadsheet. Notice that the top cell of column D and the left-most cell of row 14

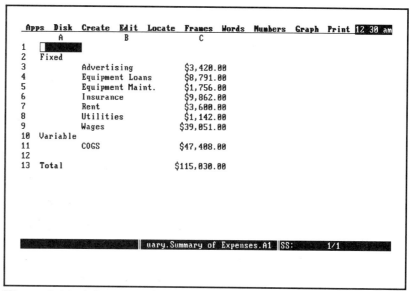

Figure 3.23: *A Summary of Expenses Spreadsheet*

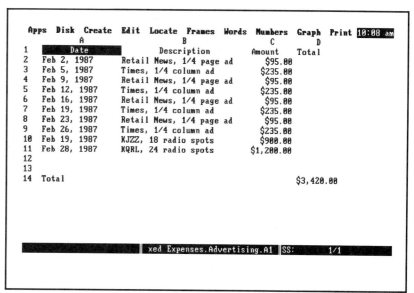

Figure 3.24: *The Sophisticated Palate—Advertising Expense Spreadsheet*

both contain the label "Total". This allows us to call cell D14 by the following English name reference:

Total.Total

Because this reference is inside the Advertising spreadsheet, the cell's expanded English name is

Advertising.Total.Total

But Advertising is a subframe inside the major outline heading "Fixed Expenses". So, finally, the full name of cell D14 is

Fixed Expenses.Advertising.Total.Total

This name can be used as a reference by any other spreadsheet inside the expenses outline. As a reference, its function will be to transfer the value contained in the Advertising spreadsheet's cell D14 to another spreadsheet location in the outline.

The Summary spreadsheet (Figure 3.23) uses a series of references like this one to fetch all the total values from the expense spreadsheets. George has been careful to organize all of the expense spreadsheets so that their totals each have the English name

Total.Total

If you were to look at the references behind the values in column C of the Summary spreadsheet, this is what you would find:

```
+ Fixed Expenses.Advertising.Total.Total
+ Fixed Expenses.Equipment Loans.Total.Total
+ Fixed Expenses.Equipment Maint.Total.Total
+ Fixed Expenses.Insurance.Total.Total
+ Fixed Expenses.Rent.Total.Total
+ Fixed Expenses.Utilities.Total.Total
+ Fixed Expenses.Wages.Total.Total
+ Variable Expenses.COGS.Total.Total
```

Each of these references links the Summary spreadsheet to one of the expense spreadsheets and transfers a data item. Finally, in cell C13 of the Summary spreadsheet, George has entered the formula that finds the total expenses for the month:

@SUM(C3:C11)

The advantage of this outline organization is this: the format of each expense spreadsheet can be designed independently and need not conform to the organization of the Summary spreadsheet. Each expense spreadsheet can be as simple or as complex as necessary. The single requirement is that the cell containing the total of each expense spreadsheet have the same English name reference—Total.Total.

With this outline, Frank can enter the data in the various expense spreadsheets daily. When the expense spreadsheets are complete, the total values will be transferred to the Summary spreadsheet.

There is only one small problem with this arrangement. References from one spreadsheet to another often need to be manually recalculated. For example, let's say Frank enters a new set of data into the Advertising spreadsheet and then George wants to open the Summary spreadsheet to examine the effect on the total month's expenses. George has to press the Recalc key (F5) from the Summary spreadsheet before the new Advertising.Total.Total value will be transferred.

LINKING THE EXPENSE SPREADSHEETS TO THE SUMMARY

But Framework II provides a solution to this problem. To complete the link between two spreadsheets, you can enter a special kind of reference in the *source* spreadsheet—that is, the spreadsheet that is sending data to a new destination. This special reference begins with the @ symbol.

For example, the Advertising expense total is located in cell C3 of the Summary spreadsheet. To provide an automatic link between the Advertising and Summary spreadsheets, George can enter the following value into a free cell in the Advertising spreadsheet:

@Summary of Expenses.C3

Now, whenever George enters a new numeric value into the Advertising spreadsheet, resulting in a recalculation of the spreadsheet, this @ reference will ensure that the Summary spreadsheet's cell C3 will also be recalculated. Transfer of data between the two spreadsheets will thus occur automatically, eliminating the need to use the Recalc key in the Summary spreadsheet.

George had to find some out-of-the-way location in the Advertising spreadsheet to store this @ reference. To avoid making a mess of the spreadsheet, he decided to add a new column for this reference. He used the Create menu to add one column at the right side of the spreadsheet—column E. Into cell E14 he entered the necessary linking reference:

@Summary of Expenses.C3

Column E does not contain information that needs to be displayed in the spreadsheet. In fact, its appearance might be a distraction from the real information of the spreadsheet. Fortunately, Framework II provides a little trick that you can use to *hide* any column in a spreadsheet. The trick is performed by the Size key. Here are the steps:

1. Place the highlight in the column you want to hide.

2. Press the Size key (F4).

3. Press the ← key until the column is 0 spaces wide.

4. Press the Return key to complete the operation.

A column thus hidden is still part of the spreadsheet; it simply is not displayed.

George used this technique to hide column E in the Advertising spreadsheet. But he found that one final adjustment was necessary to make the interspreadsheet link functional. Whenever he changed a figure in the Advertising spreadsheet, only the values that depended on that figure were recalculated. The reference linking the total to the Summary spreadsheet was not recalculated, because the reference does not depend on any other values. So his new totals did not get transferred automatically. To remedy this, he had to change the order in which Framework II recalculated the values in the Advertising spreadsheet.

The default recalculation order is called "Natural"; when Natural order is on, Framework II recalculates values in the order defined by the spreadsheet's references. For example, if a given formula depends on two other values elsewhere in the spreadsheet, those two values are recalculated before the formula. Significantly, if you change a value that does not affect any other values, no recalculation takes place.

The alternate recalculation order is called "Row-wise." Under this order, Framework II recalculates every row of the spreadsheet, from the top row to the bottom row, every time you enter a new numeric value. This order ensures that every cell of the spreadsheet will be recalculated, no matter how simple or complex a system of references the spreadsheet contains.

So to make sure the @ reference in cell E14 would be recalculated after each new entry into the Advertising spreadsheet, George pressed the following keys to change the spreadsheet's order of recalculation:

Ctrl-N	(to open the Numbers menu)
O	(to select the Options submenu)
R	(to change recalculation to Row-wise)

To summarize, here are the steps George followed to link each of the expense spreadsheets to the Summary spreadsheet:

1. Add a column at the right side of each of the expense spreadsheets.

2. At the new, lower-right corner of each spreadsheet, enter the appropriate @ reference into the Summary spreadsheet.

3. Hide the new column from view, using the Size key (F4).

4. Change each expense spreadsheet's recalculation order to Row-wise.

This may seem like a lot of trouble to go through; but remember, this outline can now be used as a template for recording and summarizing the company's expense records each month. Thanks to the rather elaborate system for linking spreadsheets inside the outline, George can be certain that his Summary spreadsheet will be developed automatically as he enters information into the individual expense spreadsheets.

EXPLORING FURTHER

As you continue to expand your knowledge of Framework II, you will find that its resources for spreadsheet programming go far beyond what we have covered in this chapter. In particular, Framework II and FRED provide a rich collection of functions and facilities that can increase the versatility and power of a spreadsheet. We'll discover many more of these functions in the chapters ahead.

THE DATE FUNCTIONS

One important group of functions consists of the date functions. You can see the @DATE function in action in George's Advertising Expense spreadsheet, Figure 3.24. For example, in cell A2, George entered the following formula:

@DATE(1987,2,2)

As you can see, this formula resulted in the display

Feb 2, 1987

George could have entered this date as a label, but he has learned that it's a good idea to enter it through the @DATE function, so that if necessary he can later perform arithmetic on the date. We'll examine the date functions in detail when we study Framework II databases in Chapter 5.

Before ending this chapter we'll look briefly at two last topics: sorting a spreadsheet, and a special spreadsheet-navigation command.

SORTING

The Locate menu has two options that allow you to rearrange spreadsheet data:

Ascending Sort
Descending Sort

These options use a selected column or portion of a column as the "key" to rearrange the spreadsheet. The sort will work on text, numbers, or dates, rearranging alphabetically, numerically, or chronologically.

To use these sorting options, follow these steps:

1. Extend the highlight over the column you have selected as the "key" for the sorting operation.

2. Open the Locate menu.

3. Select Ascending or Descending Sort.

Let's use George's Summary of Expenses spreadsheet (Figure 3.23) for a quick example of sorting. Let's say George has decided to sort the fixed expenses in the spreadsheet from the largest to the smallest expense. He extends the highlight over the expense amounts in cells C3 to C11. Then he presses these keys:

Ctrl-L   (to open the Locate menu)
D   (to select the Descending Sort)

As soon as he completes these keystrokes, the fixed expenses reappear in the following order:

Wages	$39,051.00
Insurance	$9,862.00
Equipment Loans	$8,791.00
Rent	$3,600.00
Advertising	$3,420.00
Equipment Maint.	$1,756.00
Utilities	$1,142.00

Notice that the labels in column B are also rearranged to correspond appropriately to the new order of column C.

At some point George might change his mind and decide to rearrange these expenses in alphabetical order, by the name of the expense. To do so, he would extend the highlight over the labels in cells B3 to B11 and press

Ctrl-L   (to open the Locate menu)

A   (to choose the Ascending Sort)

This will put the expenses back in the order in which you see them in Figure 3.23. We'll learn more about sorting and the Locate menu in Chapter 5.

THE GOTO COMMAND

An additional command—Goto, on the Locate menu—can be used to speed your movement through spreadsheets. To use it, press

Ctrl-L   (to open the Locate menu)

G   (to invoke the Goto command)

cell name   (to tell Framework II the name of the cell you want to move to)

Return   (to record your selection and move to the cell)

You can even use this option to move to a spreadsheet cell in a frame other than the one you are currently using.

George found this command extremely useful when he was working out his Summary of Expenses spreadsheet. He needed to know if the formula he had entered had actually succeeded in placing the summary information in the correct location. With it, he could enter the hidden formula in column E of his Advertising spreadsheet, and then move immediately to cell C3 in the Summary spreadsheet, by entering

Summary of Expenses.C3

as the name of the cell to go to.

This command has an additional feature that makes it especially useful for comparing the results of two widely separated frames. After you have moved to the specified cell, you can press the Instruct key, followed by Return, to get back to the cell from which you moved. Thus, you can make repeated adjustments to a formula in one cell and easily check to see that the results in another cell are what you intended. If they are not, two keystrokes return you to the original cell for further editing.

The Goto command is not restricted to spreadsheets. In fact, you can use it to move between any items on the desktop that have names. You can move from one subhead of an outline to another, for example, or from a frame on the desktop to one in the Library cabinet. You can even move from a spreadsheet cell in a frame nested several levels deep in one outline frame to a cell in a spreadsheet in a completely different outline. No matter how far you move, you can always return to your previous location by pressing Instruct Return Return.

SUMMARY

A Spreadsheet frame is designed to help you work with tables of numbers and to relieve you of the tedium of arithmetic. Spreadsheets also help you explore "what-if" scenarios; you can quickly find out what happens to calculated values as a result of new input data.

The rows and columns of a spreadsheet form a grid of cells. Each cell has an address, consisting of its column letter and its row number. This address can be used as a *reference* to the value the cell contains.

Formulas in spreadsheets are designed to calculate new values from already existing values. A formula can contain references to other cells, and it can perform arithmetic operations. Once you have written a formula, you can copy it to other cells in your spreadsheet. For the purposes of copying, references in formulas can be designated as *relative* or *absolute*.

To simplify the process of writing certain kinds of formulas, Framework II provides a considerable set of *functions* for you to work with in spreadsheets.

Using Framework II's menus and function keys, you can control the appearance and organization of a spreadsheet. You can change the display style of numbers and labels. You can insert or delete rows and columns. You can move blocks of data from one place to another. You can even sort data in the spreadsheet by columns.

Producing graphs from spreadsheets is an easy process in Framework II. The Graph menu offers several different types of graphs for you to choose from.

Finally, Framework II offers some rather elaborate techniques for linking spreadsheets, automating the transfer of data from one spreadsheet to another. This can be an extremely important feature when you find yourself creating complex systems of spreadsheets within an Outline frame.

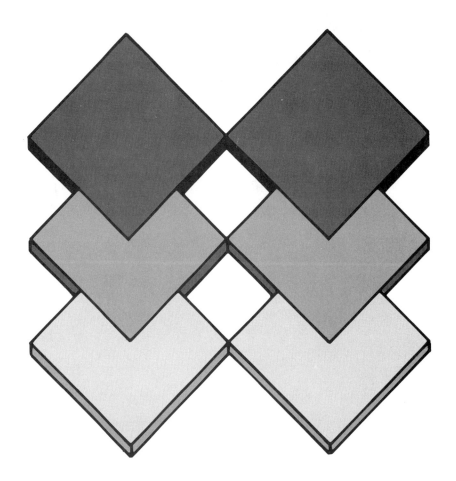

CHAPTER FOUR

WORD PROCESSING

INTRODUCTION

Word frames are designed for entering, revising, and formatting pages of text. No matter what kind of writing you do—from business letters, memos, reports, or legal documents to personal letters, essays, or poetry—Framework II's word processing capabilities will allow you to concentrate on the writing itself rather than on the mundane details of producing typewritten paper drafts of your writing.

In this chapter you'll learn how to begin writing in a Word frame, as well as how to revise your work once you've completed a written document. Here are the major topics we'll explore:

- **Entering text:** using the keyboard, understanding "word wrap," and moving the cursor

- **Formatting text:** changing the alignment of the text on the page and setting margins, paragraph indents, and tab stops

- **Editing a document:** selecting portions of the text for editing, inserting and deleting, styling text for special printing effects such as boldfacing and underlining, moving blocks of text from one place to another, using the "search and replace" feature, and correcting spelling errors

- **Printing a document:** using the submenus of the Print menu to set margins and pages, incorporate headers and footers into a document, and control the print mode. In addition, we'll look at some special FRED functions used to format a document for printing and to control the printer

As with other types of frames, your major tools for working in Word frames will be the cursor-movement keys, the special function keys at the left side of the keyboard, and the Framework II menus. The Words and Print menus are particularly important for word processing. We'll also be working with the Locate and Edit menus and, of course, the Create menu. In addition, we will learn how to place FRED functions *behind* a Word frame to control the printing process.

CREATING A WORD FRAME

The option in the Create menu that places a new Word frame on the desktop is called

Empty / Word Frame

Here are the keystrokes that place a Word frame on the desktop:

Ctrl-C   (to open the Create menu)

E   (to create an Empty frame)

You may recall from Chapter 2 that an Empty frame has two main uses. You can move other frames into it, in which case it becomes an Outline (or *containing*) frame. Or you can move inside the frame and begin word processing; it then becomes a Word frame. (You can also use an Empty frame to place a graph in or to conduct a telecommunications session; it then becomes a Graph frame or a Telecommunications frame.)

These two uses are mutually exclusive: Once you begin word processing in an Empty frame, Framework II will not allow you to move other frames inside what has become a Word frame. If you want to combine word processed text with other types of frames, you'll have to create a separate Outline frame to contain all of the various document frames you are working with. Near the end of this chapter we'll explore the use of Word frames in an outline.

As always, the first thing you'll want to do when you create a new frame is type a label into the frame's border. You'll recall that this label has two purposes: it helps you distinguish among the various frames you might have on the desktop, and it ultimately serves as a file name for your document when you save it on disk.

The Down Level key (+) moves you into the Word frame, at which point you are ready to begin word processing. As soon as you move inside a Word frame, you'll notice the *cursor* that marks your place in the frame. The word processing cursor is the same visual marker that we have worked with so often on the edit line below the desktop: a flashing underscore character, contained within a single reverse-video space.

Up to now, in our work with Outline and Spreadsheet frames, we've distinguished between the cursor, on the edit line, and the *highlight*, inside the frames themselves. The distinction may seem a little less clear in Word frames. In word processing, the cursor (the flashing underscore) always marks the current character position in a document. But the reverse-video highlight that *encloses* the cursor can be extended to block off larger parts of a document: words, sentences, paragraphs, and larger sections of text.

We will see that Framework II gives you convenient keyboard commands for *selecting* these various portions of text by extending the highlight over them. Once you have thus selected the text you want to work with, you can choose any of the word processing operations to modify the text: formatting, styling, moving, copying, deleting, and so on.

But before you can learn to use Framework II's word processing features to *revise* the appearance of text, you have to begin by *entering* some sentences and paragraphs into a frame.

ENTERING TEXT

The sample document we'll be working with in this chapter is a two-page office memorandum. Imagine yourself as the executive in charge of purchasing computer hardware and software, in a company that has recently placed a new personal computer on the desk of every manager. After considering a number of integrated software packages, you have just bought copies of Framework II for use on these PCs. You've decided to distribute a memo to all your managers, encouraging them to start using Framework II and describing some of the program's features.

Figure 4.1 is a printout of the first draft of your memo. To gain some hands-on experience with Framework II word processing, you are typing the memo yourself into your own PC. Once you have finished entering the first draft into a Word frame, you plan to begin revisions, exploring several of Framework II's formatting and editing features along the way. Don't worry if you make some mistakes in typing. You'll see in a little while how easy it is to make corrections on the screen before you print your document, and you'll also use Framework II's built-in spelling checker to catch and correct any errors you might not have noticed along the way. (If you want a preview of the final product of your work with this memo, take a look at Figure 4.11).

Create a Word frame on the desktop, and enter the following label into the border of the frame:

Memo to Managers

Press the Down Level key (+) to move the cursor into the frame.

The first several lines of our office memorandum comprise the heading, which specifies whom the memo is addressed to and who wrote it, as well as the date and the subject of the memo. After you type each line, press the Return key to move the cursor to the beginning of the next line. To place a blank space between two lines, press Return a second time.

```
Date:  March 3, 1987

To: All Managers
From: B.B.

RE: Using Framework II in the Office

We have recently purchased several copies of the integrated
software packgage called Framework II. I would like all of you to
begin working with this program as soon as possible, evaluating
its effectiveness for your own data processing tasks.

Framework has several components  that I feel will be useful to
you in the following activities:

* performing evaluations and projections,
* maintaining records and databases, and
* creating documents.

In Framework II you do all your work in special-purpose frames
that appear on the display screne. The screen becomes your
"desktop," the palce where all the action of the program takes
place. You can control exactly what part of your current work is
displayed on the desktop at a given time. You may want to work
with several frames at a time,m in which case they can all be
present on the desktop at once. Frames on the desktop are either
open--displaying their contents--or closed--temporarily placed in
a special "tray" at the side of the desktop.

You can crteate several different types of frames. Here are brief
descriptions of the frames you'll probably be working with the
most frequently:

Spreadsheet frames are designed to help you work with tables of
numbers. Any time you organize numbers and labels into columns
and rows for the purpose of calcualting totals, averages, or
other statistical values, a spreadsheet frame wil simplify the
task and increase your ability to analyze the data itself. In
addition to numbers, you can enter formulas into your
spreasheets, to take over the more tedious arithmetic tasks
involved iwth numeric record keepint. Formulas can be copied
across rows  or down columns of your spreadsheet, alowying you to
perform, in minutes, what migh otherwise turn into hours and
hours of complex aritmentic tasks.

A spreadsheet is also a projection tool, allowing you to find
answers to "what-if" questions. Change a single number on ;your
spreadsheet, and all formulas that rely on that number will be
recalculated, automatically. Those of you who do cost projections
wil particularly appreciate this feature.

Graph frames give you presentation-quality graphs from the tables
of numbers that you enter into a spreadsheet frame. Framework II
can draw a variety of different types of graphs: bar, stacked
bar, pie, mark points, line, x-y, and high-low-close. Graphs are
simple to draw, and you can even print them out ont paper, using
the printer attached to yoru PC.

Database frames allow you to organize, sotre, and work with
groups of data. You may want to create databases to handle
employee records, client information, sales records, and
inventories.

Word frames are used for working with Framework II's easy but
powerful word processor. Those of you who are used to typing your
own memos will find this to be a refereshing new way to create
documents. You can even store frequently used forms in a library
```

Figure 4.1: *Office Memorandum, First Draft*

```
on the desktop, so that you don't have to create them from
scratch every time. You may also want to introduce your
secretaries to Framework II word processing, if you can stand the
thought of sharing your desktop computers with another person.

If you can't, Framework II also has telecommunications frames,
which you can use not only for conventional telecommunications
purposes--logging on to the Central Data Processing department's
mainframe to read information processed there, for example-- but
to hook your computer directly to others in the building, and
share your work instantly with those who need to use the results
of your analyses, or the information in your files.

Please begin working with Framework II as soon as you can; ;I
think you'll find that the effort you put into learing to use the
program wil pay off almost immediately. Let me know your
impressions within a couple of weeks.

                                              B.B.
```

Figure 4.1 (continued): *Office Memorandum, First Draft*

When you begin entering the first paragraph of the text (beginning "We have recently purchased . . ."), you'll find that you do *not* have to press the Return key when you come to the end of a line. When the appropriate moment arrives, Framework II automatically moves the cursor down to the beginning of the following line on the screen. If you are in the middle of a word when you reach the end of the line, Framework II will carry that word down to the next line.

This feature is called *word wrap.* Thanks to word wrap, you need to press the Return key only when you have completed a paragraph. In fact, you should *avoid* pressing the Return key at the end of a line inside a paragraph. Otherwise, you will have unwanted *carriage-return characters* inside what you consider a paragraph, and later on you'll have trouble using Framework II's formatting tools to change the format of the paragraph.

Another important key in a Word frame is the Backspace key. Backspace does two things. It moves the cursor backward by one space, and it erases the character you had typed into that space. Backspace is a convenient key to use when you make a typing mistake and you want to move back and correct it.

Hold down the Backspace key for several seconds, and the cursor will move backward quickly, erasing several characters of the current line. If you backspace to the beginning of a line and then press Backspace again, the cursor will move up to the end of the previous line, a process that is the reverse of word wrap.

As you enter text into a Word frame, you will see a message like the following in the third section of the status panel:

Char: 36/7

This particular pair of numbers means that you are at the 36th character of the 7th line of your text. The first of these two numbers increases by 1 every time you press a key, adding a character to your line; it starts over from 0 with every new line. The second number increases whenever the cursor moves down a line. When you first create a Word frame, Framework II sets the default line length at 65 characters. We will see later how you can change that length when you want longer or shorter lines.

That's really all you need to know for the most basic word processing skill: entering text into a frame. Before you read further, spend some time entering the entire text of the memo shown in Figure 4.1. Painful a task though this may seem, you'll be glad to have this document to experiment with as we begin discussing some of the more exciting word processing features.

MOVING THE CURSOR

Once you've begun to create a document, you may find yourself wanting to move backward and forward within it, to insert, delete, or revise. Two kinds of cursor and highlight movement are possible in Word frames; both make use of the cursor-movement keys at the right side of your keyboard.

Simple cursor movement involves moving the cursor from one part of the document to another. You can move the cursor in any direction inside the document. You can also make the cursor jump a distance, from one location to another:

- □ To the beginning or end of the current line
- □ To the beginning or end of the entire document
- □ Up one frame or down one frame

Table 4.1 describes the cursor-movement keys that you will want to master for word processing in Framework II.

These cursor-movement operations do not extend the highlight; they simply move the cursor to a new character position inside the text. But for many word processing functions you'll want to use the highlight to *select* a portion of your document as the target for a certain activity. For these operations the Ctrl key works with the cursor-movement keys to extend the highlight over the text you want to select.

SELECTING BLOCKS OF TEXT

By extending the highlight over a range of text, in much the same way that you learned to extend the spreadsheet highlight over a range

Keys	Action
↑, ↓	Move the cursor up or down one line in the text.
←, →	Move the cursor one character to the left or right in the text.
Home	Moves the cursor to the first character position in the current line.
End	Moves the cursor to the last character position in the current line.
Ctrl-Home	Moves the cursor to the beginning of the entire document.
Ctrl-End	Moves the cursor to the end of the entire document.
PgUp	Moves the cursor to the top of the current frame, or scrolls one frame up.
PgDn	Moves the cursor to the bottom of the current frame, or scrolls one frame down.

Table 4.1: Cursor-Movement Keys in Word Frames

of cells, you select a portion of your document as the object of a Framework II activity. Framework II gives you pairs of keystrokes for selecting the following portions of text:

□ A word

□ A sentence

□ A paragraph

Table 4.2 describes the selection keys that extend the cursor in these three ways. To help you understand the effects of these keys, Figures 4.2 to 4.4 show examples of word, sentence, and paragraph selection, in a portion of the office memorandum that you have now entered into your Word frame.

Of course, if you want to select *several* words, sentences, or paragraphs, you should use the Extend Select key (F6). Press the key, and then use the Ctrl-key combinations described in Table 4.2 to extend the highlight over the exact block of text you want to work with.

Now we're going to look at the tools Framework II provides to help you change the appearance of your word processed document.

Key	Action
Ctrl-→	Selects the word or portion of a word immediately following, and including, the cursor position.
Ctrl-←	Selects the word or portion of a word immediately preceding, and including, the cursor position.
Ctrl-↑	Selects the sentence or portion of a sentence immediately preceding, and including, the cursor position.
Ctrl-↓	Selects the sentence or portion of a sentence immediately following, and including, the cursor position.
Ctrl-PgUp	Selects the paragraph or portion of a paragraph immediately preceding the cursor position.
Ctrl-PgDn	Selects the paragraph or portion of a paragraph immediately following the cursor position.

Table 4.2: Text-Selection Keys in Word Frames

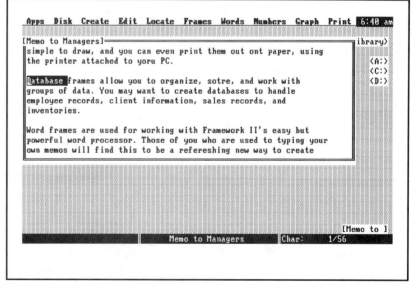

Figure 4.2: Selecting a Word (Ctrl-→)

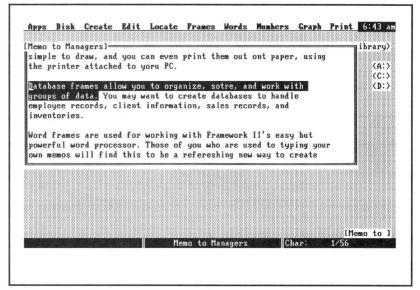

Figure 4.3: *Selecting a Sentence (Ctrl-↓)*

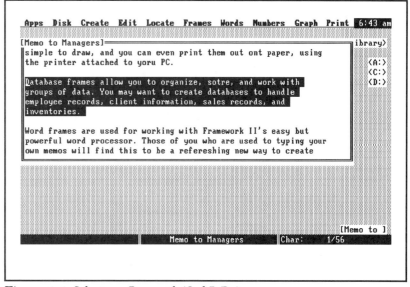

Figure 4.4: *Selecting a Paragraph (Ctrl-PgDn)*

FORMATTING YOUR DOCUMENT

Figure 4.5 shows the Words menu. It is divided into three parts, dealing with printing styles, text alignment, and margins and tabs, respectively. Here we'll look at the latter two parts of this menu. A little later in the chapter we'll examine styling, which occupies the first part of this menu.

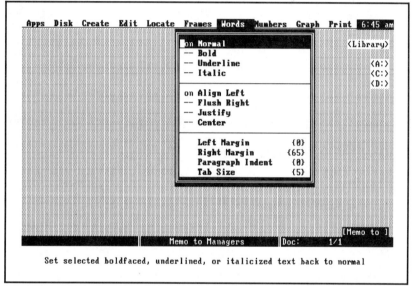

Figure 4.5: The Words Menu

GLOBAL VERSUS LOCAL FORMATTING

In the sections ahead, we'll be examining the variety of formatting and styling options available in Framework II word processing. All of these options can be used either globally—affecting the entire document—or locally—affecting only a selected portion of the document. Here are the two techniques for distinguishing between these modes of operation:

□ To assign a global format or style, move the highlight to the border of the Word frame (Up Level key, –) and select the appropriate option from the Words menu.

□ To assign a local format or style, move the cursor into the Word frame, extend the highlight over the block of text that you want to work with, and select the appropriate option from the Words menu.

We'll begin by performing some global operations on our office memorandum document. Then we'll do some local operations on certain portions of the text.

TEXT ALIGNMENT

The *format* of your document refers to the alignment of the left and right sides of the text in relation to the margins. Framework II offers four different alignment options. As we just mentioned, these can be assigned either globally or locally.

The Align Left option is the default condition for a Word frame. Under this option, the left side of the text is justified—that is, arranged in a straight line along the left margin. The Align Left option leaves the document in a "ragged-right" format. This means that each line simply ends at a random point at or near the right margin, depending on the length of the line's last word. The version of our memorandum shown in Figure 4.1 is arranged under the Align Left option, as are the displays in Figures 4.2 to 4.4. This format should seem very familiar, because most typewritten documents end up in this condition by default.

The Flush Right option is just the opposite. The right side of the document is aligned, and the left side becomes ragged. Figure 4.6 shows a paragraph displayed under the control of this option. Although this rather unusual format appears only rarely in print, you will find a use for it later in this chapter.

The Justify option aligns both the left and right sides of the document. The final version of the office memorandum, shown in Figure 4.11, is both left and right justified. To achieve this kind of justification, Framework II carefully inserts spaces inside the text, so that each line will end at exactly the same point at the right margin. Many people find that a justified document is more appealing to the eye than one that has a ragged right edge.

Finally, the Center option of the Words menu centers each line of text that you enter into a Word frame. We'll be using this option locally inside the office memorandum to center the lines of the memo's heading.

First let's try using the Justify option globally on the memorandum. Actually, you can specify a text alignment either before you begin entering text into your document or after the document is already complete. If you specify the format before you enter any text, each new line you

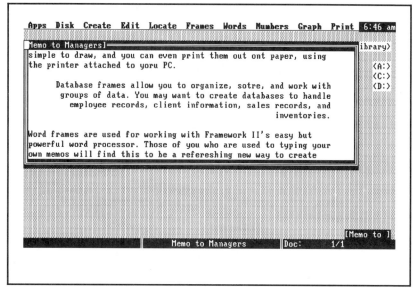

Figure 4.6: *A Paragraph Displayed in Flush-Right Format*

type will be automatically aligned according to your specification. If you wait until after the document is complete to specify a format, Framework II will quickly reformat your document, briefly displaying the following message at the bottom of the screen:

FORMATTING

Because our memorandum is already completely entered into the frame, we'll have to begin by moving the highlight to the frame's border to perform a global format operation. Here are the keystrokes:

Up Level (–)	(to move the highlight to the border)
Ctrl-W	(to open the Words menu)
J	(to justify the document)

In response, Framework II will reformat the entire document so that each paragraph is both left and right justified.

MARGINS, INDENTS, AND TABS

Formatting a document also involves several other characteristics: selecting numeric values for the left and right margins, thus determining the maximum length in characters of each line; specifying paragraph indents; and defining tab stops. The final section of the Words menu deals with these options.

The default left margin is set at 0, and the default right margin at 65. This means that each line can have a maximum of 65 characters. (The actual horizontal positioning of the text on the printed page is determined by other Framework II tools, which we will examine later.)

If you reset the margins of a Word frame before you enter any text into the frame, each line of text that you enter will be correctly formatted within the margins you have specified.

When you change the margins of an already existing document or part of a document, Framework II automatically reformats the text within the new margins. In reformatting the document, Framework II also follows the alignment option that you have selected.

Let's look at an example. The office memorandum contains six paragraphs that describe the various components of Framework II. Let's say you decide to emphasize these paragraphs by printing them within smaller margins than the other paragraphs of the document.

To make this *local* change in the document, you begin by moving inside the Word frame. Then you move the cursor to the beginning of the first target paragraph, which reads, "Spreadsheet frames are designed . . .". Now press the following keys:

Extend Select (F6)	(to extend the highlight)
Ctrl-PgDn, six times	(to select the six target paragraphs)
Ctrl-W	(to open the Words menu)
L	(to change the left margin)
11	(the new left margin)
Return	(to enter the value into the menu)
Ctrl-W	(to open the Words menu again)
R	(to change the right margin)
60	(the new right margin)
Return	(to enter the value into the menu)

Now the six paragraphs describing the components of Framework II are displayed within the margins 11 to 60. These paragraphs are also justified within the new margins, because we have already chosen justification for the entire document.

Another rather convenient Framework II word processing feature is automatic paragraph indentation. By default, this option is set at zero:

Paragraph Indent   {0}

If you would like each new paragraph in your text to be indented by a certain number of spaces, you can assign a nonzero value to this menu option. Let's try globally indenting the paragraphs of the memorandum. Place the highlight at the frame's border again, and press

Ctrl-W	(to open the Words menu)
P	(to select the Paragraph Indent option)
8	(to indent by eight characters)
Return	(to complete the operation)

When Framework II's reformatting is complete, each paragraph in the memorandum will be indented by eight characters.

If you were now to add new paragraphs to the document, you would see how the Paragraph Indent option works on newly entered text. Whenever you press the Return key to begin a new paragraph, Framework II automatically places the cursor at the indent setting rather than at the left-margin setting. The rest of the lines of each paragraph will begin at the left margin.

Framework II also allows you to create *negative indents* at the beginnings of paragraphs whose left margins are greater than zero. This means that the first line of the paragraph will begin to the left of the paragraph's own left margin. To create a negative indent, simply specify a negative number for the Paragraph Indent option. Let's try this feature out on the memorandum document.

We have set new, smaller margins for the six paragraphs in the memorandum that describe the components of Framework II. To further emphasize the importance of this information, we'll make the first line of each paragraph hang into that paragraph's left margin. Begin by entering the frame—the highlight will still be over the six paragraphs—and press the following keys:

Ctrl-W	(to open the Words menu)
P	(to select the Paragraph Indent option)
− 3	(to create a negative indent)
Return	(to complete the format change)

You can see the effect of this change in Figure 4.11.

Finally, Framework II allows you to set tab stops at regular intervals. The Tab key, located near the upper-left corner of your keyboard, is labeled with two arrows, pointing left and right. Each time you press the Tab key inside a Word frame, the cursor will move forward to the next tab stop.

You can see on the Words menu that the default tab stops occur every eight spaces. To change this default, select the Tab Size option and enter a new value.

INSERTING SOFT HYPHENS

Now that your document has been fully formatted, with both margins justified, you may find that some of the lines appear to have too much space between the words. You can correct this condition with a special character called a *soft hyphen*. A soft hyphen will cause a word to break at the right margin if there is enough room for the portion of the word that precedes the hyphen on the line before it. A regular—or *hard*—hyphen is always printed on paper; a soft hyphen is printed only if the word does break. If you add text and reformat your paragraphs, the soft hyphen will disappear. The soft hyphens are found on the Edit menu.

To start with, let's look at the telecommunications paragraph, which has a lot of "white space," particularly in the first line. It appears in Figure 4.7. Move the cursor to the first *c* in "Telecommunications" on the first line of the paragraph. Press

Ctrl-E	(to open the Edit menu)
I	(to insert a soft hyphen)

The letters "Tele" immediately move to the end of the first line, followed by a hyphen. There's still quite a bit of white space on the first line, and now there's even more on the second. Move the cursor to the first i in "Telecommunications." Press Instruct twice to insert another soft hyphen. The letters "commun" now move to the first line, the first hyphen you inserted disappears from view, and a new hyphen appears after the *n*. The paragraph reformats, and the result is shown in Figure 4.8. You can work through the rest of the document, inserting soft hyphens where they are appropriate.

DISPLAYING HIDDEN CHARACTERS

Tabs, spaces, and carriage-return characters inside your document are called "hidden characters," because they are not normally displayed in any visible way on the screen. From time to time you may want to examine these hidden characters in a document you are producing. Seeing

```
If    you    can't,    FRAMEWORK    II    also    has
Telecommunications frames,  which you can use not
only    for    conventional    telecommunications
purposes--logging    onto    the    Central    Data
Processing    department's    mainframe    to    read
information processed there,  for example--but to
hook your  computer  directly  to  others  in  the
building,  and  share  your  work  instantly with
those  who  need  to  use  the  results  of  your
analyses, or the information in your files.
```

Figure 4.7: *The Telecommunications Paragraph of the Memo, Right Justified*

```
If  you  can't,  FRAMEWORK  II  also has Telecommun-
ications frames,  which you can use  not only for
conventional telecommunications purposes--logging
onto  the  Central  Data  Processing department's
mainframe  to  read  information  processed there,
for example--but  to hook your  computer directly
to  others in the building,  and  share your work
instantly with those who need to use  the results
of  your  analyses,  or  the  information  in your
files.
```

Figure 4.8: *The Telecommunications Paragraph with Soft Hyphens*

where they are located may occasionally help you in the process of formatting your document. The Edit menu has a "toggle" option that alternately displays and hides these characters. The option is called

‐‐ Display Hidden Characters

To choose this option, press the following keys:

Ctrl-E   (to open the Edit menu)

D   (to display hidden characters)

Figure 4.9 shows a sample display of these hidden characters. The space character is represented by a small dot, the carriage-return by a paragraph symbol, the left hyphen by a double tilde, and the tab character by a line of hyphens with arrows at either end. Justified paragraphs use a large dot to represent "soft" spaces. To hide these characters once again, open the Edit menu and select the Display option.

We have examined the Words menu's formatting options, which control alignment, margins, paragraph indents, and tabs. Together, these options determine much about the ultimate shape and size of the document on the printed page. Keep in mind that all of these options may be set either before you begin entering text into a frame or after you have finished typing your document. For a final formatting exercise, let's center the heading lines at the top of the office memorandum document.

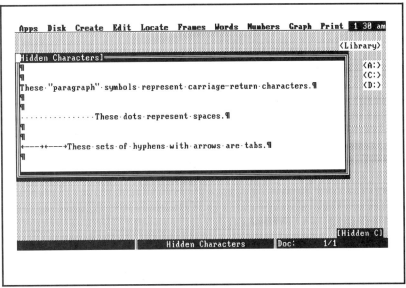

Figure 4.9: *Displaying Hidden Characters*

CENTERING A HEADING

Begin by moving the cursor to the top of the document and highlighting all four lines:

Ctrl-Home	(to move the cursor to the beginning of the document)
Extend Select (F6)	(to extend the highlight)
Ctrl-PgDn, four times	(to select all the lines of the memo heading)
Ctrl-W	(to open the Words menu)
C	(to center the heading)

Once again, check Figure 4.11 to see how this operation changes the document.

USING A WORD FRAME

In this section we'll discuss a variety of techniques for changing the appearance and content of your document, including inserting, replacing, and deleting text; styling the text; moving blocks of text; and searching for and replacing words or phrases. We'll also see how to save and print the document.

INSERTING, REPLACING, AND DELETING TEXT

Revising your text electronically, within the computer's memory, saves you the aggravation of going through multiple paper drafts of a document. These are the most basic kinds of revisions:

- □ Inserting new words
- □ Replacing parts of the document with new text
- □ Deleting portions of the document
- □ Moving blocks of text from one point in the document to another

Framework II actually has two different text entry modes for Word frames: *insert* and *typeover*. The insert mode is Framework II's default text entry mode. In the insert mode, any characters you enter from the keyboard are inserted into the document at the current cursor location. For example, let's say you have entered the following sentence into your document:

You can create different types of frames.

You decide to insert the word "several" between the words "create" and "different". Move the cursor to the "d" of "different", and begin typing the new word. As you type each character, the latter part of the sentence moves to the right to make room for the new word:

You can create several different types of frames.

In the typeover mode, the characters you type at the keyboard will *replace* the current characters in your text. To switch into the typeover mode, use the Typeover option of the Edit menu:

Ctrl-E   (to open the Edit menu)

T   (to switch to Typeover mode)

Let's look at what happens to the above sentence as we enter the word "several" in the typeover mode. Again, position the cursor at the "d" of "different" in the original sentence, and type "several". Here is what you'll see:

You can create severalnt types of frames.

The first seven characters of "different" have been replaced by "several". Now, to delete the final two characters, "nt", you press the Delete key twice. Here is the result:

You can create several types of frames.

Normally, you'll probably want to enter text in the insert mode. But keep in mind that through the Edit menu you also have the option of switching into the typeover mode. To toggle back into the insert mode, open the Edit menu and select the Typeover option a second time.

We have just seen how the Delete key erases characters from the Word frame. You can also delete blocks of text. The Delete key erases whatever portion of text is currently selected by the highlight. To delete a word, press the following keys:

Ctrl-→	(to highlight the word)
or Ctrl-←	
Delete	(to delete the word)

To delete a sentence, press

Ctrl-↓	(to highlight a sentence)
or Ctrl-↑	
Delete	(to delete the sentence)

Finally, to delete an entire paragraph, press

Ctrl-PgDn	(to highlight a paragraph)
or Ctrl-PgUp	
Delete	(to delete the paragraph)

(You can review these Ctrl-key combinations by looking back at Table 4.2.) Always keep in mind that Framework II has an Undo option that can bring back accidental deletions:

Ctrl-E	(to open the Edit menu)
U	(to select the Undo option)

Next we'll look at some of the more sophisticated word processing features that Framework II offers.

STYLING TEXT

The first section of the Words menu offers you four different text styles: Normal, Bold, Underline, and Italic. The default style is Normal.

To change to one of the other styles, extend the highlight over the target block of text and select the appropriate Words menu option.

Use the office memorandum document (Figure 4.1) to experiment with styling. Begin with the first line of the document, the memo's date:

Date: March 3, 1987

Put the word "Date" in boldface, and then underline the date itself:

Ctrl-Home	(to move to the beginning of the document)
Ctrl-→	(to select the word "Date")
Ctrl-W	(to open the Words menu)
B	(to select the Bold option)
→, three times	(to position the cursor at the "M" of "March")
Ctrl-↓	(to select the date itself)
Ctrl-W	(to open the Words menu)
U	(to select the Underline option)

Here is the result:

Date: *March 3, 1987*

To perform these operations on the rest of the headings, you can take advantage of a shortcut Framework II provides. Whenever you select an option from the menu, the menu highlight remains on the last option you selected. Therefore, if you've pressed the Instruct key to select an option, all you have to do is press Instruct again to repeat the option. We'll use this technique now. Use the cursor keys, and Ctrl-→ or Ctrl-← to select "To", "From", and "RE", and press Instruct twice after each selection. Next use the Extend Select key (F6) to select the rest of each heading in turn. When you have selected "All Managers", press

Instruct	(to open the Words menu)
U	(to select underlining)
Return	(to underline the selected text)

After that, all you have to do is select the appropriate part of each headline, and press Instruct twice.

The final version of the memorandum (Figure 4.11) has additional boldfacing: the three isolated lines below the second paragraph, and the first two words in each of the paragraphs that describe the Framework II components. Make all of these style changes in your own Word frame.

The use of the Italics option in the Words menu depends on the capabilities of the hardware in your computer system. On a monochrome monitor and on many printers, italics will be identical to underlining. However, if you have a color graphics monitor, you will see text displayed in true italics. Likewise, a printer that has an italics mode will be able to use this option properly.

Styling may also be performed globally. For example, an entire Word frame can be styled in boldface. To assign a global style, place the highlight on the frame's border before you open the Words menu. Then select the style you want for the contents of the frame.

MOVING AND COPYING BLOCKS OF TEXT

You can use the Move and Copy keys (F7 and F8, respectively) when you want to move or copy a section of text from one point to another inside your document. There are three simple steps required to perform a move or copy operation:

1. Extend the highlight over the block of text that you want to move or copy.

2. Press the Move or Copy key.

3. Move the cursor to the point in the document where you want to move or copy the text you have selected; press Return to complete the operation.

To practice with a move operation, let's turn once again to the memorandum document. We'll move the paragraph that begins "Graph frames give you . . ." to a new position, just before the last paragraph of the memo. Begin by moving the cursor to the first character of the target paragraph. Press Ctrl-PgDn to select the entire paragraph; then press the Move key (F7) to begin the move operation. Navigate the cursor to the new position, the blank line just above "Please begin working with Framework II . . .". Finally, press Return. Framework II will move the paragraph to the new location you have chosen for it.

After this paragraph move, you may have to correct the spacing between paragraphs. Press Return to insert an additional blank line or Delete to close up an unwanted blank line.

SEARCHING FOR AND REPLACING WORDS OR PHRASES

In Chapter 3 we explored the use of the Locate menu for sorting columns of data. You can't use the sorting option in Word frames, but the Locate menu does present two other important functions that *are* designed for word processing: searching and replacing. These options appear as follows in the menu:

Search	{}
Replace	{}

Actually, these options can be used in *any* type of frame. In Chapter 5 we'll look at them again in the context of Database frames.

The Search option allows you to locate a specific string of characters, if it exists in your document. Framework II moves the highlight to the string as soon as it is found. In fact, Search is a repeating function; you can continue searching for your target string of characters for as many times as the string occurs in the document. The Search option is particularly valuable for finding specific information in long documents.

The Replace option carries the process one step further. Replace also searches for a string of characters that you specify, and then it prepares to replace that string with a second string of characters that you also specify. Once again, Replace is a process that can be performed throughout the document, offering you the opportunity to replace every occurrence of the target string. You can replace selectively or globally.

We'll see that both of these operations display important messages at the bottom of the screen. To try them out, we'll first search for the word "Framework" in the office memorandum; then we'll replace that word with its uppercase equivalent, "FRAMEWORK".

You can begin the Search or Replace options from any point within your document. Let's begin with the Search operation:

Ctrl-L	(to open the Locate menu)
S	(to select Search)

At this point, Framework II moves the cursor down to the edit line and displays the following message:

Enter text to find; press RETURN to accept or ESC to exit

Enter the word "Framework" on the edit line; as you do, the word will also appear in the Locate menu:

Search: {Framework}

Press the Return key to begin the search. The highlight will immediately move to the first place "Framework" occurs after your cursor position. If you moved your cursor to the top of the document (using Ctrl-Home) before you began the search, your screen will look like

Figure 4.10. Below the desktop, you see the following messages:

TEXT FOUND

↓ – – Find Next   ↑ – – Find Previous   Any other key exits.

Following these instructions, you can press the ↓ key to move the high-light to the next occurrence of the word. If you press the ↑ key, the highlight will move backwards and find a previous occurrence of "Framework" in the document. If the highlight is currently at the first occurrence, this means that the highlight will cycle around to the *end* of the document. Similarly, if your cursor is positioned after the first occurrence of "Framework" when the search begins, pressing ↓ will continue cycling the highlight through the document, from the end back to the beginning, until it returns to your cursor position. Press any other key to end the operation.

Framework II will also tell you how many times it has found the word in the document; for example, you may see a message like this:

TEXT FOUND: 3 TIMES

If you press the ↓ key after Framework II has found the last occurrence, the following message will appear on the screen:

NOT FOUND AGAIN

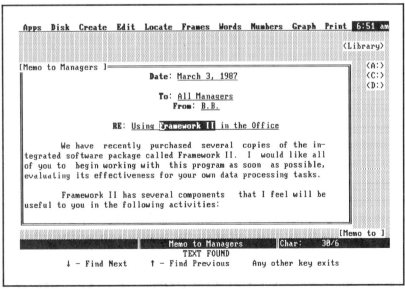

Figure 4.10: The Search Operation

At this point Framework II automatically exits from the Search operation.

After completing a search, you may sometimes decide that you want to repeat that same search. The Locate menu retains the last string you searched for, so you can simply return to the menu to begin the process again.

To use the Replace option, you must specify both a target string of characters and a replacement string. Begin by selecting the option:

> Ctrl-L   (to open the Locate menu)
>
> R   (to select Replace)

The cursor will move to the edit line, and you will first see the same message you saw for the Search operation:

> Enter text to find; press RETURN to accept or ESC to exit

Because we have just searched for the word "Framework" in the memorandum document, this target word will still be in the Locate menu and will automatically appear on the edit line. Just press Return to accept it.

Next you will see the message

> Enter Replacement text; press RETURN to accept or ESC to exit

Enter the word "FRAMEWORK" on the edit line; the word will also appear in the Locate menu:

> Replace   {FRAMEWORK}

Press the Return key to begin the replacement process. A message at the bottom of the screen offers you five different options at this point:

> RETURN −− Replace and Find Next   ↓ −− Find Next
> HOME −− Replace and Stay   END −− Replace All   ESC to exit

To replace globally, press the End key. Every occurrence of the target string will be replaced. To replace selectively, use the Return, ↓, or Home key. The Return key replaces the currently highlighted occurrence and moves the highlight to the next occurrence. The ↓ key moves the highlight forward *without* replacing the current selection. Home replaces the current selection but does not move the highlight forward. Finally, the Escape key drops you out of the operation altogether.

In the memorandum document, replace all occurrences of "Framework" with "FRAMEWORK". You'll find that the underlining under the first appearance of "FRAMEWORK" has disappeared. Go back to the Words menu and choose the Underline option again, to apply to "FRAMEWORK". You can see the result in Figure 4.11, the printout of the final draft of the office memorandum.

Date: <u>March 3, 1987</u>

To: <u>All Managers</u>
From: <u>B.B.</u>

<u>**RE:** Using **FRAMEWORK** II in the Office</u>

We have recently purchased several copies of the integrated software package called FRAMEWORK II. I would like all of you to begin working with this program as soon as possible, evaluating its effectiveness for your own data processing tasks.

FRAMEWORK II has several components that I feel will be useful to you in the following activities:

* **performing evaluations and projections,**
* **maintaining records and databases, and**
* **creating documents.**

In FRAMEWORK II you do all your work in special-purpose frames that appear on the display screen. The screen becomes your "desktop," the place where all the action of the program takes place. You can control exactly what part of your current work is displayed on the desktop at a given time. You may want to work with several frames at a time, in which case they can all be present on the desktop at once. Frames on the desktop are either open--displaying their contents--or closed--temporarily placed in a special "tray" at the side of the desktop.

You can create several different types of frames. Here are brief descriptions of the frames you'll probably be working with the most frequently:

Spreadsheet frames are designed to help you work with tables of numbers. Any time you organize numbers and labels into columns and rows for the purpose of calculating totals, averages, or other statistical values, a spreadsheet frame will simplify the task and increase your ability to analyze the data itself. In addition to numbers, you can enter formulas into your spreadsheets, to take over the more tedious arithmetic tasks involved with numeric record keeping. Formulas can be copied across rows or down columns of your spreadsheet, allowing you to perform, in minutes, what might otherwise turn into hours and hours of complex arithmetic tasks.

A spreadsheet is also a projection tool, allowing you to find answers to "what-if" questions. Change a single number on; your spreadsheet, and all formulas that rely on that number will be re-calculated, automatically. Those of you who do cost projections will particularly appreciate this feature.

Graph frames give you presentation-quality graphs from the tables of numbers that you enter into a spreadsheet frame. FRAMEWORK II can draw a variety of different types of graphs: bar, stacked bar, pie, marked points, line, x-y, and high-low-close. Graphs are simple to draw, and you can even print them out on paper, using the printer attached to your PC.

Figure 4.11: Office Memorandum, Final Draft

```
Database  frames  allow you to  organize, store, and
     work with groups of data.  You may want to create
     databases  to  handle  employee  records,  client
     information, sales records, and inventories.

Word frames are used for working with FRAMEWORK II's
     easy  but powerful  word processor.  Those of you
     who are used to  typing your own memos  will find
     this to be a refreshing  new way  to create  doc-
     uments. You can even store frequently used  forms
     in a library on  the desktop,  so  that you don't
     have to  create  them  from  scratch  every time.
     You may also want to introduce  your  secretaries
     to  FRAMEWORK II  word processing,  if  you  can
     stand the  thought  of  sharing  your  desktop
     computers with another person.

If  you  can't,  FRAMEWORK  II  also has  Telecommun-
     ications frames,  which you can use  not only for
     conventional telecommunications purposes--logging
     onto  the  Central  Data  Processing department's
     mainframe  to  read  information processed there,
     for example--but  to hook your  computer directly
     to  others in the building,  and  share your work
     instantly with those who need to  use the results
     of  your  analyses,  or the  information in your
     files.

Please  begin working with  FRAMEWORK II  as  soon as you
can; I think you'll find that the effort you put into learning to
use the program will pay off almost immediately. Let me know your
impressions within a couple of weeks.

                         B.B.
```

Figure 4.11 (continued): *Office Memorandum, Final Draft*

CHECKING YOUR SPELLING

Now that you've made your final format changes to the document, it's time to check your spelling. Framework II has a powerful spelling checker, located on the Apps menu. The Spelling Check submenu is shown in Figure 4.12. With the document that you want to check selected, press

Ctrl-A	(to open the Apps menu)
S	(to choose the Spelling Check submenu)
B	(to begin the spelling check)

If you are using a floppy disk system, you will be prompted to insert the Spell disk in drive A.

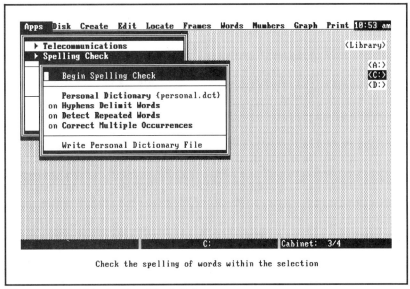

Figure 4.12: The Spelling Check Submenu.

Framework II will scan your document, checking each word against an 80,000-word dictionary. As it finds a "suspect" word, it displays something like this in the message area:

Word: B.B.   Suggest   Edit   Go On   Add Word

As you can see, you have four choices:

☐ Ask Framework II to suggest an alternative—which is selected, resulting in the message

List suggested correct spellings—ESC to exit

☐ Edit the word

☐ Ignore the (apparent) misspelling

☐ Leave the spelling-check function

Let's assume that you habitually sign your memos *B.B.* If so, it would be useful to have Framework II regard that as a legitimate word, and ignore it during spelling checks. To accomplish this, press A. This selects the Add Word option, and displays the message

Add the selected word to your Personal Dictionary—ESC to exit

The word will then be added to a file called PERSONAL.DCT, one of the dictionary files Framework II may scan during a spelling check.

If you want to edit the error, press E, and the "suspect" word will appear on the edit line. The message area will display

Edit the selected word—ESC to exit

When you have made your corrections, press Return, and the corrected word will replace the error in the document.

If you have used a word frequently in a document, but don't want to add it to your dictionary, choose Go On by pressing G. The message

Skip the selected word and continue spell checking—ESC to exit

will appear, and any other instances of the word in the document will be ignored.

If you're not sure of the correct spelling, or if you just want to see exactly how smart Framework II is, choose Suggest by pressing S. Framework II will look in its dictionaries for words that resemble the suspect word, and display several of them. More often than not, the correct word will appear among the choices. For example, on discovering the misspelling "screne" in the document, Framework II displayed the following:

Word: screne   Choose correction or ESC to previous menu
screen scene scream strewn scrounge screwing scram strain

Move the highlight to the correct word, "screen", press Return, and Framework II will replace the error in the text. Sometimes, however, you are not so lucky. On encountering the misspelling "aritmentic", Framework II offered the suggestions

arraignments arraignment aerodynamic regimented aerodynamics

When a word appears twice in a row, the second occurrence will be highlighted, with the following options displayed:

Repeated: to   Delete   Edit   Go On
Delete the selected word—ESC to exit

You can turn off this feature before the spelling check starts by selecting

on Detect Repeated Words

from the Spelling Check menu and pressing Return.

Finally, if the program finds an error that has previously been detected, you are offered the chance to correct it globally.

```
wil --> will ?                        Replace  Auto Replace  Edit  Go On
        Replace the selected word with the suggestion—ESC to exit
```

Choose Auto Replace, and every instance of "wil" will be replaced by "will".

EDITING YOUR DICTIONARIES

Framework II includes four dictionaries. In addition to the main dictionary are a dictionary of computer terms, a dictionary of business terms, and an empty dictionary. They are called COMPUTER.DCT, BUSINESS.DCT, and PERSONAL.DCT, respectively. You can use any one of them in addition to the main dictionary as a source of correctly spelled words. The default dictionary is PERSONAL.DCT. To choose another one, press

Ctrl-A	(to open the Apps menu)
S	(to choose the Spelling Check submenu)
P	(to bring the Personal Dictionary option to the edit line)
dictionary name	(enter the name of the dictionary you want to use)
Return	(to record your selection)

Whichever one you choose will be scanned during a spelling check. It will also be the dictionary to which words are added when you choose the Add Word option.

You can edit the existing dictionaries, or even create new ones. To edit any of the dictionaries, bring it to the desktop, and edit the contents as you would any Word frame. Don't be disturbed by the apparently random order of the words. Framework II optimizes the order to make it easy to search each time you bring a dictionary to the desktop.

You must be careful when editing a dictionary to use capitalization and periods exactly as you would use them in text. If you add a word that begins with a capital letter to the dictionary, Framework II will consider the word correctly spelled in the document only if it begins with a capital letter. You may inadvertently add such a word by using the Add Word option when the word is the first word of a sentence. Similarly, if you add the abbreviation *a.m.* to your dictionary, *a. m.* will not be regarded as correct.

While editing, you can add words in any order. Framework II will sort the words into optimum searching order when you save your additions.

When you have finished editing your dictionary, press

Ctrl-A   (to open the Apps menu)

S   (to choose the Spelling Check submenu)

W   (to write to the dictionary file)

If there is already a dictionary by the same name, you will be asked for permission to replace the old dictionary with the new one.

Similarly, you can create a new dictionary with any name you choose, provided the name has no more than eight characters. You may want separate dictionaries for different types of projects, or for correspondence with different organizations, each one containing personal names and technical terms appropriate to the subject. To create a new dictionary, simply enter the words in a Word frame, one to a line, then move the highlight to the label, and choose the Write Personal Dictionary File option from the Spelling Check submenu.

SAVING YOUR WORK

We have discussed the Save and Continue operation already, in the context of other types of frames. You'll recall that you can either choose the Save and Continue option from the Disk menu or just press Ctrl-Return. This command saves the current frame to disk under the label name supplied in the frame's border. If the file already exists on disk, it will be replaced by this new version.

A good piece of advice is to save your Word frame about once every 20 minutes while you are developing the document it contains. This will prevent any significant accidental loss of time and effort. If something goes wrong, the most you can lose is 20 minutes of work.

PRINTING THE DOCUMENT

The Print menu takes charge of sending the contents of a Word frame to the printer:

Ctrl-P   (to open the Print menu)

B   (to begin printing)

But before you print a word processed document, you will often want to define precisely how Framework II will carry out the printing task.

The Print menu contains several submenus to help you control many characteristics of printing. The submenu you will probably use most often is the Format Options submenu, shown in Figure 4.13. These options can be used for printing any type of frame, but many of them are especially relevant to Word frames.

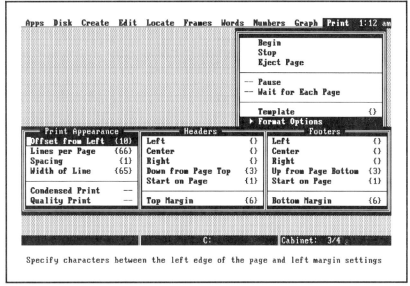

Figure 4.13: The Print Format Options Menu

POSITIONING THE DOCUMENT

The left-most menu on the Format Options submenu helps you to lay out the printed page by allowing you to establish the "offset" from the left edge of the page and the length of each line. These options must be coordinated with the margins you have already established inside the document (in the Words menu). If your paper is longer or shorter than the standard 11 inches, you can also change the number of lines per page. In addition, the last options on the center and right-most portions of the menu allow you to set a top and bottom margin.

The offset is actually the size of the left margin on the printed page. The default value is 10, but you can change it from this menu. In conjunction with the default margins for Word frames (0 on the left and 65 on the right), this value results in a page that is reasonably well centered on standard 8½ inch wide paper.

There are two ways to control the left-to-right positioning of text as it is printed. As mentioned, you can set the left margin inside the Word frame. For example, if you are using standard 8½ × 11-inch paper and an 80-column printer, you could establish margins inside your Word frame of 10 and 70, and print with no offset. It is more common, however (and easier to visualize your documents) to set the left margin so that the text you want to appear farthest to the left in the document is at a margin of 0, and to establish a right margin that formats your text as you want it to appear. In any case, you should be careful that you don't give Framework II conflicting instructions, even though it will do its best to accommodate you. If you choose an offset of 40 and a line length of 30 for a document with margins of 0 and 65, each line will break at the right margin, after 30 characters have been printed, and the rest of the line as it appeared in the Word frame will appear at the left edge of the paper on a separate line.

Let's say, for example, that you have an especially wide document— 75 characters wide. You want it to be centered on the paper. You establish margins of 0 and 75 in the Word frame. When the time comes to print, you press

Ctrl-P	(to open the Print menu)
F	(to select Format Options)
O	(to select the Offset option)
Return	(to enter your Offset selection)
2	(to set the left margin for printing two characters wide)
Return	(to record your selection)
Up Level (–)	(to return to the main Print menu)
B	(to begin printing)

By default, Framework II prints documents using single spacing, but you can use the Spacing option on the Format Options submenu to change to double or triple spacing, or even wider intervals. As with all menu options that require a value to be entered, you press Return to bring the selection to the edit line, enter the value of your choice, and press Return again.

If your paper is longer or shorter than 11 inches, you can adjust to your paper size by selecting the Lines per Page option. Most printers print six lines per inch (although some printers allow you to change this value; we'll see how to do so shortly). If your printer does print six lines per inch, you must multiply the length of your paper in inches by six.

The last options on the center and right menus are used to set a top and bottom margin, respectively. Framework II uses default values of six lines, or one inch, but you can enter different values.

PROVIDING HEADERS OR FOOTERS

A header or footer is an identifying item of information that appears on every page of your document, either at the top of the page (header) or at the bottom (footer). Headers or footers might consist of the title of the document, the date, the page number, the author's name, or some combination of these and other items. You can enter any or all of them, and position the headers or footers on the page, by using the Format Options submenu (Figure 4.13).

The central portion of the menu is for headers, and the right portion is for footers. In each section you will see the options

```
Left        {}
Center      {}
Right       {}
```

These options determine the location for the information.

To enter the information, choose the position where you want it to appear (at the top or the bottom of the page, at the left margin, the right margin, or the center), press Return, and enter the text you want to use. If the entries are not too long, you can have separate information appearing in each of the six positions.

To have Framework II print page numbers on your document, enter the text

```
<page>
```

in one of the six header or footer positions on the menu. To include a date, you must include the name of one of the FRED date-formatting functions (without the @ symbol, and enclosed in triangular brackets, as with page numbers), which you will learn about later in this chapter. For example, if the date were May 5, 1987, entering

```
<date4>
```

would print

```
May 5, 1987
```

at the specified location.

You can also choose the position of the header or footer on the page. In the center section, the option

Down from Page Top   {3}

indicates that the default position for a header is three lines from the top of the page. This is well within the default top margin of six spaces. If you change either the top margin or the vertical position of the header, be sure the values you choose don't conflict. Similarly,

Up from Page Bottom   {3}

sets a default position for a footer at three lines from the bottom, and allows you to change it.

Figure 4.14 shows a Format Options submenu filled in. When the page is printed it will appear with the header

Memo to Managers   March 3, 1987   Page 2

and the footer

Framework in the Office

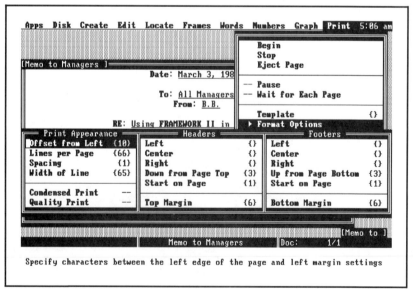

Figure 4.14: Selecting Headers and Footers

The final option regarding headers and footers controls the page they start on. You may want your opening page, for example, to have no header, as the document's title and opening remarks will contain most of the information that would ordinarily appear in a header. To have Framework II begin placing headers on page 2, select the option

Start on Page   {1}

from the central portion of the menu, press Return, enter the value 2, and press Return again. Similarly, you can have footers begin appearing on any page you choose by entering a value in the same option on the Footers portion of the menu.

STYLING YOUR TEXT

Most printers can print text in various sizes and styles. The Format Options menu provides for three different styles and sizes—normal printing, quality printing, and condensed printing. At the bottom of the left-most portion of the Format options menu are two choices:

Condensed Print   — —
Quality Print   — —

The default print style is normal printing. If your printer offers "near-letter quality" or "correspondence-quality" print style, and you have installed your printer correctly (see Appendix A), you can choose the Quality Print option. Condensed print has more than 12 characters per inch (the exact number—generally between 15 and 18—depends on your printer). If you choose Condensed Print, and your printer can handle it, your entire document is printed in this style.

FINE-TUNING YOUR PRINTOUT

Any settings you choose from the Print menu will affect the entire document. Settings chosen for a containing frame will automatically be applied to all the frames within it, unless you have previously selected settings from the Print menu for individual subframes. But what if you want more precise control over the appearance of your document? What if you want to use several type styles or print pitches in the same document? These aspects of printing are generally controlled by *printer escape sequences*. Printer escape sequences are series of characters, generally beginning with the Escape character (ASCII 27), that send instructions directly to the printer. The Escape character tells the printer that what follows is to be interpreted as instructions, rather than as characters to be printed.

There are two ways to send escape sequences to your printer through Framework II: directly in text, and through the FRED printing functions. For various purposes, you might want to combine both strategies. If you want to set a few words in a different type style—one that is not among the menu choices—you are better off inserting the escape sequence into the text. This has certain pitfalls, however. On the other hand, if you want to style a whole section differently from the body of the document, you should use the FRED printing functions. In either case, you must first consult the manual that came with your printer to see what characters have what effects. We'll look first at how to insert escape sequences into text, and then examine some of the FRED printing functions.

► INSERTING ESCAPE SEQUENCES INTO TEXT

One of Framework II's powerful features is the fact that it can accept graphics characters in text. Table C.1 in Appendix C is a complete table of all the graphics characters that you can produce in Framework II. For our present purposes, however, the most important of these are the first 32, which represent the control characters, summarized in Table C.2. The characters that affect the printer are generally among these characters. The most important of them, the Escape character (ASCII 27), can be entered by pressing Ctrl-[. This produces a small ← on your screen. If, for example, your printer expects Escape-S to print a subscript, you can cause it to make this change by typing Ctrl-[S just before the characters to be printed as a subscript. After those characters, enter the code to return to normal printing.

Some control characters, such as Ctrl-X or any of the control characters that open menus, cannot be entered by pressing a Ctrl key combination. To enter these characters, you must use a different technique. You can see in Table C.2 that Ctrl-X has an ASCII code of 24. To enter any character that cannot be entered directly, hold down the Alt and Shift keys while entering the digits of the ASCII code on the numeric keypad. To enter Ctrl-X, then, hold down Alt and Shift while pressing 2 4 on the keypad. When you release the keys, a ↑ symbol, the graphic equivalent of ASCII 24 (see Table C.1) will appear on your screen. For many printers, this character cancels all previous print settings.

The danger with this approach is that it may distort the length of your lines. When counting the number of characters per line, Framework II will treat the characters in an escape sequence just like any other character; two two-character escape sequences on a line will make that line four characters too short. It requires a great deal of experimentation with sample printouts to get the spacing exactly the way you want it.

► **THE FRED PRINTING FUNCTIONS**

Another way to mix different styles of text is to put each block of text that you want to appear in a different style in a separate frame, and place a FRED printing function in the formula area *behind* the frame. This is the normal location for any FRED formula or program, as we discussed in Chapter 1. Although Framework II will normally ignore such formulas when printing, you can force it to act on them with a Print menu option. To use a FRED printing function, press

Ctrl-P   (to open the Print menu)

C   (to open the Control Options submenu)

R   (to choose Recalc Formula during Printing)

This tells Framework II that any printing formulas anywhere among the frames to be printed should be acted upon.

From our work with spreadsheet functions in Chapter 3, you'll recall the three characteristics of FRED functions:

☐ Every function name begins with the @ character. You can type the name itself either in uppercase or lowercase, or in some combination of both.

☐ Most functions require one or more *parameters,* values that you send to define the action of the function. You place the parameters between parentheses, after the function's name.

☐ Functions return a value or produce some programmed result. In the case of the printing functions, the result is a specific characteristic of the printed page.

Let's first look at some of the kinds of printing functions that FRED offers; then we'll see exactly how to incorporate them into a Word frame.

Although you can accomplish everything on the Print menu through FRED functions (and there may be times when you want to do so), it is generally easier to use the menu options when they are available. There are circumstances, however, when the menu options do not go far enough. For this reason, Framework II contains several FRED printing functions.

Suppose, for example, that you want the header on the Memo to Managers to be in boldface. You cannot open the Words menu to boldface the text while the Print menu is open. However, you can use a FRED function to enter such a header. Instead of placing "Memo to Managers" in the left header section of the Format Options submenu, we'll see shortly how to use the function @HL to create this left header.

In particular, there are two functions you can use to select other type styles that are not available on the menus – say, double-wide enhanced type, or eight lines per inch instead of six. To enter the control codes or escape sequences that turn on these effects, use the printer setup function, @ST. This function takes as its *argument,* or *parameter,* the control code or escape sequence. There are two ways to enter it. You can enter it by name; for example, if your printer uses Escape-8 to switch to eight lines per inch, you can use the formula

@ST("{Esc}8")

If your printer uses ASCII 31, Ctrl-_, to switch to double-wide print, you could use either of the following formulas:

@ST("{Ctrl-_}")
@ST(@CHR(31))

Now we'll look at how to install FRED printing functions behind a Word frame.

USING THE PRINTING FUNCTIONS IN A WORD FRAME

To place printing functions behind a Word frame, you must first move the highlight to the frame's border and then press the Edit key:

Up Level (–)	(to select the frame's border)
Edit (F2)	(to place a formula or function behind the frame)

You will see the following message appear below the desktop:

Formula/Number editing; RETURN finishes

We saw this message many times in Chapter 3, as we entered formulas and functions into spreadsheet cells. Now we are beginning an equivalent process; the only difference is that we are placing a formula behind a frame rather than behind a cell.

In this chapter we'll be working only with the printing functions, placed behind Word frames. In Chapters 5 and 7, we'll use functions in still other contexts. The process of placing the functions behind a frame will be the same.

When you press the Edit key at the frame's border, you'll be able to begin typing the function on the edit line. Let's enter a function behind the office memorandum frame. We'll now produce the same left-justified "Memo to Managers" header, but we'll use the FRED function instead of the menu option so that it can be boldfaced. Here are the keystrokes you'll type to produce this header:

Up Level (–)	(to select the frame's border)
Edit (F2)	(to enter a formula behind the frame)
@hl("Memo to Managers. Page " & @pn)	
	(create a left-justified header including a page number)
Home	(to move the edit cursor to the beginning of the function)
→, five times	(to move the cursor forward to the "M" in "Memo")
Ctrl-↓	(to select the first sentence of the header)
Ctrl-W	(to open the Words menu)
B	(to select the Bold option)
Return	(to place the finished function behind the Word frame)

Before actually entering the formula into the frame, we have taken the necessary steps to style the header in boldface.

In the first section of the status panel, below the desktop, you'll be able to see part of the function you have just placed behind the frame. As always, this panel shows you when a frame or a cell has a formula behind it. When you print the frame, this @HL printing function will result in the display of a header and page number at the top of each page.

Framework II also allows you to enter more than one line of functions and formulas into the area behind a frame. For example, you may want to place several printing functions behind a Word frame, to control more than one characteristic of the final printed version.

To create a multi-line formula behind a frame, you use the Zoom key. In effect, this puts the edit line in full-screen mode, allowing you to enter any number of lines into the formula behind the frame. Here are the necessary keystrokes to begin this process:

Up Level (–)	(to select the frame's border)
Edit (F2)	(to enter a formula)
Zoom (F9)	(to enter a multi-line formula)

Let's say you want to print the memo at eight lines to the inch instead of six, in addition to having a boldface header. Once you've used the Zoom key to bring the edit line into full-screen mode, you can enter each function on a separate line, typing a comma to separate each function from the next. For example:

@hl(**Memo to Managers**),
@st("{Esc}"8")

NOTE: If the formula area already contains a FRED program, place the printing formulas first, and follow them with the function @PRINTRETURN to keep the rest of the formula from being recalculated while the frame is being printed. To complete the process, press the Zoom key (F9) again to drop out of full-screen mode. Finally, press the Return key to enter the multi-line formula into the frame. These two functions will produce the desired result.

In preparing the final printed version of our office memorandum, we've seen the full range of Framework II word processing features at work. The next step is to investigate the process of coordinating Word frames with other types of frames, using an Outline frame as the tool for combining these various documents. This is exactly what The Sophisticated Palate is doing to produce an invoice form, as we will see in the next section of this chapter. We'll also see some creative use of the FRED printing functions, and learn a new technique—free dragging of frames.

EXAMPLES

OUTLINING AN INVOICE FORM

The prepared trays that The Sophisticated Palate has been offering as part of its catering service for some time have been a great success. Lately, the company has been receiving increasing numbers of calls from families in the neighborhood, who want to purchase them as take-out items for cocktail parties, and from businesses, who want to serve them at conference-room luncheons during work. Eileen and George had not anticipated such business, and want to encourage it. Therefore, they have had Frank Osawa, the bookkeeper, develop monthly accounts for regular customers, and have asked Ariana Katz, the administrative assistant, to develop an invoice form for the purpose. Because

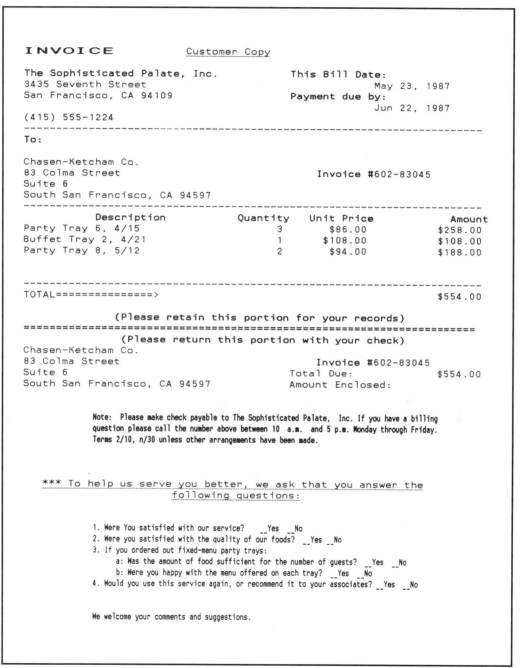

```
INVOICE          Customer Copy

The Sophisticated Palate, Inc.      This Bill Date:
3435 Seventh Street                     May 23, 1987
San Francisco, CA 94109             Payment due by:
                                        Jun 22, 1987
(415) 555-1224
-------------------------------------------------------------------
To:

Chasen-Ketcham Co.
83 Colma Street                     Invoice #602-83045
Suite 6
South San Francisco, CA 94597
-------------------------------------------------------------------
          Description         Quantity   Unit Price       Amount
Party Tray 6, 4/15                3        $86.00        $258.00
Buffet Tray 2, 4/21               1       $108.00        $108.00
Party Tray 8, 5/12                2        $94.00        $188.00


-------------------------------------------------------------------
TOTAL================>                                   $554.00
          (Please retain this portion for your records)
===================================================================
          (Please return this portion with your check)
Chasen-Ketcham Co.
83 Colma Street                     Invoice #602-83045
Suite 6                             Total Due:            $554.00
South San Francisco, CA 94597       Amount Enclosed:
```

Note: Please make check payable to The Sophisticated Palate, Inc. If you have a billing
question please call the number above between 10 a.m. and 5 p.m. Monday through Friday.
Terms 2/10, n/30 unless other arrangements have been made.

    *** To help us serve you better, we ask that you answer the
                    following questions:

    1. Were You satisfied with our service?   __Yes __No
    2. Were you satisfied with the quality of our foods? __Yes __No
    3. If you ordered out fixed-menu party trays:
          a: Was the amount of food sufficient for the number of guests? __Yes __No
          b: Were you happy with the menu offered on each tray? __Yes __No
    4. Would you use this service again, or recommend it to your associates? __Yes __No

    We welcome your comments and suggestions.

Figure 4.15: *A Corporate Invoice Form*

the invoice form is an odd combination of numbers and text, it is an ideal application for an Outline frame—combining a Spreadsheet frame and some Word frames.

Figure 4.15 shows a filled-in example of the invoice that she has developed, using Framework II spreadsheet programming and word processing. The top half of the invoice is the customer's copy, with itemized orders and a total bill amount. The lower half is to be returned to the Grocery with the customer's payment. Ariana decided to include a short survey at the bottom of the invoice, to see if she could elicit some information on customer satisfaction.

The invoice actually consists of four different frames, held inside an Outline frame that Ariana calls "Corporate Invoice and Survey". Figure 4.16 shows the containing frame, in Outline view.

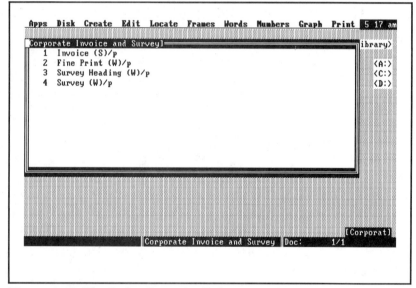

Figure 4.16: The Outline Frame for the Corporate Invoice Form

THE INVOICE SPREADSHEET

The first frame in the outline is a spreadsheet, called "Invoice", which contains all the numeric calculations of the invoice. The spreadsheet actually takes up a little more than half of the final invoice page, down to the line that is just above the invoice's fine print (see Figure 4.15). The first part of the Spreadsheet frame, zoomed to full-screen view, is shown in Figure 4.17. Let's review it briefly.

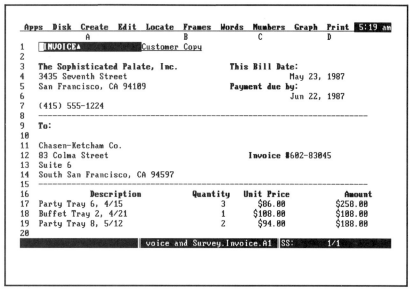

Figure 4.17: The Sophisticated Palate's Invoice Spreadsheet

Ariana has written formulas into the spreadsheet to calculate the total amount of each order (the quantity multiplied by the price) and the total for all the orders itemized on the bill. For this total she used the @SUM function. To display the invoice date in cell D4, she has used the @TODAY function, which provides today's date. Since all payments are due 30 days after billing, Ariana has also taken advantage of Framework II's @SUMDATE function, to add 30 days to the date in cell D4. She entered the following formula into cell D6:

@sumdate(D4,30)

As you can see in Table 3.3, the @SUMDATE function takes two parameters, a date and the number of days you want to add to the date. Ariana uses this function to determine the date payment is due.

Notice the graphics symbols in cell A1 of the spreadsheet in Figure 4.17. These represent control codes for the printer. The first turns double-wide printing on, and the second turns it off, so that the word "INVOICE" appears twice as wide as any other text.

THE INVOICE WORD FRAMES

Below the Spreadsheet frame are three Word frames. The first of these, called "Fine Print", contains payment instructions and some contractual information about the invoice. To format this frame, Ariana worked with the following four options in the Words menu:

    on Bold
    on Justify
        Left Margin   {19}
        Right Margin   {108}

She also selected

    Condensed Print on

from the Print Format Options submenu. When she prints this frame on a dot-matrix printer, the result is the condensed, boldface paragraph that you can see in Figure 4.15.

The second of the Word frames, called "Survey Heading", simply contains a two-line title for the survey at the bottom of the invoice. Ariana retained the default margins for this frame, but she changed the following two Words menu options:

    on Underline
    on Center

Because neither Quality Print nor Bold Print was turned on for the containing frame, both the Invoice and Survey heading frames will be printed in normal print.

Finally, the last of the three frames, "Survey", has the same margins as "Fine Print". It also requires the Condensed Print menu option to switch the printer once again into condensed mode. Figure 4.18 shows the Format Options submenu for the containing frame, with Ariana's chosen settings.

PRINTING AND SAVING THE INVOICE AND SURVEY OUTLINE

A number of interesting steps are required to print this outlined document properly. First, Ariana moves the highlight to the outer border of the outline and presses the View key (F10) to place the outline in Frames view.

Normally when you print an entire outline of documents, Framework II also prints the labels of the frames contained in the outline. Ariana does not, of course, want the labels of the various frames of her Invoice

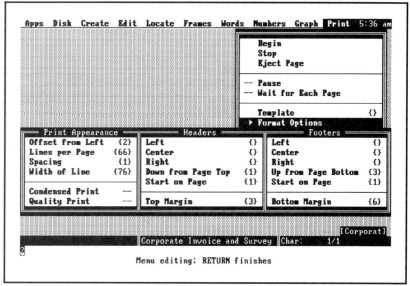

Figure 4.18: *A Filled-in Format Options Menu*

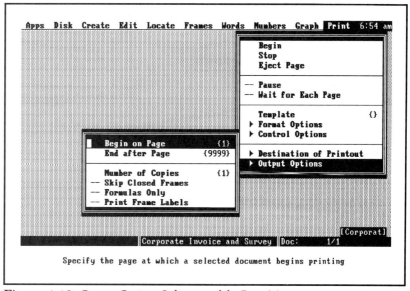

Figure 4.19: *Output Options Submenu of the Print Menu*

and Survey outline to appear in the printed invoice form. To prevent Framework II from printing the labels, Ariana has to go into the Output Options submenu of the Print menu (shown in Figure 4.19) and disable the following option:

-- Print Frame Labels

Next, she has to go to the Control Options submenu of the Print menu and choose one of these two options:

-- Keep Frame on One Page

-- Begin Frame on New Page

Ariana chooses Keep Frame on One Page, so that all the subframes will be printed one after the other on the same sheet. The result is shown in Figure 4.20.

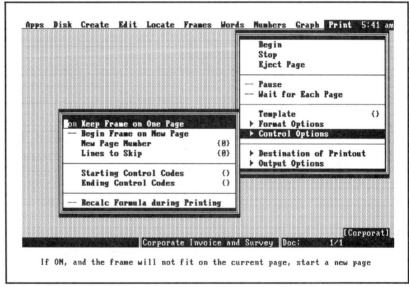

Figure 4.20: *Control Options Submenu of the Print Menu*

Once the format options have been selected, then, the entire process of printing the invoice requires the following sequence of keystrokes:

Ctrl-Up Level (–)   (to select the outer border of the Outline frame)

View (F10)   (to place the outline in Frames view)

Ctrl-P	(to open the Print menu)
O	(to open the Output Options submenu)
P	(to disable the Print Frame Labels option)
Up Level (–)	(to move back into the main part of the Print menu)
C	(to open the Control Options submenu)
Up Level (–)	(to return to the Print menu)
B	(to begin printing)

Ariana finds that she can easily use this Outline frame again and again, each time she has a new invoice to send. She simply changes the customer address, the invoice number, and the order information in the original Spreadsheet frame. Then she prints out the new invoice.

There are a few final steps to take. First, she creates an Empty frame, and labels it with the customer's name. Next, she changes the label of the Outline frame to the current date, and moves the Outline frame into the frame with the date label. Third, she creates another Empty frame labeled "Invoices", moves all the customer frames into it, selects it, and uses the Ascending Sort option of the Locate menu to place the customer names in alphabetical order. Now she can have a single file of customer invoices, conveniently arranged in order by date. This is the form in which she will save the information on disk.

EXPLORING FURTHER

STORING TEMPLATES IN THE LIBRARY

Ariana realized that she would need several blank invoice forms every month, so she made use of the Library to keep a blank on hand. First, she copied a completed invoice. Next, she blanked out all the values, such as dates, invoice numbers, customer names, and dollar amounts, that change from one invoice to the next. Here are the keystrokes she used to place the blank invoice in the Library:

Shuttle (Scroll Lock)	(to select the Library)
Return	(to open the Library cabinet)

Down Level (+)	(to enter the Library cabinet)
↓, seven times	(to place the cursor below {Alt-F6}, the Memos and Letters macro)
Shuttle	(to return to the desktop)
↑, several times	(to select the blank invoice)
Move (F7)	(to invoke the move function)
Shuttle	(to return to her location in the Library cabinet)
Return	(to complete the move)

You can use a similar procedure to store printing templates, as well as blank forms. Once you have created a frame with format and control options that you want to use again, press

Ctrl-F	(to open the Frames menu)
B	(to select the Blank All option)

This will erase all the text from the frame. However, Framework II will remember the printing options you selected even if the frame is empty. Give the frame an appropriate name (one that you will remember) and move it into the Library cabinet under the Printing Templates heading. Next time you want to use the same print options, press

Ctrl-P	(to open the Print menu)
T	(to select the Template option)
Template name	(enter the name of the template)
Return	(to record your selection)
B	(to begin printing)

That way, once you have a set of satisfactory settings, you don't have to go through the tedium of reentering them every time you want to use them.

PAGE BREAKS

Normally Framework II will print two blank lines between frames, unless you specify otherwise in the Print Control Options submenu. There are, however, several ways to control the spacing between frames. First, the

Print Control Options submenu includes these options:

－－ Keep Frame on One Page
－－ Begin Frame on New Page
    Lines to Skip   {0}

The first two options can be applied to a containing frame with many subframes, or to any frame within a containing frame. For example, if you have an outline that includes a graph, you will not want to break the graph across pages. If you select the Graph frame and then select Keep Frame on One page, the graph will not be printed on the current page if there is not enough space left to hold it. If you select Begin Frame on New Page, the graph will begin on a separate page regardless of whether it might fit on the previous page.

If you choose Begin Frame on New Page for a containing frame, every frame will begin on a new page. This may be useful when you are printing an outline that contains many different types of frames—Graph and Spreadsheet frames intermixed with Word frames, for example.

If you want more than the normal three lines between frames, select Lines to Skip, and enter the number of lines you want skipped between frames.

Yet another way of controlling the appearance of the printed page is to select Hide Borders from the Frames menu. Normally, Framework II inserts a line for each top and bottom frame border. If the borders are hidden, you can overlap them, and no space will be skipped between frames. With this option selected, frame labels will also not be printed. This may be useful if you are setting up a document in outline form and want to use the outline headings to keep track of your work, but want to print the document as a continuous piece of text.

On the other hand, if you are creating a rather long document in a Word frame, you may want certain parts of the text to begin on new pages. First, you might want to find out where the page breaks will fall. To do so, press

    Ctrl-F   (to open the Frames Menu)
    V   (to choose the View Pagination option)

The message area will display

    CALCULATING PAGE NUMBERS

and after the screen scrolls a bit, your text will be broken up by lines that look like this:

－ － － － － － － － － － － － 24 － － － － － － － － － － －

As you insert text at varous points in your document, these lines will adjust themselves to the text. Each of these lines represents the beginning of a new page, and the number tells you the page number.

If these do not fall where you want them, Framework II allows you to insert a "hard page break." To do so, press

Ctrl-E   (to open the Edit menu)

B   (to select the Begin New Page option)

A heavy line will appear across the screen. The text immediately following that line will begin on a new page.

PRINTING PARTS OF FRAMES

There are times when you don't want to print all of a document. Framework II provides several ways for you to print only part of a document. First, if your document has many subframes and you only want to print some of them, select and open the containing frame, and follow these keystrokes:

Down Level (+)   (to enter the frame)

↑ or ↓   (to select the frames that you don't want to print)

Return   (to close those frames)

Ctrl-Up Level (–)   (to select the containing frame)

Ctrl-P   (to open the Print menu)

O   (to open the Output Options submenu)

S   (to turn on the Skip Closed Frames option)

If you want to print only one of several subframes, all you have to do is make sure that that frame is selected before you go to the Print menu. As with so many other features of Framework II, the Print menu commands operate only on what is selected. Therefore, if you are inside a Word frame, you can print part of the frame just by using Extend Select (F6) to highlight the part of the frame that you want to print, and then using whatever print options you choose.

If you have turned on the View Pagination option, you can also print a specific series of pages within the document. This is useful especially if you have made a small change to a single page, and don't need to reprint the rest of the document. To do so, press

Ctrl-P	(to open the Print menu)
O	(to open the Output Options submenu)
B	(to choose Begin on Page)
number	(enter the starting page number)
Return	(to record your selection)
E	(to choose End after Page)
number	(enter the ending page number)
Return	(to record your selection)
Up Level (–)	(to return to the main Print menu)

You can then go on and choose any other options you want to use.

SPECIAL EFFECTS IN HEADERS AND FOOTERS

There are several more special effects that can be used in headers and footers. In this section, we'll take a brief look at ways to use multi-line headers and footers and alternate headers or footers on opposite pages, and explore a bit further the method of inserting dates into headers and footers.

DATE STRINGS

In Chapter 3 we learned how to use the @DATE function to put dates into a spreadsheet, and a few pages ago we learned how Ariana used the @TODAY function in the same way. The result of these two functions is a *date value*, on which you can ultimately perform two kinds of *date arithmetic:*

- ☐ You can find the number of days between two dates (using the @DIFFDATE function, which we'll examine in more detail in Chapter 5).

- ☐ You can add a number of days to a given date (using the @SUM-DATE function).

You cannot use @DATE or @TODAY in a context that requires a *text value;* the result of these two functions is not text. However, Framework II does provide four different functions for converting date values into text, or *string values*. These functions are called @DATE1, @DATE2, @DATE3, and @DATE4, and they all require date-value parameters. Each displays the date in a different format. Here are examples of the formats:

Function	Result
@date1(@date(1987,6,20)	Jun 20, 1987
@date2(@date(1987,6,20)	Jun 1987
@date3(@date(1987,6,20)	Jun 20
@date4(@date(1987,6,20)	June 20, 1987

To insert today's date into a header, we don't actually have to use these FRED functions; just their names. Thus, if today's date were July 4, 1999, entering

<date4>

in any of the six menu options that place headers or footers on a page would result in

July 4, 1999

being displayed at the chosen location. A similar series of functions allows you to print the time in various formats. We'll look at these functions in Chapter 5.

MULTI-LINE HEADERS AND FOOTERS

To create a header or footer that continues on an additional line, include the symbol

<return>

within the text that you enter in the menu option. Anything following this symbol will be printed on a separate line. You can create headers or footers that are several lines long by using more than one such symbol in your text. Be sure that your margin and your placement of the header or footer allow for the number of lines you want to use.

ALTERNATING HEADERS AND FOOTERS

An additional symbol lets you place different headers and footers on opposing pages. Suppose, for example, that you were printing out this book, and wanted the book title as the header on left-hand pages and the chapter title on right-hand pages. Framework II makes the distinction with respect to even and odd numbered pages, however, rather than left and right. To separate the text appropriately, the symbol

<even/odd>

is used. Since odd numbered pages traditionally fall on the right, choosing the center position for headers and entering the text

Word Processing<even/odd>Mastering Framework II

would give you the result you want.

PAGE LAYOUT

A special technique allows you to lay out your pages in a "what you see is what you get" fashion. This technique is called "free dragging." To use it, choose the containing frame, and press

Ctrl-F   (to open the Frames menu)

A   (to select Allow Free Dragging)

You can then drag the frames to any position on the screen, and the printout will reflect their relative position. There are several important limitations to this technique:

- Only the text that actually appears in the frame will be printed; if the text extends beyond the frame border, any text that does not appear will not be printed. The only exception to this rule is that printing starts at the upper-left corner of the frame. Thus, if the frame contains 16 lines, and is set at 14 lines in length, the last two lines will not be printed.

- Any print options that have been selected for the subframes will be ignored; only those for the containing frame will have any effect. Therefore, any styling of text in subframes must be done by inserting escape sequences directly in text.

- No FRED printing formulas will be executed.

- If any open frames overlap physically, their text will be intermixed in the printout.

In this connection, we can see a use for the Flush Right option in the Words menu. Figure 4.21 shows another way of laying out part of

Ariana's invoice. The Hide Borders option from the Frames menu has been selected, and the frame near the upper-right corner of the screen has the following options selected from the Words menu:

    on Flush Right
        Right Margin   {0}

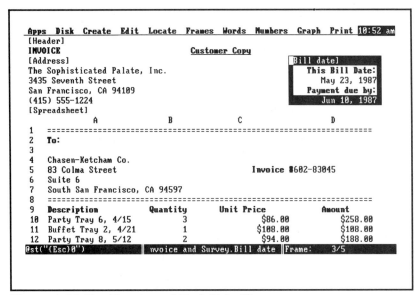

Figure 4.21: *Free Dragging and Flush Right Alignment*

The right margin of 0 is necessary to make sure that there is no irrelevant "white space" that is theoretically inside the frame to the left of the text. To see the trouble you can get into, try setting the right margin of such a frame to 65, entering the frame, and pressing Ctrl-Home. You will find that all the text will be pushed to the right, out of view of the frame; it will therefore not be printed at all.

The Free Dragging option is one of the most complex print options available. Be aware that it may take numerous printouts to have everything appear exactly as you want it.

When you have repositioned frames through free dragging, you may find that, when you revert to Outline view, they appear to be in the wrong order. You can use the Move key (F7) to move the outline headings into the correct order without affecting the layout in Frames view. Thus, you can have the advantages of both an orderly outline and a precise page layout.

PRINTING A FRAME TO DISK

We have learned a number of ways to format and control the final printed appearance of a document. Not all of these characteristics show up in the Word frame on the screen. For example, if you enter a header or footer function in the Format Options submenu, you won't be able to see the result of that function until you actually print the frame.

Sometimes you may want to check to see if a document looks the way you want it to before you go to the trouble of putting it on paper. The Destination submenu of Framework II's Print menu (shown in Figure 4.22) gives you an option that allows you to create a *print file* on disk. This file will contain the same information that Framework II will send to your printer when you ultimately print the file.

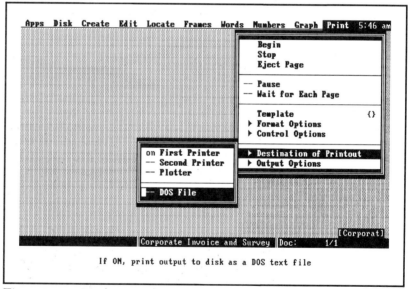

Figure 4.22: *Destination Submenu of the Print Menu*

To create a print file, follow these steps:

Ctrl-P	(to open the Print menu)
D	(to open the Destination submenu)
D	(to select the DOS File option)
Up Level (–)	(to move back to the main Print menu)
B	(to begin printing)

These commands produce a print file on disk, using the frame's label as the file name. The extension name of a print file is ".PRT". So, for example, if the frame you are printing is called "Invoice", the name of the print file will be

INVOICE.PRT

To see exactly how your document will look when you print it onto paper, just load this print file onto the desktop. If you have included any styling, it will be represented in this file by printer escape sequences. Similarly, any format options you have selected—such as headers, footers, and margins—will be reflected in the layout of text in the file. Page breaks will be represented by a female symbol, which is the displayable version of the form-feed character (ASCII 12).

COUNTING YOUR WORDS

An additional feature on the Edit menu is especially useful if you need to know how many words a Word frame contains. Word Count, the final option on the menu, will count the number of words in a frame, displaying

WORD COUNTING

in the message area while the process proceeds, and then displaying a count of the number of words in the frame.

SUMMARY

Framework II's word processing tools include keyboard functions, menu options, and special frames in the Library cabinet. Here is an inventory of these tools:

> □ *Cursor-movement keys.* You can use the four arrow keys to move the cursor backward, forward, up, and down inside your

document. Ctrl-Home and Ctrl-End move the cursor to the beginning and the end of the document, while PgUp and PgDn move up and down one screen at a time, respectively.

☐ *Text-selection keys.* You can select a word (Ctrl-→), a sentence (Ctrl-↓), or an entire paragraph (Ctrl-PgDn) for some subsequent activity in a Word frame. Similarly, you can select the same units going upward or backward using Ctrl-←, Ctrl-↑, and Ctrl-PgUp, respectively. You can also use the Extend Select key (F6) for extending the highlight over larger portions of text.

☐ *Other function keys.* The Move (F7) and Copy (F8) keys will move or copy a selected block of text from one location to another inside your document.

☐ *The Words menu.* This menu controls styling, text alignment, margins, paragraph indentation, and tabs in a Word frame. Style and format specifications can be assigned globally or locally.

☐ *The Edit menu.* This menu includes six functions that are important in word processing. Four of them—switching between insert mode and typeover mode; displaying the "hidden" characters—space, tab, paragraph beginning, carriage return, and soft hyphen; inserting soft hyphens; and inserting hard page breaks—are used almost exclusively in Word frames. In addition, the Undo option lets you restore text that has been deleted, or restore text that has been moved to its former position, and the Word Count option displays a count of the number of words in a frame.

☐ *The Locate menu.* Through this menu you can search for specific strings of text inside your document, or you can replace one string with another throughout the document.

☐ *The Print menu.* This menu prints your document, either on paper or to a print file on disk. It also allows you to specify many aspects of the final printed version of your document: the paper margins and dimensions, the spacing, the headers and footers, the printing mode of the printer, and the relationship between frames and pages. If these options do not give you all the printing features you want, special FRED printing functions can be placed in the formula area behind a Word frame (which you reach by pressing the Edit key, F2), and you can also insert printer escape sequences directly into your frame.

□ *Printing templates.* A frame that has been formatted for printing can be stored in the Library with its text deleted. Entering the name of this frame in the Printing Template option of the Print menu when you print a frame will automatically cause the frame to be printed with the formats you have stored in the Library.

□ *Document templates.* You can store a partially completed frame, containing text in a form that you use regularly, as a document template in the Library. To do so, copy the frame to the Library cabinet, beneath the heading for the macro labeled {Alt-F6}.

Finally, we have seen how the effectiveness of word processing can be combined with other Framework II components to produce mixed documents. Framework II outlining is the tool that makes this kind of integration possible.

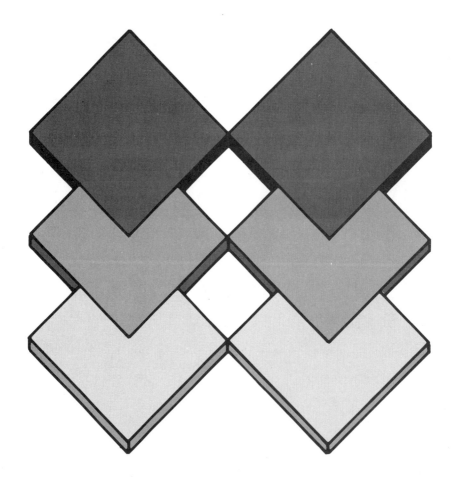

CHAPTER FIVE

DATABASES

INTRODUCTION

A Database frame is designed for organizing, storing, and working with information. The primary unit of information in a database is called a *record*. A record consists of all the relevant information describing one event, one asset, one employee, one sales transaction, one client, one inventory category—or one item of whatever kind of information you are working with. A *database* is a collection of many such records, all organized in the same way.

Framework II's database management capabilities are designed to simplify the process of working with records of information. Specifically, Framework II gives you these capabilities:

- ☐ You can add new records to your database.

- ☐ You can delete records.

- ☐ You can change the information contained in records.

- ☐ You can change the structure of the database.

- ☐ You can search for a specific record.

- ☐ You can sort the records of the database in any order that you specify.

- ☐ You can calculate values for each record in the database.

- ☐ You can find groups of records that have certain characteristics in common.

These are the activities that we'll be studying in this chapter. Before we start, however, we should discuss a few general database characteristics.

THE STRUCTURE OF A DATABASE

When you set out to organize a new database, Framework II does not dictate the *structure* of the records you'll be working with. Because each different data processing job has its own particular requirements, Framework II leaves you with the task of deciding how to organize the database. You will determine the specific items of information that each record will contain. These items are called *fields*.

Figure 5.1 shows a database that we are going to be working with in this chapter; it stores information about a group of sales people and summarizes their sales activities over a half-year period. Each record, or *row*, in the database contains six fields of information, one field for each of the six columns of the table. Together, these six fields in a given row describe one sales person: the employee number ("EmpNo"), the last name ("Last"), the first name ("First"), the region in which the person works ("Reg"), the person's total sales for the half-year period ("SixMo-Sales"), and finally, the date the person was hired ("Hired").

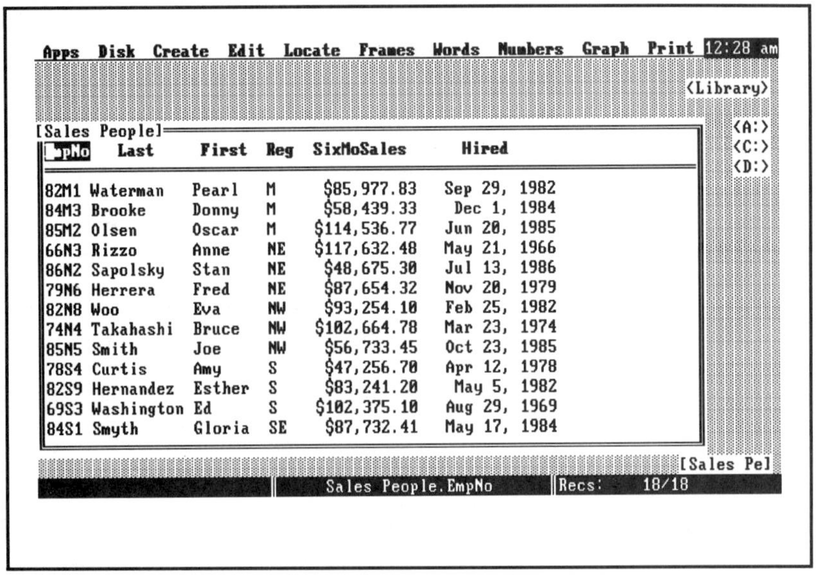

```
 Apps  Disk  Create  Edit  Locate  Frames  Words  Numbers  Graph  Print 12:28 am
                                                                    <Library>
                                                                         <A:>
[Sales People]                                                           <C:>
  EpNo   Last      First   Reg  SixMoSales      Hired                     <D:>

 82M1 Waterman    Pearl    M    $85,977.83   Sep 29, 1982
 84M3 Brooke      Donny    M    $58,439.33   Dec  1, 1984
 85M2 Olsen       Oscar    M   $114,536.77   Jun 20, 1985
 66N3 Rizzo       Anne     NE  $117,632.48   May 21, 1966
 86M2 Sapolsky    Stan     NE   $48,675.30   Jul 13, 1986
 79N6 Herrera     Fred     NE   $87,654.32   Nov 20, 1979
 82M8 Woo         Eva      NW   $93,254.10   Feb 25, 1982
 74N4 Takahashi   Bruce    NW  $102,664.78   Mar 23, 1974
 85N5 Smith       Joe      NW   $56,733.45   Oct 23, 1985
 78S4 Curtis      Amy      S    $47,256.70   Apr 12, 1978
 82S9 Hernandez   Esther   S    $83,241.20   May  5, 1982
 69S3 Washington  Ed       S   $102,375.10   Aug 29, 1969
 84S1 Smyth       Gloria   SE   $87,732.41   May 17, 1984
                                                                    [Sales Pe]
                              Sales People.EmpNo      Recs:    18/18
```

Figure 5.1: The Sales People Database

This example illustrates Framework II's normal way of organizing and displaying a database—in Table format. Each row of the database table contains one record; each column, one field category. A database is similar to a spreadsheet in many ways, but there are some essential differences. While a spreadsheet has a free structure, the design of a database requires that rows represent records and columns represent field categories.

When you design a Database frame, one of your first jobs will be to determine the characteristics of each field in the database. Field categories are normally defined by three elements:

1. A name

2. A width, in characters

3. A data type

Notice in Figure 5.1 that the top row of the frame is reserved for the *field names*. These names express, in an abbreviated way, the nature of the data contained in each field category. Framework II draws a line below this row of names, to separate the names from the actual data. The importance of these names will become clear as soon as we begin working with databases: names give you a way of identifying the field or fields upon which you want to perform specific database operations.

The column widths in a database table determine the maximum number of characters that can be displayed in the field categories. Just as in a spreadsheet, the width of each column can be controlled independently. Using the Size key (F4), you can increase or decrease the width of the database columns. You'll generally want to arrange the size of each column in the table to accommodate the maximum number of characters that you anticipate in a given field.

For example, consider the field called "First" in Figure 5.1; this field contains the sales people's first names. If the longest first name in your database contains seven characters, you might set this column at a width of 8, allowing an extra space to separate this field from the next one to the right.

Near the end of this chapter, we'll find that the length of a field is not truly limited by the width of the column in the database table. Framework II offers you three ways of looking at a database: the Table format displayed in Figure 5.1, a special *Forms* view, and a view similar to the one used in Ashton-Tate's dBASE products. In the Table format, your concern will be to design a frame that will display all the important information for each record; in this context, the column widths are significant. In the Forms view, however, you look at only one record at a time on the screen. This format allows you to work with fields that contain more than one line of text. In effect, the Forms view allows you to incorporate a small word processed document as a field in each record of your database. We'll look at examples of the Forms and dBASE views later. In the meantime, as we work with databases in the Table format, we'll think of the column width as the limiting factor on the width of a field.

The final characteristic of a field is its data type. You are responsible for making sure that all the information in a given column, or field, of your database is of the same type. We'll be working with four data types in this chapter: text, numbers, dates, and logical values. When you define a field, you will determine the type of data the field will contain; this data type should remain constant from one record to the next.

Once you have organized the structure of your database, you can begin entering the actual data. Field values can be entered manually, or they can be calculated. When you devise a formula for a calculated field, the entire column that represents that field is filled in at once. We'll find out exactly how to work with calculated fields later in this chapter.

You may need to increase or decrease the number of records and fields in your database during the course of your work with the information in the database. The total size of your database is limited by the amount of memory in your computer. Let's briefly discuss this issue before we begin looking at the details of Framework II database management.

MEMORY CONSIDERATIONS WITH DATABASES

A frame that is currently on your desktop is stored in its entirety in the computer's random-access memory (RAM) if there is room for it. (The largest frame on your desktop is *always* stored in RAM.) Of course, a frame can also be saved as a file on disk; but during the course of your work with a frame, the whole frame must reside in the computer's memory.

This arrangement contrasts with some other personal computer programs that automatically take care of shifting portions of a long file between the computer's memory and a storage area on disk. This shifting back and forth may take place whenever you work with a long file; only the portion of the file that you are currently working with needs to reside in RAM at any one time. When this automatic shifting procedure is included in a database management program, the result is a potential for larger databases: the size of a database is limited by the storage area available on your disk rather than by the amount of RAM in your computer. If your computer has a hard disk, with storage capacity measured in megabytes, this kind of database management program will allow you to work with very large databases, containing thousands of records.

Framework II, however, always keeps the largest frame on the desktop entirely in RAM. This has serious implications for the size of a database. Database frames require more memory than other types of frames (even Spreadsheet frames that have the same number of cells) so they tend to be large. Second, even empty cells in a Database frame take up a significant amount of memory. The implications are twofold: first, you can assume that Framework II will want to keep Database frames entirely in RAM; second, this means that the dimensions of a database in Framework II are limited by the amount of memory you have installed in your computer.

This arrangement has advantages and disadvantages. The main disadvantage is, as noted, that although the theoretical limit on the dimensions of a database is 32,000 columns by 32,000 rows, as a practical matter Framework II limits the size of your database to what will fit in your available memory—a maximum of about 32,000 cells. (However, as a consolation, Framework II can be configured to take advantage of any memory resources you have available: expanded or extended memory up to 16 megabytes, RAM disks, or even, if all else fails, your hard disk. The latter is not recommended, however. See Appendix A for details.)

On the other hand, given an appropriate small- to medium-sized project, Framework II database management has two advantages over other database programs: simplicity and efficiency. You'll be able to master Framework II's database operations in a short time, yet these operations will allow you as much flexibility with your data as you would expect with more complex programs. Furthermore, because all your data are stored in memory, the Framework II database operations will be performed quickly. In particular, during sorting and searching operations, you won't have to wait for the computer to shift various parts of your database between disk and RAM to complete the operation.

Now let's begin creating a database and finding out how to work with it.

CREATING A DATABASE

The Database option of the Create menu places a new Database frame on the desktop:

Ctrl-C   (to open the Create menu)

D   (to create a Database frame)

However, before you create a Database frame, you should determine the dimensions you want to begin with: the number of fields and the number of records your database will initially contain. The Create menu options that allow you to specify these dimensions are the same as those used for creating a Spreadsheet frame:

Width   (#Cols/Fields)   {50}
Height (#Rows/Records)   {100}

As we saw in Chapter 3, the default dimensions of a new Database (or Spreadsheet) frame are 50 columns by 100 rows. If you want to change these dimensions, you should select the Width and Height options and enter new numeric values to match your own specifications.

The Sales People database that we have been examining has 6 columns and 18 rows, although only 13 rows are shown in Figure 5.1. In working with this database, you'll imagine yourself the manager of a national sales force, with sales people stationed in six regions: northeast, southeast, midwest, south, northwest, and southwest (abbreviated NE, SE, M, S, NW, and SW, respectively, in the database itself). You have accumulated total sales figures for each of your sales people over the last six months. You are creating this database to store the information and to provide a tool for analyzing the relative merits of your employees' performances over this half-year period.

Your first task is to create a frame for the database; here are the necessary keystrokes:

Ctrl-C   (to open the Create menu)
W   (to select the Width option)
6   (to specify 6 fields)
Return   (to enter this value into the Create menu)
H   (to select the Height option)
18   (to specify 18 records)
Return   (to enter this value into the Create menu)
D   (to create the Database frame)

The resulting frame appears in Figure 5.2. You can see that Framework II automatically supplies a row at the top of the frame for the field names. (This row is not considered one of the 18 record rows of your database.) A double line separates this row from the data section of the frame.

Enter the following title into the frame's border:

Sales People

Then press the Down Level key (+) to move the highlight into the frame. The highlight will initially land in the upper-left corner of

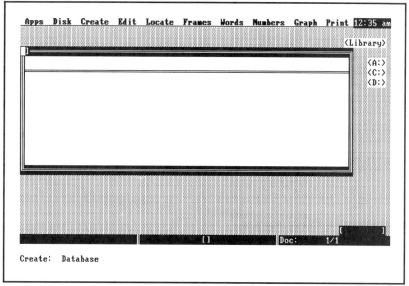

Figure 5.2: *A New Database Frame*

the frame. Just as in a Spreadsheet frame, you can use the four arrow keys, ↑, ↓, ←, and →, to move the highlight, one row or column at a time, inside the Database frame. Unlike a Spreadsheet frame, however, a Database frame does not contain column letters and row numbers. The actual organization of a Database frame is invisible until you begin entering field names and data into the frame, although the status panel does tell you how many record rows the frame contains:

    Recs: 18/18

Press the → and ↓ keys several times now, and you will see that the frame is indeed organized into columns and rows. Each time you press →, the highlight moves one column to the right. The first ↓ keystroke moves the highlight from the field-name row into the data section of the frame; subsequently, ↓ continues to move the highlight down the rows of the frame.

Table 5.1 reviews the keys and keystroke combinations that you can use to move the highlight from one place to another inside the Database frame. These keystrokes should seem quite familiar to you after your work with Spreadsheet frames.

Keys	Action
←, →, ↑, ↓	Moves the highlight one field or record in the direction indicated.
Home	Moves the highlight to the first field of the current record.
End	Moves the highlight to the last field of the current record.
Ctrl-↑	Moves the highlight up to the first row (the field-name row) in the current field column.
Ctrl-↓	Moves the highlight down to the last record in the current field column.
PgUp	Scrolls one frame up.
PgDn	Scrolls one frame down.
Ctrl-Home	Moves the highlight to the first field name, in the top row of the frame.
Ctrl-End	Moves the highlight to the last field in the last record of the frame.
Return	Enters data, or moves the highlight one record down.
Tab	Enters data and/or moves the highlight one field to the right.
Shift-Tab	Enters data and/or moves the highlight one field to the left.

Table 5.1: *Keys for Moving the Database Highlight*

The next step is to prepare the frame to conform to the specifications of your database. You do this in three stages:

1. First, enter the field names.

2. Then size the columns appropriately.

3. Finally, assign data display styles, where necessary, corresponding to the fields' data types and appropriate to the overall appearance of the database table.

We'll work on all of these details in the next section.

PREPARING THE DATABASE FRAME

Figure 5.3 shows the structure of the Sales People database as a spreadsheet containing the name of each field, the width of each column, the type of data that will go into each field, and the purpose of each field. You may find it useful to set up a spreadsheet containing a table similar to this one for each Database frame that you create in Framework II; the table reminds you at a glance exactly how your database is organized and what purposes it serves. You can store the two in a single containing frame.

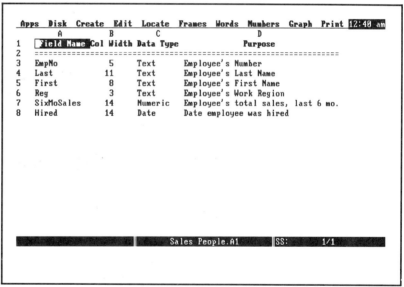

Figure 5.3: *Structure of the Sales People Database*

With only 6 fields and 18 records, Sales People is a very small example of a database. But imagine a database that has, say, 20 fields of information and a few thousand records; you can see how a table like the one shown in Figure 5.3 could become an essential tool for reminding you exactly what kind of information your database contains. Throughout this chapter, keep in mind that all the database management operations we examine will work effectively on much larger databases than Sales People.

Following the specifications in Figure 5.3, you need to prepare each column of the Database frame for the field information that the column will ultimately contain. Let's begin with the first column. Press Ctrl-Home to move the highlight to the upper-left corner of the frame, and type the field name

EmpNo

The name appears in the top row of the database table as you type it. Press Return to enter the name. Now press the Size key (F4), to adjust the width of the column. This first column is to have a width of 5 spaces. Because the default width of database columns is 9 spaces, you'll press the ← key four times to reduce the width of the first column appropriately. A message in the right section of the status panel will tell you the current width of the column; this is how it will look when the column is correctly sized:

Size: 5/1

Press Return to end the sizing operation.

Continue this process for each column of the Database frame: first enter the field name; then size the column. When all the field names are in place, you may want to center them inside their respective column widths. To do so, use the Middle option of the Numbers menu:

Ctrl-Home	(to move the highlight to the first field)
Extend Select (F6)	(to extend the highlight)
End	(to extend across the entire row)
Ctrl-N	(to open the Numbers menu)
M	(to select the Middle option)

Figure 5.4 shows what your frame should look like at this point. Notice that we use the Numbers menu, not the Words menu, to align text entries in the Table format of a database.

Finally, before you begin entering the actual data into the frame, you may want to specify display styles. In Figure 5.1 you can see that the numbers in the SixMoSales field are displayed as currency values, and the dates in the Hired field are right justified, to allow a little more space between the figures in SixMoSales and the dates. To select Currency style, you'll extend the highlight over the entire SixMoSales column and once again use the Numbers menu. To right justify the Hired column, follow the same process. Begin by moving the highlight to the field name SixMoSales. Then press the following keys:

Extend Select (F6)	(to extend the highlight)
Ctrl-↓	(to extend down the entire column)

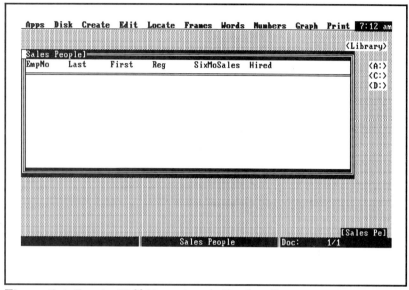

Figure 5.4: *Entering Field Names into the Database Frame*

Ctrl-N	(to open the Numbers menu)
C	(to select the Currency option)
→	(to move the highlight to the Hired column)
Ctrl-N	(to open the Numbers menu)
R	(to select the Right option)

Now when you enter numbers into the SixMoSales column, they will automatically be displayed in Currency style, with dollar signs and commas. And the dates in the Hired column will automatically be right justified within the column width.

Now we are ready to begin the data entry process.

ENTERING DATA INTO THE DATABASE FRAME

Figure 5.3 shows that the Sales People database contains three types of data: text, numbers, and dates. As we enter the data for each record and field, we have to make sure that Framework II is accepting the data as the correct type. The techniques we learned in Chapter 3 for spreadsheet data entry also apply to Database frames. Let's review those techniques as we enter the first record of the Sales People database.

The employee-number field, EmpNo, contains a four-character identification code for each employee. Notice, though, that these are actually text values—because they contain a mix of digits and letters, Framework II would not be able to accept them as numeric values.

However, the format of these values imposes a small complication on the data entry process. Each value begins with a digit; for example:

82M1

We know from Chapter 3 that the first keystroke of a data entry determines Framework II's reading of the data type. In this case, if you were to enter the digit 8 as the first character, the following message would be displayed at the bottom of the screen:

Formula/Number editing; RETURN finishes

But numeric entry is not the correct mode for the EmpNo field. You may recall the solution to this problem. Press the Space bar before you enter the number. As soon as you do, you will see the correct data entry message:

Text editing; RETURN finishes

Use the Space bar to begin text data entry whenever the text begins with a digit (or other character) that Framework II would normally read as the beginning of a numeric data entry. Each time you enter one of the employee numbers in the database, use the Space bar to indicate that this code is a text value.

After typing each field value, you can use the Tab key to perform two functions: to complete the data entry and to move the highlight one field to the right. This is the equivalent of pressing

Return   (to complete the entry)

→   (to move the highlight)

The next three fields, Last, First, and Reg, are simple text values—the last name, first name, and region of the first sales person:

Waterman   Pearl   M

Because each of these values begins with a letter, Framework II will put you immediately in the correct data entry mode as you enter them. You do not need to preface the data entry by pressing the Space bar.

The SixMoSales field is numeric. Enter the value for the first record as follows:

85977.83

Upon reading the first digit, 8, Framework II will display the correct data entry message:

Formula/number editing; RETURN finishes

When you press the Tab key to complete the data entry, you will see the following value in the SixMoSales field:

$85,977.83

The Currency style that you specified earlier determines the display style of the new value.

The last field, Hired, is a date value. To enter it we'll use the FRED function called @DATE. Enter the following formula into the Hired field of the first record:

@date(1982,9,29)

When Framework II reads the @ character, you will once again see the "Formula/number editing" message at the bottom of the screen. The result of entering this function will be a display of the following date:

Sep 29, 1982

You may wonder why you can't simply enter this date as a text value rather than use the @DATE function. The answer is that you can, if you never intend to perform any special operations involving this date. The @DATE function, while *displaying* the date itself, privately records a *numeric* version of the date. This numeric version, sometimes called a *scalar date*, allows you to use the date information in these ways:

1. You can find the difference, in days, between two dates.

2. You can add a number of days to one date, yielding a second date.

3. You can sort dates in chronological order.

We'll see examples of these activities later in the chapter.

You have now entered one entire record. Before reading further in this chapter, finish entering the entire database—the 6 fields of information for all 18 sales people. Press the Zoom key (F9) to shift into full-screen mode; you'll be able to see all 18 rows of the database table at once.

You'll need the complete database for the exercises that follow. Once you have finished the data entry, you should save the database on disk, using the shortcut Save and Continue command:

Ctrl-Return   (to save and continue)

Now we'll begin learning how to work with this database.

USING THE DATABASE

In the sections ahead we'll study a number of database management operations, including sorting, searching, changing the structure of the database, writing formulas to calculate field values, and writing "filter" formulas to select groups of records that have specific characteristics in common. In the course of this discussion we'll find ourselves expanding the contents—and the usefulness—of the Sales People database.

SORTING

We saw in Chapter 3 that sorting means rearranging information in some specified order: alphabetical, numerical, or chronological. The Locate menu offers two sorting orders: ascending or descending.

Sorting a Framework II database is remarkably easy and fast. You always begin by selecting a field in the database that will act as a *key* for the sort. For example, you might choose to sort the Sales People database in any of the following ways:

- □ Placing the records in alphabetical order by the employees' last names (using the Last field as the key for the sort)

- □ Placing the records in numerical order by the total sales for the six-month period (with SixMoSales as the key field)

- □ Placing the records in chronological order by the date employees were hired (using Hired as the key field)

Framework II can sort any type of data. An alphabetical sort generally follows ASCII code order. Look at the ASCII listing in Appendix C, and you will see that the code is arranged as follows:

1. Punctuation characters

2. Digits

3. Uppercase letters, A to Z

4. Lowercase letters, a to z

An *ascending* alphabetical sort follows this ASCII order; a *descending* alphabetical sort goes in the opposite order.

However, in many alphabetical sorts you may want Framework II to ignore case; that is, you'll want uppercase and lowercase to be sorted together. This sorting characteristic is controlled by the following Locate menu option:

Ignore Capitalization

The Ignore option is a toggle: when it is on, a sorting operation will mix uppercase and lowercase; when it is off, sorting follows strict ASCII order, isolating uppercase from lowercase.

To perform a sort operation, follow these three steps:

1. Move the highlight to the name of the field that you wish to sort by (that is, the *key* for the sort).

2. Open the Locate menu.

3. Select either the Ascending or Descending sort option.

Notice that you do not have to extend the highlight over the entire field column; it is sufficient to place the highlight anywhere in the first row of the database table.

Let's try a few sorting operations. First we'll sort by the total sales for the period, from best to worst. Begin by moving the highlight to the SixMoSales column, and then press the following keys:

Ctrl-L   (to open the Locate menu)

D   (to sort in descending order)

The result will be an instant rearranging of the entire database table in order of total sales—starting from the best record of $117,632.48, down to the worst record of $47,256.70.

Now let's sort by the dates the employees were hired, from the oldest to the newest employee. Move the highlight to the Hired column, and press

Ctrl-L   (to open the Locate menu)

A   (to sort in ascending order)

You can see the result of this sort in Figure 5.5.

```
 Apps  Disk  Create  Edit  Locate  Frames  Words  Numbers  Graph  Print 12:53 am
 EmpNo    Last      First  Reg   SixMoSales   ▐ Hired ▌

 66N3 Rizzo      Anne     NE   $117,632.48   May 21, 1966
 69S3 Washington Ed       S    $102,375.10   Aug 29, 1969
 72S6 Schroeder  Art      SE    $94,243.22   Jan 24, 1972
 74N4 Takahashi  Bruce    NW   $102,664.78   Mar 23, 1974
 78S4 Curtis     Amy      S     $47,256.70   Apr 12, 1978
 78S1 Smithfield Frank    SW    $51,623.62   Jul 22, 1978
 79N6 Herrera    Fred     NE    $87,654.32   Nov 20, 1979
 81S5 Petrakis   Bill     SE   $112,312.34   Aug 24, 1981
 82N8 Woo        Eva      NW    $93,254.10   Feb 25, 1982
 82S9 Hernandez  Esther   S     $83,241.20   May 5, 1982
 82M1 Waterman   Pearl    M     $85,977.83   Sep 29, 1982
 83S9 Goldberg   Jack     SW   $103,254.67   Oct 29, 1983
 84S1 Smyth      Gloria   SE    $87,732.41   May 17, 1984
 84M3 Brooke     Donny    M     $58,439.33   Dec 1, 1984
 85M2 Olsen      Oscar    M    $114,536.77   Jun 20, 1985
 85N5 Smith      Joe      NW    $56,733.45   Oct 23, 1985
 86S2 Smith      AshleighSW     $67,132.45   Mar 4, 1986
 86N2 Sapolsky   Stan     NE    $48,675.30   Jul 13, 1986

                          Sales People.Hired        Recs:    18/18

 Locate:  Ascending Sort
```

Figure 5.5: *Sorting by Dates*

Finally, let's sort by the employees' last names. Move the highlight to the Last field, and press

Ctrl-L   (to open the Locate menu)

A   (to sort in ascending order)

The records will be reordered by last names, from Brooke to Woo. But there is a problem with this particular operation. You have two sales people named Smith on your staff, and this sort has left them in the wrong alphabetical order:

Smith   Joe
Smith   Ashleigh

You need some way of making sure that Framework II will sort by first names when two or more last names are identical.

The solution to this problem is simple. You will have to sort the database twice: first by first names, then by last names. When you complete these two operations, the Smiths will be in the correct order:

Smith   Ashleigh
Smith   Joe

In this case we say that the Last field is the *primary* key and the First field is the *secondary* key for the sort. It may seem that the terminology is backwards, but the secondary sort must be performed *before* the primary sort.

You may think of other situations in which it would be appropriate to sort by more than one key. For example, consider the following two problems, and try performing the suggested solutions:

1. You would like to separate the sales people by region, and, within the regions, arrange the people in order of their total sales, from best to worst. Solution: sort first by SixMoSales (descending), then by Reg (ascending).

2. You want to arrange the sales people by employee number, within each region. Solution: sort first by EmpNo (ascending), then by Reg (ascending).

SEARCHING AND REPLACING

In Chapter 4 we saw how the Locate menu's Search and Replace options work in Word frames. Search helps you find every occurrence of a specified string of characters. Replace will change every occurrence of a specified string to a new string of characters. The options work almost the same way in Database frames, except that they operate exclusively within the field you have selected.

For example, let's say you want to find all the Smiths in your database. Begin by placing the highlight over the field name Last, and then press the following keys:

Ctrl-L   (to open the Locate menu)

S   (to select the Search option)

Smith   (specify the text you want to search for)

Return   (to begin the search)

You'll recall that Framework II supplies you with a message below the desktop, explaining how to use the Search operation. In brief, you can press the ↓ key to move down to the next occurrence of the text you are searching for, or the ↑ key to move up to the previous occurrence.

If you try this particular search operation, you'll discover that Framework II finds the two Smiths in your database, but it does *not* find the person named Smyth. To help you find related words, or variant spellings, Framework II allows you to use "wild cards" in both Search and Replace operations. As with the computer's operating system, the character "?" will stand for any character in the position it occupies, and the character "*" for a group of any characters in the positions including and following the asterisk. Thus, if you wanted to find Smyth as well as Smith, you would enter

Search   {Sm?th}

in the Search option in the Locate menu. You can use wild cards while searching in *any* type of frame. Thus, to search for any day of the week, you could enter

Search   { *day}

in the Locate menu.

At the same time, you may have noticed that your search operation turned up not only the two Smiths, but also a person named Smithfield. To search only for the name "Smith", ignoring any names that *begin with* "Smith", include a space (press the Space bar) as the last character of the target text, so that the Search option in the Locate menu will look like this:

Search   {Smith }

You can also use this little trick for specifying a precise target text for the Replace operation.

Replace requires that you first enter a text for which Framework II will search in the field column you have selected. Then you enter a string to replace the text you're searching for. You'll recall from Chapter 4 that Framework II allows you either to replace all occurrences at once or to step through the occurrences one by one, making individual decisions to replace or not to replace. (Detailed instructions are supplied below the desktop.) Pressing the End key results in the replacement of every occurrence.

Try using the Replace operation on the column that contains the sales people's work regions. Let's say you've decided to change the abbreviation for the midwestern region from "M" to "MW". Move the highlight to Reg, and press the keys shown opposite.

Ctrl-L	(to open the Locate menu)
R	(to select the Replace option)
M	(specify the target text)
Return	(to enter the target text into the Locate menu)
MW	(specify the replacement text)
Return	(to enter the replacement text into the Locate menu)
End	(to replace all occurrences)

The results of this particular Replace operation are not very dramatic; there are only three occurrences to be replaced. But keep in mind that this operation, like the sort and search operations, works as well on a database containing thousands of records as it does on a small database like this one.

ADDING RECORDS OR FIELDS

At various points in your work with a database you may want to increase the dimensions of the database table. The Create menu contains two options that allow you to do so; these are the same options that we used in Chapter 3 to increase the size of a spreadsheet:

Columns/Fields: Add
Rows/Records: Add

Adding rows to the database table is simply a way of making room for more records. In the case of the Sales People database, you'd want to add a row whenever you hire a new salesperson. In the event that you open up a new sales region, you might have to add several rows at a time, to accommodate all the salespeople in the new region.

Adding a column, however, means changing the *structure* of the database. You may discover that there is some new piece of information that you want to keep about each record in your database. This information will become a new field in the structure of the database.

In some database management programs, changing the structure of an already existing database (by adding new fields) can be a difficult operation, if it is possible at all. Framework II makes the operation very simple, again partly because the entire database is held in the computer's active memory during your work.

Despite the simplicity of the operation itself, the addition of a new field into your database is an event you may have to prepare for carefully. First, if you are keeping a structure table for your database (see Figure 5.3), you will want to revise it, adding a description of the new field. Second, you'll have to decide exactly how you are going to fill the new field with data. There are two possibilities:

1. You can enter the data manually, typing a new field value for each record in the database.

2. You can instruct Framework II to enter *calculated* values into the new field.

Your choice between these two approaches will, of course, depend on the nature of the data itself.

We are going to add three new fields to the Sales People database, which we'll call "AvgPerMo", "Pbn", and "Yrs". Here are the descriptions of the new fields:

□ AvgPerMo will contain the average monthly sales for each sales person, during the six-month period covered by the database.

□ Pbn will indicate whether a given sales person has been placed on probation, based on the sales for the period.

□ Yrs will show how many years each sales person has worked for the company.

All three of these will be *calculated* fields; no new manual data entry will be necessary.

Figure 5.6 shows a new structure table for the expanded database. (You will have to add rows to the database to complete this table.) Our first step in changing the structure is to add columns for the new fields. The first two fields, AvgPerMo and Pbn, will be located immediately after SixMoSales. The field Yrs will become the final field of the database, located after Hired. Adding the three new columns will thus be a two-step operation.

Begin by placing the highlight in the SixMoSales column. Press the following keys to add two new columns to the right of the SixMoSales column:

Ctrl-C	(to open the Create menu)
C	(to add new columns)
2	(to specify two columns)
Return	(to complete the operation)

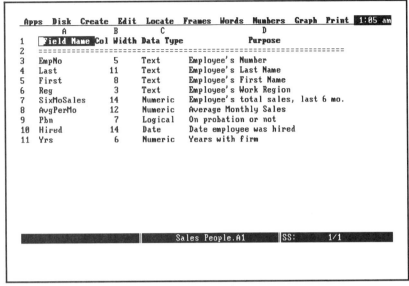

Figure 5.6: *Structure of the Expanded Database*

Now place the highlight in the Hired column, and press

Ctrl-C	(to open the Create menu)
C	(to add new columns)
1	(to specify one column)
Return	(to complete the operation)

You now have three empty columns in your database, for three new fields of information. In the next section of this chapter, we'll learn how to write formulas that will fill these columns with data. But first we need to prepare the columns properly for the data they will contain. In making these preparations, we'll follow the specifications outlined in Figure 5.6. Here are the steps:

1. Enter the three field names into the first row of the database table: AvgPerMo, Pbn, and Yrs.

2. Revise the column sizes. Use the Size key (F4) to initiate the procedure and the → or ← key to increase or decrease the size of the column. The AvgPerMo column should be 12 spaces wide; Pbn, 7 spaces; and Yrs, 6 spaces. Use the Middle option of the

Numbers menu to center the field names inside their column widths.

3. Select appropriate styles for the two numeric fields. Assign the Currency style to the AvgPerMo column. Extend the highlight over the entire column, and select the Currency option of the Numbers menu. For the Yrs column, specify the Fixed Decimal style, with one decimal place. Extend the highlight over the entire Yrs column, and press the following keys:

Ctrl-N	(to open the Numbers menu)
D	(to select the Decimal Places option)
1	(to specify one decimal place)
Return	(to enter the value into the Numbers menu)
Ctrl-N	(to open the Numbers menu again)
F	(to select the Fixed Decimal style)

Figure 5.7 shows what the database should look like at this point in your work.

WRITING FORMULAS TO CALCULATE FIELD VALUES

One of the most useful features of Framework II database management is its ability to calculate values for a field column, based on a defining formula that you supply. In a way, this feature has the same effect as the process of writing and copying formulas in a spreadsheet. But the procedure is even simpler in a Database frame, because you need to enter only one formula to define an entire calculated field category.

The top row of the database table, which up to now we have used exclusively for displaying field names, is also the correct location for formulas that calculate field columns. Formulas that you enter into this row will reside *behind* the field names. In Chapter 4 we saw how a formula can reside behind a frame; we used the Edit key to place FRED printing functions behind our Word frames. Likewise, the Edit key (F2) will also give us access to the area behind the field names in a Database frame. Entering such a formula does not affect the display of the field name itself, because the result of the formula appears in the data portion of the frame, as a column of calculated field values.

Database formulas for calculating fields can be written in one of two formats. The result of these two formats is identical; you can use whichever format seems clearer and easier to you. Both formats have two

```
 Apps  Disk  Create  Edit  Locate  Frames  Words  Numbers  Graph  Print  1:11 am
 EmpNo    Last     First  Reg  SixMoSales    AvgPerMo    Pbn      Hired       Yrs

 66N3  Rizzo       Anne    NE   $117,632.48                     May 21, 1966
 69S3  Washington  Ed      S    $102,375.10                     Aug 29, 1969
 72S6  Schroeder   Art     SE    $94,243.22                     Jan 24, 1972
 74N4  Takahashi   Bruce   NW   $102,664.78                     Mar 23, 1974
 78S4  Curtis      Amy     S     $47,256.70                     Apr 12, 1978
 78S1  Smithfield  Frank   SW    $51,623.62                     Jul 22, 1978
 79N6  Herrera     Fred    NE    $87,654.32                     Nov 20, 1979
 81S5  Petrakis    Bill    SE   $112,312.34                     Aug 24, 1981
 82N8  Woo         Eva     NW    $93,254.10                     Feb 25, 1982
 82S9  Hernandez   Esther  S     $83,241.20                     May  5, 1982
 82M1  Waterman    Pearl   MW    $85,977.83                     Sep 29, 1982
 83S9  Goldberg    Jack    SW   $103,254.67                     Oct 29, 1983
 84S1  Smyth       Gloria  SE    $87,732.41                     May 17, 1984
 84M3  Brooke      Donny   MW    $58,439.33                     Dec  1, 1984
 85M2  Olsen       Oscar   MW   $114,536.77                     Jun 20, 1985
 85N5  Smith       Joe     NW    $56,733.45                     Oct 23, 1985
 86S2  Smith       AshleighSW    $67,132.45                     Mar  4, 1986
 86N2  Sapolsky    Stan    NE    $48,675.30                     Jul 13, 1986

                                     Sales People.EmpNo    Recs:    18/18
```

Figure 5.7: *Adding New Fields to the Database*

essential parts: first, the name of the field category that will be calculated, and second, the formula that defines the calculation.

The first format uses a FRED function called @SET to establish a defining formula for a given field:

    @set(field, formula)

You might read this function as, "Set each value in the *field* column to the result of *formula.*" The second format uses a special symbol, ":=", to *assign* a formula to a field:

    field : = formula

This statement could be read as, "Assign the result of *formula* to each value in the *field* column." This is the format we will use in this chapter. Remember, the two formats perform exactly the same task.

You can place defining formulas behind any field name in the top row of the database. A formula does not necessarily have to reside behind the name of the field that it defines; but usually the most convenient place to write a formula will be in the column that actually receives the resulting calculated values.

See over for the steps involved in writing a defining formula.

1. Move the highlight to the field name where you want the formula to reside.

2. Press the Edit key (F2).

3. Type the formula itself, on the edit line, in either of the two legal formats.

4. Press the Return key to enter the formula into the area behind the field name.

When you complete this process, assuming you have written a valid formula, Framework II will immediately begin calculating results for the entire field category that you have defined. You will also see the formula itself displayed in the left section of the status panel. (You can always review the formula by placing the highlight over the field name where the formula resides; the formula will appear in the status panel.)

We're going to enter three formulas to calculate values for the three new field categories of the Sales People database: AvgPerMo, Pbn, and Yrs. Figure 5.8 shows the database after these three formulas have been entered. As we write each formula, you should examine this final version of the database and make sure you can find the specific calculated values that result from the formulas.

```
 Apps  Disk  Create  Edit  Locate  Frames  Words  Numbers  Graph  Print  12:08 am
 EmpNo   Last      First     Reg   SixMoSales    AvgPerMo       Pbn      Hired        Yrs

 82M1 Waterman   Pearl     MW    $85,977.83    $14,329.64  #FALSE   Sep 29, 1982   4.6
 84M3 Brooke     Donny     MW    $58,439.33    $9,739.89   #TRUE    Dec  1, 1984   2.5
 85M2 Olsen      Oscar     MW    $114,536.77   $19,089.46  #FALSE   Jun 20, 1985   1.9
 66N3 Rizzo      Anne      NE    $117,632.48   $19,605.41  #FALSE   May 21, 1966  21.0
 79N6 Herrera    Fred      NE    $87,654.32    $14,609.05  #FALSE   Nov 20, 1979   7.5
 86N2 Sapolsky   Stan      NE    $48,675.30    $8,112.55   #TRUE    Jul 13, 1986    .8
 74N4 Takahashi  Bruce     NW    $102,664.78   $17,110.80  #FALSE   Mar 23, 1974  13.2
 82N8 Woo        Eva       NW    $93,254.10    $15,542.35  #FALSE   Feb 25, 1982   5.2
 85N5 Smith      Joe       NW    $56,733.45    $9,455.58   #TRUE    Oct 23, 1985   1.6
 69S3 Washington Ed        S     $102,375.10   $17,062.52  #FALSE   Aug 29, 1969  17.7
 78S4 Curtis     Amy       S     $47,256.70    $7,876.12   #TRUE    Apr 12, 1978   9.1
 82S9 Hernandez  Esther    S     $83,241.20    $13,873.53  #FALSE   May  5, 1982   5.0
 72S6 Schroeder  Art       SE    $94,243.22    $15,707.20  #FALSE   Jan 24, 1972  15.3
 81S5 Petrakis   Bill      SE    $112,312.34   $18,718.72  #FALSE   Aug 24, 1981   5.7
 84S1 Smyth      Gloria    SE    $87,732.41    $14,622.07  #FALSE   May 17, 1984   3.0
 78S1 Smithfield Frank     SW    $51,623.62    $8,603.94   #TRUE    Jul 22, 1978   8.8
 83S9 Goldberg   Jack      SW    $103,254.67   $17,209.11  #FALSE   Oct 29, 1983   3.6
 86S2 Smith      AshleighSW       $67,132.45    $11,188.74  #FALSE   Mar  4, 1986   1.2

                         Sales People.EmpNo          Recs:    18/18
```

Figure 5.8: Placing Calculated Field Values in the Database

The simplest of the three formulas is for the field category AvgPerMo. We know that the field SixMoSales contains total sales amounts for a six-month period. So to calculate the average monthly sales for each record, we will simply divide the SixMoSales value by 6.

Move the highlight to the AvgPerMo field name. Press the Edit key (F2), and enter the following formula onto the edit line:

AvgPerMo : = SixMoSales/6

The ":=" symbol assigns the formula to AvgPerMo, and the "/" symbol performs the division in the formula itself. Press the Return key to enter the formula into the database. As soon as you do so, the AvgPerMo column will be filled with dollar-and-cent values. (Recall that we have already specified the Currency display style for this column.)

If you wanted to use the alternative format for this defining formula, this is what it would look like:

@set(AvgPerMo, SixMoSales/6)

You may find a small advantage in using this format: You are not required to press the Edit key before you begin entering the formula. Framework II reads the "@" symbol as the beginning of a formula, and therefore automatically puts you in the correct data entry mode.

Next we'll enter the formula for calculating the number of years each employee has worked for the firm. This formula will go into the last column of the database, the field named Yrs. To compute the values for this field, we'll use the FRED function @DIFFDATE, which supplies the number of days between any two dates. The @DIFFDATE function takes the following format:

@diffdate(*date1, date2*)

Assuming that *date1* is later in time than *date2*, @DIFFDATE yields the positive number of days that separate the two dates. Both *date1* and *date2* have to be Framework II date values, not text expressions that represent dates.

We saw in Chapter 4 that the @TODAY function supplies today's date, which is read from the DOS system calendar. For each employee in the Sales People database, we want to find out how much time has elapsed between the date the person was hired and today's date. Here is the @DIFFDATE function that will supply the information:

@diffdate(@today, Hired)

But this expression yields the difference between the two dates in days. Because we want the value to be expressed in years, we'll have to divide the result by 365, the number of days in a year:

@diffdate(@today, Hired)/365

So, finally, here is the defining formula that we'll enter into the area behind the Yrs field name:

Yrs : = @diffdate(@today, Hired)/365

You can see the result of this formula in the last column of the final version of the database, in Figure 5.6. (Actually, because these values depend on the value of @TODAY, the Yrs column you produce on your own computer will undoubtedly display larger values than those in Figure 5.6.)

The last of the three formulas that we'll enter into the Sales People database will result in a field of *logical values* for Pbn. You'll recall the purpose of the Pbn field: to indicate whether a given sales person is on probation. As manager of the sales force, you have decided to place on probation any employee whose average monthly sales level was less than $10,000 for the six-month period covered by the database.

The FRED programming language supplies Framework II with a pair of *logical constants* for the conditions *true* and *false*. These constants are expressed as the values

#TRUE

and

#FALSE

(The "#" symbol designates any of several categories of special built-in constants in Framework II and FRED.)

Up to now we have written formulas that result in numeric values. In these formulas, Framework II evaluates the calculation expressed in the formula and produces the resulting numeric values for the field category. In the Pbn formula, we will see that Framework II can also accept a logical expression as part of a formula. A logical expression is simply a statement that Framework II evaluates as either #TRUE or #FALSE.

Logical expressions are easy to write in Framework II, because they correspond exactly to statements we might make in plain English. For example, consider the following statement:

The average monthly sales level is less than $10,000.

For each one of your sales people, this statement will be either true or false. If the statement is true, the sales person will be placed on probation. If the statement is false, that is, if the person's sales level is greater than or equal to $10,000, the employee will remain in good standing with the company.

In the context of the Sales People database, we would express this logical statement as follows:

```
AvgPerMo < 10000
```

The "<" symbol means "is less than." This symbol is called a *relational operator*, because it expresses a relation between two values. Framework II uses a set of six relational operators:

<	(is less than)
>	(is greater than)
=	(is equal to)
<=	(is less than or equal to)
>=	(is greater than or equal to)
<>	(is not equal to)

Any time you write a statement with one of these relational operators, Framework II will evaluate the statement as either true or false. If you enter such a statement into a spreadsheet cell or a database field, Framework II will display one of the two logical constants, #TRUE or #FALSE.

So to place logical values into the Pbn field of the Sales People database, here is the formula we'll enter:

```
Pbn : = AvgPerMo < 10000
```

This formula tells Framework II to examine the AvgPerMo field in every record of the database. If the AvgPerMo field is less than 10,000, the record's Pbn field will receive the value #TRUE; if the AvgPerMo field is greater than or equal to 10,000, the record's Pbn field will receive the value #FALSE.

Enter the formula into the database, behind the field name Pbn. The resulting column of logical values is shown in Figure 5.8. Looking down the database, you can tell exactly who is on probation (Pbn is #TRUE) and who is not (Pbn is #FALSE).

Actually, Framework II has not one but two pairs of logical values. The two pairs are simply different ways of saying the same thing. By default, Framework II uses #TRUE and #FALSE to evaluate the result of a logical statement. But you can also use the constants #YES and #NO to express the same meaning:

#YES is equivalent to #TRUE.

#NO is equivalent to #FALSE.

In the case of the Pbn field you might actually prefer to use #YES and #NO to express the status of each employee. In response to the question, "Is this person on probation?", the #YES and #NO values seem to make a little more sense than #TRUE and #FALSE.

As a quick but completely optional exercise in formula writing, let's change the Pbn values to the alternative logical constants #YES and #NO. The exercise will lead us to yet another important FRED function, one that deals specifically with the results of logical statements. The function is named @IF; its role in spreadsheets, databases, and FRED programs is to provide a kind of decision-making tool.

The @IF function takes three parameters, in the following format:

@if(*logical statement, expression1, expression2*)

The @IF function evaluates its first parameter, the *logical statement*, as either true or false. The ultimate result of the function depends upon this evaluation:

□ If the *logical statement* is true, @IF returns the value of *expression1*.

□ If the *logical statement* is false, @IF returns the value of *expression2*.

The @IF function is extremely valuable in any Framework II task that needs to choose between two values, depending on the result of a logical statement.

Perhaps you've already figured out how we are going to use @IF in the new version of our Pbn formula. In order to replace the #TRUE and #FALSE values with #YES and #NO values, we'll replace the former Pbn formula with the following one:

Pbn := @if(AvgPerMo < 10000, #YES, #NO)

Examine the three parameters in the @IF function. The logical statement is the same as before:

AvgPerMo < 10000

If, for any given record in the database, this statement is true, the Pbn field of that record will receive the value #YES. Otherwise (if the logical statement is false), the Pbn field will receive the value #NO.

To revise the Pbn formula, you need only move the highlight to the field name Pbn and press the Edit key (F2). You can either delete the previous formula and then enter the new one, or you can insert the necessary characters of the new formula into the original version. Press Return when the revision is complete, and you will see the Pbn values begin changing immediately. Figure 5.9 shows the resulting revised database.

```
  Apps  Disk  Create  Edit  Locate  Frames  Words  Numbers  Graph  Print 12:10 am
  EmpNo   Last      First    Reg   SixMoSales    AvgPerMo   [ Pbn      Hired        Yrs

  82M1 Waterman   Pearl    MW    $85,977.83   $14,329.64 #NO      Sep 29, 1982   4.6
  84M3 Brooke     Donny    MW    $58,439.33    $9,739.89 #YES     Dec  1, 1984   2.5
  85M2 Olsen      Oscar    MW   $114,536.77   $19,089.46 #NO      Jun 20, 1985   1.9
  66N3 Rizzo      Anne     NE   $117,632.48   $19,605.41 #NO      May 21, 1966  21.0
  79N6 Herrera    Fred     NE    $87,654.32   $14,609.05 #NO      Nov 20, 1979   7.5
  86N2 Sapolsky   Stan     NE    $48,675.30    $8,112.55 #YES     Jul 13, 1986    .8
  74N4 Takahashi  Bruce    NW   $102,664.78   $17,110.80 #NO      Mar 23, 1974  13.2
  82N8 Woo        Eva      NW    $93,254.10   $15,542.35 #NO      Feb 25, 1982   5.2
  85N5 Smith      Joe      NW    $56,733.45    $9,455.58 #YES     Oct 23, 1985   1.6
  69S3 Washington Ed       S    $102,375.10   $17,062.52 #NO      Aug 29, 1969  17.7
  78S4 Curtis     Amy      S     $47,256.70    $7,876.12 #YES     Apr 12, 1978   9.1
  82S9 Hernandez  Esther   S     $83,241.20   $13,873.53 #NO      May  5, 1982   5.0
  72S6 Schroeder  Art      SE    $94,243.22   $15,707.20 #NO      Jan 24, 1972  15.3
  81S5 Petrakis   Bill     SE   $112,312.34   $18,718.72 #NO      Aug 24, 1981   5.7
  84S1 Smyth      Gloria   SE    $87,732.41   $14,622.07 #NO      May 17, 1984   3.0
  78S1 Smithfield Frank    SW    $51,623.62    $8,603.94 #YES     Jul 22, 1978   8.8
  83S9 Goldberg   Jack     SW   $103,254.67   $17,209.11 #NO      Oct 29, 1983   3.6
  86S2 Smith      AshleighSW     $67,132.45   $11,188.74 #NO      Mar  4, 1986   1.2

 Pbn := @if(AvgPerMo <1000         Sales People.Pbn        Recs:     18/18
```

Figure 5.9: Using #YES and #NO

Because we have added three columns of new information to the database, now is a good time to perform the Save and Continue operation again, to produce a disk copy of the new version of the database. In the next section of this chapter we'll continue to gain experience with using logical statements and relational operators.

FILTERING THE DATABASE

One of the most commonly used features of any database management program is called *filtering*. Filtering gives you the power to isolate specific groups of records that have one or more characteristics in common. You can then perform operations on this subset of records as though it constituted an independent database. Framework II's database filtering mechanism is simple and efficient.

To filter a database, you must first determine at least one criterion that Framework II can use to select a subset of records from the entire database. You then translate your criterion into a logical statement, which in this context becomes a *filtering formula.* You must enter this formula into the area behind the Database frame. When you do, Framework II instantly filters the database for you and displays the subset of records that match your criterion.

Before we start writing filtering formulas, let's examine five different examples of selection criteria that you might want to try on the Sales People database. These examples identify five different groups of records, selected from the entire database. The purpose of each of the following expressions is to identify the characteristic (or characteristics) that each record in a selected group will have in common:

1. All the sales people who have achieved total half-year sales of over $100,000

2. All the employees who have worked for the company for five years or less

3. Everyone who is currently on probation

4. All the people who work in the eastern regions (northeast or southeast)

5. All probationary employees who have worked more than two years for the company

Given the small size of the Sales People database, you might easily be able to pick out the groups of records that each of these criteria represent. But once again, imagine working with a database of several hundred records, only a score of which can fit on the display screen at a time. Scrolling screen by screen through the database to pick out a specific group of records would be a time-consuming process. The larger your database, the more useful Framework II's automatic filtering feature will become to you.

To translate the above criteria into filtering formulas, we'll make use of what we've learned about logical statements and relational operators. For example, consider the first example: employees with total half-year sales over $100,000. Here is the formula that expresses the criterion for selecting this group:

    SixMoSales > 100000

For each record in the database, this statement will be either true or false. Only those records for which the statement is true will appear in the filtered database. As a first experiment with filtering, then, let's enter this formula into the area behind the Database frame.

You may recall from Chapter 4 that the first step for entering a formula behind a frame is to move the highlight to the frame's border. Here are the keystrokes for entering the filtering formula:

Up Level (–)	(to move the highlight to the border of the Database frame)
Edit (F2)	(to place a formula behind the frame)
SixMoSales > 100000	(the formula itself)
Return	(to complete the formula entry)

That's all there is to it. When you complete these steps, Framework II will instantly filter the database according to your criterion. Only those records that pass the criterion will be displayed in the Database frame. Figure 5.10 shows the filtered database; you can see the six sales people who achieved total sales of over $100,000.

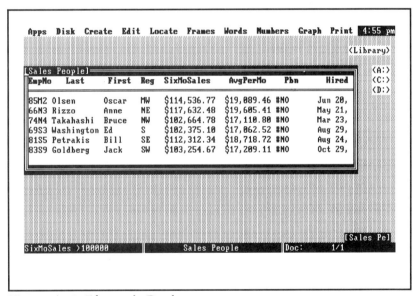

Figure 5.10: *Filtering the Database*

When you move the highlight inside a filtered database, the right side of the status panel will tell you both the total number of records in the database and the number of records that were selected by the filtering formula; for example:

    Recs: 6/18

This message means that you are examining a filtered subset of 6 records out of a total database of 18 records.

Where are the rest of the records, the ones that didn't make it into the filtered group? They are still in the computer's memory, temporarily hidden from view. They must be retrieved before you impose a new filtering formula, or the formula will work only on the filtered subset. There are two ways to get the hidden records back:

1. Move the highlight back to the frame's border, and press the Edit key (F2). Delete the filtering formula from the edit line. When you press the Return key, the frame will be "recalculated," without the filtering effect, and all the previously hidden records will return.

2. Use the Open All option in the Frames menu, while the highlight is positioned on the border of the frame. This option will result once again in a display of the complete database, without eliminating the filtering formula from behind the frame. If you want to refilter the database, move the highlight to the frame's border and press the Recalc key (F5).

Note that when you bring back hidden records, the group of previously filtered records remains at the top of the database, and the previously hidden records follow. If you want to return your database to some other order, use either the Ascending or Descending sort option of the Locate menu.

Now let's write formulas for the other criterion examples we discussed. Try entering each of these formulas, one at a time, into the area behind the Database frame. Make sure you delete the previous filtering formula and bring back all the hidden records before you enter each new formula.

In the second example, we want to find all the employees who have worked for the company for five years or less. Here is the filtering formula:

    Yrs < = 5

Notice the use of the relational operator that means "less than or equal to." In the filtered database resulting from this formula, you'll see that half the employees meet this criterion.

The third example is to find all the employees who are currently on probation. The filtering formula for this example is surprisingly simple. It consists of a lone reference to the field name itself:

    Pbn

Recall that the Pbn field contains logical values. For this reason, the field reference itself stands as a logical statement, which Framework II will evaluate as either true or false for each record. Figure 5.11 shows the filtered database. You can see that Framework II has selected all the records that contain a value of #YES in the Pbn field.

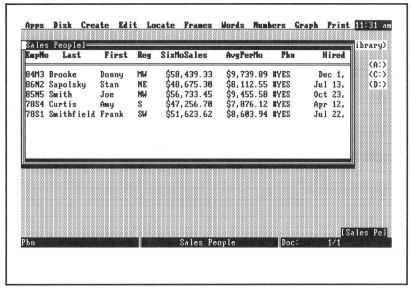

Figure 5.11: *Filtering on a Logical Field*

By the way, this filtering formula, consisting of only the name Pbn, will work correctly with either pair of logical constants: #TRUE and #FALSE or #YES and #NO. It doesn't matter which of these values you currently have in the Pbn field. Framework II selects either all the #TRUE values or all the #YES values.

USING @OR AND @AND TO FILTER

Our final two criterion examples involve *compound* logical statements. Let's review the original expressions of these final two examples:

4. All the people who work in the eastern regions (northeast or southeast)

5. All probationary employees who have worked more than two years for the company

We could rephrase these examples as pairs of criteria, connected by the words "or" or "and":

4. People who work either in the northeast region *or* in the southeast region

5. People who are on probation *and* have worked more than two years for the company

Translating these criteria into pairs of Framework II formulas, we might write them as follows:

4. Reg = "NE"   *or*   Reg = "SE"

5. Pbn   *and*   Yrs > 2

Clearly, we need some way of expressing two selection criteria at once for filtering the database.

The solution to these problems comes in the form of a pair of FRED functions, called

@or

and

@and

Along with @IF, we call these *logical functions*, because they deal primarily with logical expressions. The two functions @OR and @AND take, as parameters, a series of logical expressions; we can describe the format of the functions as follows:

@or(*expression1, expression2, expression3, . . .*)
@and(*expression1, expression2, expression3, . . .*)

Both @OR and @AND return a logical value, #TRUE or #FALSE. Here is how the two functions operate:

□ @OR returns a value of #TRUE if any one of its parameters is evaluated as true. Only if *all* of its parameters are false does @OR return a value of #FALSE.

□ @AND returns a value of #TRUE if *all* of its parameters are evaluated as true. If any one or more of its parameters are false, @AND returns a value of #FALSE.

Given these two functions, we can easily express compound filtering formulas for the last two examples. The following formula will select all the eastern sales people:

@or(Reg = "NE", Reg = "SE")

Enter this formula into the area behind the Database frame, and Framework II will display the six eastern employees, as shown in Figure 5.12.

The following formula will find any employee who is on probation and has worked more than two years for the company:

@and(Pbn, Yrs > 2)

Enter this formula into the area behind the Database frame, and you will find that there are only three employees who meet both these criteria. You can examine the filtered database in Figure 5.13.

In summary, the @OR and @AND functions allow you to create compound filtering formulas for a Database frame. When you want to find all the records that match *any one or more* elements of a set of criteria, use the @OR function. When you want to find the records that match *all* elements of a set of criteria, use the @AND function.

USING FILTERED DATABASES

Once you have created a filtering formula to select a group of records from your database, you can treat the group of selected records as a database in its own right. You can perform any of the following database

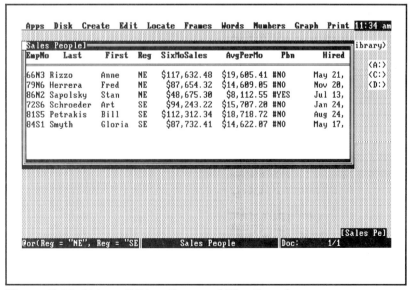

Figure 5.12: Using @OR in a Compound Filter Formula

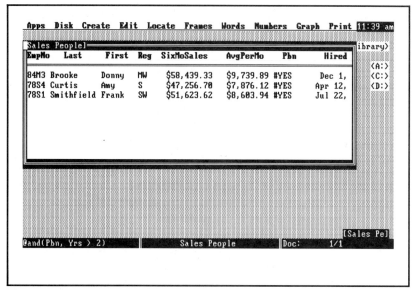

Figure 5.13: *Using @AND in a Compound Filter Formula*

management activities on the selected records:

- Sorting by fields
- Searching for field values
- Replacing field values
- Deleting records
- Filtering the database
- Printing the database table

None of these operations will include or have any effect on the records that have been temporarily hidden by the filter operation.

For example, let's say you want to delete a set of records that you have isolated through a filter operation. First use the Extend Select key (F6) to extend the highlight over the filtered records. Then press the Delete key. At that point you can bring back the hidden records to restore the database, minus the group of records that you have deleted.

The ability to print a group of filtered records can also be important. The process of printing a database is the same as printing any other frame:

Ctrl-P   (to open the Print menu)

B   (to begin printing)

If the database has been filtered, the Print menu will print only the records that are currently displayed in the frame.

You can use any of the styling options from the Words menu, and any of the submenus to the Print menu, as well as the FRED printing functions, to control the way the frame is sent to the printer. There are several factors to be aware of, however:

☐ If the data in any field exceeds the column width allowed for it, only the data that is visible on the screen will be printed.

☐ If the entire database exceeds your page width, additional columns will be printed separately, just as they are with a spreadsheet.

☐ If a record contains numeric data that exceeds the column width, asterisks will be printed.

As we'll see later, you can use the other two views of a database—Forms and dBASE—to overcome these limitations.

There are also other ways to control the way a database is printed. As with any other type of frame, you can print only part of a database by selecting the portion you want to print and then beginning the printing process. You can also make special adjustments to a database just for printing purposes. For example, you can widen frames that are too narrow to display their entire contents. If there are particular fields that you *don't* want to print, you use the Size key (F4) to reduce their width to 0. Moreover, if the database is to be part of a larger document, you can use the Allow Free Dragging option discussed in Chapter 4 to center a narrow database on the page, for a more pleasing appearance.

We have examined Framework II's impressive database management facilities; now it is time to turn once again to The Sophisticated Palate to look for an example of these facilities in action.

EXAMPLES

CREATING AN INVENTORY DATABASE

Eileen Wilcox is in charge of tracking the inventory of packaged wholesale goods in the warehouse portion of the business. Her main problem with inventory has always been to determine when it is time to reorder a given item. The warehouse space is limited, so Eileen reorders packaged goods once every two weeks. She wants neither to run out of popular items nor to build up too large a stock of any one product.

A secondary problem is determining wholesale pricing. The wholesale division calculates a 45 percent markup on all packaged goods. However, after this calculation, Eileen likes to adjust prices to retailers slightly, to introduce an "attractiveness" factor. Her adjustment simply assures that the last digit of each price will be either a 5 or a 9. For example, rather than marking the price of an item as $12.37, she increases the price by two cents, to $12.39.

Eileen has created a Database frame called Inventory. The database has seven field categories, with the following field names:

Stock No
Description
CostPerCase
Whsl Pr
Units Avail
Reorder
Supplier

Each record in the database describes one inventory item; Eileen has initially made room for 50 items. Before actually creating the database she took the time to prepare a structure table, which you can examine in Figure 5.14.

A printout of the inventory database that Eileen created is shown in Figure 5.15. Because this database is relatively long, Eileen was interested in finding as many shortcuts as possible for the data entry process. For some of the field categories there was no alternative to manual data entry, record by record; this was true of the Description, CostPerCase, Units Avail, and Reorder fields. However, for the other three fields, Eileen discovered simple ways to let Framework II fill in the data for her.

The Supplier field displays the supplier of each inventory item. The Sophisticated Palate regularly uses only six wholesale suppliers for its packaged retail goods:

Scandinavian Fine Foods, Inc.
Mediterranean Importers, Inc.
Whole Earth Foods
United Distributors
Produits de France, Lté.
Celestial Spice Co.

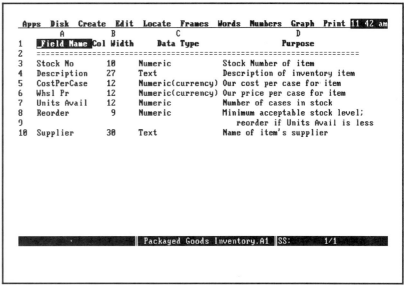

Figure 5.14: The Sophisticated Palate's Inventory Database Structure

Rather than typing these six long names many times, Eileen simply entered the single-character abbreviations S, M, W, U, P, or C in the Supplier field. Then she used the Locate menu's Replace option to replace each of the abbreviations with the supplier's full name. Here is how she entered the name "Scandinavian Fine Foods, Inc." into the database:

Ctrl-L	(to open the Locate menu)
R	(to select the Replace option)
S	(the target text)
Return	(to enter the target text into the menu)
Scandinavian Fine Foods, Inc.	(the replacement text)
Return	(to enter the replacement text into the menu)
End	(to replace all occurrences)

Eileen decided to assign stock numbers starting from 1001 to the packaged retail goods. (If she later decides to include other inventories in the database—such as a list of perishable goods—she can code them with another starting point, for example, 2001.) To enter the consecutive

```
The Sophisticated Palate, Inc.        Packaged Goods Inventory              May 17, 1987


Stock No      Description      CostPerCase   Whsl Pr   Units Avail  Reorder        Supplier
===================================================================================================
  1001 Pate de foie gras          $14.50     $21.05        13        8 Produits de France, Lte.
  1002 Capers                     $19.83     $28.75        14       10 Produits de France, Lte.
  1003 Spanish saffron            $16.20     $23.49         5        8 Mediterranean Importers, Inc.
  1004 Cold pressed olive oil     $65.32     $94.75        10        5 Mediterranean Importers, Inc.
  1005 Tortellini (dried)         $13.20     $19.15         9       12 United Distributors
  1006 Norwegian Crispbread, lt.   $8.12     $11.79        36       20 Scandinavian Fine Foods, Inc.
  1007 Norwegian Crispbread, dk.   $8.12     $11.79        18       20 Scandinavian Fine Foods, Inc.
  1008 Norwegian Crispbread, heavy $8.12     $11.79        32       20 Scandinavian Fine Foods, Inc.
  1009 Artichoke hearts, marinated $72.00   $104.45        40       35 United Distributors
  1010 Dijon mustard              $21.00     $30.45        15       12 Produits de France, Lte.
  1011 Creole Mustard             $19.60     $28.45         6       12 Whole Earth Foods
  1012 Hungarian Paprika           $8.62     $12.55         2        8 Celestial Spice Co.
  1013 Coriander seeds             $6.78      $9.85        12        8 Celestial Spice Co.
  1014 Anchovy paste               $9.22     $13.39        15       12 United Distributors
  1015 Turmeric                    $8.62     $12.55        12        8 Celestial Spice Co.
  1016 Lingonberry jam            $14.53     $21.09         8        5 Scandinavian Fine Foods, Inc.
  1017 Sardines in olive oil      $17.22     $24.99        40       20 Mediterranean Importers, Inc.
  1018 Escargots                  $43.12     $62.55        23       10 Produits de France, Lte.
  1019 Caviar, red                $56.40     $81.79         7        8 United Distributors
  1020 Caviar, black              $76.40    $110.79        12        8 United Distributors
  1021 Lemon curd                 $23.53     $34.15         9        5 Whole Earth Foods
  1022 Scots Shortbread           $19.76     $28.65        27       12 United Distributors
  1023 Miso                        $7.33     $10.65        15        5 Whole Earth Foods
  1024 Spaghetti, fresh           $12.60     $18.29        11        7 Whole Earth Foods
  1025 Spaghetti, spinach, fresh  $12.60     $18.29        12        5 Whole Earth Foods
  1026 Herring, in wine sauce     $13.54     $19.65        14        8 Scandinavian Fine Foods, Inc.
  1027 Herring, in sour cream     $13.54     $19.65        11       12 Scandinavian Fine Foods, Inc.
  1028 Herring, in tomato sauce   $13.54     $19.65        16        8 Scandinavian Fine Foods, Inc.
  1029 Herring, in mustard sauce  $13.54     $19.65        20        8 Scandinavian Fine Foods, Inc.
  1030 Minestrone                  $4.22      $6.15        27       12 Mediterranean Importers, Inc.
  1031 Beef Consomme               $4.77      $6.95         6       10 Produits de France, Lte.
  1032 Sage leaves, whole          $6.17      $8.95        13        8 Celestial Spice Co.
  1033 Couscous                    $9.45     $13.75         2        5 Mediterranean Importers, Inc.
  1034 Falafel mix                $13.21     $19.15        17        8 Mediterranean Importers, Inc.
  1035 Hoummous                    $8.52     $12.35         6        5 Mediterranean Importers, Inc.
  1036 Tomatoes, dried/olive oil   $9.12     $13.25        14        8 Mediterranean Importers, Inc.
  1037 Tuna/olive oil             $13.46     $19.55        11       12 Mediterranean Importers, Inc.
  1038 Whole rice flour            $6.85      $9.95        10        6 Whole Earth Foods
  1039 Filo                        $8.10     $11.75         8        6 Mediterranean Importers, Inc.
  1040 Major Grey's Chutney       $14.88     $21.59        12        8 Whole Earth Foods
  1041 Darjeeling Tea             $11.80     $17.15         9       10 Celestial Spice Co.
  1042 Oolong tea                 $11.80     $17.15        16       10 Celestial Spice Co.
  1043 Keemun tea                 $11.80     $17.15        17       10 Celestial Spice Co.
  1044 Bean thread noodles         $4.22      $6.15        11       20 Whole Earth Foods
  1045 Japanese horseradish        $8.48     $12.35         8        3 Whole Earth Foods
  1046 Dried seaweed               $3.17      $4.65         6        5 Whole Earth Foods
  1047 Bombay curry powder        $28.60     $41.49        13        7 United Distributors
  1048 Pineapple marmalade        $23.57     $34.19        12        8 United Distributors
  1049 Macadamia nuts             $57.60     $83.55        20       20 Whole Earth Foods
  1050 Cream of Coconut           $14.41     $20.89                 12 United Distributors
```

Figure 5.15: *The Sophisticated Palate's Inventory Database*

stock numbers into the database, Eileen used a FRED function named @FILL.

This is exactly the kind of task that @FILL is designed for: entering a column of consecutive, or evenly incremented, numbers into a database or spreadsheet. The format of the @FILL function is as follows:

@fill(*range, start, increment*)

where *range* is a database or spreadsheet range that will receive the numbers, *start* is the starting point of the numbers, and *increment* is the amount by which each number is increased (or decreased).

The @FILL function is an odd sort of tool, for a couple of reasons. Once it has performed its initial task, it is of no further use to the database or spreadsheet in which it was entered. Eileen therefore realized that once @FILL had done its work, she would be deleting the formula from the database. Furthermore, although @FILL does fill a range with values, it is not a field calculation formula. To prevent the database from treating it as though it were a field calculation formula, Eileen did not enter it behind a field name. Instead, she entered the function into the first record position of the Description column, before she had begun filling that column with data. (This location was an arbitrary choice; Eileen simply wanted to avoid placing the function in any location that already had data in it.) Here is the formula she entered:

@fill(Inventory.Stock No, 1001, 1)

The formula instantly filled in the Stock No column, with numbers from 1001 to 1050. Eileen remembered to delete the formula, by pressing the Delete key, before she began entering the item descriptions into the Description column.

CALCULATING THE RETAIL PRICES CATEGORY

Finally, Eileen wanted the retail prices for the inventory items to be calculated automatically, based on the wholesale price. Eileen knew she could simply enter the following formula into the area behind the Whsl Pr field name:

Whsl Pr : = 1.45 * CostPerCase

She tried this formula, and it worked just fine, computing each wholesale price as a 45 percent markup from cost. But Eileen was not satisfied; she wanted to find some way to incorporate her concept of "attractive pricing" into the formula for retail prices.

Looking at the Whsl Pr column in Figure 5.15, you can see that she found a solution to this problem. The last digit of each price is either 5 or 9, following Eileen's specifications. In order to achieve this, she had to write a small FRED program behind the Whsl Pr field name, rather than just a simple calculation formula. We will look at Eileen's program in Chapter 7; for now, simply keep in mind that the program has two purposes:

1. To compute the 45 percent markup

2. To increase each retail price by a few cents, when necessary, to ensure a final digit of 5 or 9.

PRINTING THE INVENTORY DATABASE

Once Eileen had completed the database, she of course wanted to print it out on paper. Because of the width of the columns, she realized that to fit all the information across a standard $8\frac{1}{2} \times 11$ inch page, she would have to print the database in a condensed mode. She used the many options of the Print menu for the purpose. First she opened the Format Options submenu, and entered the values shown in Figure 5.16. She selected

Condensed Print   on

Then she set the margins. A page offset of 2 and a line length of 128 assured that the entire line would be printed in condensed mode. A top margin of 8 and a bottom margin of 5 allowed plenty of room for a header.

Next, Eileen inserted the Header text. She wanted three headers, one left, one centered and one right. The left would read

The Sophisticated Palate, Inc.

The center header would contain the text

Packaged Goods Inventory

The right header would display the date.

There was only one problem: Eileen wanted the company name to be in boldface type. Now, as we've seen, you can get boldface type into a header by using one of the FRED printing functions. But the @HL function, which creates a header at the left margin, also destroys the spacing of the headers established in the menus, so they print continuously:

The Sophisticated Palate, Inc. Packaged Goods InventoryMay 17, 1987

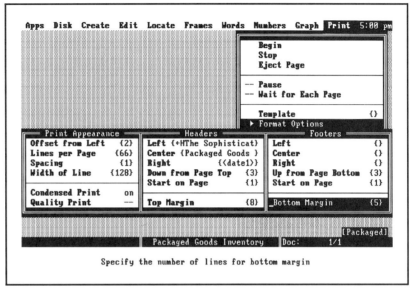

Figure 5.16: *Print Format Options for the Inventory Database*

She solved the problem by inserting a printer control code in the header text. For the Left Header, she entered

←HThe Sophisticated Palate, Inc←I

starting the text with the code her dot-matrix printer uses to begin bold-facing and ending it with the code to stop boldfacing. As you can see from Figure 5.15, this worked perfectly.

FILTERING TO DETERMINE INVENTORY REORDER TIMES

Finally, Eileen is ready to deal with her most important inventory problem: determining which products she needs to reorder at any given point. She has entered numeric values into the Reorder column; these values represent what she considers the minimum acceptable stock level for each item. She has also entered the current stock levels into the Units Avail column, and she plans to update this field on a weekly basis. Here is the filtering formula she'll use each week to find the items that need to be reordered:

Units Avail < Reorder

Eileen moves the highlight to the Database frame's border and presses the Edit key (F2) so she can enter her filtering formula.

At that point, Eileen decides to add some more information to the header, so she revises the center header as follows:

Packaged Goods Inventory < return > < return >Reorder List

As you may remember, inserting the symbol

< return >

into header text creates a multi-line header. With this new center header, the text "Reorder List" will be centered two lines below the "Packaged Goods Inventory" portion of the header, as shown in Figure 5.17.

As Eileen examines the filtered database, she finds that it is time to reorder a dozen items. She sorts the filtered database into alphabetical order by supplier and then prints out the Reorder list.

EXPLORING FURTHER

To complete our discussion of Database frames, we'll look at several more topics in this section as listed on the following page.

The Sophisticated Palate, Inc.		Packaged Goods Inventory					May 17, 1987
		Reorder List					
Stock No	Description	CostPerCase	Whsl Pr	Units Avail	Reorder	Supplier	
1012	Hungarian Paprika	$8.62	$12.55	2	8	Celestial Spice Co.	
1041	Darjeeling Tea	$11.80	$17.15	9	10	Celestial Spice Co.	
1003	Spanish saffron	$16.20	$23.49	5	8	Mediterranean Importers, Inc.	
1033	Couscous	$9.45	$13.75	2	5	Mediterranean Importers, Inc.	
1037	Tuna/olive oil	$13.46	$19.55	11	12	Mediterranean Importers, Inc.	
1031	Beef Consomme	$4.77	$6.95	6	10	Produits de France, Lte.	
1007	Norwegian Crispbread, dk.	$8.12	$11.79	18	20	Scandinavian Fine Foods, Inc.	
1027	Herring, in sour cream	$13.54	$19.65	11	12	Scandinavian Fine Foods, Inc.	
1005	Tortellini (dried)	$13.20	$19.15	9	12	United Distributors	
1019	Caviar, red	$56.40	$81.79	7	8	United Distributors	
1011	Creole Mustard	$19.60	$28.45	6	12	Whole Earth Foods	
1044	Bean thread noodles	$4.22	$6.15	11	20	Whole Earth Foods	

Figure 5.17: *The Reorder List Filtered from the Inventory Database*

- Working with databases in *Forms view*
- Printing a mailmerge letter
- Printing mailing labels
- Using the dBASE view of databases
- Linking spreadsheets with databases

At the beginning of this chapter we learned that there are three ways of looking at a Framework II database: the Table format, the Forms view, and the dBASE view. Up to now, we have seen databases only in the Table format. You may find yourself using the Forms and dBASE views less often than the Table format, but you should nonetheless know about the special features offered by these formats.

USING THE FORMS VIEW OF A DATABASE

Let's return briefly to the Sales People database that we developed in the first part of this chapter. Bring back the database onto the desktop, and move the highlight inside the frame. Press the View key (F10) to switch into Forms view. Figure 5.18 shows approximately what your screen will look like.

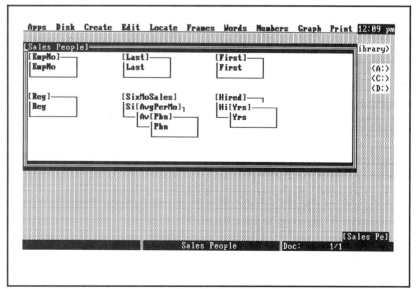

Figure 5.18: *The Sales People Database in Forms View*

The Forms view of a database displays a single record at a time. Each field within the record becomes an individual frame inside the containing Database frame. You can use the arrow keys, located at the right side of your keyboard, to move the highlight from field to field or to display a new record:

       ←   (to move the highlight to the previous field)
       →   (to move the highlight to the next field)
       ↑   (to display the previous record)
       ↓   (to display the next record)

You can enter a new field value into a record simply by moving the highlight to the frame that represents the field and then typing the new value. Thus the Forms view presents not only a different kind of display of the database, but also a new way to enter data into individual records.

The Forms view allows you to customize the organization of the screen for the display of a single record. You can use the Drag key (F3) to move the field frames to new locations on the screen, and the Size key (F4) to change the display dimensions of the field frames. (The modifications that you make on the Forms view arrangement will have no effect on the Table format.) By thus rearranging the fields on the screen, you can devise a record display that will be convenient both for viewing and for entering data.

Figure 5.19 shows a rearranged Forms view of the Sales People database. In this arrangement, the six input fields appear first, followed by the calculated fields. If you were using the Forms view to enter data, you might find this to be a more useful input screen than the original Forms view in Figure 5.18. Before you read on, try your hand at rearranging the Forms view screen on your own computer. Press the Zoom key (F9) to switch the Forms view into full-screen mode. Then experiment with the Size (F4) and Drag (F3) keys, and try to duplicate (approximately) the arrangement of Figure 5.19.

Forms view also allows you to expand the size of a text field so that you can enter multiple lines of information into the field. In this way, you can actually include a small word processed document in each record in your database. (NOTE: You can add multiple lines to any text field simply by bringing the field to the edit line and pressing the Zoom key (F9).) Figure 5.20 shows an example. A new field, Notes, has been added to the database; the purpose of the field is to keep evaluative and personal notes about each Sales Person. Let's examine the steps for creating and using this new field.

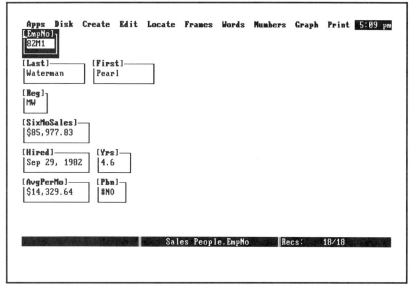

Figure 5.19: *Rearranging the Forms View*

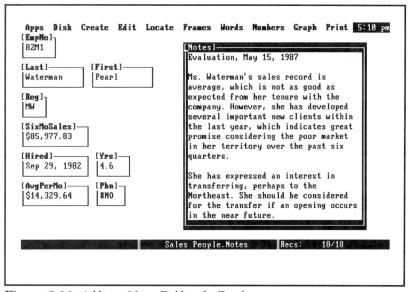

Figure 5.20: *Adding a Notes Field to the Database*

We should begin by adding a new field column to the Table format of the database. Press the View key (F10) twice to return to the Table format. Move the highlight to the last column of the database, Yrs, and press the following keys to add a new column:

Ctrl-C	(to open the Create menu)
C	(to add a column)
1	(to specify one column)
Return	(to complete the operation)

Move the highlight to the top of the new column, and enter the following field name:

Notes

Now press the View key (F10) to switch back to Forms view. You will find a new field frame devoted to the Notes field. Use the arrow keys to find the first record of the database, and move the highlight to the new Notes frame. Perform the following modifications:

□ Press the Drag key (F3) to move the frame; use the → and ↑ keys to drag the frame to the empty upper-middle portion of the screen. Press the Return key to complete the Drag operation.

□ Press the Size key (F4) to change the visual dimensions of the frame; use the ↓ key to enlarge the frame vertically and the → key to enlarge the frame horizontally. Try to match, approximately, the dimensions of the Notes frame shown in Figure 5.20. Press the Return key to complete the Size operation.

□ Press the Down Level key (+) to move the highlight into the frame. Using the Words menu, change the right margin of the text to 35.

Now start typing some notes; follow the example in Figure 5.20 if you like. You will find that the word processing features we discussed in Chapter 4 are in effect inside this frame. Wrap-around will occur when you get near the end of each line. We have already seen that you can control the margins of the text from the Words menu. You can also change the alignment and the styling of the text. Be aware that the frame size controls only the *appearance* of the frame in Frames view; you can enter more text than will be visible in the frame. Press the Up Level key (–) to move the highlight back up to the frame's border.

As you move forward to subsequent records of the database, each new forms screen will present you with a new empty Notes field. Using the

Forms view, you can thus keep word processed notes about each member of your sales staff.

The Forms view can also be useful for printing your database. When you print a Database frame that is in Forms view, each record of the database is printed on a separate page. So, for example, if you were to print the new version of the Sales People database in Forms view, you would receive a one-page report, including all the information fields and the new Notes field, for each employee.

In summary, the Forms view of a database can be useful for four major activities:

☐ Viewing records, one at a time, in a customized screen format

☐ Entering data into a customized record input screen

☐ Incorporating a field of word processed text into each record of your database

☐ Printing each record of the database on a customized page format

MAILMERGE PRINTING

Framework II includes two powerful features for sending out form letters—mailmerge printing and label printing. Both are found in the Apps (Applications) menu, shown in Figure 5.21.

With mailmerge printing, you can create a form letter to be sent to several different people, and fill in the names, addresses, and any other relevant information, from a database. Figure 5.22 shows a new database, called Supervisors. This database, which we'll be returning to in Chapter 7, contains the names and addresses of the sales supervisors in each of your six national regions. The database has eight fields of information:

Reg
Last (name)
First (name)
Address
Suite
City
ST
Zip

You can see that the region abbreviations, in the first column of the database, correspond to the regions in the Sales People database.

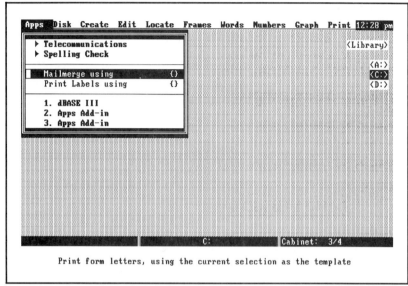

Figure 5.21: The Apps Menu

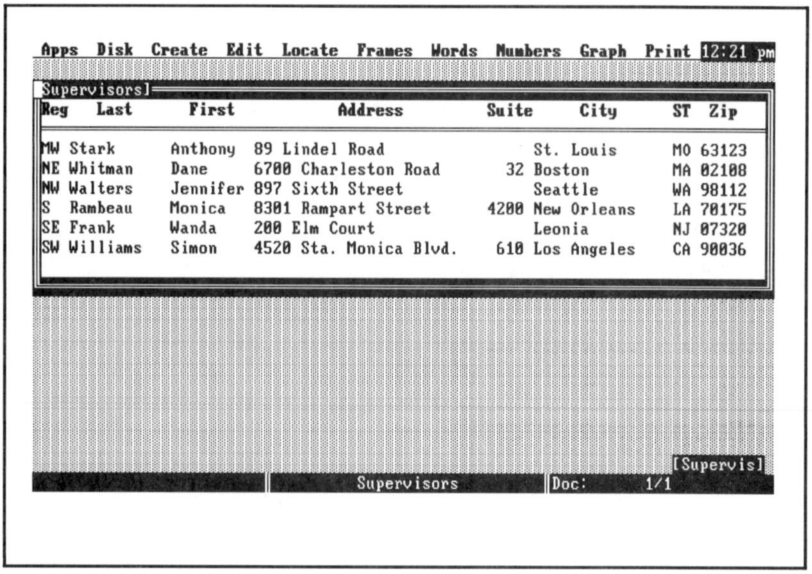

Figure 5.22: The Supervisors Database

We are going to send a form letter to each of the supervisors, but we will type this letter only once. The basic technique in creating a form letter for mailmerge printing is to substitute the names of the database fields that you want to appear in the letter for the actual text that those fields contain. As with keywords in the Print Format Options menu, these field names are enclosed in triangular brackets. Thus, the opening of the form letter might appear as in Figure 5.23.

Notice the marker

<Optional>

before the word *Suite*. This marker is used when the following field may be empty. It means, "If the following field contains data, print the text and the data, otherwise leave this line blank." Thus, you can use the same form letter for people whose addresses include a second line of information and for those who don't.

To print this letter, with the supervisors' names and addresses filled in appropriately, you must first have both the letter and the database on the desktop. Next, follow these keystrokes:

Ctrl-A	(to open the Apps menu)
M	(to select Mailmerge using)

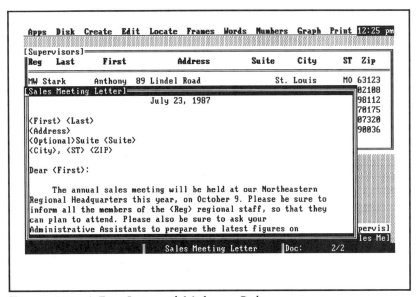

Figure 5.23: *A Form Letter with Mailmerge Codes*

| *supervisors* | (enter the name of the database to be used) |
| Return | (to record your selection) |

Framework II will print one copy of the letter for each supervisor, with no further intervention from you.

PRINTING MAILING LABELS

Now that you have your form letter ready to go, you can have Framework II print your mailing labels, either from a roll of labels one label wide, or from sheets two or three labels wide. To print on a single-label roll, you will design a Word frame to match the label. Create a Word frame, and size it so that it is 5 lines deep and 40 characters wide. Set the right margin to 35. The text of your frame will read:

```
<First> <Last>
<Address>
<Optional>Suite <Suite>
<City>, <ST> <Zip>
```

Since the labels come on a continuous roll, you will print them as though each label were a "page." Thus, you should set the following options on the Print Format Options menu:

Offset from Left	{1}
Lines per Page	{6}
Spacing	{1}
Width of Line	{34}
Top Margin	{0}
Bottom Margin	{0}

Leave all the header and footer settings blank. Keep the Supervisors database on the desktop, and mount the labels in your printer. Select the frame that contains the label information. Finally, press

Ctrl-A	(to open the Apps menu)
P	(to select Print Labels using)
supervisors	(enter the name of the database to be used)
Return	(to record your selection)

Printing three-up labels is slightly more complicated. You must copy the single label into a containing frame, turn Allow Free Dragging on, and make three copies of the label frame. Line the frames up alongside each other so that they are laid out exactly the same as three labels across the page. It may take several attempts before your labels are printed correctly, so it might be a good idea to test with a small sample of records from your database (at least nine, so that you can see how several consecutive rows of labels will appear) before you print the entire list. Once you have a format that works, you might want to store it in the Library for future reference.

USING THE dBASE VIEW OF A DATABASE

As you switched back and forth between the Table and Forms views of the Sales People database, you may have noticed a third view appearing. This is the dBASE view. This screen layout is identical to the data entry format used by the dBASE programs marketed by Ashton-Tate (as is Framework II). If you are accustomed to using any of the dBASE programs, you may find this view, which is illustrated in Figure 5.24, more congenial. The dBASE view has another distinct advantage: even though it shows you only one record at a time, it allows you to size the records so that all characters are displayed, no matter how wide the database is, or how narrow the columns in Table view are (except for multiple lines of text). It may even show you more information per record than Forms view.

To display dBASE view, press the View key (F10) twice. As you can see in Figure 5.24, only one record is displayed. The field names appear on the left, in square brackets, and the contents of the field to the right of the field name. Only a few of Framework II's special keys function in the dBASE view of a database. These keys are summarized in Table 5.2.

LINKING SPREADSHEETS WITH DATABASE FRAMES

Another typical database management function involves calculating statistical values from database fields. For example, consider the following three values that you might want to calculate from the Sales People database:

    □ The total sales, of all the sales people, during the six-month period covered by the database

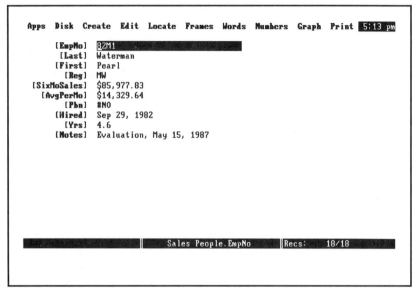

Figure 5.24: *dBASE View of a Database*

□ The average sales per employee

□ The average number of years employees have worked for the firm

There is no convenient way to incorporate bottom-line statistics like these into a Database frame. Each row of a Database frame is supposed to represent a consistently formatted record of information; a bottom line of totals and statistics would go against the nature of a database.

Fortunately, you can easily draw database statistics into a Spreadsheet frame. We have already seen how different spreadsheets can contain interframe references for transferring information from one spreadsheet to another. A similar kind of linking is possible between spreadsheets and databases.

For an example, look at Figure 5.25. This figure shows two frames on the desktop: the Sales People Database frame, and a Spreadsheet frame called Sales Statistics. The spreadsheet contains three calculations from data drawn off the Database frame: the total nationwide sales for the six-month period, the average sales per person, and the average years of work for the firm.

To arrive at these calculations, we enter references to database fields into the appropriate cells of the Spreadsheet frame. From outside the Database frame, a reference to an entire field consists of the name of

Keys	Action
↑	Moves the highlight to the previous field.
↓	Moves the highlight to the next field.
←, →	Moves the cursor within the current field.
Return	Moves the highlight to the next field.
Ctrl-↑	Moves to the equivalent field of the previous record.
Ctrl-↓	Moves to the equivalent field of the next record.
Home	Moves to the first field of the record.
End	Moves to the last field of the record.
Ctrl-Home	Moves to the name of the first field.
Ctrl-End	Moves to the last record of the last field.
PgUp	Moves to the equivalent field of the previous record.
PgDn	Moves to the equivalent field of the next record.
Up Level (–)	Moves to the frame border.
Down Level (+)	No effect.
Size (F4)	Changes the size of the field.

Table 5.2: Framework II Special Keys in dBASE View

the frame and the name of the field. For example, here is the correct reference to the SixMoSales field:

Sales People.SixMoSales

Cell A3 in the Sales Statistics spreadsheet contains the following formula:

@sum(Sales People.SixMoSales)

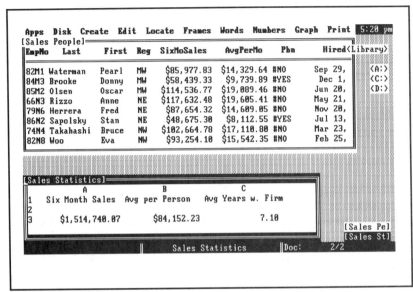

Figure 5.25: *Linking a Spreadsheet with a Database Frame*

This formula tells Framework II to find the sum of the entire SixMo-Sales column.

The formula in cell B3 of the Sales Statistics spreadsheet contains the same reference but a different function:

@avg(Sales People.SixMoSales)

This formula finds the average of all the numbers in the SixMoSales column.

Finally, cell C3 of the spreadsheet contains the formula

@avg(Sales People.Yrs)

This formula yields the average of the numeric values in the Yrs column of the database.

In short, whenever you want to calculate values from entire columns in a database, you can simply create a Spreadsheet frame and write formulas that refer to the fields of the database.

SUMMARY

A Database frame is designed to store records of information in rows and columns. Each row holds one record, and each column represents a field category. The top row of the database is reserved for the field names. The adjustable width of each column determines the maximum number of characters that can be *displayed* in a given field of the database table. Once you have determined the data type of a field, you can use the Numbers menu to specify an appropriate display style for the column.

Framework II menus and function keys provide all the most important database management tools for a Database frame. The Locate menu allows you to sort the database, search for specific information in the database, and replace specified strings of text in the database. Using the Create menu, you can add new field columns or record rows to the database table.

The Edit key (F2) gives you access to the formula area behind the field names. Formulas that you enter in these areas can calculate values for entire columns of the database. There are two acceptable formats for such formulas: you can use the FRED @SET function to assign a calculation to a specific field, or you can use the assignment symbol, "$:=$".

Formulas of another variety can be placed behind the Database frame itself. Specifically, you can write filtering formulas that express criteria for selecting specific groups of records from the database. A successful filtering formula will result in the display of a subset of the database. You can use the filtered database as you would the whole database; operations such as sorting, searching, deleting, and printing are all available for the filtered subset of records.

The Forms view of a database displays one record at a time on the screen. The Forms view is useful for producing customized data forms—for viewing, entering, or printing data. You can also expand the size of a field's frame in Forms view, to produce space for a word-processed text to become part of each record.

You can link databases to Word frames to print form letters with the Mailmerge Using option of the Apps menu. You can also print mailing labels for all records in a database or for a filtered database with the Print Labels Using option of the same menu.

A third view of databases, the dBASE view, adds compatibility with the dBASE programs, and also affords you the opportunity to see complete records when the Table view is larger than the screen or has columns narrower than the data they contain.

Finally, you may sometimes want to link a spreadsheet to a database, to compute statistics from database fields. The tool that creates the link is simply a reference, in the spreadsheet, to a field name in the database.

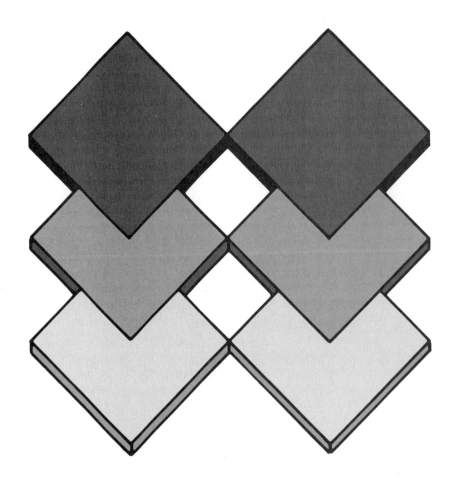

CHAPTER SIX

TELECOMMUNICATIONS

INTRODUCTION

In addition to its many other capabilities, Framework II can be used to communicate with other computers. Through its telecommunications component, you can send information to computers anywhere in the world, and you can capture and store information received from remote computers. You can receive information from services such as Dow Jones News/Retrieval, CompuServe, or The Source, or you can establish a direct connection with a computer on another desk.

Before you begin, you should be aware that telecommunications is the least standardized function in the nonstandardized world of computers. To use telecommunications you need patience, dogged persistence, and a willingness to experiment.

When you want two computers to talk to each other, there are a great many aspects of the process that must be attended to. The computers must be matched carefully in a number of respects before any communication can take place. In addition, there are many different types of telecommunications equipment and many different brands of each type. Each of them has quirks that can disrupt the smooth flow of data communications if it has not been set up properly. The various computer programs that make telecommunications possible also have quirks, and Framework II is no exception.

In this chapter we'll cover the basics of telecommunications, and then we'll practice using Framework II's telecommunications component. Later, we will walk through a communications session ourselves, and then watch as Eileen Wilcox of The Sophisticated Palate performs several communications tasks. Finally, we'll discuss some of the other telecommunications features available in Framework II.

We'll begin by introducing some of the background information you need to run a telecommunications program effectively. If you are already familiar with telecommunications, you may want to skip the following section.

TELECOMMUNICATIONS BASICS

Before any PC can communicate with another computer, both computers must have a *serial communications port,* either a *modem* or an

RS-232 interface, and some form of *communications software*. Let's start with the hardware.

THE SERIAL PORT

The serial port is the physical connection through which a computer communicates with the outside world. A serial port is *not* standard equipment on the IBM PC, although most compatibles do have one. If you do not have one, you must purchase a *serial board*. IBM sells a serial board called the IBM Asynchronous Communications Adapter. However, if you have a memory-expansion board installed in your computer, chances are excellent that it includes a serial board with a serial port. If you are not sure whether you have a serial port, look on the back of your computer. If there is a 25-pin connector (in the shape of a trapezoid) that is *not* directly below the monitor interface, you have a serial port.

The serial board is more than just a place to plug in a connection to another computer. To understand its importance, you must understand the way computers normally transmit information.

The smallest meaningful unit of information in a computer is a *bit*—represented in data communications as a voltage level. Each bit has one of two voltage levels, which are represented by 0 and 1, or off and on. It generally takes eight of these bits, grouped together into a *byte*, to convey meaningful information. Each byte represents a single character.

Ordinarily, when information is transmitted among the various parts of a computer, or to peripheral devices such as monitors and printers, it is transmitted in *parallel* form. This means that the eight bits that make up a byte are all transmitted at the same time, along eight parallel electrical paths.

In *serial* communication, however, the eight bits in a byte are transmitted one after the other, in sequence. This is the mode of transmission normally used in telecommunications. (Some printers also use serial communication.) The reason for this is that most telecommunication involves transmitting signals along telephone wires, and telephone wires contain only two channels—one for receiving information and another for transmitting it. So the computer's eight-bit characters must be converted into a stream of consecutive bits before transmission. When these consecutive bits are received, they must be reconstructed into bytes. This rearranging of the data is the principal function of the serial board.

THE RS-232 INTERFACE

The serial board is connected to the outside world by means of an *RS-232 interface.* This is a more-or-less standard type of cable having a 25-pin trapezoidal connector, called a DB-25 connector, at each end. Although only two of the possible 25 pins are actually used in data communications, several other pins perform related functions, such as carrying commands from the computer to the modem.

If you are communicating directly with another computer, you will need one type of RS-232 cable. If you are using a modem, you will probably need a different type. In any case, successful communications depend on the pins of your serial board being connected correctly to those on the device at the other end of the cable. Check with your dealer to be sure that the cable you are using is suitable for your intended purpose.

THE MODEM

If you want to communicate with a computer that is more than a few feet away, you will also need a *modem.* A modem is a device that links a computer to a telephone line. The term is a contraction of *modulator-demodulator,* terms that describe the modem's principal functions: translating the digital information that arrives at the serial port into sound frequencies that can be transmitted by telephone, and converting arriving sound frequencies back into the digital information that a computer can understand.

Modems vary greatly. Some, such as the Hayes Smartmodem 1200B, are boards that plug directly into slots in the computer. While they take less desk space, they also usurp some of the computer's expansion room. Free-standing modems come in two basic types: *acoustic couplers,* on which the telephone's handset is rested during transmission, and *direct-connect* modems, which are wired directly into the telephone lines. The latter generally transmit information more accurately than the former, because room noises cannot leak in and distort the signal.

COMMUNICATIONS SOFTWARE

To communicate with another computer, you also need *communications software.* This is where Framework II's telecommunications component comes in. It allows you to control the modem and the serial board, and to configure the information being sent and received so that it matches the requirements of the computer with which you are communicating. It also takes care of such chores as storing incoming data, preparing frames on the desktop for sending, and setting up disk files to receive data directly.

You configure the information that passes through the serial port by setting a series of *communications parameters*. These parameters control the way the computers make sense of the electrical pulses arriving at their serial ports.

The communications parameters that must be set include the *baud rate*, the number of *data bits*, the *parity* setting, the *stop bits*, and the *source* and *direction* of communication. These terms will be explained shortly.

In addition to the parameters that determine the form of the data to be communicated and the rate at which it travels, there are a number of routines that check for errors when data is being sent or received. These routines are called *communications protocols*. All you really need to know about communications protocols is that the sending and receiving computers must both be using the same protocol. Framework II includes five different protocols, so that you can transfer files to and from computers using other communications programs:

☐ *XMODEM*. This is one of the most popular communications protocols, used on virtually all CP/M-based remote bulletin boards and available in most microcomputer telecommunications packages.

☐ *Batch XMODEM*. This is a multifile, wild-card version of the XMODEM protocol.

☐ *CLINK/Crosstalk*. This is a protocol designed for use with IBM PCs running the popular communications program Crosstalk.

☐ *HAYES*. This protocol is used by the Smartcom program supplied with the Hayes Smartmodem 1200B.

☐ *CRC*. This is an additional error-checking protocol for use in conjunction with either of the XMODEM protocols. In order to use it, both computers must have it available.

BASIC TELECOMMUNICATIONS MODES

There are three fundamentally different ways to send and receive information through telecommunications.

- *Terminal mode.* In terminal mode you converse directly with another computer.

- *Uploading and downloading.* These processes transfer text files informally (character-by-character, without error-checking) from one computer to another.

- *Protocol transfers.* Protocol transfers use error-checking routines that can be applied to all types of files.

Let's see how these operations work.

Before you can engage in any of these activities, your telecommunications software must be configured to match the software running on the computer you want to communicate with. When dealing with mainframes and on-line services, you must ensure that your computer conforms to the remote computer's communications parameters. In connecting to another PC, you and the user of the other PC must agree on the parameters you will use.

Once you have configured your telecommunications software properly, you can converse directly with other computer users or access the various on-line information services and electronic bulletin boards. In this mode, which is called *terminal mode,* you type the information you want to send at the keyboard, and it appears almost simultaneously on the remote computer's screen. Similarly, information generated by the remote computer will appear on your screen. A great deal of recreational telecommunications consists of this type of conversation.

If the conversation is not too long, it will all be saved in the Telecommunications frame. You can also open a file into which the text generated during the session will automatically be sent. In addition, you can use the Text Transfer options on the Telecommunications menu to receive a complete text file from another computer. These processes—saving information in a desktop frame, saving the session to a file automatically, and receiving files through a text transfer—are referred to as *downloading.*

In addition to downloading, you can also *upload* text files from the Framework II desktop, that is, transmit them to a remote computer through terminal mode. This process is also controlled by the Text Transfer submenu.

In the *protocol transfer* mode, controlled by the File Transfer options of the Telecommunications menu, you can send or receive any disk file, including programs. This mode of file transfer scrupulously checks the transmission for errors. It is especially appropriate for the following:

- Transmitting and receiving files in Framework II's format.

Framework II files contain a great deal of formatting information along with the data you have entered into them. If you are sharing files with another Framework II user, you should use a protocol transfer method to ensure that the receiver can use the files within Framework II.

☐ Transmitting and receiving word processed text files created by other programs. The control codes used to format text in word processing programs may also be used to control terminal communications, and they may have undesirable effects when transmitted through the terminal as part of a file. (Other options of the Telecommunications menu allow you to control this process, too, however.) A protocol transfer prevents these undesirable effects from occurring.

☐ Transmitting and receiving program code. In a program, every character is significant, so you want to be sure that none are lost in the transfer process. Text files, in contrast, are relatively easy to reconstruct.

Figure 6.1 shows the main Telecommunications menu, which is displayed when you select Telecommunications from the Apps menu.

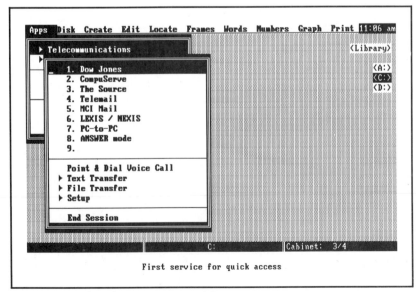

Figure 6.1: The Telecommunications Menu

CREATING A TELECOMMUNICATIONS FRAME

Unlike all other types of frames, which are created from the Create menu, Telecommunications frames are created from the Apps menu. A Telecommunications frame is essentially a Word frame, but one that receives some of its contents from another computer. As your session proceeds, the frame will fill with text until it contains 32,000 characters, after which the first part of the session will be lost, as new text comes in and replaces it. You can, however, increase this figure from one of the Telecommunications submenus. When you have finished a telecommunications session, you can treat the contents of a Telecommunications frame as you would any other Word frame—edit the text, save the contents to a file, move or copy portions of the text to another frame.

To create a Telecommunications frame, press

Ctrl-A	(to open the Apps menu)
T	(to select the Telecommunications submenu)
S	(to select the Setups submenu)
B	(to begin a telecommunications session)

If a Word frame is currently selected, Framework II will display the message

Use this frame for Telecommunications session? (y/n)

If you press Y, the session will begin after the last character in the frame.

Otherwise a new frame, occupying the full desktop except for the bottom line, will be created, with the label

Telecommunications.

In the third section of the status panel, the message

Tcom

will appear. Figure 6.2 shows a Telecommunications frame.

What happens when you choose to begin a session (which is what you did in order to create the frame) depends on whether you have a modem connected and turned on. If your computer is not connected to a modem, or if the modem is turned off, a peculiarity of the RS-232 interface makes your computer respond as if a call is in progress. You will see, in quick succession, the messages

Dialing... (Ctrl-Break to cancel)

Waiting for carrier detect... (Ctrl-Break to cancel)

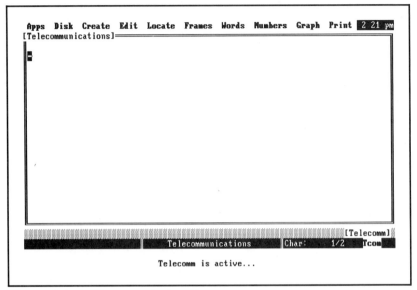

Figure 6.2: *A Telecommunications Frame*

Telecomm is active

in the message area at the bottom of your screen. If your computer is connected to a modem and the modem is turned on (or if you have an internal modem), Framework II automatically attempts to dial a phone number and link with another computer. It will wait 45 seconds for the other computer's telephone to respond, displaying the message

Waiting for carrier detect... (Ctrl-Break to cancel)

In any case, once you have selected the Begin/Resume session option, Framework II regards telecommunications as active. You can press the Up Level key (–) and leave the frame, and you can use most of Framework II's menu options, but you cannot delete the frame until telecommunications becomes inactive. If you do not have a modem active, you must return to the Telecommunications menu and formally end the session. Press

Ctrl-A	(to open the Apps menu)
T	(to open the Telecommunications submenu)
E	(to end the session)

If your modem is active, on the other hand, you can just press Ctrl-Break while the modem waits for a response, or wait 45 seconds, and telecommunications will become inactive.

As you can see, before you can actually use a Telecommunications frame for telecommunications, you must make certain preparations in advance. We'll now turn to the Telecommunications Setup Options menu, where you make these preparations.

PREPARING FRAMEWORK II FOR TELECOMMUNICATIONS

In a little while, we'll be logging onto Telenet, one of the major national *networks* through which you can log onto information services. Before we do so, however, we'll have to configure telecommunications for the purpose. To do so we'll have to set the communications parameters. These parameters are controlled by the Setup Options menu, which is shown in Figure 6.3. To display this menu, press

Ctrl-A	(to open the Apps menu)
T	(to select Telecommunications)
S	(to select the Setup submenu)
S	(to select the Setup Options submenu)

You will see that the Setup Options menu is divided into three sections. The left-hand section of the menu contains most of the communications parameters mentioned briefly at the beginning of this chapter. Two more parameters, the source and direction of communications, are in the right-hand section of the menu. We'll discuss the communications parameters at greater length here.

BAUD RATE

The *baud rate* is the rate at which bits are transmitted. Roughly, the baud rate divided by ten will yield the number of *characters* transmitted per second. Most modems allow baud rates of 110 or 300. Others can handle baud rates of up to 1200, and some of the newer models can transmit at baud rates as high as 2400. It is essential that the baud rates of both systems be the same. If they are not, the information you receive or transmit will be meaningless. You will know that the two computers are not using the same baud rate if your screen resembles the one shown in Figure 6.4.

DATA BITS

The Data Bits parameter represents the number of bits used to transmit a single character. To transmit the characters from 0 to 127 in the ASCII code (see Appendix C), only seven bits are required. These characters include the standard alphabet and the Ctrl-key combinations; the codes are almost completely standardized from computer to computer. The characters with ASCII codes greater than 127 vary greatly from one computer to another, however, and may even be modified by the software. Eight bits are required to transmit these characters.

The vast majority of intercomputer communication requires only seven bits. The number of data bits, however, like so many aspects of data communications, varies from one system to another, and both systems must agree before successful communication can occur.

PARITY

Parity is a primitive means of checking transmitted data for errors. If the system you are communicating with uses seven data bits, the eighth bit is a *parity bit*. If the parity is set to *even*, the software will place 1 in the parity bit if the addition of the seven data bits results in an odd number. If the result is already even, the software will place 0 in the parity bit. If the parity is set to *odd*, the reverse happens. Thus, when checking incoming data, the receiving computer will know that an error has occurred if the value of the eight bits does not conform to the parity setting. If the system uses eight data bits, no parity is used.

STOP BITS

If the receiving computer is to make sense of the stream of apparently random bits arriving at its serial port, the data has to be formatted in some way. Therefore, every 8-bit byte is preceded by a *start bit*, which is a binary 0. At the end of a byte are either one or two *stop bits*, which are binary 1s. This is the representation of the line signal's "resting" voltage. When stop bits are detected, the receiving computer waits until

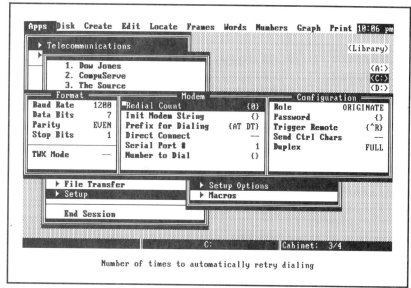

Figure 6.3: The Telecommunications Setup Options Menu

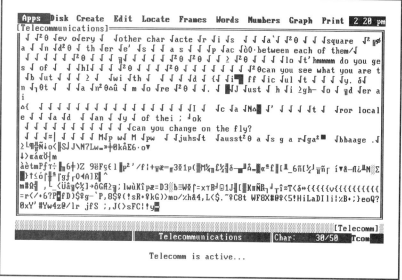

Figure 6.4: The Result of Telecommunicating with Unmatched Baud Rates

the next start bit is received. Different systems require different numbers of stop bits. Two stop bits are commonly used at low baud rates,
while one stop bit is more prevalent at higher speeds.

CHANGING THE SETTINGS

The default settings shown in Figure 6.3 for the baud rate, data bits,
parity, and stop bits are all correct for logging onto Telenet:

Baud Rate	1200
Data Bits	7
Parity	EVEN
Stop Bits	1

Telenet can also function with 300-baud modems, however. If you have
a 300-baud modem, select Baud Rate from the Setup Options submenu.
The baud rate will cycle through the values 2400, 4800, 9600, 100, and
300, changing each time you press Return. Press Return one more time
to return to 1200 baud.

You might want to try changing the other settings just for practice.
Try selecting Data Bits and pressing Return. This setting will toggle
between 7 and 8 each time you press Return. Similarly, the Stop Bits
setting will toggle between 1 and 2. The Parity setting might be considered a "throggle"—it has three possible values instead of two. Press
Return once and EVEN will be replaced by NONE. Press Return again,
and NONE will change to ODD. Press Return a third time, and EVEN
will reappear.

SOURCE OF COMMUNICATION

In the right section of the Setup Options menu are two more communications settings that must be established before you make a call
(which is called *going on-line*). The first is called Role and refers to the
source of communication.

When two computers communicate, one must be designated as the
source, or originator, of the communication, and the other as the answer-
ing computer. It doesn't much matter which is which, so long as they are
different. When dialing on-line services such as CompuServe, however, or
logging onto electronic bulletin boards, the Role must be set to ORIGI-
NATE (the default setting), because the remote service will always be set
up to answer.

DIRECTION OF COMMUNICATION

Data communications also involve "directionality." The transmission of data can occur in one of three ways: in only one direction, in both directions at different times, or in both directions at the same time.

Transmission in only one direction is called the *simplex configuration.* It is rarely used with microcomputers. The other two configurations, *half duplex* (both directions at different times) and *full duplex* (both directions at the same time) are much more common, but most communication between microcomputers takes place in full duplex mode, which is the default value for this option.

When you type characters at your keyboard for transmission, they do not automatically appear on your screen. Rather, they go directly to the serial port. What you see on your screen is an "echo" of the characters that are received at the remote computer. This may seem a roundabout way of getting characters on your screen, but it assures that what you send is being received. This echoing process is possible only in full duplex mode. If you do not see characters when you type, try changing the Duplex setting to FULL (in case it has been switched away from the default) by selecting it and pressing Return. Sometimes, you'll get a double echo—so that when you type

    hello

you see

    hheelllloo

on your screen. In this case, try changing your Duplex setting to HALF.

The Role and Duplex default settings on the Setup Options menu are both correct for use with Telenet.

INTERACTING WITH YOUR MODEM

The center section of the Setup Options menu is where you set up telecommunications to make your call and interact properly with your autodial modem. (If you have a manual-dial modem, you do not need to enter anything in this section of the menu, unless your modem automatically goes on-line whether or not you are in communication with another computer. If it does, select Direct Connect and press Return. You must, however, set the ORG/ANS switch on the modem to ORG.) In this menu, you will see the following options and their current values:

Redial Count	{0}
Init Modem String	{}
Prefix for Dialing	{AT DT}

```
Direct Connect          --
Number to Dial          {}
```

The Redial Count specifies the number of times you want your auto-dial modem to redial a number after it reaches a busy signal. You can change this setting to any number up to 99.

Now check the manual that came with your modem to see if you need a *modem initialization string* and a *dial prefix*. If your modem requires an initialization string, select Init Modem String, press Return, and enter the characters that your manual indicates exactly as they appear. If any of them are control characters, enter them by pressing ^ (Shift-6), followed by the letter of the control character. Press Return a second time to record your selection. (If your modem does not require an initialization string, don't enter anything here.)

If your modem requires a dial prefix other than the one shown, select Prefix for Dialing and follow the same procedure, entering the dial prefix for your modem. If it requires none, select Prefix for Dialing, press Return, and type a space before pressing Return a second time.

Framework II will automatically attempt to dial a number whenever you begin a telecommunications session. In order to succeed, however, it must have a valid number to dial. It looks for this number in the Number to Dial option on the Setup Options menu. The fact that you have not yet installed one is the reason for the bizarre results you encountered when you created a Telecommunications frame. A bit later, when we log onto a network, we'll install a phone number in this space.

Let's summarize the setup procedure:

☐ The baud rate must be set to match *both* that of your modem and that of the remote computer (some modems offer the option of several different baud rates, and some of the remote services can communicate at either 300 or 1200 baud).

☐ The number of data bits, the parity, the number of stop bits, and the telephone number (when using an autodial modem) must be set to match those of the remote computer.

☐ The initialization string and dial prefix must be set to match your autodial modem.

LOGGING ONTO A NETWORK

Now that we have covered some of the basics of telecommunications, let's try using Framework II's telecommunications function. First be sure that the following hardware requirements are met:

☐ Your modem is connected to your computer with the correct type of cable.

☐ The modem switches are set correctly (check page 2-5 of the Framework II Advanced Topics manual if you are not sure).

☐ The telephone is attached to the modem (if you have an auto-dial modem).

☐ The modem is turned on.

Next, you will need somebody to communicate with. We will log onto Telenet, a *communications network* through which you can gain access to such remote services as CompuServe, The Source, and The Knowledge Index. Telenet has a number of services that can be used without charge, and we will begin with one of those, so you can practice using telecommunications without paying for the time.

To use the services Telenet offers, you need Telenet's local phone number. You can get it through Telenet's toll-free customer-service numbers:

(800) 336-0437
(800) 572-0408 (in Virginia)

First check whether your modem is 300, 1200, or 2400 baud. Then call the appropriate number and ask for the nearest phone number you can use with your baud rate.

When you have the phone number, press

Ctrl-A	(to open the Apps menu)
T	(to select Telecommunications)
S	(to select the Setup submenu)
S	(to select the Setup Options menu)
→ or ←	(to select the center section)
N	(to select Number to Dial)
Return	(to enter the number)
phone number	(the number to dial)
Return	(to record your entry)

MAKING THE CONNECTION

To actually start communications, make sure your modem is connected and turned on, then press the keys to begin the session.

Up Level (–)   (to back up to the Telecommunications Setup
                 menu)

B   (to begin the session)

As before, a Telecommunications frame will be created, and if you
have an autodial modem, it will immediately dial the number you just
installed. (If you have a manual-dial modem, just dial the number.
When you hear a high whining sound, either place the receiver on the
acoustic coupler or unplug the modular cord from the receiver and plug
it into the appropriate jack on the modem.)

Within the Telecommunications frame, the dial prefix and phone
number you installed will appear, while the message

   Dialing... (Ctrl-Break to cancel)

appears in the message area. After the modem finishes dialing the number, the message

   Waiting for carrier detect... (Ctrl-Break to cancel)

will replace it. If you have a direct-connect modem with a speaker,
you will then hear either a busy signal or a phone ringing, followed by a
high-pitched tone. (If you dialed manually, these sounds will come from
your telephone handset. Place the handset on the acoustic coupler, or
unplug the handset and plug the wire into your modem, depending on
which type of modem you have.) The message area will now read

   Telecomm is active

You should now press Return twice, to alert the remote computer to
your presence. The word

   TELENET

will appear, followed on the next line by your local area code along with
another code. When you see

   TERMINAL =

type

   d1

and press Return. This is your *terminal identifier code*. Telenet's system
prompt is the @ sign. When you see it, type

   mail

and press Return. This is the service you can have access to without charge. The next prompt asks for your user name:

    User name?

For this service, type

    phones

and press Return. When you see the prompt

    Password?

type

    phones

again and press Return. This time the word will not appear on your screen. This dialogue is illustrated in Figure 6.5.

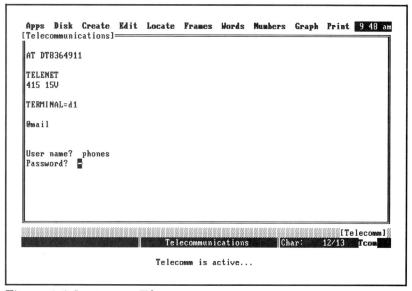

Figure 6.5: *Logging onto Telenet*

Be careful when you type your responses to the prompts, because you cannot edit them. The Delete key, while it appears to be deleting on your screen, instead sends a delete character (ASCII 127), and the Backspace key sends a backspace character (ASCII 8, or Ctrl-H) in addition to the character you have deleted. If, for example, you typed "maio" instead of "mail", and you tried to correct it before pressing Return,

maio ^H!

would be transmitted. (Your screen will look perfectly normal, but you can see graphic symbols representing the Backspace and Delete characters in a capture file, which you will learn how to establish shortly.) You will know you mistyped a response if you get a question mark followed by a repetition of the previous prompt. If that happens, do not be alarmed. Simply retype your response. Telenet is fairly forgiving at this level, and you can make quite a few mistakes before the network throws you off.

In a short time a number of commercial messages will appear. There will be prompts you can answer to get more information about Telenet local access numbers in various parts of the country. They will scroll across your screen, pausing periodically when the program sends a certain message. The pause is normal and is nothing to worry about. A sample section of Telenet's messages, with appropriate responses to Telenet's prompts, appears in Figure 6.6.

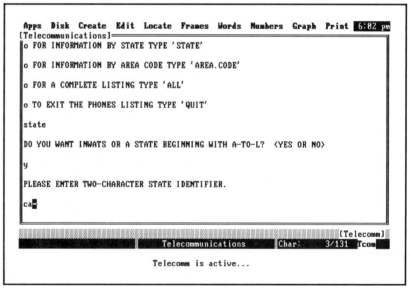

Figure 6.6: *Messages, Prompts, and Responses from Telenet*

You can continue as long as you like. When you are ready to stop, if you are at a Telenet prompt, type

    quit

To disconnect your own phone, or to quit when you are not at a prompt, press

    Ctrl-A   (to open the Apps menu)

    T   (to open the Telecommunications menu)

    E   (to end the session)

RECORDING A CONVERSATION

You have now completed your first on-line session. If it was short, the complete transcript of what you have seen will still be in the Telecommunications frame. But what if you want to record more extensive dialogues for future reference?

You can send the contents of the active Telecommunications frame to a disk file at any time by pressing Ctrl-PrtSc. The first time you press this combination of keys, you will be prompted to

    Please enter a name for file to capture to

After you enter the file name, the message

    Capture file open

will appear. Thereafter, you can toggle capturing on and off by pressing Ctrl-PrtSc.

You can also create a file in advance into which the entire text of the dialogue will be written, at the same time as it appears in the Telecommunications frame. To do so, you will use the Text Transfer submenu, shown in Figure 6.7, which controls uploading and downloading of text. To set this option, press

    Ctrl-A   (to open the Apps menu)

    T   (to open the Telecommunications menu)

    T   (to open the Text Transfer menu)

    →   (to move to the Download portion of the menu)

    Return   (to select Capture to File)

You will be prompted with

    Please enter a name for file to capture to

Enter the file name and press Return. When you begin your next session, text will automatically be sent to the file you have named. If a file by that name exists, the new text will be appended to it.

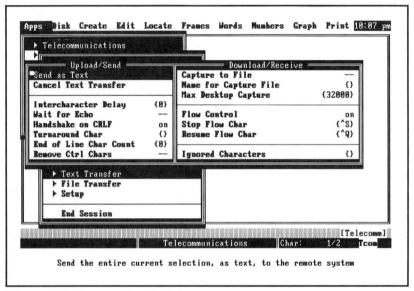

Figure 6.7: *The Text Transfer Submenu*

If you are already involved in a session, you can begin to send text to a file at any point by using the Capture to File option. The text sent to the file, however, will include only what appears after you have named the file. You can also toggle the capturing process off and on at any point during a session by selecting this menu option and pressing Return. This is useful if, for example, you want to record a menu the first time it is displayed, for further perusal, but do not want to save all succeeding instances of the same menu.

Let's log onto Telenet again, but this time we'll save the conversation, to get some practice in downloading a file. Follow the steps just outlined, and type in the name under which you will save the dialogue, preceded by the drive designator of the disk on which you want the file to appear, and press Return. For example, you might type

    C:TELENET.TXT

You can open the disk directory by pressing the Shuttle key (Scroll Lock) at any time during or after the session, and you will see this file name in the directory. Once your session is over, you can load this file (which will be a Word frame) to the desktop and edit, print, or read it at leisure.

TRANSFERRING FILES

Strictly speaking, *all* computer files are binary files—that is, files of eight-place, binary-coded numbers whose values range from 0 to 255. Text files are simply a special case of binary files, in which these values are interpreted as ASCII character codes.

When files are transferred by means of telecommunications, text file transfer means that the information in the file is sent as a stream of characters, departing through the serial port one character at a time. Only files that are prepared as text files can be sent through text file transfer. If you want to send information from a Framework II frame to someone who does not use Framework II or who wants to use the information in another program, the frame *must* be prepared as a text file, so that the nontextual information that only Framework II uses is filtered out.

However, text files can also be sent by means of a binary transfer, in which the information is sent and received in blocks of bytes rather than as a stream of characters. The advantage of sending a text file through a binary transfer is that special error-checking routines are used that ensure the integrity of each block of bytes. This is also a useful means of sending word processed files, which may contain control codes that would interrupt the smooth flow of communication if the file were sent character by character.

When you send a file that is on the desktop, it is always sent as a text file. Framework II automatically converts the frame to an ASCII text file, just as if you had selected the DOS File option from the Destination submenu of the Print menu (or if you had converted it to an ASCII text file yourself, as will be explained in Chapter 8). To send a file in this manner, first exit from the Telecommunications frame. Then select the file you want to send, and press

Ctrl-A	(to open the Apps menu)
T	(to open the Telecommunications menu)
T	(to select the Text Transfer submenu)
S	(to send the file as text)

You can, in fact, send any selected material from the desktop in this manner—parts of frames, whole frames, or several frames. Anything that would affect the printed appearance of the frame – such as title locking in a spreadsheet (except for special type styles, such as underlining)—will affect the appearance of the material that is sent. You can interrupt the transfer at any time by selecting Cancel Text Transfer from the same menu.

When you select Send as Text, Framework II creates a temporary file, just as it does when it prepares to print a file, and displays the message

PREPARING TO UPLOAD

As soon as the file is ready, the message area displays

Waiting for "trap" character from remote system...
(Ctrl-Break to cancel)

When the awaited character is received, a graphics character appears in the Telecommunications frame, and a message flashes briefly before the next segment of the file is sent. The "trap" character message then reappears. When the entire file has been sent, the message area displays

Upload Completed

While this is going on, you can leave the Telecommunications frame and work elsewhere in Framework II. A beep will sound when the upload is completed, to remind you to return to communication. Be aware that telecommunications messages appear only while the Telecommunications frame is selected.

Once again, note that you need not use the Text Transfer option if your files are already on disk in the proper form. Any file that has been saved on disk through the DOS File Destination option from the Print submenu or the ASCII Text Export option (discussed in Chapter 8) on the Disk menu is a text file. These files can be sent either as text files from the desktop, or as binary files using an error-checking protocol, from the File Transfer menu (which will be discussed shortly).

SETUP FILES

If you communicate on a regular basis with telecommunications services, such as Dow Jones News/Retrieval or CompuServe, or with electronic bulletin board services, you will find that each service uses a particular set of communications parameters, as well as a particular telephone number. Most of them will also require you to have an account number and a password.

For your convenience, you can save all the settings for a given remote computer or service in a *setup file*. As you can see from the Telecommunications menu in Figure 6.1, Framework II comes with eight preconfigured files: items 1 through 8. Included are files for connecting to Dow Jones News/Retrieval, CompuServe, The Source, GTE's Telemail service, MCI Mail, the Lexis/Nexis information databases, connecting to another personal computer, and placing your computer into answer mode. These files, which are identified on disk by a .TCM extension, contain the communications parameters necessary to connect with these services. Before you can use them, however, you must insert the service's local phone number, your account number, and your password. After the necessary information has been inserted, selecting any of these options from the Telecommunications menu will automatically dial the phone number (assuming you have an autodial modem) and initiate the log-on sequence, leaving you ready to communicate. We'll learn how to perform these steps in the next section.

If the setup file you need is on the menu, you can load it simply by selecting it from the Telecommunications menu. (Doing so will automatically initiate a telecommunications session.) If not, you can load a setup file by pressing

Ctrl-A	(to open the Apps menu)
T	(to open the Telecommunications menu)
S	(to select the Setup submenu)
L	(to select the Load Setup File option)
Return	(to enter the name of the file)
filename	(enter the name of the file)
Return	(to record your selection)

The message area will then say

Your options have been set from setup file

Next time you begin a telecommunications session, the communications parameters, telephone number, and log-on sequence from this file will be used (until you reset the computer or load another setup file).

A setup file is really nothing more than a "snapshot" of the settings on all the Telecommunications submenus. You can create such a file at any time by selecting the Write Setup File option from the Setup submenu, and entering the file name. If you haven't changed the settings since your conversation with Telenet, you could write a setup file for Telenet just by selecting Write Setup File and entering the file name

telenet

To change the default settings that are automatically loaded when you start Framework II, establish the menu settings you want to use, then choose the Write Setup File option and enter the file name

    telecomm

CONFIGURING SETUP FILES: TELECOMMUNICATIONS MACROS

There is, however, a bit more to organizing your setup files so that they will perform all their chores automatically. For this we need yet another submenu—the Macros submenu of the Setup submenu. To open this menu, which is shown in Figure 6.8, press

Ctrl-A	(to open the Apps menu)
T	(to open the Telecommunications menu)
S	(to select the Setup submenu)
M	(to open the Macros submenu)

Here you can add macros to your setup that will be sent by a combination of the Ctrl key and a function key. The right half of the menu gives you a place to add a comment explaining the purpose of the macro.

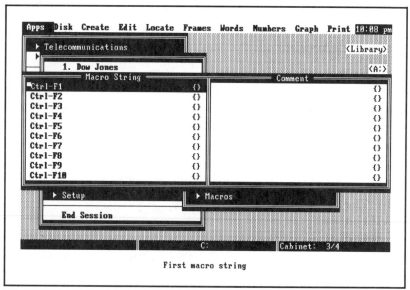

Figure 6.8: The Telecommunications Macros Menu

The macros on this menu can be used anywhere in Framework II, as well as in telecommunications. This means that you can load an additional ten macros by loading a setup file, even if you are not going to use telecommunications. (Macros established in the Library can be used in telecommunications as well.) Thus, you can send a series of characters to the remote computer by calling them from a macro, just as you can insert them anywhere else in a frame on the desktop. These macros differ from Library macros, however, in that they must be created on the edit line, rather than recorded from your keystrokes.

You can add macros that will smooth your communication with a particular remote computer. Ctrl-F10, in particular, is reserved for a macro that will be sent automatically as soon as connection is established with the remote computer. Thus, you can use it to perform your log-on sequence automatically. To accomplish this, however, you may need to use some special codes that act as telecommunications commands. These codes and their effects are listed in Table 6.1.

Character	Function
@W	WAIT code—waits for one second before sending the next character.
@T*char*	Waits for the character *char* to be received.
@L*n*	Links to macro number *n*. Used if a single macro cannot hold enough keystrokes to complete your command. (Ctrl-F10 is macro number 0.)
@@	Sends a Ctrl-@, an ASCII 0 or Null.
^	Makes the following character a control character.

Table 6.1: Special Codes for Telecommunications Macros

The WAIT code, @W, is extremely useful if you use a long-distance service such as MCI. You can insert it between your local number and your access code, so that the access code will not be sent until you have connected with your local access number.

To see how the other codes are used, let's create an automatic log-on macro for Telenet. Your first response upon connection to Telenet is two carriage returns, so your Ctrl-F10 macro will begin with

^M ^M

(As you can see from Table C.2, Ctrl-M is the equivalent of a carriage return.) You do not need to respond again until Telenet gives you the prompt

TERMINAL =

so you want your macro to wait for this prompt. When the equal sign is received, you want to send your terminal identifier, so add

@T = d1 ^M

to your macro. This tells the computer to wait for an equal sign, and then send

d1

followed by a carriage return. The next prompt you need to respond to is an @ sign, to which you reply

mail

so you will add

@T@mail ^M

The next two prompts both end in a question mark and receive the response

phones

so you can add the rest of the string. Your macro should now read:

^M ^M@T = d1 ^M@Tmail ^M@T?phones ^M@T?phones ^M

You might want to try adding this macro to your Telenet setup and beginning another session, to make sure that it works.

It's also extremely helpful to include (probably in Ctrl-F1) your log-off sequence. Many services use

OFF

or

BYE

as their log-off command. However, you should find out what each system that you communicate with regularly uses, and install that command as the macro for Ctrl-F1. In addition, you will need to tell your modem to hang up the phone. As you will remember, you hang up the phone by pressing

Ctrl-A   (to open the Apps menu)

T	(to select Telecommunications)
E	(to select End Session)

to get to the End Session command. However, you do not want to transmit the Ctrl-A T E characters to the remote system—you want to send them to Framework II. Therefore, you must record them in Framework II's format. The log-off macro, therefore, should be in the form

BYE ^M@W{ctrl-a}te

If you had used ^A instead of {ctrl-a}, telecommunications would have attempted to send the Ctrl-A character to the remote computer. The @W is included so that the modem will wait until the remote computer's response to your log-off command has been received before hanging up.

CONFIGURING EXISTING SETUP FILES

If you use any of the services for which a setup file is included, you will find that the log-on and log-off sequences are already installed in Ctrl-F10 and Ctrl-F1 on the Macros menu. All you have to do is add your local access number, your password, and your account number. Begin by loading the setup file by means of the Load Setup File option on the Setup submenu. Otherwise, Framework II will immediately try to dial the number (which you have not yet installed) and connect to the service. You will need to install the phone number in the appropriate location, as we did in our Telenet setup file. Then you should go to the Macros menu and install your personal information. For example, the macro assigned to Ctrl-F10 for the Dow Jones setup is

^M ^M@T = d1 ^M@T@c 60942 ^M@T?@Wdjns ^M@TE@Wacct# ^M

To customize this macro, bring it to the edit line with Return, delete the characters

acct#

and insert your Dow Jones account number in their place. If there are particular subsections of a service that you use regularly, you can install the series of commands needed to reach them in other macros on this menu, and execute the commands whenever you like just by pressing the appropriate Ctrl-function key combination. When you are finished, press

Ctrl-A	(to open the Apps menu)
T	(to open the Telecommunications menu)

S	(to open the Setup submenu)
W	(to choose the Write Setup File option)
Return	(to write the file using the name of the same file that you originally loaded)

The changes you made will be written to the setup file, and the next time you want to use the service, you can just select it from the main Telecommunications menu. If the services on the Telecommunications menu are not the ones you use, you will learn in Appendix A how to delete the ones you don't need and add the ones that you use. You will create the setup files necessary for the process simply by entering the appropriate values in all the menus and then using the Write Setup File option.

Now that you are familiar with the basics of telecommunications and have experienced an on-line session, we'll look at some examples of telecommunications at work. At The Sophisticated Palate, Eileen Wilcox is in charge of telecommunications. We'll watch as she uses telecommunications to receive a spreadsheet file from the recently established branch store, to place an advertisement on an electronic bulletin board, and to log onto an on-line service. Finally, we'll watch her put telecommunications into answer mode and send some spreadsheet files to the firm's accountant. In Chapter 8, we'll learn how George Farley prepared the spreadsheet file for the accountant, and how he integrated the information from the branch store into his own spreadsheets.

EXAMPLES

It was after hours at The Sophisticated Palate. Frank Osawa had just finished posting the day's expenses to a spreadsheet and George was taking care of the bank deposit. As soon as Frank finished, Eileen would begin a telecommunications session. She prepared her work carefully in advance, because some of her calls would be long distance, and connect time on the on-line services could be expensive. She wanted to save time and money.

During the course of her session, Eileen had several tasks to accomplish:

- □ Scanning a local bulletin board service to find advertisements for used equipment that could be used in the new branch store

- □ Receiving a spreadsheet from the newly opened branch store, to be integrated with the main store's spreadsheet

- □ Logging onto a major on-line service

- □ Sending a spreadsheet to the firm's accountant

There were quite a few steps Eileen could take to ensure efficient use of her telecommunications time. First, she put a blank data disk in drive A. Next, she used Framework II's wordprocessor to prepare an "Equipment Wanted" notice she would post if there were no appropriate items listed. When it was finished, she pressed Ctrl-P D D to save the frame as a DOS text file. That way, it could be used again without further preparation if she received no response during the two weeks that notices were permitted to remain on the bulletin board. She also left the notice in a tray on the desktop, so she could transmit it as a text file.

Now Eileen was ready to go on-line. She opened her Telecommunications menu, shown in Figure 6.9. (Notice that she has tailored her Telecommunications menu for her own purposes.)

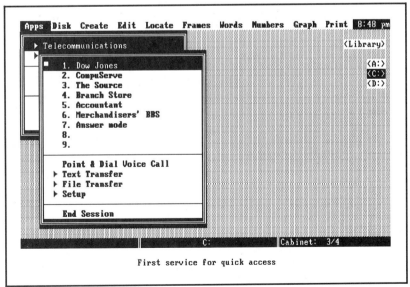

Figure 6.9: *The Sophisticated Palate's Telecommunications Menu*

Her first on-line task would be to receive a spreadsheet from the branch store. She wanted to finish that first so that Joe Escovedo, the branch store manager, could leave for the evening.

RECEIVING A FILE THROUGH A PROTOCOL TRANSFER

The branch store, which did not need to keep as extensive records as the main store, had an Apple IIe computer. George and Eileen had chosen the VisiCalc spreadsheet program for that computer, because Framework II can convert VisiCalc spreadsheets to Framework II spreadsheets, as we'll learn in Chapter 8. For telecommunications, they had chosen a package called Easycom/Easygo, because it included the XMODEM error-checking routine for file transfer, as well as an adequate word processor. It was important to have an error-checking protocol, because the information in the spreadsheets was too important to risk sending through a simple text transfer.

Although VisiCalc spreadsheets themselves are not compatible with Framework II, VisiCalc can create a special type of file, called a DIF file, which is a simple sequential text file. Framework II's file-conversion options include converting DIF files to Framework II files.

First, to make sure that Joe was ready, Eileen called him on the telephone. Having assured herself that Joe was prepared, she hung up the phone, switched on her Hayes Smartmodem 1200, moved the cursor to the Telecommunications menu, and pressed Return to load the Branch Store setup and begin the session. At that point she was in terminal mode, and her parameter file for the branch store had been set up to make the call automatically. Her parameter file had set the baud rate to 300, to match that of the Apple modem at the other end.

To make sure the connection was good, she typed

Are you there, Joe? –o–

(The symbol –o– is used in telecommunications to indicate "over.") Joe responded with

Everything looks good at this end. –o–

Then she typed

OK, let's go. –oo–

(The symbol –oo– is used to indicate "over and out.")

Next, she pressed these keys:

Ctrl-A   (to open the Apps menu)

T   (to open the Telecommunications menu)

F   (to open the File Transfer submenu)

R   (to select the Receive a File option)

This brought the cursor to the edit line, so she could enter the file name

    a:brnchsls.dif

This would be the name under which the VisiCalc file would be stored on her disk. She chose the name to indicate that the file contained the branch store's sales for the fourth quarter. She did not need to select the XMODEM protocol, because XMODEM is Framework II's default protocol.

Telecommunications responded to her file name with

    T

Attempting to Synchronize

Now Receiving A:BRNCHSLS.DIF

The T indicates that Transfer mode has been entered. The two messages tell Eileen that telecommunications has prepared the space she requested on disk and is waiting for the other computer to enter the XMODEM protocol transfer mode.

After a few moments, an R appeared on Eileen's screen. This indicated that the first block of the file had been transmitted incorrectly, and was being retransmitted. This is quite a common occurrence in protocol file transfers, and nothing to worry about unless it happens repeatedly. As each block of the file was transmitted, a period appeared on Eileen's screen to indicate the progress of the transfer. During this period Eileen could do nothing but wait. While a protocol transfer is being completed, the only action available to the user is to cancel the transfer by pressing Ctrl-Break. After about two minutes, the message

    File Received

appeared. Eileen said goodbye to Joe and logged off. When she was finished, her screen looked like Figure 6.10. She hung up the phone by pressing Ctrl-F1, to activate the hang-up macro.

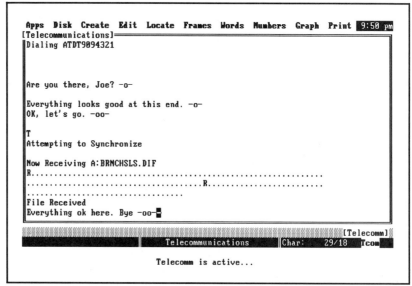

Apps Disk Create Edit Locate Frames Words Numbers Graph Print `9:50 pm`
[Telecommunications]
Dialing ATDT9094321

Are you there, Joe? -o-

Everything looks good at this end. -o-
OK, let's go. -oo-

T
Attempting to Synchronize

Now Receiving A:BRNCHSLS.DIF
R...
....R..........................
....
File Received
Everything ok here. Bye -oo-

[Telecomm]
Telecommunications |Char: 29/18 Tcom

Telecomm is active...

Figure 6.10: *Completing a Protocol Transfer*

LOGGING ONTO A BULLETIN BOARD

Eileen's next task was to place an advertisement on the Merchandisers' Bulletin Board Service. She pressed

Ctrl-A   (to open the Apps menu)

T   (to open the Telecommunications menu)

6   (to select the Merchandisers' BBS setup file)

She had already set up her Ctrl-F10 macro to transmit her identification code and password automatically. When the log-on procedures were completed, her screen displayed the menu shown in Figure 6.11. Notice that it is only 40 columns wide, to accommodate those computers that can display only 40 columns of text. This is quite common on electronic bulletin boards.

Eileen opened a download file from the Text Transfer menu, and chose the fourth option, Scan Mail. While any messages that might have been left for her were being written to disk, she took care of some paperwork. When she heard the computer beep, Eileen returned to it and closed the download file.

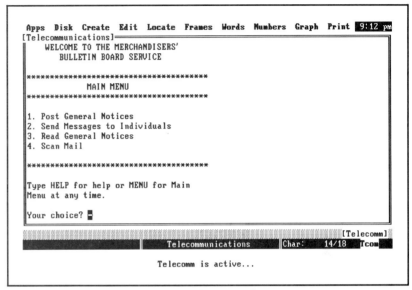

Figure 6.11: The Merchandisers' Bulletin Board Service Menu

Next she chose the third option, Read General Notices, selecting

Merchandise for Sale—Equipment

from a submenu, to see if anyone was advertising any of the equipment The Sophisticated Palate needed. She found an ad for a restaurant stove, and returned to the main menu to select the second option, Send Messages to Individuals. The remote computer prompted:

Enter name of new file, a / and your ID code:

Then she waited while the remote bulletin board responded with

Please wait. . .checking disk space.

When the remote computer had verified that there was enough disk space, it displayed the message

OK to begin sending.
Press Ctrl-C when done.

Eileen typed a response, right in the Telecommunications frame,to be posted as a message to the individual who had placed the ad. She finished by pressing Ctrl-C, and after a short time, the text

ished by pressing Ctrl-C, and after a short time, the text

Message Received
Your Choice?

appeared on her screen. Eileen typed MENU and then pressed 1, to post her own advertisement. Finally, she typed MENU, and then chose the third option again, to assure herself that her notice had been posted. When she saw that it had, she pressed Ctrl-F1, to send the bulletin board's log-off message and hang up the phone. At her next telecommunications session, she would choose Scan Mail, to see if she had received any responses to her ad.

USING ANSWER MODE

Eileen's final task for the evening was to send a spreadsheet to the firm's accountant. Although the accountant used Lotus 1-2-3 rather than Framework II, this posed no problem, because one of the formats that Framework II can convert its files to is that of Lotus 1-2-3. She had previously broken George's Income and Expenses spreadsheets into two separate frames, because that was how the accountant wanted them, and converted them to 1-2-3 format using the procedures that we'll look at in Chapter 8. Using a method we'll look at shortly, she used Framework II to dial the accountant's number by way of the modem, and made sure he was ready.

She then turned to the Setup submenu, changed the Role setting from Originate to Answer, and opened the File Transfer submenu to select the Batch XMODEM protocol, which allows you to send several files at once. Then she set her modem to auto-answer, and waited for the accountant to call back. When the connection was made, the message

Welcome to Framework Telecommunications

appeared on both screens. This telecommunications session appears in Figure 6.12. When the end of the file was reached, the messages

File Sent
Now Sending EXPENSES.WKS

appeared. After saying goodbye, Eileen used the Ctrl-F1 macro to hang up the phone, and proceeded to her final telecommunications activity for the evening.

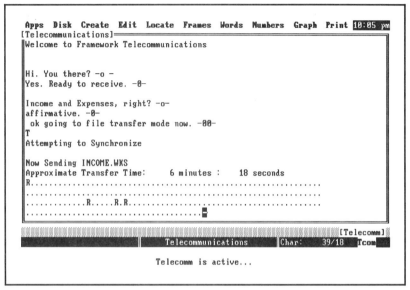

Figure 6.12: Beginning a Telecommunications Session

LOGGING ONTO COMPUSERVE

Eileen liked to keep up-to-date with the latest developments in her areas of interest, one of which was, of course, Framework II. Ashton-Tate maintains a bulletin board on CompuServe for users of its products, and Eileen wanted to see if the library of technical notes had been updated. She opened a file on drive A to receive the contents of her session, selected CompuServe from the Telecommunications menu, and logged in automatically. At the top-level (main) menu, shown in Figure 6.13, she typed

    GO ASHTON

and after a short pause was in the Ashton-Tate Support Library. The library is divided into sections by product, and the Framework II section includes two subcategories—Reference Notes, and Anomalies and Workarounds.

Eileen scanned Anomalies and Workarounds to see if there were any bugs that had been discovered or fixed. She scanned the screens quickly, knowing that she was paying for her time and that the information was secure in her download file, where she could peruse it at

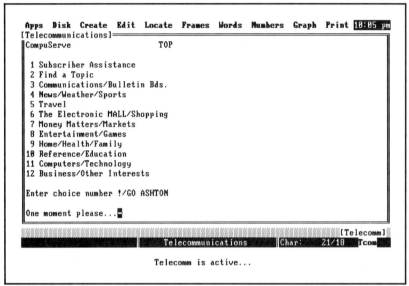

Figure 6.13: CompuServe's Top-Level Menu in a Telecommunications Frame

leisure. Having completed her scan, she typed

    GO MAIL

to check her electronic mailbox. She found a request for a recipe from another CompuServe user, whom she had "met" earlier via one of the service's Citizens' Band Simulators. Not wanting to spend her on-line time composing a response, Eileen made a mental note to check the download file for her correspondent's electric mailbox number, so she could prepare a response to send the next time she used CompuServe. By this time it was quite late, so Eileen bypassed the opportunity to chat on the Citizens' Band Simulator, and logged off instead.

Her work done for the evening, Eileen quit Framework II, shut down the computer, and closed up for the night.

EXPLORING FURTHER

Before we leave telecommunications, we should discuss several more telecommunications features of Framework II. First, we'll learn how you can use several features of the Library to have your modem dial your phone automatically. Then we'll take a brief look at Framework II's terminal emulation capabilities and at transferring files directly between computers without a modem.

AUTOMATIC PHONE DIALING

As you may remember, the Library cabinet includes a frame called the Phone Book. This frame is a four-column database, with headings

    Last Name
    First Name
    Home Phone
    Work Phone

Having your telephone directory at hand on the desktop is, of course, a great convenience. Moreover, it need not be in the form supplied—you can tailor it as you see fit. You might want to add addresses, notes, or other information.

The Library also includes two preconfigured macros to help you: Alt-F9 and Alt-F10. Pressing Alt-F9 will display a Zoom view of the Phone Book, no matter where in Framework II you are currently working. To locate a number, follow these keystrokes:

Alt-F9	(to display the Phone Book frame)
Home	(to move to the first column)
Ctrl-L	(to open the Locate menu)
S	(to select the Search option)
name	(enter the name to find)
Return	(to record your selection)
Tab, as many times as necessary	(to move the highlight to the phone number)

If you have a modem, Framework II will dial any number in this directory (or anywhere on the desktop) automatically, by means of another preconfigured macro. First, you must be sure that your modem is plugged in and turned on. Next, when the number you want to call is highlighted, press Alt-F10. The message

DIALING

will appear in the message area, along with your selected phone number. You will hear your modem play the tones of the number as it dials.

The message area will then display

Pick up phone, then when dialing complete, press Spacebar

That's all there is to it! If you keep all your frequently used phone numbers in the Library's Phone Book, this feature can be a real time-saver. In the next chapter, we'll look at a couple of programs you can write that will use these features to maintain a log of the calls you make.

TERMINAL EMULATION

Terminal emulation is a feature included principally for people who need to log onto a corporate mainframe computer. Such computers generally expect those who use their files to be working from a "dumb terminal"—a workstation including a keyboard and screen, but no computing powers of its own. Generally, a terminal will allow you full-screen editing, which is not available in most telecommunications software, although you have a form of it in Framework II's telecommunications component. To use terminal emulation, press

Ctrl-A	(to open the Apps menu)
T	(to select the Telecommunications menu)
S	(to open the Setup submenu)
E	(to turn Emulation on)

You can begin terminal emulation at any time during a telecommunications session by following these keystrokes. However, you will then have to press B to select the Begin/Resume Session option.

You may choose from among these five types of terminals:

DEC VT-100
Televideo 920
IBM 3101
Admiral 3A
Adds Viewpoint

To select a terminal, select the Terminal option from the Setup submenu and press Return. The selected terminal will cycle through these five types, changing each time you press Return.

If you subscribe to an on-line service such as Dow Jones, CompuServe, or The Source, you can try out terminal emulation on these services. The most common type of terminal is the VT-100. Choose the appropriate menu from the service to let it know you will be using terminal emulation, and turn emulation on in the Setup menu.

Framework II behaves somewhat differently when terminal emulation is on:

□ The screen will change to a form like that shown in Figure 6.14.

□ Even if you have a color screen, the terminal screen will be black and white.

□ If you press Ctrl-PrtSc while using terminal emulation, a snapshot of the screen, rather than the entire contents of the Telecommunications frame, is sent to the capture file.

□ Control characters typed at the keyboard, or contained in macros, are sent to the remote computer, even if they normally activate Framework II menu commands.

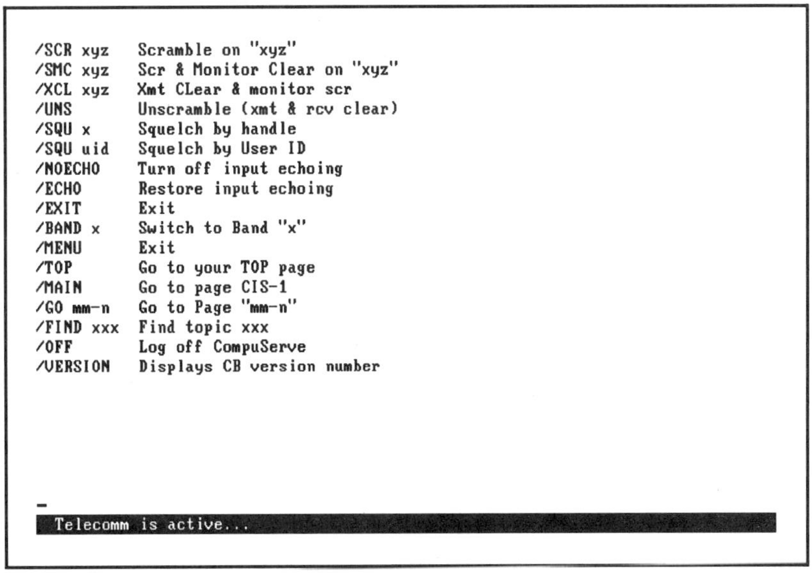

```
/SCR xyz     Scramble on "xyz"
/SMC xyz     Scr & Monitor Clear on "xyz"
/XCL xyz     Xmt CLear & monitor scr
/UNS         Unscramble (xmt & rcv clear)
/SQU x       Squelch by handle
/SQU uid     Squelch by User ID
/NOECHO      Turn off input echoing
/ECHO        Restore input echoing
/EXIT        Exit
/BAND x      Switch to Band "x"
/MENU        Exit
/TOP         Go to your TOP page
/MAIN        Go to page CIS-1
/GO mm-n     Go to Page "mm-n"
/FIND xxx    Find topic xxx
/OFF         Log off CompuServe
/VERSION     Displays CB version number




-
Telecomm is active...
```

Figure 6.14: *The Telecommunications Screen during Terminal Emulation*

To leave emulation mode while engaged in a telecommunications session, press Ctrl-Break or Instruct. This will not interrupt communications, but it will return you to the desktop. You can then move the cursor into the active Telecommunications frame, but you will have to use the Begin/Resume Session option to return to the terminal screen and resume communications. Alternatively—if the remote computer will permit it—you can turn emulation off, and resume communications inside the active Telecommunications frame.

HARDWIRE TRANSFERS

If you need to send information to another computer that is nearby—perhaps to send a text file to a computer that cannot read disks formatted under MS-DOS—you might consider the "hardwire" method. This involves connecting your computer's serial port directly to that of the other computer by means of a special type of RS-232 interface. (The technical description is that it has "pins 2 and 3 crossed," which simply means that the wires are crossed so that your computer's output channel is connected directly to the other computer's input channel, and vice versa.) The only other change you need to make is to select the Direct Connect option by pressing D while in the Setup Options submenu.

Assuming that the other computer has telecommunications software that is compatible with Framework II, you can then proceed just as though you were dealing with another computer by means of a modem. The advantages are twofold:

- ☐ There is less chance of interference in the signal, because you won't be dealing with potentially noisy phone lines.

- ☐ You are not limited by the speed of your modem. PCs can comfortably handle baud rates up to 9600. If the other computer can be set to a comparable baud rate, you can communicate at 9600 baud instead of the more common 1200 or 300 baud that most modems can handle. In any case, you can communicate at the other computer's highest baud rate.

SUMMARY

Telecommunications is Framework II's final productivity component. With this component, you can perform all of the standard telecommunications tasks:

- ☐ Conversing in terminal mode

- □ Uploading text files

- □ Downloading text files

- □ Performing protocol transfers in either direction

- □ Emulating a dumb terminal

Framework II telecommunications can be used easily from the desktop. You have access to all of Framework II's features while using it, and you can even work elsewhere on the desktop while telecommunications is proceeding.

Framework II will save the communications parameters you use most frequently in setup files, which you can install on the main Telecommunications menu and recall with three keystrokes. It will also automatically capture the contents of your telecommunications dialogues to disk.

CHAPTER SEVEN

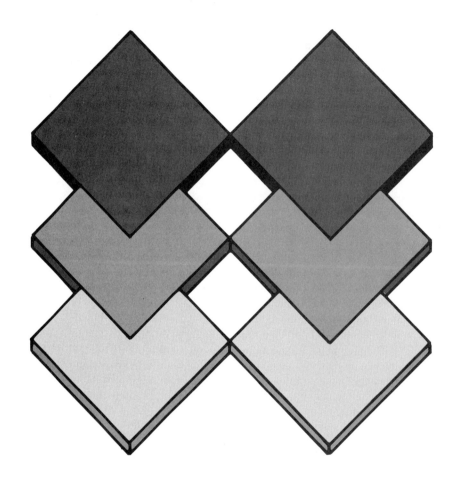

AN INTRODUCTION TO FRED

PROGRAMMING

INTRODUCTION

While studying Spreadsheet, Database, and Word frames, we have learned to write formulas and to use several categories of functions that begin with the @ character. Formulas and functions are the elements of Framework II's built-in programming language, called FRED.

We've seen two general uses for formulas: producing calculated values and performing certain "programmed" activities. In spreadsheets and databases we've written formulas primarily for the purpose of calculating values. We've learned that a single formula can result in many calculated values. In spreadsheets, formulas can be copied down or across a range of cells; in databases, a single formula, entered into the area behind a field name, results in calculated values for an entire field column.

But we've also used formulas to perform tasks that deal with entire frames rather than a single cell or range of cells. Specifically, we've written formulas behind Database frames to *filter* the database according to a specific criterion for selecting records. Once again, the primary result of such a formula, from our point of view as Framework II users, is a process, not a value. We've also written some printing formulas that affect entire frames.

In this chapter we'll expand upon the subject of writing formulas and using functions. We'll now begin to think of these formulas and functions as *FRED programs*. However, this shift in our thinking is taking place at an arbitrary moment in our study of Framework II. In fact, every formula in Framework II, no matter how large or small, is a FRED program; furthermore, any spreadsheet cell, database field, or frame can store a FRED program. In this sense, we have been writing FRED programs all along.

But much more is possible with FRED programming than what we have been doing up to this point. As we begin to explore the versatility of FRED—and to see the range of processes that FRED can control—keep in mind that FRED's resources are available in any Framework II context. We'll examine a variety of programming examples in this chapter, but these examples will represent only a brief first glimpse at the full power of FRED. The purpose of this chapter is not so much to provide a text on how to program in FRED as it is to show you the capabilities available to you through FRED.

WHY WRITE PROGRAMS?

Given all the Framework II features we have discussed in previous chapters, you might well wonder why we need a programming language at all. What powers can the complexities of programming add to the considerable capabilities that are already built into Framework II?

The answer is not simple, primarily because you can exploit FRED at several levels—beyond what you have already learned about writing formulas and using functions. Your use of FRED will depend on your own programming requirements, as well as on the extent to which you are inclined to explore and master the sometimes intricate details of the programming language. Some personal computer users enjoy learning the logic of computer programming; others prefer to work within the simpler confines of a predefined software environment.

Thinking in very general terms, we could propose three potential levels of FRED programming. From first to last, these levels offer progressively more power and assume a progressively more sophisticated understanding of FRED:

1. The first level involves writing "convenience" programs that save time and give you shortcuts to accomplishing essential Framework II activities. At this level we'll be discussing a special kind of FRED program called a *macro*. Macros are accessible to anyone—even people who do not care to learn how to program. A macro can streamline your day-to-day use of Framework II, allowing you to perform the most common tasks with just a couple of keystrokes.

2. The second level involves writing programs that actually add new computational or procedural capabilities to Framework II. In this category you might write formulas—long or short—that perform specific arithmetic tasks for which Framework II does not already have a built-in function. Or you might write programs that work with Framework II documents in new ways—combining data, producing reports, controlling procedures, and automating complex activities. This kind of programming delves more deeply into FRED's resources, as we will see in examples later in this chapter.

3. The most advanced level of programming involves writing "turnkey" programs that take complete control over an entire session with Framework II. Writing turnkey programs (in FRED or in any other computer language) is one of the jobs of the professional programmer. Turnkey programs are generally designed

for users who want to accomplish a specific computerized task without having to learn anything about a particular software environment. The main goal of such a program is "user friendliness"—hiding the intricacies of computer operations and making the computer seem like a machine devoted exclusively to a single task.

As you explore FRED and gain experience with Framework II's features, you will find your own place in this range of programming levels. One guiding rule is that when Framework II is accomplishing everything you bought it for, you have reached your own appropriate level of expertise. A second rule is that Framework II, along with FRED, can always be stretched further than your current level, to achieve new kinds of versatility and usefulness.

FRED PROGRAMMING

The programming features of FRED are represented by special categories of functions. Like the other functions we have seen, each programming function has its own name, beginning with the "@" symbol.

Through these functions, FRED offers all the capabilities of other, more traditional PC programming languages, such as BASIC and Pascal. If you have already programmed in one of these languages, you will recognize the vocabulary that programmers use to describe these capabilities. Otherwise, the following brief descriptions of the various categories of programming activities and structures will help to introduce you to some of the concepts involved in programming:

- *Control over input and output.* Input and output activities involve accepting values from the keyboard, displaying information on the screen, sending data to the printer, and creating interactive "dialogues," in which the computer reacts appropriately to values entered from the keyboard.

- *Variables and arrays.* These programming structures allow you to set aside specific places for values that are required during a program's performance. You can establish "global" variables, available throughout the program, or "local" variables, available in only a certain section of the program.

- *Decisions and flow of control.* Often a program will have to choose among alternative courses of action, depending on some current condition in the program. For this reason, programming languages provide ways of expressing logical conditions on which decisions can be made.

□ *Structured loops.* A loop allows a program to repeat the performance of a certain sequence of activity a controllable number of times.

□ *Subroutines.* Subroutines make it possible to organize a program into functional "modules," each of which is responsible for accomplishing a distinct task. Subroutines can operate on "parameters," information passed to them from other parts of the program.

Unlike other languages, FRED is designed to operate exclusively in the Framework II environment and to take advantage of all of Framework II's features. A FRED program can access and perform any of Framework II's menu and keyboard operations—including creating new frames, sorting and searching, formatting and styling, graphing and printing, moving and copying information, selecting frames, recalculating formulas, and even placing a new formula behind a frame. In short, FRED and Framework II rely on each other for the resources that build upon each other's power.

GETTING READY TO WRITE A FRED PROGRAM

The Edit key and the Zoom key are the tools that allow us to enter a formula into the area behind a frame. We have seen the process a number of times: you begin by moving the highlight to the border of the frame (or to the spreadsheet cell or database field) where you want to store a formula. Then you press

Edit (F2)   (to move the cursor to the edit line)

Zoom (F9)   (to expand the edit line into full-screen mode)

The full-screen edit mode allows you to create a formula—or a FRED program, as we are now saying—that consists of multiple lines of text. While you are writing a program, you can use Framework II's menus and keyboard functions to edit or style your program. For example, the Locate menu allows you to perform search and replace operations on a program. The Words menu permits styles such as boldfacing and underlining in programs.

You'll often want some way of *documenting,* in English, the activities that a program performs, especially when a program is long or complex. Like most programming languages, FRED allows you to incorporate "comments" into your program. Any line of your program can contain a comment or a part of a comment. The semicolon character (";") marks the beginning of a comment.

A line can be entirely devoted to a comment, in which case you'll place the semicolon at the beginning of the line:

> ; FRED will read this line as a comment.

Or you can place a comment at some point following, but on the same line as, a part of the program itself. FRED ignores any text that you enter to the right of the semicolon character:

> ; The following line contains a formula and a comment:
> SixMoSales > 100000   ; filter the database

In either case, the purpose of commenting is to provide explanations of the logic and structure of your program. Liberal use of commenting will help other people understand the programs you write. Commenting will also remind you of the logic of your own program, several weeks or months after you have written it.

Later in this chapter, we'll be writing some fairly complex programs. You should get into the habit of writing comments while you are developing a program. Many programmers promise themselves that they'll go back and insert comments after the program is complete; this promise is frequently broken. As we proceed, you'll see many examples of fully commented programs.

When you have finished writing a program behind a frame, press the Zoom key (F9) to move back to the single edit line. The Return key enters the formula into the frame and calculates its result. To enter a formula without immediately calculating it, press the Escape key. You can calculate a frame's formula at any time by moving the highlight to the frame's border and pressing the Recalc key (F5).

Framework II's Print menu allows you to print a FRED program at any stage of the programming task. To do so, first move the highlight to the border of the frame that contains the formula. Open the Output Options submenu of the Print menu, and toggle the Formulas Only option to its *on* status:

> on Formulas Only

Finally, select the Begin option of the Print menu. Framework II will print the formula that resides behind the frame, rather than the contents of the frame.

We refer to a printed copy of the lines of a program as a *listing*. Obviously, producing a program listing is a good way for you to study your work, search for mistakes, and consider ways to improve the program's performance.

In the remaining sections of this chapter we will move rather quickly through the elements of FRED programming. First we'll look at the Library's tools, learning what they can do and how they are organized. Then we'll survey some of the most important FRED programming functions, and we'll learn about Framework II's help facilities for programming.

During our visit to The Sophisticated Palate, we'll return to Eileen Wilcox's Packaged Goods Inventory database, to look at a short program we talked about briefly in Chapter 5.

Finally, in the "Exploring Further" section of this chapter we'll examine a complete example of a significant FRED program and learn how to create a user-defined function. The example program controls the process of merging information from two databases and producing printed documents from the combined data. Mastering the details of this program will be difficult if you have no programming background; however, you should read through to the end of this chapter anyway. Even if you don't understand the workings of the program itself, you'll finish with a better sense of what FRED can do.

THE USES OF THE LIBRARY

Framework II gives you a powerful tool to aid you in your programming—the Library. Within the Library cabinet you will see, among other things, four major subheadings, as shown in Figure 7.1:

Macros
Abbreviations
User-defined functions
Assumptions

Each of these headings contains examples of different types of FRED formulas and programs, some of which you can use as they stand. Others you can modify to suit your needs.

```
        Macros
          -  {Alt-F1}        ; Display Library Frame
          -  {Alt-F2}        ; Save Library Frame
          -  {Alt-F3}        ; Type Current Date
          -  {Alt-F4}        ; Type Current Time
          -  {Alt-F5}        ; Available Memory
             1  {Alt-F6} ; Memos and Letters
             -  1.1  Memorandum
             -  1.2  Company Letter
             -  1.3  Personal Letter
             -  1.4  Exit
          -  {ALT-F7}        ; Cut
          -  {ALT-F8}        ; Paste
          -  {Alt-F9}        ; Display Phone Book
          -  {ALT-F10}       ; Point and Dial Voice Call
          -  Return to Caller
          -  Cut Paste Buffer
        Abbreviations
          -  CA     ; California
          -  MA     ; Massachusetts
          -  fed    ; federal government
          -  fw     ; Framework II
        Printing Templates
        User-defined functions
          -  weekday
          -  hour
          -  minute
        Assumptions
          -  Your Name            ;For letters, memos
          -  Your Address 1       ;Street address
          -  Your Address 2       ;City, state, zip
          -  Your Company         ;Company name
          -  Company Address 1
          -  Company Address 2
          -  Inflation            ;Avg rate for past qtr
          -  Interest             ;Prime rate for past wk
        Phone Book
```

Figure 7.1: *The Framework II Library*

In addition, you can create new programs of each of these types. In this section, we'll examine each of these types of programs, and experiment with at least one of each. We'll look into the macros that are supplied with the Library in some detail, as they are quite powerful and useful. Since any frame in the Library can be called directly by other frames, this is an excellent way to keep handy any special blocks of text, formulas, or even complex programs that you will want to use often.

CREATING LIBRARY MACROS

You have already heard about Framework II's ability to create macros—strings of characters that can be invoked with a single keystroke combination. The command to create a macro is

Ctrl-C   (to open the Create menu)

M   (to create a Macro or Abbreviation)

You will then see the message

Enter macro or abbreviation for recording—ESC cancels entry

Before you create the macro, you must decide which key will execute it. It must be a combination of the Alt key and another key. All of the following characters are available for representing FRED macros:

- The 26 letters of the alphabet
- The 10 digits
- The 10 function keys

When you have entered the key you want to use, a frame will be created in the Library, under the Macros subheading, with a label containing the name of your chosen key. The message area then displays

Recording library macro/abbreviation entry—press Ctrl-Break to finish

All the keystrokes you type, until you press Ctrl-Break, will be recorded in the contents area of this special frame. This is probably the easiest way to write FRED programs, since you can include any keystrokes you might use in any task, as well as text, and Framework II takes care of all the syntax and structure for you. The only catch is that the keystrokes must be valid – you can't create text on an empty desktop, for example; there must be a frame of some sort to contain it. Similarly, if you issue commands among your keystrokes, they must be valid in the environment in which you issue them. Let's try a few examples. Then we'll look into the frames, to see what has happened.

A SIMPLE MACRO EXAMPLE

First, we'll create a macro that enters your first and last names into a frame. It's quite simple. Press

Ctrl-C   (to open the Create menu)

E   (to create an Empty frame where your keystrokes can be recorded)

Ctrl-C   (to open the Create menu)

M	(to create a macro)
Alt-N	(to select the key to which the macro will be assigned)
Fred Masters	(your name, followed by a space)
Ctrl-Break	(to terminate recording)

Now that you've recorded your macro, press Alt-N to invoke it. The macro will play back the keys that you have specified, entering your name into the contents area of the frame:

Fred Masters

Try it several more times, pressing Alt-N repeatedly. Each time you press Alt-N, the macro will perform its keystrokes:

Fred Masters Fred Masters Fred Masters

You can, of course, use a macro along with other keystrokes that you enter into the frame yourself. Press the Return key to move to the next line of what has now become a Word frame. Enter the following text:

My name is

Be sure to enter a space after "is". Now press Alt-N once again, and the frame will read:

My name is Fred Masters

The name macro, though perhaps a bit trivial, illustrates a typical use of macros: to store a sequence of frequently used keystrokes that can be recalled with a single keystroke combination. But the power of macros goes well beyond this. Let's elaborate the name macro a bit, and incorporate a few commands.

We'll create a macro that enters your name and address into a frame, centered so that you can use it as a letterhead. In the steps that follow, substitute your own name and address for those in the example. Here are the keystrokes:

Ctrl-C	(to open the Create menu)
E	(to create an Empty frame where your keystrokes can be recorded)
Ctrl-C	(to open the Create menu)
M	(to create the macro)

Alt-N   (to select the key to which the name macro will be assigned)

Since you have already used Alt-N, this message will appear:

Library entry exists; overwrite it?
(y to overwrite, n to append, ESC to cancel)

Framework II warns you if you have already used a key for a macro, and gives you a chance to replace it, edit it, or choose another key. (Of course, you can also edit a macro by opening its frame in the Library and editing it as you would any other text.) Press

Y	(to create a new macro with the same name)
Ctrl-W	(to open the Words menu)
C	(to center the text)
Fred Masters	(your name)
Return	(to start a new line)
123 Calc Street	(your address)
Return	(to start a new line)
Ashton, TX 54321	(the rest of the address)
Return	(to start a new line)
Ctrl-W	(to open the Words menu)
A	(to align the following text of the letter with the left margin)
Ctrl-Break	(to terminate recording)

Now let's take a look at what has happened. Follow these steps:

Shuttle (Scroll Lock)	(to shuttle to the cabinets)
↑ or ↓	(to select the Library cabinet)
↓	(to select the frame labeled Alt-N)
Zoom (F9)	(to look at the contents area of the frame)

You should see the text

{CTRL-W}cFred Masters{RETURN}123 Calc Street
{RETURN}Ashton, TX54321{RETURN}{CTRL-W}a

Note that this is the exact series of keystrokes you used to enter the macro. Notice also that if you made any mistakes, and corrected them with the Backspace or Delete keys, the incorrect keys will also appear, followed by

{BACKSPACE}

or

{LEFTARROW}{DEL}

FRED gives a name to each keystroke, placing the nonalphabetic keys in curly braces, and records exactly what you type. You can see a sampling of nonalphabetic keys in Table 7.1.

Library macros are different from other programs in several important respects. First, as you noticed, the keystrokes you entered were recorded in the *contents* area of the frame, rather than the formula area. In our previous encounters with FRED programming, we used the formula area behind the frame, which we reached by pressing the Edit key (F2). Second, Library macros require no FRED language commands other than the names of the keys. Third, because the macros are in the Library, you can call them whenever you are using Framework II.

ABBREVIATIONS

As we also noted in Chapter 1, you can store complex series of keystrokes in an abbreviation in the Library, as well as in a macro. If your macro is primarily a text macro to be used in a Word frame, as are the ones we've tried out so far, it might be more advantageous to store the text as an abbreviation. There is no limit on the number of abbreviations you can use, but you are limited as to how many macros you can create. Moreover, it's much easier to create a mnemonic abbreviation than a mnemonic macro name. For example, you might want to make your Alt-N macro into an abbreviation called NAD, for name and address, or LH, for letterhead (as in all other aspects of FRED, it doesn't matter whether you use uppercase or lowercase names).

It's easy to change a macro into an abbreviation. Select the frame in the Library labeled {alt-n}, edit the label so that the label is the abbreviation you want, and use the Move key (F7) to move the frame from the Macros subheading into the Abbreviations subheading.

Let's try creating an abbreviation from scratch.

Suppose you were writing a letter to a friend describing the wonders of Framework II. Naturally, you would be using the words "Framework

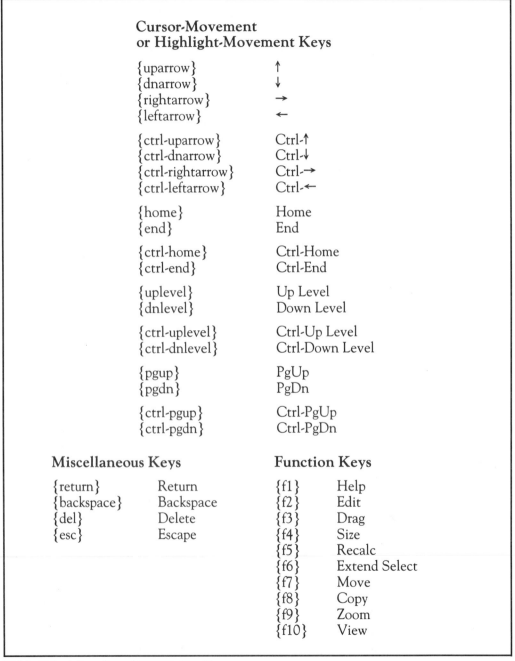

**Cursor-Movement
or Highlight-Movement Keys**

{uparrow}	↑
{dnarrow}	↓
{rightarrow}	→
{leftarrow}	←
{ctrl-uparrow}	Ctrl-↑
{ctrl-dnarrow}	Ctrl-↓
{ctrl-rightarrow}	Ctrl-→
{ctrl-leftarrow}	Ctrl-←
{home}	Home
{end}	End
{ctrl-home}	Ctrl-Home
{ctrl-end}	Ctrl-End
{uplevel}	Up Level
{dnlevel}	Down Level
{ctrl-uplevel}	Ctrl-Up Level
{ctrl-dnlevel}	Ctrl-Down Level
{pgup}	PgUp
{pgdn}	PgDn
{ctrl-pgup}	Ctrl-PgUp
{ctrl-pgdn}	Ctrl-PgDn

Miscellaneous Keys

{return}	Return
{backspace}	Backspace
{del}	Delete
{esc}	Escape

Function Keys

{f1}	Help
{f2}	Edit
{f3}	Drag
{f4}	Size
{f5}	Recalc
{f6}	Extend Select
{f7}	Move
{f8}	Copy
{f9}	Zoom
{f10}	View

Table 7.1: *A Sampling of FRED's Key Names*

II" quite frequently, so they would be a natural candidate for an abbreviation. To set up an abbreviation, press the following keys:

Ctrl-C   (to select the Create submenu)

M   (to select Macros and Abbreviations)

You will then see the message

Enter macro key or abbreviation for recording—
ESC cancels entry

in the message area. You now type

fw

and the message

Recording library macro/abbreviation entry—press Ctrl-Break to finish

appears in the message area. Type

Framework II

and press Ctrl-Break. Your abbreviation is now recorded in the Library. To use the abbreviation, press Alt-Backspace, and in place of the letters "fw", "Framework II" will appear.

THE @PERFORMKEYS FUNCTION AND SPECIAL KEY NAMES

There may be times when you want something that is similar to a macro—that is, a series of keystrokes to be entered automatically—but you don't want to create it "on the fly." The FRED function @PERFORMKEYS can accomplish the same thing as a macro in other contexts.

Significantly, FRED allows you to place *any* combination of keystrokes inside the @PERFORMKEYS string, including the cursor-movement keys, the Up Level and Down Level keys, the Ctrl key, the function keys, and all the other keys that are so essential to the Framework II environment.

@PERFORMKEYS recognizes special names for all these keys; Table 7.1 lists some of the most important of these names. Notice that all of these names must be enclosed in curly braces. They must also be included inside the quotation marks of the @PERFORMKEYS function's string parameter.

Here is a quick sequence of examples. Suppose you want to write a macro that creates an Empty frame. You could prepare the following function:

@performkeys("{ctrl-c}e")

The "{ctrl-c}" keyboard command opens the Create menu, and the "e" selects the Empty/Word Frame option. If you want to expand your macro to assign the label "Test" to this new frame, you would edit the formula to read like this:

@performkeys("{ctrl-c}eTest{return}")

After the Empty frame has been created, the keystrokes "Test" represent the label, and the "{return}" key enters the label into the frame's border. Finally, if you want the macro to move the highlight down into the contents area of the frame, you will add one more element:

@performkeys("{ctrl-c}eTest{return}{dnlevel}")

The "{dnlevel}" keystroke moves the highlight into the frame. Notice that a @PERFORMKEYS string can contain any combination of regular characters and special keys.

To implement this simple program, you create an Empty frame, and place the program in the programming area behind the frame by pressing the Edit key (F2), just as you did for spreadsheets and databases. When you select this frame and press Recalc (F5), the program will be executed, producing the Empty frame shown in Figure 7.2.

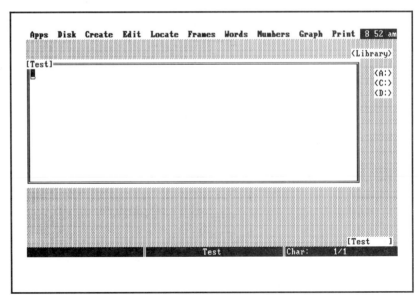

Figure 7.2: *An Empty Frame Created by a Macro*

Keyboard Name	Function	Description
Alt-F1	Display Library Frame	When the Library frame is selected, displays a full-screen (Zoom) view of the Library.
Alt-F2	Save Library Frame	Saves the current version of the library to disk.
Alt-F3	Current Date	Enters the date from the system clock at the current location of the cursor.
Alt-F4	Current Time	Enters the time from the system clock at the current location of the cursor.
Alt-F5	Available Memory	Displays the amount of unused memory still available in your system.
Alt-F6	Memos and Letters	Allows you to select a any of several predefined formats for letters and memos from a menu.
Alt-F7	Cut	Cuts text selected with the cursor keys or the Extend Select key (F6) to the Library frame labeled Cut Paste Buffer.
Alt-F8	Paste	Pastes text from the Cut Paste Buffer to the current cursor location.
Alt-F9	Display Phone Book	If you have a Phone Book frame in the library, displays a full-screen (Zoom) view of that frame.
Alt-F10	Dial Phone	Dials a phone number currently displayed on the desktop and selected with a highlight.

Table 7.2: Functions of the Library Macros

MACROS SUPPLIED WITH THE LIBRARY

Let's look now in greater depth at the macros that are supplied with the Library. Figure 7.1 shows you the names of these macros as they appear in the Library, and Table 7.2 briefly explains their functions. You are of course free to modify them as you see fit, or to assign completely different macros to the function keys. However, the ones supplied are quite useful.

There are three ways to view the Library. (Remember that you select the Library by pressing Shuttle [Scroll Lock] and the ↑ or ↓ key.) First, you can select the Library and press Return, which gives you a narrow frame much like a disk drive cabinet. Second, you can get a full-screen (Zoom) view by selecting it and pressing Recalc (F5). This recalculates the formula that is behind the Library cabinet itself. Third, you can use the Alt-F1 key, the first macro in the Library. This gives you a full-screen view of the Library cabinet from anywhere in Framework II. This is the same as selecting the Library and recalculating it, but with two advantages. First, you need not leave your current location to select the Library before viewing it. Second, as the message area will indicate, you can return immediately to your previous working location by pressing the Escape key. This can save quite a few keystrokes. (The cryptically named "Return to Caller" frame in the Library does the work of remembering where you were working and returning you there.)

The macro assigned to Alt-F2, called "Save Library Frame," is also used to manage the Library. It will save the current version of the Library to disk any time you invoke it. Again, you can accomplish the same thing by selecting the Library and pressing Ctrl-Return, but, like Alt-F1, Alt-F2 works no matter where you are located. If you have just created a new macro or abbreviation, you might want to use this key, for the same reason that you should always save your work frequently.

Alt-F3 and Alt-F4 will type the date and the time, respectively, as strings, in their most common formats. For example, pressing Alt-F3, followed by a space, then Alt-F4 in a Word frame will produce a result of the following form:

August 24, 1987 10:20 AM

This is accomplished with simple @PERFORMKEYS statements. The formula executed by Alt-F3 is

@performkeys(@date4(@today))

Alt-F4's formula is

@performkeys(@time1(@today))

Notice that these formulas do *not* include the quotation marks usually found in @PERFORMKEYS statements. If they did, the formula would be entered, rather than the result of the formula.

You cannot perform date arithmetic with the results, because they are string values, not date values. Later, however, we'll modify the time for use in conjunction with a user-defined function so that we can use the string value to do time arithmetic. We'll also look at an application where this can be extremely useful.

Alt-F5 tells you how much memory is currently available in your computer. It uses a FRED function called @MEMAVAIL, which you can use behind any frame or cell for the same purpose. However, Alt-F5 will supply the information in the message area, in a form that is easily readable:

You have 488,992 more bytes of memory available.

Moreover, like other Library macros, it can be used at any point in Framework II, without disturbing your current working environment.

Alt-F6 is a menu of templates for letters and memos. Later in the chapter, you'll learn how to write a program that produces a menu like this one. You can, of course, add your own templates to the outline contained under the Alt-F6 subheading, or modify the existing ones.

Alt-F7 and Alt-F8 are a cut-and-paste tool. Alt-F7 will copy any selected text to a special frame called Cut Paste Buffer, without disturbing that text in its original location. Alt-F8 will restore the text from this special frame to the cursor location. You could use the Copy key (F8) to perform these functions, but the macros provide considerably greater flexibility.

Together, Alt-F7 and Alt-F8 allow you to move text freely among different types of frames, and different parts of frames. You can use these keys to move text from the formula area behind a frame into the text area, or vice versa. You can also paste from a text area to a label (provided that you place the label on the editing line by pressing the Space bar first). You can even cut text from a Word frame into a Spreadsheet or a Database frame. Moreover, you can use Alt-F8 to paste the same text repeatedly into different locations.

When you get involved in programming, you will find these macros indispensable, because the Move key (F7) cannot move text from one formula area to another. If you want to use similar formulas behind several different frames, the only way to do so without retyping is to use the macros.

Alt-F9 and Alt-F10 are used to display the Phone Book frame in the Library and to dial a selected phone number, respectively. We looked at these macros in Chapter 6, in the section on "Automatic Phone Dialing."

WRITING A MACRO PROGRAM

Let's look at an example of the Library macros in use. First, we'll write the macro as a program, and then move it to the Library, just to get a feel for programming and for the power of the Library macros. Suppose you need to log your phone calls for business purposes. You set up a database called Phone Log in the Library, with the following column heads:

Date
Time
Number
Party

We'll use a number of Library macros to fill in the column entries. Follow these steps:

Alt-F9	(to open the Phone Book)
Home	(to move to the first column)
Ctrl-L	(to open the Locate menu)
S	(to select the Search option)
Name	(the name of the party you want to call)
Tab, several times	(to move to the phone number)
Alt-F10	(to dial the number)
Alt-F7	(to copy the number to the Cut Paste Buffer)
Zoom (F9)	(to close the Phone Book)

Next, you'll open the Phone Log, and move to the first empty cell in the Date column (later, you'll incorporate some FRED functions into a macro that will do this for you automatically). Continue with:

Alt-F3	(to record the date)
Tab	(to move to the Time column)
Space bar	(to begin entering text)
Alt-F4	(to enter the time, which begins with a number, as text)
Tab	(to move to the Number column)
Space bar	(to begin entering text)
Alt-F8	(to bring back the phone number from the Cut Paste Buffer)

Return   (to record the number)

Now we'll write the macro that accomplishes this task automatically. We'll create the macro as a frame on the desktop, to practice programming, and then use the Move key (F7) to move it to the Library.

There are a few considerations to be taken into account when setting up this Phone Log. Most obviously, why not simply enter the formula

@date(@today)

in the cells of the first column, and the formula

@time1(@today)

in those of the second? Principally because, if you used date and time formulas, they would all be recalculated automatically if you hit the Recalc key (F5) for any reason. If the dates and times were formulas rather than strings, every one of them would be reset to today's date and the current time whenever you used the log, which would result in no log at all. Thus, the string dates and times supplied by the Alt-F3 and Alt-F4 macros are much more useful for the purpose.

Second, what about pasting times and phone numbers into database cells? We want to treat them as text, but they begin with digits, with the result that they will be treated as invalid formulas. The way we set up our @PERFORMKEYS statement will take care of this, and will also show you the power of this function.

Begin by creating an Empty frame. Label it

{Alt-P}

and use the Edit Formula (F2) and Zoom (F9) keys to get to the full-screen programming mode. Figure 7.3 shows the formula that will be entered behind this frame.

Again, we'll assume that you have called the Phone Book by pressing Alt-F9, and already dialed your call. When you press Alt-P, your call will be recorded automatically. The statement

@performkeys("{alt-f7}{uplevel}")

copies the phone number to the buffer, and gets you out of the Phone Book. Next, the @SETSELECTION function, which you will learn a bit more about in the following section, tells Framework II to look for the frame that is specified in its parameter. The next problem is finding the first empty cell in the Phone Log. The next @PERFORMKEYS statement opens the log with the Zoom key. Ctrl-Home makes sure that you start in the upper-left corner of the database. Ctrl-↓ automatically

```
{Alt-P}        ; Log Phone calls:
    ; This macro must be used after a phone number is selected
    ; from the Phone Book. It will automatically log the date,
    ; time, and number called.

    ; First copy the phone number to the buffer with the Cut macro;
    ; then leave the Phone Book.

    @performkeys("{alt-f7}{uplevel}"),

    ; Next select the Phone Log

    @setselection("library.phone log"),

    ; Open the log and locate the first empty cell in the
    ; first column:

    @performkeys("{f9}{ctrl-home}{ctrl-dnarrow}{dnarrow}"),

    ; Enter the date, time, and phone number

    @performkeys("{alt-f3}{tab} {alt-f4}{tab} {alt-f8}{tab}"),

    ; Remind the user that the Library will disappear when you
    ; press the Escape key:

    @prompt("Press ESC when finished")
```

Figure 7.3: *A Macro to Call the Phone Log*

moves the highlight to the last cell in the column that contains data. (NOTE: You must have something—perhaps a dotted line—in cell A2 of the Phone Log, or the Ctrl-↓ command will automatically jump to the last row of the spreadsheet. A second ↓ moves down to the next cell, which is the first cell in the first empty row.)

The third @PERFORMKEYS statement could be included as part of the previous one, but it is separated here for clarity. This statement pastes the three essential items of data into the proper cells in the spreadsheet: date, time, and phone number.

Notice the spaces between several of the key names. These spaces bring the cells to the edit line as text cells, so that the time and phone number can be entered as text, rather than as numeric data.

Each of the macro keys included in the last @PERFORMKEYS statement generates prompts in the message area that will replace the prompt

Press ESC to return to where you were

which appeared when the Phone Book was opened with Alt-F9. Therefore, a prompt reminds you to press the Escape key after you have finished entering the details of the conversation.

Now that the Alt-P macro is complete, you may open the Library and move the frame into it, under the Macros subheading, using the Move key (F7).

ASSUMPTIONS

"Assumptions" can be any values that you use repeatedly. The usual reason for storing Assumptions in the Library is to have them on hand for recalculating spreadsheets. Suppose, for example, you have made various cost-price-profit analyses for different purposes in different spreadsheets. Each of these spreadsheets includes some assumptions you have made about the current interest rate and the current rate of inflation. You can store these values in frames (in the contents area, not in the formula area) under the Assumptions subheading in the Library. In order to use them, just refer to them as if they were FRED functions. For example, if you want to use the inflation rate as part of a formula in a cell, you might write a formula like

@sum(B3:B17) * @inflation

If the inflation rate changes, replace the figure in the Library Assumptions frame labeled Inflation with the new value, and any spreadsheet that refers to that frame will automatically take on the new value when you recalculate it.

As you can see from a cursory glance through the Assumptions in the Library, these frames can also store text. If you place the name of your company in the frame labeled Your Company, then any cell behind which you enter the formula

@your company

will display the name of your company. This may not be so useful for text values such as a name (an abbreviation might be more appropriate). However, it is a distinct advantage when you want to treat numbers as text, as in addresses and zip codes.

USER-DEFINED FUNCTIONS

One of the joys of a programming language such as FRED is its extensibility—if you need a function that it doesn't include, you can write it.

Suppose, for example, that you use a computer at home. The Internal Revenue Service requires you to log the time you spend on your computer for business purposes. FRED has functions that will perform date arithmetic—@SUMDATE and @DIFFDATE. But it has no equivalent functions for time. After we have looked further at FRED programming functions, we'll write a new function that will find the time elapsed between two times—the @DIFFTIME function. We'll also look at how the log should be set up, and suggest some ways of making it work automatically.

The FRED macro functions, @PERFORMKEYS and @SETSELEC-TION, are only two of many available programming functions. The next section of this chapter presents a survey of several other programming categories.

FRED PROGRAMMING FUNCTIONS

In this section we'll look briefly at the various categories of programming activities and structures we discussed earlier, and we'll mention some of the functions FRED provides in these categories. These are the programming categories we'll look at:

- Input and output
- Variables and arrays
- Decisions
- Loops
- Subroutines
- Control of frames

For more information about the functions we discuss here, consult Appendix B, which presents a complete glossary of all the FRED functions. Also, the sample program in the final section of this chapter shows examples of many of these functions in use.

INPUT AND OUTPUT

Programs are said to be *interactive* if they can accept information that is entered from the keyboard during the course of the program's performance. Such programs often present *prompts* on the screen, to tell the user what kind of input information is expected at that point in the program. FRED includes a group of functions that allow you to plan and write interactive programs. These functions present messages on the display screen and accept input information from the keyboard.

The @PROMPT and @ERASEPROMPT functions allow you to make programmed use of the message area below the Framework II desktop. @PROMPT places a message on the screen; @ERASE-PROMPT erases any information currently in the message area.

For receiving information from the keyboard, using the edit line as the input location, FRED offers the @INPUTLINE function. This function can display a prompt at the bottom of the screen, and if you wish you can make it imitate several of the usual edit line characteristics.

@INPUTLINE causes FRED to wait for a value to be entered from the keyboard. When the user presses the Return key (to complete the input process), the input value itself is returned as the value of the @INPUTLINE function. Within a program, this value can be assigned to a variable for storage; for example:

```
Company : = @inputline("What company do you work for?")
```

If a program needs to display more information than will fit in the message area at the bottom of the screen, the @DISPLAY function can be used for displaying an entire existing frame on the desktop.

FRED also offers the @MENU function for displaying programmer-prepared menus on the screen and waiting for the user to select an option from the menu. To set up a menu, you create an Outline frame, with subframes that represent the menu's options. The formula residing behind each subframe provides instructions that FRED will follow when the user selects the corresponding menu option. @MENU takes, as its single parameter, a reference to the Outline frame that represents a menu of options. We'll see an example of @MENU later.

VARIABLES AND ARRAYS

Programs often require temporary storage space for numeric and string data values that are generated during the course of a program's performance. Programming languages provide various means of defining *variables*, to which a program can refer by name, to store and later recall specific values when they are needed. FRED offers two kinds of structures that can act as variables: frames on the desktop or variables created through the @LOCAL function.

In FRED programs, any frame that is on the desktop during a program's performance, or in the Library, can act as a *global* variable in a program. Such space is available to any section of the program, even if the program is divided into many "subroutine" modules. In Chapter 5 we found two ways to assign values to a frame, spreadsheet cell, or database field: using the @SET function or the symbol ":=".

You can also set up *local* variables, for the private use of one individual subroutine in a program. The @LOCAL function defines such variables simply by giving them names. Once you have defined local variables, the @SET function or the ":=" symbol can be used to assign values to those variables. However, when the work of a subroutine is complete and control passes to some other section of the program, any local variables defined by the previous subroutine are lost.

Sometimes it is convenient for a program to be able to work with lists or tables of variables; in programming languages such as BASIC and Pascal, such groups of variables are called *arrays*. In FRED, a programmer can simulate the structure of an array by providing a spreadsheet or a database of values for the program to work with.

Two special FRED functions, @GET and @PUT, allow the programmer to read from and write to a range of spreadsheet cells or database fields. These functions are used within a *loop* structure to process an entire range of cells or fields, one value at a time.

This *range* processing, using @GET and @PUT, is similar to the way a BASIC program might process the information in an array, using a FOR loop. However, there is an important difference. Arrays in BASIC and Pascal are numerically *indexed*. If you want to access any particular value in an array of variables, you refer to the correct index value in the array.

The @GET and @PUT functions, on the other hand, set up a pointer in the range. As the range of values is processed, the @NEXT function is used to move the pointer forward in the range, value by value. Thus the processing must occur sequentially, from the beginning of the range to the end. Direct access of one particular value in the range is not possible with @GET and @PUT, although the more complicated @HLOOKUP and @VLOOKUP can accomplish this.

FRED also has the @ITEM function, which is useful for passing up to 16 parameters of information from one subroutine to another. We'll examine this function when we discuss subroutines.

DECISIONS

The @IF function is a tool for introducing decision making into a FRED program. We had some experience with @IF in Chapter 5. @IF takes three parameters—a logical expression and two values or formulas:

@if(*logical expression, formula1, formula2*)

If the *logical expression* has a value of #TRUE, the @IF function evaluates *formula1* and returns its value; otherwise, @IF evaluates and returns the value of *formula2*.

Sometimes the three-parameter structure of the @IF function is too confining. A programmer may want to choose between two *groups* of formulas, depending on the value of the logical expression. For times like this, FRED provides the @LIST function.

@LIST allows you to place a group of formulas in a location where structurally there is room for only one. In an @IF function, we might picture the use of @LIST as follows:

```
@if(logical expression,
    @list(formula1,
    formula2,
    formula3,
    formula4),   ; end of first list
@list(formula5,
      formula6,
      formula7,
      formula8) ; end of second list
)               ; end of @if
```

In this example, a value of #TRUE for the logical expression will result in evaluation of the first list of formulas. A value of #FALSE sends control to the second list of formulas.

For building compound and complex logical expressions, FRED provides the three functions @AND, @OR, and @NOT. Both @AND and @OR take a series of parameters and result in a logical value, #TRUE or #FALSE.

For @AND to return a value of #TRUE, *all* its parameters must be #TRUE. @OR, however, returns a value of #TRUE if *any* of its parameters are true.

The @NOT function negates the value of its single parameter. If the parameter is #TRUE, @NOT returns a value of #FALSE. If the parameter is #FALSE, @NOT returns a value of #TRUE.

LOOPS

A programming loop provides a structure for repeated processing of a series of formulas. Different programming languages provide different kinds of looping structures. Loops in FRED are created by the @WHILE function.

@WHILE takes an unspecified number of parameters. Its first parameter is a logical expression; subsequent parameters are formulas to be processed:

```
@while(logical expression,
        formula,
        formula,
        formula, ...
        )                           ; end of @while
```

The formula parameters of the @WHILE function are processed repeatedly, in sequence from first to last, as long as the logical expression remains #TRUE.

Normally some event within the repeated activity will ultimately switch the logical value to #FALSE. When this occurs, processing of the formulas stops after the current iteration. (If the logical expression is #FALSE from the outset, the formulas will never be evaluated at all.)

We discussed earlier the use of the @GET and @PUT functions to process a range of values within a loop. A special FRED constant called #NULL! is available for this kind of range processing. The @GET function returns a value of #NULL! when it reaches the end of the range of values it is processing.

In an @WHILE function that uses @GET to process a range of values, #NULL! will appear as part of the logical expression; for example:

```
@while(@get(range) < > #NULL!,
        formula,
        formula,
        formula, ...
        @next(range)
        )
```

After @GET processes each value in the range, the @NEXT function (at the end of the @WHILE loop) moves the range pointer forward by one value. When the last range value has been processed and @NEXT tries to move the pointer forward again, the next evaluation of @GET will return a value of #NULL!, thus ending the @WHILE loop.

We'll see an example of this kind of range processing in the sample program at the end of the chapter.

SUBROUTINES

Framework II's outlining function makes it easy to write FRED programs that are well planned, modularized, and structured into logical levels of control. Frames at every level of the outline can contain subroutines, stored in the formula area behind the frame itself. The outer, containing frame might make a series of subroutine calls to the frames within the outline. Each subframe, in turn, might call upon the subroutines located in frames at lower levels.

Ideally, the frames located at the higher levels of the outline will control the broad structure of the program; they will be devoted primarily to subroutine calls to frames lower in the outline. The frames at the lowest levels will contain the FRED code for accomplishing specific details of the task at hand. This kind of organization leads to subroutines that are short, easy to identify, and easy to debug if necessary.

The structure of a subroutine call in FRED is identical to a function call. To perform a program contained in a given frame, simply place the "@" symbol before a reference to the frame:

@frame name

This call causes FRED to transfer control of the program to the frame you have referenced and to perform (or "recalculate") the formula residing behind the frame.

You can also send up to 16 parameter values to a subroutine, again in the same format that you would use for a FRED function:

@frame name(1st value, 2nd value, 3rd value, . . . , 16th value)

To make use of the parameter values sent to it, the subroutine you are calling simply refers to the functions @ITEM1, @ITEM2, @ITEM3, . . . , @ITEM16. These functions return the values of the corresponding parameters that have been passed to the subroutine.

When the work of a subroutine is complete, control of the program returns to the program location from which the subroutine was originally called. The @RETURN or @RESULT functions can be used to return a specific value from the subroutine.

CONTROLLING THE FRAMES ON THE DESKTOP

FRED also has a special set of functions that allow you to manipulate and work with frames from within a program. These functions are unique, with no real parallels in other programming languages. Through these functions, FRED and Framework II manage to work even more closely together than we have seen up to now.

These functions include @EXECUTE, for changing and then recalculating the formula behind a frame; @PRINT, for printing a frame from within a FRED program; @SETSELECTION, for moving the highlight to a specific frame on the desktop; and @PERFORMKEYS, a function that we have already seen can be useful for performing keyboard commands that affect frames.

Together, these functions allow you to perform, from within a FRED program, any frame operation that is available in Framework II. In the program example at the end of the chapter, we'll see how efficiently all these functions can be used.

GETTING HELP

As you learn to program in FRED, several sources of help are available to you in Framework II. They include

- Sample programs

- The on-line help system

- the @TRACE function

Let's look briefly at these facilities.

SAMPLE PROGRAMS

One of the most effective ways of learning to program is to study examples of programs that work, and modify them. To assist you, Framework II includes sample programs on the System 2, Apps, Spell, and Tutorial 1 disks. These programs are not designed as fully functioning applications. However, they provide samples of the kinds of applications you can create, and the code needed to create them. Following is a brief description of the sample programs, the data files they use, and their locations on disk. All these files have the .FW2 extension.

- *FRAMEDEX* is a program designed to maintain and filter a database, log phone calls, and set up a call-back system. It is located on the Spell disk. It is designed to work with the database file FD_NAA (FrameDex name and address), on the same disk. It includes an ad for a program called Time Frame, which functions as an "appointment calendar and office assistant," available from Ashton-Tate.

☐ *LEGALDOC*, also on the Spell disk, is a set of instructions and a loader program for a sample document designed to demonstrate the use of "boilerplate" text. The document itself is the file LEGAL2. It contains a sample agreement between a software developer and a software publisher.

☐ *RUNDBASE*, on System Disk 2, is designed to run dBASE III from the desktop. We'll look at this program, and make some modifications to it, in the next chapter.

☐ *CROSSTAB* is a program designed to filter a database and perform numeric operations on the resulting database—a more elaborate version of what we did with the Sales People database in Chapter 5. It is supplied on the Apps disk, along with the sample file CRSTABDB.

☐ *HISTOGRM*, also on the Apps disk, produces a histogram in an Empty frame from spreadsheet data.

☐ *DSUMDCNT*, on the Apps disk, contains a pair of user-defined functions: one to sum all items in a range matching certain criteria, and one to count them. Both functions also provide further demonstration of the use of @WHILE loops.

☐ *REFORMAT*, on the Apps disk, strips hard carriage returns from a Word frame and reformats the text with a right margin that you specify at a prompt.

☐ *DBREPORT*, on the Tutorial 1 disk, is a menu-driven program to create reports from a database. The menu includes options for creating a printing template, loading a printing template from disk, filtering the database, and setting up the printing formats.

☐ *NEWSLETR*, also on the Tutorial 1 disk, contains sample text for a newsletter and a client database, with a menu for mailmerge printing of the newsletter and mailing labels.

ON-LINE HELP

As with the rest of Framework II, on-line help is provided for programming in FRED via the Help key (F1). The help system includes an overview of the language, complete with descriptions of every constant, error code, and operator. There is also a brief tutorial on writing user menus. An additional portion of the help system is devoted to an index to FRED functions, containing brief descriptions of every FRED function and its syntax, and a quick review of the key names used in FRED.

THE @TRACE FUNCTION

When you have written a program that doesn't quite work as you intended, it is extremely helpful to be able to follow the code, step by step, as it executes. For this purpose, the FRED language includes a function called @TRACE. To use this function, follow these steps:

1. Create two Empty frames.

2. Label one frame A and the other B (you can use other labels, but since the frames will probably be temporary, you might as well use something simple).

3. Select frame B, and press the Edit key (F2) to access the formula area.

4. Enter the formula

   @trace(a, #ON)

Once you have entered this formula, the name of every function that is executed will appear in frame A, followed on the next line by the result of that function's execution. For example, as soon as you enter the formula in frame B, frame A will display

   TRACE Result: #ON

The results of formulas that make selections will appear underlined. Tracing will continue until you enter the formula

   @trace(a, #OFF)

or delete either frame A or frame B from the desktop.

Now it's time for a short visit to The Sophisticated Palate to follow up on a FRED program that we talked about in Chapter 5.

EXAMPLES

Look back at Eileen Wilcox's Packaged Goods Inventory database in Figure 5.15. Recall Eileen's dilemma as she prepared to write a formula to calculate the wholesale prices of her inventory items. Eileen wanted this field, called Whsl Pr, to contain values showing a 45 percent markup on the prices cost per case. She could have stored a simple calculation formula behind the Whsl Pr field name:

Whsl Pr : = CostPerCase * 1.45

But when Eileen tried this formula, she didn't like the wholesale prices that were calculated. Prices ended in odd numbers of cents; for example:

$2.31
$2.64
$1.82
$3.55
$2.97

She knew that her customers would be used to seeing wholesale prices assigned in a more consistent manner.

COMPUTING "ATTRACTIVE" PRICES

To achieve this effect, Eileen wrote the small FRED program shown in Figure 7.4. She entered this entire program behind the field name Whsl Pr at the top row of her database table. The program then calculated the final wholesale prices that you can see in Figure 5.15.

```
Packaged Goods Inventory.Whsl Pr:
  ; Formula for "Attractiveness Pricing"

  @local(pr,        ; the calculated wholesale price
        temp,       ; the last digit aver the decimal point
        add         ; the amount, in cents, to add on
        ),
  pr := @round(CostPerCase * 1.45,2),          ; find the price
  temp := 10 * (pr * 10 - @int(pr * 10)),      ; isolate the last digit
  add := @if(temp>5, 9-temp, 5-temp),          ; find how much to add
  Whsl Pr := pr + add/100
```

Figure 7.4: Formula for Computing "Attractive" Prices

Let's examine this program. As you can see, the program contains rather extensive comments that describe what is happening on each line.

The program begins by defining three local variables, using the @LOCAL function:

```
@local(pr,
        temp,
        add
        ),
```

These variables are used in the various steps of the calculation that the formula performs.

In the next line of the program, the variable PR receives the wholesale markup, calculated as a simple 45 percent increase over the cost per case:

```
pr := @round(CostPerCase * 1.45, 2),
```

The @ROUND function rounds a value to a specified number of decimal places. @ROUND takes two parameters: the value to be rounded and the desired number of decimal places. As you can see, this formula rounds the calculated wholesale price, PR, to two decimal places.

The next line isolates the last digit in the value of PR and assigns it to the variable TEMP:

```
temp := 10 * (pr * 10 - @int(pr * 10)),
```

This rather convoluted algorithm uses the @INT function to find the integral value of PR * 10. When this integral value is subtracted from the product of PR * 10, the last digit of PR is the result; this result needs to be multiplied by 10 again to yield a single-digit integer.

The value of the variable ADD, calculated in the next line, represents the number of cents that need to be added to the calculated wholesale price, PR, to yield a price ending in 5 or 9. The @IF function is instrumental in determining this value:

```
add := @if(temp>5, 9 - temp, 5 - temp),
```

If the digit TEMP is greater than 5, Eileen will add enough pennies to yield a price ending in 9. Otherwise, if TEMP is less than or equal to 5, she will add enough pennies to yield a price ending in 5. Given ADD, the number of pennies to add, the last line of the program actually calculates the field Whsl Pr:

```
Whsl Pr := pr + add/100
```

Writing programs like this one can prove useful in many Spreadsheet and Database frames. Because you can use the full-screen edit mode to produce a formula for any spreadsheet cell or database field, you can easily write and experiment with customized, multistep arithmetic formulas like Eileen's.

EXPLORING FURTHER

THE LETTERS PROGRAM

In this section we'll examine a complete and somewhat detailed FRED program. The program works with two databases we studied in Chapter 5: the Sales People database and the Supervisors database. (You can review these two databases by looking back at Figures 5.9 and 5.22.)

Sales People, you'll recall, contains the following fields of information about a group of 18 sales employees: employee number, last name, first name, work region, total sales for the last six months, average monthly sales, probation status (#YES or #NO), date hired, and years with the firm. The Supervisors database contains information about the six regions in which these sales people work: the region name, the regional supervisor, the regional office address, the city, the state, and the zip code.

The program we're going to look at is called Letters. Its task is to write two sets of form letters to two different groups of sales people. To create the letters, the program merges information from the Sales People and Supervisors databases.

The first group of sales people consists of all the employees who are on probation. Each person in this group is to receive a warning letter like the example shown in Figure 7.5. Along with its actual message, the letter contains the sales person's name and complete regional address; the average monthly sales that the person achieved; and the name of the person's supervisor, on the "cc:" line at the bottom of the letter.

The second group of sales people who are to receive letters consists of those who achieved sales of $100,000 or better during the six-month period. Figure 7.6 shows an example of the congratulatory letter written for these people. The letter contains the same individual information as the warning letter—name, address, average monthly sales, and supervisor.

The Letters program automatically prepares and prints these letters to all the sales people in both groups. This exercise may be performed repeatedly over time. For example, suppose that you revise and update the Sales People database after six more months; the Letters program could once again generate two sets of letters to the sales people who at that time fall into the two special groups.

In the process of preparing these letters to the sales force, the program works its way through a sequence eight of rather interesting programmed tasks.

```
                                    June 9, 1987

          Donny Brooke
          89 Lindel Road
          St. Louis, MO 63123

          Dear Donny:

                We are sorry to  note that your  sales record for
          the  last  six months  has not been  satisfactory. Your
          average monthly sales were  $9,739.89.  We hope you can
          do better than this in the future;  we'll be keeping an
          eye on your progress.

                                       Sincerely yours,




          cc: Anthony Stark
```

Figure 7.5: *Warning Letter to Probationary Sales People*

```
                                    June 9, 1987

          Anne Rizzo
          6700 Charleston Road
          Suite 32
          Boston, MA 02108

          Dear Anne:

                We are  delighted to note that  your sales record
          for the last six months has been  excellent. Your aver-
          age monthly sales were  $19,605.41.  Congratulations on
          your very high  achievement.  We hope you will continue
          to do as well in the future.

                                       Sincerely yours,




          cc: Dane Whitman
```

Figure 7.6: *Congratulatory Letter to Best Sales People*

1. It creates a new database, called Sales Addresses, with room for all the pertinent fields of the Sales People database, plus space to append the correct address to each record.

2. It copies the Sales People database into the containing frame, and moves the information from it into the Sales Addresses database, deleting the Sales People database when the task is completed.

3. It copies the Supervisors database into the containing frame, and merges data from this database (supervisor's last name and first name, address, suite, city, state, zip) into the Sales Addresses database, then deletes the Supervisors database.

4. It presents a menu on the screen, allowing you, the user, to select which group of letters you wish to produce. Figures 7.7 and 7.8 show two views of this menu. The menu has only two options, but the explanatory message displayed at the bottom of the screen changes according to the option that is highlighted.

5. Once you have chosen one of the two menu options, the program filters the Sales Addresses database according to the criterion that you have selected: all those who are on probation, or all those who achieved sales over $100,000.

6. The program uses the filtered database to perform a mailmerge with one of two predesigned letter templates, representing the warning letter and the congratulatory letter. These templates contain the text of the two letters, with mailmerge fields included for the information from the database.

7. The program then prints the filled-in form letters onto paper, generating one letter for each sales person in the selected group.

8. Finally, before returning you to the desktop, the new Sales Addresses database is deleted.

Since this is a task that might be performed every six months, why not simply save the new database, with the information from both of the original databases, within the frame for later use? There are several reasons. First, there is no reason to store the same information (the address of every regional office, and the name of the local supervisor) twice. Second, by avoiding the redundancy of having two copies of the

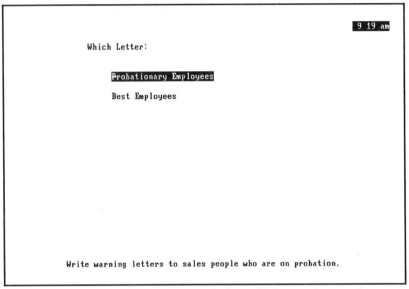

Figure 7.7: *The Which Letter Menu, with the Highlight over the First Option*

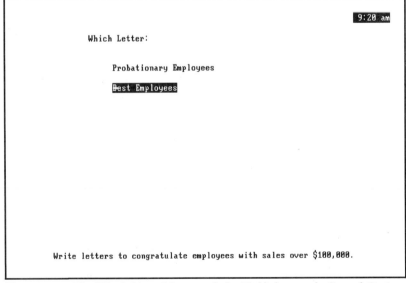

Figure 7.8: *The Which Letter Menu, with the Highlight over the Second Option*

same information, you make it easier to keep the information current. If a new supervisor is hired, for example, only one database needs to be updated. Third, your information is more likely to be accurate. If a sales person transfers to a different region, you need only change the "Reg" field in the Sales People database. There is no danger of your copying the address incorrectly, because it is safely stored in another database. For these reasons, it is much safer to create the database with the combined information only when you need it.

THE STRUCTURE OF THE LETTERS PROGRAM

The modules of the Letters program, along with the documents that the program works with, are stored in a single Outline frame called Letters. The frame is shown, in Outline view, in Figure 7.9. You can see that the first two subframes contained inside the outline are the form letters: Good and Bad. The print formatting for these frames has been set up on the Print menu. The date, which does not appear in the form letter templates, is added by using the formula

<date4>

as a header, centered, on line 11. The top margin is set at 13 lines, to allow space for the company letterhead. Figure 7.10 shows the template for the "Good" letter.

The third subframe in the Letters frame is an outline within the outline. It is called Program, and its frames and subframes contain the FRED program modules that perform the letter-writing tasks.

The first two subframes under the Program heading represent the global-variable storage space that the program requires:

- Region is a frame that will contain the name of the region for which the addresses are being transferred to the merged database.

- Letter Code is a frame that is assigned one of two codes, depending on which kind of letter is currently being prepared— "P" for "probation" letter and "B" for "best" letter. This variable is used throughout the program, to determine which letter template should be used, to determine the formula that filters the Sales Addresses database, and to determine which letter template should receive the information from the Supervisors database.

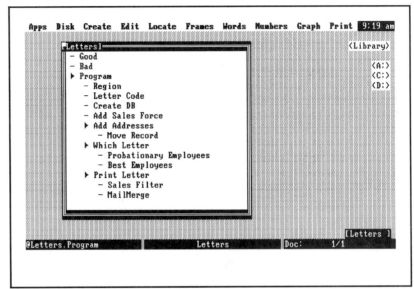

Figure 7.9: Outline of the Letters Program

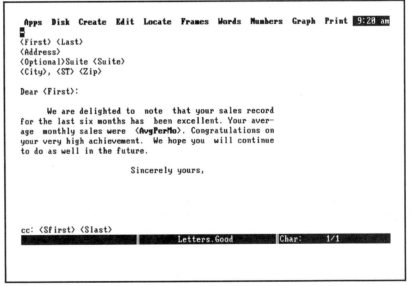

Figure 7.10: The "Good" Form Letter

The following three frames do most of the work of the program:

- □ Create DB uses a complex @PERFORMKEYS statement to create a database frame of appropriate dimensions for Sales Addresses and fill in some of the column heads (the rest of the column heads will be transferred directly from the Sales People database).

- □ Add Sales Force brings the Sales People database into the frame from disk (it is assumed that this database is on the default drive and directory), and copies all but the last two columns of that database ("Hired" and "Yrs", which are not needed for this task) into the Sales Addresses database.

- □ Add Addresses begins by bringing the Supervisors database into the frame from disk. It then repeatedly filters the Sales Addresses database so that the records for only one region are displayed. After the Sales Addresses database has been filtered, this frame calls a subroutine called Move Record, which performs the actual copying of information from the Supervisors database to the Sales Addresses database.

Continuing down the program outline, you'll see a frame called Which Letter. This frame is itself a short outline that the program uses for displaying the menu on the screen:

> ► Which Letter
> 　–Probationary Employees
> 　–Best Employees

We will see later how the @MENU function works with this outline, as well as the formulas that the outline contains.

Finally, the Print Letter outline contains two simple modules:

- □ Sales Filter filters the Sales Addresses database so that it includes only the records that are appropriate for the letter you want to print.

- □ MailMerge selects the correct form letter and performs the mailmerge.

Let's look at the Letters program, module by module, and see what it can teach us about FRED programming.

INSIDE THE LETTERS PROGRAM

To run the program, first load the Letters Outline frame from disk. Make sure that the Supervisors and Sales People databases are in the default directory of the default drive. Then select the Letters frame, and press the Recalc key (F5). The first formula that is executed is behind the containing frame itself. As you may recall, you can cause the formula in a frame to be executed by referring to the frame with an @ symbol:

@Letters.Program

This formula simply directs FRED to execute the program in the frame called Program, which is shown in Figure 7.11.

```
Letters.Program:
    ; Call the subroutines to create the merged database.

@Letters.Program.Create DB,
@Letters.Program.Add Sales Force,
@Letters.Program.Add Addresses,

    ; Call the menu to choose the letter to be printed.

@menu(Letters.Program.Which Letter),

    ; When the program is finished, delete the new database.

@setselection("Letters.Sales Addresses"),
@performkeys("{del}"),

    ; If the program is interrupted, restore Outline view.

@if(@isabend, @performkeys("{f10}{ctrl-uplevel}"))
```

Figure 7.11: The Formulas behind the Letters.Program Outline

The formulas behind the Letters.Program frame contain the master program. The first four formulas do nothing but call the subroutines that do the actual work:

@Letters.Program.Create DB,

@Letters.Program.Add Sales Force,

@Letters.Program.Add Addresses,

@menu(Letters.Program.Which Letter),

The remainder of the frame contains some cleanup routines to be performed after the program is finished. First the new database is selected and deleted:

```
@setselection("Letters.Sales Addresses"),
@performkeys("{del}"),
```

Finally, we have one of FRED's *error-trapping* functions. @ISABEND stands for "is abnormal end." It is contained in the formula

```
@if(@isabend, @performkeys("{f10}{ctrl-uplevel}"))
```

Since most of the work of the program consists of entering data into the Sales Addresses database, the Letters frame must be switched from Outline view to Frames view before the work can begin, because you cannot go inside a frame in Outline view. If you interrupt the program by pressing Ctrl-Break before it has finished executing, this formula will notice the "abnormal end" to the program, and restore the containing frame to Outline view, placing the highlight on the outer frame.

CREATING THE SALES ADDRESSES DATABASE

The new database is created by three subroutines, one of which has a subroutine of its own:

```
–Create DB
–Add Sales Force
► Add Addresses
   –Move Record
```

Each of these subroutines begins by displaying a message and then halting the screen display. The latter is accomplished by a call to the FRED function @ECHO, which controls whether the effects of FRED functions are displayed on the screen. @ECHO takes one of two FRED constants, #ON or #OFF. @ECHO is set to its OFF status during the execution of these frames for two reasons. First, it spares the user from having to watch as the screen changes frantically. Second, the program executes much more quickly if it does not have to display every change on the screen as it proceeds.

The @PROMPT function displays a message as each subroutine begins, so you know that the program is still working while nothing changes on the screen. The second parameter in the @PROMPT statement, a number, determines how many spaces from the left margin the message will appear. Each subroutine ends by restoring screen echoing to #ON, so that the initial message of the next subroutine can be displayed.

Figure 7.12 shows the Create DB frame. It consists mostly of one long @PERFORMKEYS statement. Notice the use of the *string concatenation operator,* "&". This symbol allows you to add a string to the end of the previous string. Although a FRED program statement can be as long as 255 characters, it is much easier to read if it is broken into small sections that will fit on the screen. You could, alternatively, create a whole series of short @PERFORMKEYS statements, but a single statement executes much more quickly than a series of statements, because Framework II has to look up the meaning of each FRED function before it executes it.

```
Letters.Program.Create DB:
  ; Create the empty Sales Addresses database.

  @prompt("Please wait . . . creating database.", 22),  ; Display message.

  @echo(#OFF),       ; Freeze screen activity during program performance.

  ; Use the Create menu to create a database of appropriate dimensions,
  ; inside the Letters frame.

  @performkeys("{f10}{dnlevel}{ctrl-c}w14{return}h18{return}d"

            ; Label the database frame.

          & "Sales Addresses{return}"

            ; Widen the SixMoSales column.

          & "{f9}{tab}{tab}{tab}{tab}{tab}{f4}"
          & "{rightarrow}{rightarrow}{rightarrow}{return}"

            ; Label the columns for the new data.

          & "{tab}{tab}Slast{tab}Sfirst{tab}Address"
          & "{tab}Suite{tab}City{tab}ST{tab}Zip{return}{uplevel}"),

  @echo(#ON)       ; Restore screen activity so next message can be displayed.
```

Figure 7.12: The Create DB Subroutine

Breaking up the statement into several lines also allows you to add comments, so that you will remember what each segment of the statement is supposed to do. In the first line,

```
@performkeys("{f10}{dnlevel}{ctrl-c}w14{return}h18{return}d"
```

F10 first switches to Frames view, so that the frame can be entered. Next, the Down Level key ensures that the database will be created within the Letters frame, but not within the Program frame. The rest of this line issues the Create menu commands to create a Database frame with appropriate dimensions.

The following lines place a label in the new frame, move the high-light to the fifth column and widen it, and place labels in the columns that will hold the new data, so that the fields can be referred to by name in the mailmerge form letter. It is necessary to widen the fifth column, which contains the AvgPerMo field, because it is not wide enough to display the numbers, displaying asterisks instead. This is no problem when the formulas are recalculated, because the formula resides behind the frame. When a mailmerge is performed, however, it is the text displayed in the cells that is copied into the form letter. If the AvgPerMo field were not widened, asterisks would appear in the form letters, instead of the correct sales figures. It is not necessary to widen the Six-MoSales column because, although the column is used to determine the best employees, the figures themselves are not used in the letters.

Finally, column labels are placed in the right-hand columns of the database, to be used as field names in the form letter. This is not necessary for the left-hand columns because they will be copied from the Sales People database.

If you want to see exactly how this routine works, you can place a semicolon before the

    @echo (#OFF)

statement, or type in all the keystrokes of the @PERFORMKEYS statement.

The Add Sales Force subroutine, shown in Figure 7.13, has the job of transferring the data from the Sales People database to the new Sales Addresses database. With one exception, this routine is also essentially one long @PERFORMKEYS statement.

First the database is brought from disk into the Letters frame by the following menu command:

    @performkeys("{ctrl-d}gSALES_PE{return}"

Next, the Open All command from the Frames menu is issued, in case the database had been stored on disk in a filtered state, and the cursor is placed in the upper-left corner:

    & "{ctrl-f}o{dnlevel}{ctrl-home}"

The highlight is extended over the entire contents of the frame, and then moved back two columns by the keystokes

    {leftarrow}{leftarrow}

This is the quickest way to select the portion of the database that we want to use.

```
Letters.Program.Add Sales Force:
     ; Transfer the data from the Sales People database to the Sales
     ; Addresses database.

     @prompt("Adding Sales People to database", 25),      ; Display message.
     @echo(#OFF),       ; Freeze screen activity during program performance.

     ; Load the Sales People database from disk.

     @performkeys("{ctrl-d}gSALES_PE{return}"

     ; Initialize the database by opening all frames and placing
     ; the cursor in the upper-left corner.

               & "{ctrl-f}o{dnlevel}{ctrl-home}"

     ; Select the columns to be copied.

               & "{f6}{ctrl-end}{leftarrow}{leftarrow}{f7}{uplevel}"),

     ; Copy the data to the Sales Addresses database.

     @setselection("Letters.Sales Addresses"),
     @performkeys("{dnlevel}{ctrl-home}{return}{uplevel}"),

     ; Delete the Sales People database.

     @setselection("Letters.Sales People"),
     @performkeys("{del}"),

     @echo(#ON)       ; Restore screen activity so next message can be displayed.
```

Figure 7.13: The Add Sales Force Subroutine

It is difficult, when issuing keystrokes by means of a program, to know exactly where a frame will be located, especially if it has been created or put in place by the program itself. Therefore, instead of using

{uparrow}

or

{dnarrow}

to move to another frame, the @SETSELECTION statement is used. It makes the frame named in its argument the currently selected frame. In this instance, it selects the destination we want to move the data to:

@setselection("Letters.Sales Addresses")

In a FRED program like this one, the @SETSELECTION statement can function as though it were part of the @PERFORMKEYS statement. The move, which was started in the previous @PERFORMKEYS statement, is still waiting for the Return key to establish its destination while the @SETSELECTION statement is executed. The move is finally completed by the statement

@performkeys("{dnlevel}{ctrl-home}{return}{uplevel}"),

after which the Sales People database is deleted.

The third subroutine, Add Addresses, is the most complex part of the program. It appears in Figure 7.14. The complexity arises from the use of two *region-walking* functions, @GET and @NEXT. Because of its complexity, it deserves a thorough explanation.

```
Letters.Program.Add Addresses:
    ; Copy addresses from Supervisors database to the proper records
    ; in the Sales Addresses database.

    @prompt("Transferring addresses to database", 23),    ; Display message.
    @echo(#OFF),       ; Freeze screen activity during program performance.

    ; Load the Supervisors database from disk.

    @performkeys("{ctrl-d}gSUPERVIS{return}"),

    ; Initialize the database for both copying and region walking.

    @performkeys("{dnlevel}{ctrl-home}{uplevel}"),
    @reset(Letters.Supervisors.Reg),

    ; Process the first record.

    Letters.Program.Region := @get(Letters.Supervisors.Reg),
    @execute(Letters.Sales Addresses, Reg = Letters.Program.Region),
    @Add Addresses.Move Record,

    ; Process the remaining records.

    @while(@next(Letters.Supervisors.Reg) <> #NULL!,
        @setselection("Letters.Sales Addresses"),
        @performkeys("{ctrl-f}o"),       ; Reopen the database after filtering.
        Letters.Program.Region := @get(Letters.Supervisors.Reg),
        @execute(Letters.Sales Addresses, Reg = Letters.Program.Region),
        @Add Addresses.Move Record,
    ),                                   ; End of the @WHILE loop.

    ; Delete the Supervisors database.

    @setselection("Letters.Supervisors"),
    @performkeys("{del}"),

    @echo(#ON)       ; Restore screen activity so next message can be displayed.
```

Figure 7.14: *The Add Addresses Subroutine*

Like the Add Sales Force subroutine, the Add Addresses subroutine begins by displaying a message, bringing the appropriate database from disk into the Letters frame, and initializing it. This frame, however, requires two types of initialization. Because the region-walking is quite separate from any cursor movement, the @PERFORMKEYS statement places the cursor in the upper-left cell to prepare for copying, while the statement

@reset(Letters.Supervisors.Reg),

places the range pointer at the beginning of the range.

The bulk of the subroutine is an extensive @WHILE loop, but because of some peculiarities of the region-walking functions in FRED, the first record must be processed before the loop begins. The first step in processing each record is to use the @GET statement to read the name of the next region in the Reg column. However, the @NEXT statement, which determines when the loop should end, moves the pointer to the next record. If the first record were not processed before the loop began, it would be skipped.

The @WHILE loop steps through the Supervisors database, repeatedly filtering the Sales Addresses database for each region, and copying the supervisor's name and regional office address to the appropriate records. The Reg field is used to control iterations of the loop itself:

@while(@next(Letters.Supervisors.Reg) < > #NULL!,

@NEXT, like @GET, takes a *range* parameter. In the case of a Database frame, the field name itself represents a range—that is, an entire column in the database.

If the @GET statement were used to control the loop instead of the @NEXT statement, the column would be read until the condition indicated by #NULL! (the end of the database column) were reached. However, since the copying occurs *after* the @WHILE statement, the last record would be read twice. Since the @GET statement is used to filter the database, the final pass through the loop would copy the last record to a database filtered on a null value. That is, the database would appear to have no records in it; as a result, the last record would be copied into the column heads, replacing the field names, with disastrous results. The peculiar construction of this subroutine avoids the problem.

The statement

Letters.Program.Region : = @get(Letters.Supervisors.Reg),

reads the first record in the Reg column, and assigns it to the global variable contained in the frame Region. This is necessary if the result of the reading process is to be available to the Sales Addresses database, because otherwise the results of region-walking functions are known only in the frame in which they occur.

The next statement filters the Sales Addresses database so that it contains only the sales people for the region whose name is stored in the

Region frame. The main tool for doing this is the @EXECUTE function. @EXECUTE, you may recall, places a new formula behind a specified frame and then recalculates the formula. One of its most useful applications is filtering databases during a program's performance. The format of @EXECUTE is

> @execute(*frame name, formula*)

After the database is filtered, the Move Record subroutine, which we will look at shortly, performs the actual copying of the data. You will note that these three statements—the statement containing @GET, the @EXECUTE statement, and the call to the Move Record subroutine—also appear inside the @WHILE loop.

The only other statements in the @WHILE loop are in charge of reopening the database before it is filtered again. The database is selected, and the Frames menu is used to restore it:

> @setselection("Letters.Sales Addresses"),
> @performkeys("{ctrl-f}o"),

Because these statements are at the end of the loop, the database will be fully open after all the addresses have been added, so that it can be filtered to select the employees to whom letters will be written.

At the end of the subroutine, the Supervisors database is deleted, in the same manner as the Sales People database was deleted.

The Move Record subroutine, which is called after the first record in the Supervisors database is selected, and then again during each pass through the loop, simply selects the appropriate records of the field to be transferred, and copies them to all the records in the filtered database. It is illustrated in Figure 7.15. Since, if the program executes properly, you will never see the Sales Addresses database in its final form, part of it is illustrated in Figure 7.16.

THE MENU

Now that we have created a database that contains all the information we need, we are ready to begin creating the letters. The @MENU statement in the Program frame begins this portion of the program by displaying the menu on the screen (see Figures 7.7 and 7.8).

The @MENU statement calls the Outline frame Which Letter, and causes it to act as a menu:

> @menu (Letters.Program.Which Letter)

```
Letters.Program.Add Addresses.Move Record:
    @setselection("Letters.Supervisors.Last"),
    @performkeys("{dnarrow}{f6}{end}{f8}{uplevel}"),
    @setselection("Letters.Sales Addresses.Slast"),
    @performkeys("{dnarrow}{f6}{ctrl-dnarrow}{return}{return}")
```

Figure 7.15: The Move Record Subroutine

Apps	Disk	Create	Edit	Locate	Frames	Words	Numbers	Graph	Print	6:21 am
Last	First	Reg	SixMoSale	AvgPerMo		Pbn	Slast	Sfirst	Addre

Last	First	Reg	SixMoSale	AvgPerMo	Pbn	Slast	Sfirst	Addre
Smithfiel	Frank	SW	*********	$8,603.94	#YES	Williams	Simon	4520
Goldberg	Jack	SW	*********	$17,209.11	#NO	Williams	Simon	4520
Smith	Ashleigh	SW	*********	$11,188.74	#NO	Williams	Simon	4520
Petrakis	Bill	SE	*********	$18,718.72	#NO	Frank	Wanda	200 E
Schroeder	Art	SE	*********	$15,707.20	#NO	Frank	Wanda	200 E
Smyth	Gloria	SE	*********	$14,622.07	#NO	Frank	Wanda	200 E
Smith	Joe	NW	*********	$9,455.58	#YES	Walters	Jennifer	897 S
Takahashi	Bruce	NW	*********	$17,110.80	#NO	Walters	Jennifer	897 S
Woo	Eva	NW	*********	$15,542.35	#NO	Walters	Jennifer	897 S
Sapolsky	Stan	NE	*********	$8,112.55	#YES	Whitman	Dane	6700
Rizzo	Anne	NE	*********	$19,605.41	#NO	Whitman	Dane	6700
Herrera	Fred	NE	*********	$14,609.05	#NO	Whitman	Dane	6700
Brooke	Donny	MW	*********	$9,739.89	#YES	Stark	Anthony	89 Li
Olsen	Oscar	MW	*********	$19,089.46	#NO	Stark	Anthony	89 Li
Waterman	Pearl	MW	*********	$14,329.64	#NO	Stark	Anthony	89 Li
Curtis	Amy	S	*********	$7,876.12	#YES	Rambeau	Monica	8301
Washingto	Ed	S	*********	$17,062.52	#NO	Rambeau	Monica	8301
Hernandez	Esther	S	*********	$13,873.53	#NO	Rambeau	Monica	8301

Sales Addresses.Reg   Recs: 18/18

Figure 7.16: The Sales Addresses Database

To display and work with a menu, the @MENU function makes use of every part of this outline—the frame labels, the frame contents, and the formulas residing behind the frames. This is how @MENU operates:

□ The frame labels—in this case, the labels "Probationary Employees" and "Best Employees"—become the actual menu options.

□ Any contents of the option frames are displayed as explanatory messages at the bottom of the screen. The two messages seen in Figures 7.7 and 7.8 are stored in the contents areas of the Probationary Employees frame and the Best Employees frame, respectively.

☐ When the user selects an option from the menu, control of the program passes to the formula residing behind the frame that represents the selected option.

From the user's point of view, a menu created by the @MENU function has the same operational features as a regular Framework menu. You can use the ↑ and ↓ keys to move the highlight over a menu selection. Pressing the Return key selects the current selection. Alternatively, you can simply press the first letter of the option you want to select—in this case P or B. If you want to exit from the menu without selecting an option, press the Escape key.

As we have seen, selecting a menu option results in execution of the formula that resides behind the corresponding Outline frame. Figure 7.17 shows a listing of the formulas behind the two frames Probationary Employees and Best Employees.

```
Letters.Program.Which Letter.Probationary Employees:
    ; Prepare to write letters to the
    ; employees who are on probation.

    ; Begin by placing a "P" in Letter Code:

    Letters.Program.Letter Code := "P",

    ; Now call the Print Letter Program:

    @Letters.Program.Print Letter


Letters.Program.Which Letter.Best Employees:
    ; Prepare to write letters to the
    ; employees whose sales levels are above $100,000.

    ; Begin by placing a "B" (for "Best") in Letter Code:

    Letters.Program.Letter Code := "B",

    ; Now call the Print Letter Program:

    @Letters.Program.Print Letter
```

Figure 7.17: The Formulas behind the Which Letter Menu Outline

Both routines are simple. They begin by assigning a single-character code to the variable frame Letter Code. If the user has selected the Probationary Employees option from the Letter menu, a "P" is placed in Letter Code:

Letters.Program.Letter Code : = "P",

If the user selected the Best Employees option, the frame receives a "B":

Letters.Program.Letter Code : = "B",

The value stored in this frame, Letter Code, will be used to determine which of the two letters is being processed, the warning letter or the congratulatory letter.

Finally, both of the menu option formulas end by sending control of the program to the Print Letter frame. Notice the form of the subroutine call:

@Letters.Program.Print Letter

As we have discussed, a subroutine call consists simply of a reference to the frame that contains the subroutine. The reference must be preceded by the @ symbol.

PRINTING THE LETTERS

The Print Letter program module appears in Figure 7.18. It consists primarily of subroutine calls to the two lower-level subroutines that do the real work of the module:

@Letters.Program.Print Letter.Sales Filter

@Letters.Program.Print Letter.MailMerge

As we will see, Sales Filter selects the appropriate group of sales people, and MailMerge selects the appropriate letter template and prints the letters.

```
Letters.Program.Print Letter:
  ; Write letters to selected sales people

  @echo(#OFF), ; Freeze screen activity during program performance

  ; Filter the Sales People database and process each
  ; person in the filtered group:

  @Letters.Program.Print Letter.Sales Filter,
  @Letters.Program.Print Letter.MailMerge,

  ; End the program:

  @echo(#ON),
  @quitmenu,
  @performkeys("{ctrl-uplevel}{f10}")
```

Figure 7.18: The Print Letter Subroutine

The Print Letter subroutine contains a call to another FRED function, @QUITMENU. This function exits the menu and returns the user to the desktop.

The Sales Filter subroutine, shown in Figure 7.19, is in charge of filtering the Sales Addresses database according to the appropriate criterion for the selected group. Once again the filtering is performed by the @EXECUTE function. The task of this subroutine is to choose one of two different filter formulas. You may recall the two filters we used in Chapter 5 to examine different groups of employees. If we want to print warning letters to probationary employees, the formula will be simply

    Pbn

If we will print congratulatory letters to the most successful sales people, the filter formula will be

    SixMoSales > 100000

```
Letters.Program.Print Letter.Sales Filter:
    ; Filter the Sales Addresses database so that
    ; only the selected employees (Probationary or Best)
    ; will be displayed.

    @if(Letters.Program.Letter Code = "P",
        @execute(Letters.Sales Addresses, Pbn),
        @execute(Letters.Sales Addresses, SixMoSales > 100000)
        )
```

Figure 7.19: The Sales Filter Subroutine

To choose between these two formulas, Sales Filter examines the value currently stored in the variable frame Letter Code. If the frame contains a "P", we are writing to probationary employees; otherwise, we are dealing with the best employees. Sales Filter uses the @IF function to decide between two possible @EXECUTE commands:

    @If(Letters.Program.Letter Code = "P",
        @execute(Letters.Sales Addresses, Pbn),
        @execute(Letters.Sales Addresses, SixMoSales > 100000)
)

Once the Sales Addresses database has been correctly filtered, the MailMerge subroutine can print the letters. A listing of MailMerge is shown in Figure 7.20.

```
Letters.Program.Print Letter.MailMerge:
   ; Select the correct letter.

@if(Letters.Program.Letter Code = "P",
     @setselection("Letters.Bad"),
     @setselection("Letters.Good")
     ),

 ; Call the Mailmerge using function from the Apps menu.

@performkeys("{ctrl-a}mLetters.Sales Addresses{return}")
```

Figure 7.20: *The MailMerge Subroutine*

The MailMerge subroutine uses the value stored in Letter Code to identify the correct letter template to use:

```
@if(Letters.Program.Letter Code = "P",
    @setselection("Letters.Bad"),
    @setselection("Letters.Good")
    ),
```

Finally, the @PERFORMKEYS statement calls the "Mailmerge using" option from the Apps menu, and tells it to use the Sales Addresses database for the mailmerge.

As you can see, the Letters program is a rather complex example of what you can do using FRED and Framework II's outlining capability to organize a program. This example is provided not to confuse you, but rather to show you how many of the functions and capabilities you learned about in Framework's other components – databases, mailmerge, and so on—can be used to provide power and flexibility in the context of FRED programming.

CREATING A USER-DEFINED FUNCTION

Now that we have some experience with programming in FRED, let's try writing the @DIFFTIME function. This function should calculate the time elapsed between two times, just as the @DIFFDATE function calculates the time elapsed between two dates.

We could conceivably write a version of the function that would work with the time displayed in *any* form. However, to simplify our work, the function we'll write will assume that the time is given as a string value, as hours and minutes on a *24-hour* clock, the same form as given by the function

@time2(@time)

We've chosen not to use a 12-hour clock because 1PM would be later than 11AM, for example, and we'd have to find a way of converting the PM times so that we could easily perform arithmetic. There *are* ways to convert a date-type function into numbers. However, there are also ways to convert strings into numbers, and any date-type function will also include extraneous information, such as seconds. In addition, after we've created the function, an application will be suggested where you'll want to use strings to prevent recalculation, just as you did with the Phone Log example.

The basic form of the function, when used in (or as) a formula, will be

@difftime(*early, late*)

where early and late are two times, the second one being later than the first. Since we will ultimately generate the times on which we work by using the @TIME2 function, which presents times in the form

HH:MM

the strategy will be to:

1. Select the first two characters from the string: HH.

2. Convert the characters to numbers to find the number of hours.

3. Multiply the number of hours by 60 to find out how many minutes they represent.

4. Select the last two characters, MM, and convert them to numbers.

5. Add these minutes to the number of minutes represented by the hours.

We'll do this for both the early time and the later time, and then subtract the early time from the later time. Since the operation for determining both times is identical, we'll use a subroutine so we don't have to write the code twice. This subroutine, called Calculate, is shown in Figure 7.21. The two times that serve as the function's parameters are treated within the program as @ITEM1 and @ITEM2. However, since each of the times is sent to the subroutine separately, each one is treated by the subroutine as @ITEM1.

```
Library.User-defined functions.difftime.Calculate:
   @local(hours, minutes),
                                ; First find the colon in the time string
                                ; colon is third character
   hours := @mid(@item1,1,2),   ; hours are characters to left of colon
   minutes := @mid(@item1,4,2), ; minutes are characters to right of colon
                                ; convert strings to numbers
                                ; calculate total number of minutes,
                                ; return to main program

   @return((@value(hours)*60) + @value(minutes))
```

Figure 7.21: *The Calculate Subroutine of the @DIFFTIME Function*

The Calculate routine does three things. First, it uses the @MID function (which behaves virtually the same as BASIC's MID$ function), to count two characters from the beginning of the string, and assign them to the local variable HOURS. Second, it starts with the fourth character (the third is the colon), and assigns the following two characters to the local variable MINUTES. Finally, these strings are converted to numbers by the @VALUE function, which returns the value of a string consisting of numbers, and the arithmetic is performed. The result is returned to the main program at the same time. The following formula accomplishes the last three tasks:

@return((@value(hours)*60) + @value(minutes))

The main program is shown in Figure 7.22. Again, local variables called HOURS and MINUTES are defined. They are not the same as those used in the Calculate subroutine, because they are defined as local. One statement passes both times to the subroutine, receives the result from the subroutine, and divides the result by 60, to find out how many hours have elapsed:

hours : = (@difftime.calculate(@item2)
    − @difftime.calculate(@item1))/60,

The rest of the routine is designed to convert the fraction left over after dividing by 60 into a number of minutes, and put together a string representing hours and minutes elapsed in conventional format. First, the formula

minutes : = (hours − @int(hours))*60

finds the fraction left over after dividing HOURS by 60. Subtracting the integer part of the number leaves the fraction. This is multiplied by 60 to convert the fraction into minutes, which is then converted back

```
Library.User-defined functions.difftime:
  ; @difftime(early, late)
  ; Calculates the number of minutes and hours between two specified times.
  ; Times should be recorded as strings generated by @time2, that is
  ;   hours and minutes on a 24-hour clock.

  ; The Calculate subroutine breaks apart the string into minutes and hours,
  ;   and performs the arithmetic to convert each time string into a number of
  ;   of minutes, on which arithmetic can be performed.

  @local(minutes, hours),

  ; @item1 is the early time, @item2 the later time.
  ; The following formula sends both values to the Calculate subroutine,
  ; and subtracts the later from the earlier, then divides by 60 to
  ; get the number of hours elapsed.

  hours := (@difftime.calculate(@item2) - @difftime.calculate(@item1))/60,

  ; Minutes is the remainder after subtracting whole hours. This decimal
  ; fraction must be multiplied by 60 to convert to minutes.

  minutes := (hours - @int(hours))*60,

  ; The result is converted to a string by the @integer function.

  minutes := @integer(minutes),

  ; If the string is one character long, a zero is placed before it,
  ;   to conform to conventional time formats.

  @if(@len(minutes) = 1, minutes := "0" & minutes),
      ; Hours is converted to a string value.
      hours := @integer(@int(hours)
      ),

  ; A string of the form "HH:MM" is returned.

  @return(hours & ":" & minutes)
```

Figure 7.22: The Difftime Program

into a string by the @INTEGER function. This is the inverse of the @VALUE function, and can be used to convert both date and numeric data into strings.

Finally, for a touch of elegance, the length of the MINUTES string is checked. If the number of minutes is less than ten, the resulting string might appear in the form

7:3

Therefore, the @LEN function is used to see if the MINUTES string is only one character long. If so, the concatenation operator, "&", is used to add a zero before the number of minutes. Finally, HOURS is converted to a string by the @INTEGER function, and a string of the proper form is created:

```
hours := @integer(@int(hours)),
@return(hours & ":" & minutes)
```

If the elapsed time were seven hours, three minutes, the display would now be

7:03

AN APPLICATION FOR THE @DIFFTIME FUNCTION

You may wonder what the @DIFFTIME function is good for. Consider the fact that, if you use a computer at home for business purposes, the Internal Revenue Service requires you to keep a log of the percentage of time you use it for such purposes. This function is very handy in maintaining such a record.

The programming details will not be presented, so you can work them out as an exercise, but here are the outlines of the problem. To start, create a spreadsheet with five columns, labeled

Date
Start Time
Project
End Time
Time Elapsed

You can use Alt-F3 to enter the date. Create a modified version of the Alt-F4 macro that places a string of the proper form in the second column. You'll have to fill in the name of the project by hand. Use your new macro to log the ending time when you have finished your work. Finally, place the formula

@difftime(B2,B4)

in cell E2, and copy it downward into every cell in column E.

If you want to get elaborate, you can create a program that will do most of the work automatically. The outline for the program is shown in Figure 7.23. Create an Empty frame. Move your spreadsheet into it, and copy it twice with the Copy key (F8). Label the frames

Business
Personal
Financial

Now you can create a menu, following the principles you learned in the Letters program. But this menu will have submenus. The menu is the frame called

Which function

and each of its options displays a second menu with the options

Begin session
End session

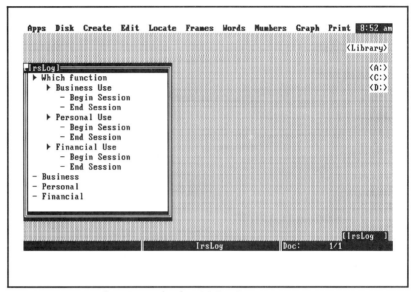

Figure 7.23: *Outline Frame for the IRS Log Program*

With what you have learned from the Phone Log example, you should be able to construct a program that will let you choose the appropriate spreadsheet and enter the starting or ending time into the appropriate cell. Later, you can create an @SUMTIME function, to add up the total hours for each function. You might even want to create a Library macro that automatically calls the program from disk and begins execution, and stores the frame on disk again as soon as the new data has been entered.

SUMMARY

FRED programming is attractive for a range of Framework II applications, from simple to complex. Your own programming level will depend partly on your inclination to learn about and work with the details of the FRED language. Your motivation for writing a program might include any of the following:

- A desire to streamline your work with Framework II, using keyboard macros

- The need to add new calculating or processing power to Framework II applications

- The ambition to produce turnkey applications for professional programming projects

One feature of Framework II that is extremely helpful to both novices and experienced programmers is the desktop Library. Items in the Library can be called by FRED formulas anywhere on the desktop. It also provides a home for programs that you write automatically, as macros or abbreviations. In it you can store:

- Macros, which capture a series of frequently used keystrokes, ready to be performed whenever you enter an Alt-key command from the keyboard.

- Abbreviations, which allow you to type a simple mnemonic, and recall a block of text by pressing Alt-Backspace.

- Assumptions, which you can reference from a spreadsheet cell or database field, which will automatically take on the values stored in them upon recalculation.

- User-defined functions, which allow you to extend the scope of the FRED language, and which can be called from any point in Framework II.

FRED is also a complete programming language, with facilities for all the usual processes and structures that such a language must offer. In particular, FRED includes functions for handling all of the following:

- Keyboard input and screen output

- Local and global variables

- Decisions and flow of control

- Structured loops

- Subroutines

In addition, FRED has several unique functions that allow you to perform any Framework II operation from within a program. In short, the individual resources of Framework II and FRED are designed to work together to accomplish more than either could do alone.

CHAPTER EIGHT

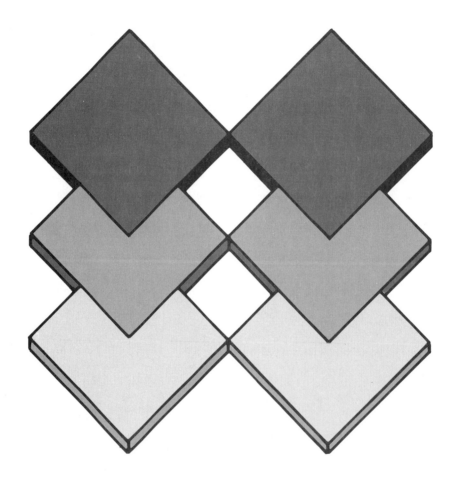

WORKING WITH

OTHER PROGRAMS

OVERVIEW

INTRODUCTION

One of Framework II's advantages is that as an integrated software package it allows you to perform all the important productivity functions—word processing, spreadsheet analysis, database management, creating business graphs, telecommunications, outlining, and printing documents and reports—in the same environment. The same commands, which you enter with the same keystrokes, are used in all activities. Framework II thus spares you from having to learn a different set of commands—and keystrokes to activate them—for different purposes. If you had separate programs for each function, each one would undoubtedly require you to learn different commands. In addition, Framework II's outline-based structure, and its move, copy, and cut-and-paste functions, allow you to move data between different types of frames with ease.

However, not everyone uses Framework II. Sometimes even people who do use Framework II have to use other programs to accomplish tasks for which they normally use Framework II. And sometimes you may have a need for a specialized program that performs some function more efficiently than Framework II's generalized components.

You may, for example, have an accounts receivable program that efficiently handles all your accounts receivable transactions, and needs no design or programming on your part. You might not want to invest the time needed to create a spreadsheet that would perform all the functions of this program equally well. Or, you might want to use some sort of paint or graphics program to enhance Framework II's graphs for presentation—changing the colors or smoothing out the edges of the labels, for instance.

You might also want to use files created by your accounts receivable program within a Framework II spreadsheet or in conjunction with other data, or use data created by a dedicated database management program in a Framework II database. In addition, you may need to share your data with people who use other programs to accomplish the tasks you perform with Framework II.

Framework II is designed for maximum flexibility in these areas. In this chapter, we'll explore:

- *Importing files into Framework II:* What kinds of files Framework II can read, how to load them into a Framework II frame, and what you can do to make other types of files readable

- *Exporting files from Framework II:* What kinds of files Framework II can write

- *Ways to run other programs:* By using a DOS Access frame, by running a FRED program on the desktop, or by adding programs to the Apps menu

You'll learn how to write a program that allows you to run another program right from the desktop, and we'll take our first look at the Setup program (which is explored more fully in Appendix A), which we'll use to add the program to the Apps menu. In our visit to The Sophisticated Palate, we'll see how George Farley integrates the Visi-Calc DIF file, which Eileen downloaded in the previous chapter, into his Activity Comparisons spreadsheet. Finally, we'll look at ways of importing types of files that are not on the menus, and ways of approaching the process of transferring files between applications to minimize potential problems and difficulties.

CONVERTING FILES

If you open the Disk menu, you will notice that it includes two options we have not yet explored: Import and Export. Each of these options opens a submenu. The Import submenu is shown in Figure 8.1, and the Export submenu in Figure 8.2. The items on these menus call up special FRED programs (which are on the Apps disk if you are using a floppy disk system) that convert files from one format to another.

IMPORTING FILES INTO FRAMEWORK II

Framework II includes options to import seven types of files. If a file on a disk is (or appears to be) in any one of these formats, you can load it to the desktop simply by selecting the file name in a disk drive cabinet.

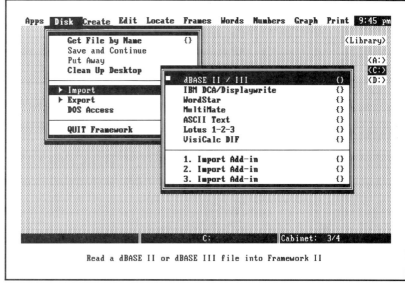

Figure 8.1: The Import Submenu

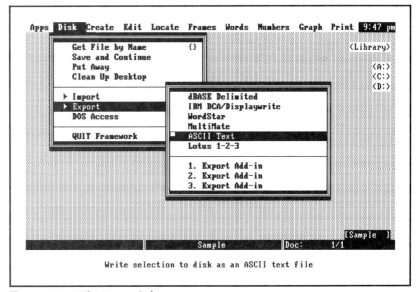

Figure 8.2: The Export Submenu

(If you prefer, however, you can choose any of these file formats from the Import submenu, entering the name of the file to be converted.) Framework II can import files specific to four programs, and three more general formats. The four specific formats are as follows:

- Database files from the programs *dBASE II, III, and III Plus*. These programs are products of Ashton-Tate, as is Framework II, and are fully compatible with Framework II. These files normally have the extension ".DBF". They will appear on the desktop as Database frames.

- *Lotus 1-2-3 worksheet files*. If you select a Lotus file with the .WKS extension from a disk drive cabinet, it will be brought to the desktop as a Framework II Spreadsheet frame. Only the contents of the cells will be read by Framework II, however, not the formulas.

- *WordStar* word processing files. These files need not have any special extension.

- *MultiMate* word processing files. These files generally have the extension ".DOC".

If you select a file of any of these types, Framework II will perform the conversion automatically. (If you have a floppy disk system, you will be prompted to insert the Apps disk in drive A.) Framework II will load a conversion program and check to see that there is no frame on the desktop with the same name. If there is, it will prompt you

> **Name conflict: rename desktop frame and try again—**
> **Press SPACE to continue**

Otherwise, it will create the appropriate type of frame on the desktop and convert the data, displaying various messages in the message area and in a special frame called "Messages". You can cancel the conversion by pressing Ctrl-Break. Figures 8.3 and 8.14 show examples of the Messages frame.

In addition, Framework II includes programs to convert three more general types of files to its own format:

- DCA. A DCA (*Document Content Architecture Revisable-Form Text*) file is a special type of file format owned by IBM, which is used by both the DisplayWrite word processing programs and by many programs that run on IBM mainframe and mini-computer programs. If you download text files from an IBM

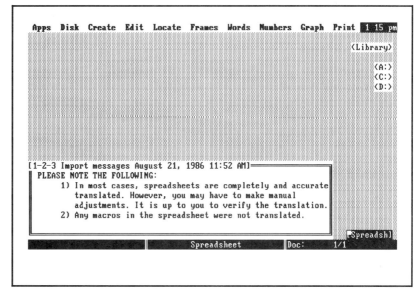

Figure 8.3: A Messages Frame Created by Importing a Lotus 1-2-3 Worksheet

mainframe, the chances are good that they will be in this format. These files have the extension ".DCA". They are completely unreadable without some means of converting them to text.

□ *ASCII text files.* These files contain nothing but the standard ASCII characters, and are similar to the files created by selecting the DOS File option from the Print Output Destination submenu, except that, as a rule, they do not contain printer escape sequences or the results of selecting printing formats. (DOS files created by way of the Print menu are loaded as ASCII text files, however.) ASCII text files may have almost any extension. If you select an ASCII text file in a disk drive cabinet, it will be loaded directly, without the intervention of a conversion program.

□ *DIF files.* A DIF (*data interchange format*) file is a special type of ASCII text file that contains the data from a spreadsheet (but not the formulas), plus enough additional information to reconstruct the spreadsheet. DIF files have the extension ".DIF".

These types of files can be created by many different programs. If you need to import a file from a program other than the four named earlier (dBASE, Lotus 1-2-3, WordStar, or MultiMate), the chances are fairly good that that program can create a file in one of these formats (DCA, ASCII, or DIF). We'll look at some details of these formats shortly.

If you select a file that is neither in Framework II format nor in any of the formats that Framework II includes conversion programs for, Framework II will load it to the desktop without attempting to perform any type of conversion. If the file is a text file of any type, there is some chance that you will be able to read it, although you may have to reformat it extensively before you can do anything else with it. If it is a program file, most of the contents will probably be lost. Later in this chapter, we'll look at ways to read files of other types.

WRITING FILES FOR OTHER PROGRAMS

Also on the Disk menu is an Export submenu of file formats that Framework II can create on request. They include formats specific to three of the four programs that Framework II can import files from:

- □ WordStar

- □ MultiMate

- □ Lotus 1-2-3

(This is how Eileen Wilcox created a Lotus 1-2-3 file for the accountant.) Framework II can also write ASCII text files and DCA files. Although it cannot write DIF files, Framework II can write a third general file format, the *comma-delimited* file, which appears on the menu as

dBASE Delimited

This is one of several formats used by the dBASE programs, and some others as well, for exchanging data with other programs. Most programs that can write comma-delimited files can also read them. A comma-delimited file is like a DIF file for database programs – it contains the data plus enough information to reconstruct the table.

You cannot create the file types on the Export submenu automatically. You must first bring the frame you want to convert to the desktop. Next, you must select it. Finally, you must select the export format from the menu. For example, to export a frame called LETTER to WordStar, you must select the frame, then press

Ctrl-D   (to open the Disk menu)

E   (to open the Export submenu)

W   (to export to WordStar)

If you are using a floppy disk system, Framework II will prompt you to place the Apps disk in drive A. Framework II will then load the appropriate conversion program and perform the conversion, writing the result to disk. You can interrupt the process at any time by pressing Ctrl-Break, but you may end up with an empty file on the disk anyway.

WordStar files are written with the extension ".WSD" so you can identify them, although WordStar does not require an extension. ASCII text and comma-delimited files are written with the extension ".TXT", although comma-delimited files created by dBASE programs have the extension ".CDF".

The export format must be appropriate to the frame you want to convert. You cannot export a Database or a Spreadsheet frame directly to a word processing format, for example. You can, however, export such frames to ASCII text files.

SOME CHARACTERISTICS OF THE ASCII FILE FORMATS

An ASCII text file contains nothing but the displayable characters of the ASCII code. These are the characters from 32 through 127 in Table C.1. They include all the characters that you can type at the keyboard, and none of the control characters. Since most word processing programs (with the notable exception of WordStar) can produce ASCII text files, you can probably arrange to read files from almost any word processing program if you plan your work carefully. Virtually all word processing programs can also read ASCII text files, so you can use the ASCII format to create files for word processors that are not on the Export menu, and for many spreadsheet and database programs as well. However, you will lose any print styling that was in the original frame. DIF and comma-delimited files are special types of ASCII text files, so they have some of the same advantages.

► **ROW-ORDER DIF FILES**

Although the VisiCalc spreadsheet program was the first to produce DIF files, many spreadsheet programs (and, indeed, quite a few other programs) can produce DIF files. These files can be set up so that the information is recorded row-by-row or column-by-column. However, Framework II can read only DIF files that are in *row order*. Such files will be converted into a normal Framework II spreadsheet frame. If the DIF file is in *column order*, however, the information in the resulting spreadsheet will appear sideways, with the row labels in row 1, the column labels in column A, and the data correspondingly rearranged. This may not be a problem with a small spreadsheet, but if you are importing a spreadsheet that is a few columns wide and many rows long, you may have trouble reading the result. Later in this chapter, we'll look at the DIF file that Eileen Wilcox downloaded from the branch store.

If you find yourself dealing extensively with DIF files, you may find the book *Mastering VisiCalc*, by Douglas Hergert (SYBEX, 1983), extremely useful. It contains an extensive description of the characteristics of DIF files, including BASIC programs to write and read them. If you must interact with a program that can create DIF files only in column order, you may be able to adapt some of these programs to convert the files to row order. Indeed, if you become adept at FRED programming, you may be able to write the program in FRED.

► **COMMA-DELIMITED FILES**

Comma-delimited files convert the data from a database or spreadsheet one row at a time. Each field (or cell) in a row is separated from the next by a comma. Non-numeric data is also surrounded by quotation marks. There are three potential hazards in exporting comma-delimited files:

□ Since quotation marks delimit text fields, a text field that contains quotation marks will be broken into several fields. To prevent this, replace double quotation marks with single quotation marks before you perform the conversion.

□ Since numeric fields are delimited only by commas, attempting to import a spreadsheet or database in which the numeric format includes commas will result in the numeric information being broken into several fields. Convert numeric fields to general or integer format before performing the conversion.

□ If the columns are not wide enough to display their entire contents on the screen, some characters will be lost. The conversion program converts only those characters that would be displayed in the tabular form of the original frame.

Figure 8.4 shows a comma-delimited file created from the Sales People database we worked with in Chapter 5. If you want to try this for yourself, bring the file to the desktop and press

Ctrl-D   (to open the Disk menu)

E	(to open the Export submenu)
D	(to export a dBASE Delimited file)
Sales People	(enter the name of the file to export)
Return	(to record your selection)

(If you're using floppy disks, you need to insert the Apps disk first.) When you see the message

Export file written

select the file SALES_PE.TXT from your default disk drive cabinet, and press Return. The file will be brought to the desktop as an ASCII text file, exactly as it appears in Figure 8.4. Later in this chapter, we'll look at some specialized techniques for dealing with comma-delimited files.

```
"EmpNo","Last","First","Reg","SixMoSales","AvgPerMo","Pbn","Hired","Yrs"
"82M1","Waterman","Pearl","MW",85977.83,14329.64,"#NO","Sep 29, 1982",4.6
"84M3","Brooke","Donny","MW",58439.33,9739.89,"#YES","Dec 1, 1984",2.5
"85M2","Olsen","Oscar","MW",114536.77,19089.46,"#NO","Jun 20, 1985",1.9
"66N3","Rizzo","Anne","NE",117632.48,19605.41,"#NO","May 21, 1966",21.0
"79N6","Herrera","Fred","NE",87654.32,14609.05,"#NO","Nov 20, 1979",7.5
"86N2","Sapolsky","Stan","NE",48675.30,8112.55,"#YES","Jul 13, 1986",.8
"74N4","Takahashi","Bruce","NW",102664.78,17110.80,"#NO","Mar 23, 1974",13.2
"82N8","Woo","Eva","NW",93254.10,15542.35,"#NO","Feb 25, 1982",5.2
"85N5","Smith","Joe","NW",56733.45,9455.58,"#YES","Oct 23, 1985",1.6
"69S3","Washington","Ed","S",102375.10,17062.52,"#NO","Aug 29, 1969",17.7
"78S4","Curtis","Amy","S",47256.70,7876.12,"#YES","Apr 12, 1978",9.1
"82S9","Hernandez","Esther","S",83241.20,13873.53,"#NO","May 5, 1982",5.0
"72S6","Schroeder","Art","SE",94243.22,15707.20,"#NO","Jan 24, 1972",15.3
"81S5","Petrakis","Bill","SE",112312.34,18718.72,"#NO","Aug 24, 1981",5.7
"84S1","Smyth","Gloria","SE",87732.41,14622.07,"#NO","May 17, 1984",3.0
"78S1","Smithfield","Frank","SW",51623.62,8603.94,"#YES","Jul 22, 1978",8.8
"83S9","Goldberg","Jack","SW",103254.67,17209.11,"#NO","Oct 29, 1983",3.6
"86S2","Smith","Ashleigh","SW",67132.45,11188.74,"#NO","Mar 4, 1986",1.2
```

Figure 8.4: *A Comma-Delimited Version of the Sales People Database*

You might also try the following experiments:

1. Create a spreadsheet, convert it to 1-2-3 format, and then read it back.

2. Create a Word frame, convert it to WordStar, DCA, or Multi-Mate format, and then read it back. To see the other program's format, use the Import submenu to import the file into Framework II as an ASCII text file.

You will find that 1-2-3, MultiMate, and DCA files are completely unreadable when imported as ASCII text files. When you attempt to import files using an importing standard that appears to be incorrect for the type of file, you will see a message of the form

> File appears to be (1) MultiMate, not (2) ASCII
> Load as (1), (2), or Cancel (ESC)?

To force Framework II to load the file in the format you want to see, press 2.

You now have a sense of the ways in which Framework II can talk to other programs—how it can read files they have created and write files they can read. Let's look now at ways of running other programs while using Framework II.

MORE ABOUT DOS ACCESS FRAMES

The easiest way to run another program while using Framework II is to create a DOS Access frame, and enter the command that invokes the program when the DOS prompt appears in the frame. If you wanted to run WordStar, for example, you would simply type

> WS

DOS commands will actually be executed in the DOS frames. Many other programs, however, will take over the whole screen. When you exit a program like WordStar, your screen will look as though Framework II has disappeared. In fact, it has not. To return to Framework II from DOS or any other program, you simply enter the DOS command

> exit

If the desktop seems to have disappeared, no text will be captured in the DOS Access frame after its disappearance. You can keep the DOS Access frame from capturing characters by issuing the CLS ("clear screen") command at the DOS prompt. You can also increase the amount of text Framework II will store in a DOS Access frame by means of the Setup program, which we will look at in Appendix A. If you use the ANSI.SYS device driver, it will be impossible to capture any text in a DOS Access frame, as the desktop will disappear as soon as the DOS prompt appears.

What if you want to capture the information displayed on the screen while you are working in DOS, or in another program, and the desktop has disappeared? If you are working in another program, you may be able to write a file in a format that Framework II can read, and import it when you return to the desktop.

If you are working in DOS, you may be able to use "output redirection" to create a file. For example, suppose you wanted to keep copies of the directories of several different diskettes on the desktop for easy reference. If your DOS Access frame does not disappear, this is no problem—simply type the command

    dir

at the DOS prompt, and keep the frame after you return to the desktop. If the desktop does disappear, however, you can have DOS send the directory to a file instead of to the screen, and then read the file as an ASCII text file when you return to the desktop. For example, you might type

    dir > disk1.dir

to have the directory sent to a file called DISK1.DIR. The ">" symbol tells DOS to send the output to whatever is specified after it.

Alternatively, if you use a RAM-resident "background" program such as SideKick or SuperKey that has a "cut and paste" feature, you can capture anything on the screen with it. When you return to Framework II with the EXIT command, create an Empty frame, and use the background program's paste feature to send the text from the screen into the frame.

A FEW WORDS OF CAUTION

Some kinds of programs must be run *before* you start Framework II, rather than from within it. DOS programs that include a portion that remains in memory, such as MODE.COM and GRAPHICS.COM, will place an upper limit on the memory available to Framework II. If you load such a program from a DOS frame, it will be located at the upper limit of the memory currently in use, and you will no longer have access to any of the computer's memory that is located above the point at which the resident program now ends. The same thing will happen if you load a RAM-resident "background" utility program.

If any of the programs you plan to run from the desktop requires a special device driver, such as a mouse driver program, it, too, must be loaded before Framework II, to prevent the same kind of limitation.

ADDING APPLICATIONS TO THE APPS MENU

In addition to using DOS Access frames, you can run other applications directly from the desktop. Figure 8.5 shows the Apps menu. As you can see, the third section of the menu includes three numbered items: dBASE III, and space for two application "add-ins." Thus, you can run dBASE III directly from the desktop (if you have it) by pressing

Ctrl-A   (to open the Apps menu)

1   (to run dBASE III)

If you press these keys, the desktop will clear, and a frame will appear displaying the text shown in Figure 8.6. If you have dBASE III, then the program will create an output frame for it, and display messages and prompts to guide you in running dBASE III from the desktop. Of course, if you don't have dBASE III, after a bit of disk whirring and opening and closing of menus, you will be returned to the desktop.

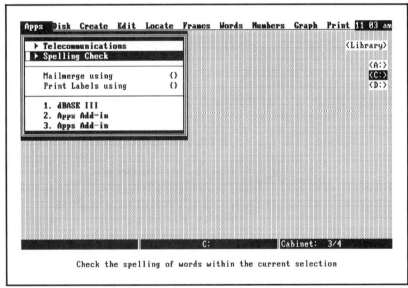

Figure 8.5: The Apps Menu

The key to this process is a FRED program called RUNDBASE.FW2, which is on System Disk 2. Careful study of the program will show you how to deal with running a complex program such as dBASE III. However, most programs are much simpler to run than dBASE III. Let's imagine that you have an accounting program called AP-AR.EXE, which

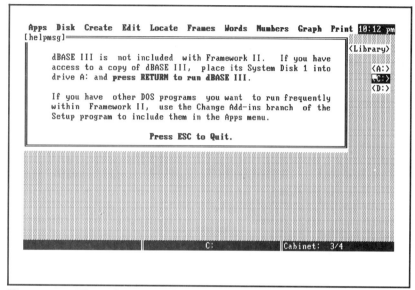

Figure 8.6: *The Help Message from RUNDBASE.FW2*

handles your accounts payable and receivable quite effectively, and you would like to run it from the desktop. We will write a relatively simple program to accomplish this. We'll assume that the program is in a separate directory on your hard disk, called \ACCOUNTS. We'll start with a very simple version of the program, and then add a few niceties.

Let's call the program Accounts. Create an Empty frame and label it ACCOUNTS. Next, press Down Level (+) to enter the frame, and create another Empty frame inside the first. Label this frame OUTPUT. (FRED programs always need a destination for their output.)

Now select the frame labeled ACCOUNTS. Press the Edit key (F2) to get to the programming area, and then press the Zoom key (F9) to get a full screen on which to write your program. The program will have to direct your computer to find the proper directory and select it, and then run the program, finally returning you to your Framework II directory when it is finished.

The key function for running another program is the @RUN function. For example, to run the program AP-AR.EXE, you would need a statement of the form

    @run(accounts.output, "c:ap-ar.exe"),

This tells Framework II to run the program, using the OUTPUT frame within the ACCOUNTS frame for its output. But you also need to tell your computer where to find the program to be run. The following program is really all you need:

```
@setdirectory("c:\accounts"),
@setdrive("c:"),
@run(accounts.output, "c:ap-ar.exe"),
@setdirectory("c:\framewk"),
```

The @SETDIRECTORY function is the FRED's equivalent of the DOS CHDIR ("change directory") command. The @SETDRIVE function has the same effect as selecting a different directory at a DOS prompt. This short program will select the \ACCOUNTS directory, make sure you are logged onto drive C, run the accounting program, and return you to the \FRAMEWK directory before returning you to the desktop. To run the program, select it and press the Recalc key (F5).

A MORE ELABORATE PROGRAM

Let's try a somewhat more advanced version of the same program. Create another Empty frame inside the ACCOUNTS frame, and label it HELPMESSAGE. In Outline view, use the Move key (F7) to move the OUTPUT frame below the HELPMESSAGE frame.

If you need to give a user some special instructions, such as "Insert a disk in drive A", you can enter the text in the HELPMESSAGE screen. We'll assume that you do not. Use the Size key (F4) to make the frame relatively small. Then press

Ctrl-F   (to open the Frames menu)

S   (to select Size All)

This will make all the inner frames small enough to be fully displayed in the containing frame. Press Down Level (+) twice to enter the HELP-MESSAGE frame, press Return to get to the second line, and perform the following keystrokes:

Ctrl-W   (to open the Words menu)

R   (to set the right margin)

36   (to select a right margin of 36, the size of the frame)

Return   (to record your selection)

Instruct   (to reopen the Words menu)

C   (to center the text)

Enter the text

> Press Return to run **AP/AR**

using the Words menu to boldface the program name. Now press

Up Level (–)	(to move the highlight to the frame's border)
Ctrl-F	(to open the Frames menu)
D	(to turn Display Labels off)

Your frame should look like Figure 8.7.

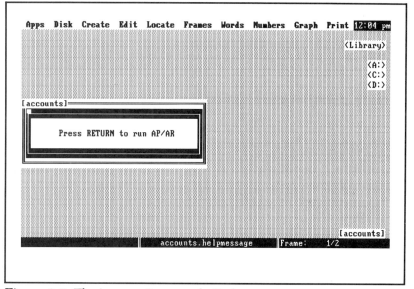

Figure 8.7: *The Accounts Frame on the Desktop*

Next, select the outer frame and enter the programming area. Modify the program so that it matches the one shown in Figure 8.8.

Again, to run the program, select it and press Recalc (F5). This version of the program begins by cleaning up the desktop, which conserves memory, and then using the @DISPLAY function to display the HELP-MESSAGE frame in the upper-left corner of the desktop. When you press Return, check to see if there is enough memory available in your computer to run the AP/AR program, which we'll assume requires 128K, or somewhat over 131,000 bytes. If there's not enough memory,

```
@performkeys("{ctrl-d}c"),
@display(accounts.helpmessage),
@eraseprompt,
@local(ch),ch := @nextkey,
@echo(#on),
@if(@memavail < 132000,
        @list(
                @eraseprompt,
                @prompt("Not enough memory to run AP/AR -- Press a key to continue"),
                @beep,
                @nextkey,
                @eraseprompt,
                @return(#FALSE)
               )
        ),
@if(ch = {return},
    @list(
                @setdirectory("c:\accounts"),
                @setdrive("c:"),
                @eraseprompt,
                @prompt("Loading AP/AR . . . Please Wait"),
                @echo(#OFF),
                @performkeys("{ctrl-d}c"),
                @run(accounts.output, "c:ap-ar.exe"),
                @setdirectory("c:\framewk"),
                @echo(#ON),
            )
    )
```

Figure 8.8: *The Accounts Program*

your computer will beep and tell you so:

```
@if(@memavail < 132000,
    @list(
        @eraseprompt,
        @prompt("Not enough memory to run AP/AR—Press a key to
continue"),
        @beep,
        @nextkey,
        @eraseprompt,
        @return(#FALSE)
        )
    )
```

The statement

```
@return(#FALSE)
```

ends the program immediately at that point.

If there is enough memory, however, the program proceeds to the second @IF statement. This statement waits for the Return key to be pressed, and then executes substantially the same program that we wrote the first time. The only differences are that it displays a prompt while loading the accounting program, and that screen echoing is turned off, so you don't have to watch menus opening and closing.

You can use variations on this program to run almost any program that will fit in your available memory from the desktop. If you plan to run the program from a different disk drive, change the @SETDRIVE and @SETDIRECTORY statements accordingly. (If you are using a floppy disk system, you will probably want the application program you will run to be in drive B, because ultimately the FRED program will reside on System Disk 2 in drive A.)

You can also execute almost any DOS commands within your FRED program. For example, if you want your FRED program to copy data files to a RAM disk before running the application, you can use a series of statements such as

```
@prompt("Insert data disk in drive B and press a key"),
@nextkey,
@eraseprompt,
@run(accounts.output, "\command.com /c copy b:*.dat d:"),
@prompt("Insert AP/AR Program Disk in drive B and press a key"),
@nextkey,
@eraseprompt,
```

before the @RUN statement that actually runs the application program.

Notice the form of the @RUN statement in this segment of the program. The syntax

```
\command.com /c
```

must be used when you want to use any of the DOS commands. The other statements in this segment simply display a prompt, wait for a key to be pressed, and then erase the prompt.

If you include statements like these, you will probably also want to prompt the user to place the data disk in drive B and use an @RUN statement to copy the modified files back onto it:

```
@run("\command.com /c copy d:*.dat b:")
```

ADDING YOUR PROGRAM TO THE APPS MENU

Up to now, you've been using a frame on the desktop to run other application programs. Presently we're going to install the accounting program on the Apps menu, so you can select it without having to load the FRED program first. To do this we'll have to leave Framework II. Use the Move key (F7) to save your program on System Disk 2 if you are using floppy disks, or simply save the program to the Framework II directory on your hard disk before you exit from Framework II.

To install the program on the menu, we need the Setup program. (Floppy disk users will find it on the Setups disk.) We'll look at the program in detail in Appendix A. For now, just follow the steps outlined below. When your screen displays the appropriate drive prompt, type

> setup

Once the program is loaded, the screen should look like Figure A.1 in Appendix A. Press

> 2   (to select All Other Uses of the Setup Program)

If you have a hard disk, you will probably then press 2 again, if the Setup program is in your Framework II directory. If you have a floppy disk system, insert System Disk 2 in drive A and press 1. Next, press

> 6   (to select Add-ins)
>
> 1   (to select Applications Add-ins)

You will see the screen shown in Figure 8.9. We'll assume for now that you want to keep dBASE III on the menu. Press

> 4   (to enter the Add-in 2 menu name)
>
> AP/AR   (enter the name of the application to appear on the menu)
>
> Return   (to record your entry)

as shown in Figure 8.10. Next, press

> 5   (to enter the Add-in 2 file name)
>
> *accounts.fw2*   (enter the name of the FRED program to run the application)
>
> Return   (to record your entry)
>
> 6   (to enter the Add-in 2 user message)
>
> *Run Accounting from*   (enter the message to be displayed
> *the Desktop*   in the message area)
>
> Return   (to record your entry)

At this point, your screen will look like Figure 8.10. Now press

> M   (to return to the main menu)
>
> 7   (to record the changes you have made)

You will be prompted if you need to change disks. Figure 8.11 shows the completed entry.

```
APPLICATIONS ADD-INS                    CURRENT SETTING        NEW SETTING
(1) Add-in 1 menu name                      dBASE III              same
(2) Add-in 1 file name                    rundbase.fw2             same
(3) Add-in 1 user message              Run dBASE III within        same
(4) Add-in 2 menu name                     Apps Add-in             same
(5) Add-in 2 file name                                             same
(6) Add-in 2 user message              Use Setup to add you        same
(7) Add-in 3 menu name                     Apps Add-in             same
(8) Add-in 3 file name                                             same
(9) Add-in 3 user message              Use Setup to add you        same
================================================================================




================================================================================
           PRESS A NUMBER to indicate which setting you want to change.
  Or press      [F1] for Help      [Esc] to back up one screen     M for Main menu.
```

Figure 8.9: *The Applications Add-ins Setup Menu*

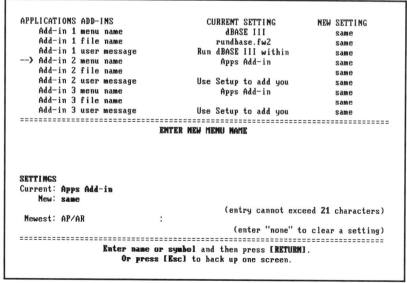

```
APPLICATIONS ADD-INS                    CURRENT SETTING        NEW SETTING
    Add-in 1 menu name                      dBASE III              same
    Add-in 1 file name                    rundbase.fw2             same
    Add-in 1 user message              Run dBASE III within        same
--> Add-in 2 menu name                     Apps Add-in             same
    Add-in 2 file name                                             same
    Add-in 2 user message              Use Setup to add you        same
    Add-in 3 menu name                     Apps Add-in             same
    Add-in 3 file name                                             same
    Add-in 3 user message              Use Setup to add you        same
================================================================================
                          ENTER NEW MENU NAME



SETTINGS
Current: Apps Add-in
    New: same
                                      (entry cannot exceed 21 characters)
  Newest: AP/AR                :
                                      (enter "none" to clear a setting)
================================================================================
                Enter name or symbol and then press [RETURN].
                     Or press [Esc] to back up one screen.
```

Figure 8.10: *Entering an Application Add-in*

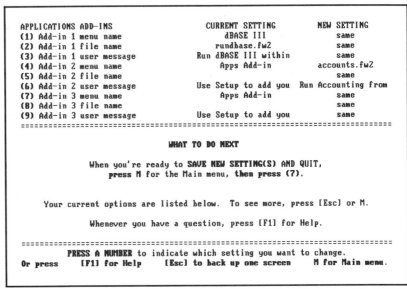

Figure 8.11: A Completed Application Add-in

If you would rather replace dBASE III, select 1, 2, and 3 in place of 4, 5, and 6, respectively, on the Applications Add-ins menu screen. Figure 8.12 shows the Apps menu with three applications added and one selected. Next time you want to run the AP/AR program, open the Apps menu and press the appropriate number key. The HELP-MESSAGE frame will appear on the desktop as shown in Figure 8.13, waiting for you to press Return.

EXAMPLES

When we last looked in on The Sophisticated Palate, Eileen Wilcox had completed a telecommunications session in which she downloaded a spreadsheet from Joe Escovedo, manager of the new branch store. It was in the form of a VisiCalc DIF file. The next morning, George wanted to integrate those figures into the spreadsheet he developed in Chapter 3.

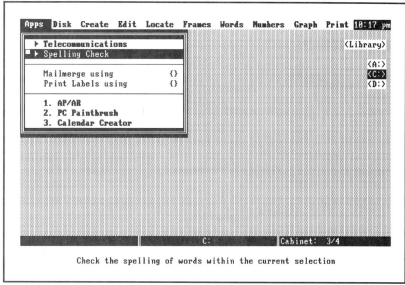

Figure 8.12: The Apps Menu with Three Add-in Applications Installed

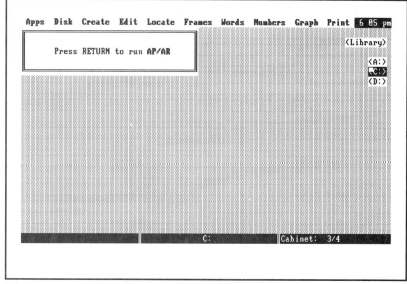

Figure 8.13: Running the Accounting Application Program from the Apps Menu

INTEGRATING THE VISICALC DIF FILE

Before he could do anything with Joe's spreadsheet, George first had to convert the VisiCalc DIF file into a form that Framework II could read. Since DIF is one of the formats that Framework II recognizes, it converted the spreadsheet automatically. Next, George watched as Framework II created a spreadsheet and transferred all the figures from the file to the spreadsheet. When the process was finished, the spreadsheet shown in Figure 8.14 appeared on his screen. You'll notice that the title on the screen is spaced rather strangely, because Framework II adjusted the column widths automatically after all the figures were transferred. For comparison, the text of the original BRNCHSLS.DIF file is shown in Figure 8.15.

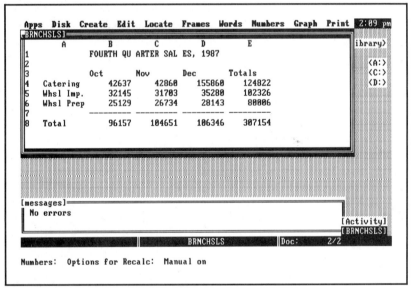

Figure 8.14: A Framework II Spreadsheet from a DIF File

Now George had to integrate the information into his Activity Comparisons spreadsheet, so he could see the totals for both stores combined. He had already loaded the Activity Comparisons Outline frame to the desktop. (This frame contains the spreadsheet and graph we first saw in Chapter 3, Figures 3.18 and 3.19. The spreadsheet and graph have been updated and now reflect the sales figures for the second half of the year.) Next he renamed his new spreadsheet (which was still called BRNCHSLS) "Activity Comparisons: Branch Store" and

```
TABLE                  1,0                    V                      V
1,0                    " "                    0,15586                -1,0
" "                    1,0                    V                      BOT
VECTORS                " "                    0,124822               1,0
0,5                    1,0                    V                      " "
" "                    " "                    -1,0                   1,0
TUPLES                 1,0                    BOT                    "_____"
0,8                    " "                    1,0                    1,0
" "                    -1,0                   "Whsl Imp."            "_____"
DATA                   BOT                    0,32145                1,0
0,0                    1,0                    V                      "_____"
" "                    " "                    0,31703                1,0
-1,0                   1,0                    V                      "_____"
BOT                    "Oct"                  0,35280                -1,0
1,0                    1,0                    V                      BOT
" "                    "Nov"                  0,102326               1,0
1,0                    1,0                    V                      "Total"
"FOURTH QUA"           "Dec"                  -1,0                   0,96157
1,0                    1,0                    BOT                    V
"RTER SALES"           "Totals"               1,0                    0,104651
1,0                    -1,0                   "Whsl Prep"            V
", 1987"               BOT                    0,25129                0,106346
1,0                    1,0                    V                      V
" "                                           0,26734                0,307154
-1,0                   "Catering"             V                      V
BOT                    0,42637                0,28143                -1,0
1,0                    V                      V                      EOD
" "                    0,42860                0,80006
```

Figure 8.15: *The BRNCHSLS.DIF Text File (one long column on disk)*

moved it inside the Outline frame. He also renamed his original spreadsheet "Activity Comparisons: Main Store".

To make comparing and combining the spreadsheets easier, he had to change the format of Joe's spreadsheet to match his own. First, he deleted Joe's title and the blank line beneath it. Second, he added three columns after column A, so the last three months of the quarter were at the right side of the spreadsheet. Third, he centered the month headings of Oct, Nov, and Dec. Then he moved the highlight to the border of the Branch Store spreadsheet, set the Decimal Places option in the Numbers submenu to 0, and chose the Currency format, to make the display of numbers match his spreadsheet. Finally, he locked the titles.

Now his spreadsheets were laid out identically. He copied the Main Store spreadsheet to a new frame within the Sales Activity outline. He labeled it "Activity Comparisons: Both Stores". Behind the cell for July Wholesale Prepared Food sales, he created a formula to add the values from the equivalent cells of the spreadsheets for each store. He used Framework II's pointing mode to create the formula, which read

@sum([Activity Comparisons: Main Store].B2,
[Activity Comparisons: Branch Store].B2)

He copied this formula to all the cells in the spreadsheet except the titles and the cells containing dotted lines, and then waited as Framework II recalculated all the values. When the process was complete, he printed out the Outline frame so he could compare the spreadsheets easily. His printout of the spreadsheets is shown in Figure 8.16. Next July, when George would prepare another activity comparisons summary, he could just copy the formulas into a new "Activity Comparisons: Both Stores" spreadsheet.

```
Activity Comparisons: Main Store

            Jul       Aug       Sep       Oct       Nov       Dec       Totals
Catering  $83,639   $79,243   $75,621   $77,821   $84,260   $87,402   $487,986
Whsl Imp. $60,218   $61,732   $61,482   $59,709   $64,821   $65,201   $373,163
Whsl Prep $45,521   $45,443   $42,879   $43,826   $47,365   $47,888   $272,922
          -----------------------------------------------------------------
Total     $189,378  $186,418  $179,982  $181,356  $196,446  $200,491  $1,134,071


Activity Comparisons: Branch Store

            Jul       Aug       Sep       Oct       Nov       Dec       Totals
Catering                                $39,325   $42,637   $42,860   $124,822
Whsl Imp.                               $31,703   $35,280   $35,343   $102,326
Whsl Prep                               $25,129   $26,734   $28,143    $80,006
          -----------------------------------------------------------------
Total                                   $96,157   $104,651  $106,346  $307,154


3  Activity Comparisons: Both Stores (S)

            Jul       Aug       Sep       Oct       Nov       Dec       Totals
Catering  $83,639   $79,243   $75,621   $117,146  $126,897  $130,262  $612,808
Whsl Imp. $60,218   $61,732   $61,482   $91,412   $100,101  $100,544  $475,489
Whsl Prep $45,521   $45,443   $42,879   $68,955   $74,099   $76,031   $352,928
          -----------------------------------------------------------------
Total     $189,378  $186,418  $179,982  $277,513  $301,097  $306,837  $1,441,225
```

Figure 8.16: Integrating a DIF File into a Framework II Spreadsheet

EXPLORING FURTHER

Before we leave our discussion of working with other programs, let's look at ways to import and export file formats that are not included on Framework II's Import and Export menus. We'll explore ways to integrate columnar data from an ASCII text file into a spreadsheet or database, import a comma-delimited file, and export a spreadsheet or database to a word-processing program.

INTEGRATING A COLUMNAR ASCII FILE
INTO A SPREADSHEET OR DATABASE

As you may have discovered, you can transfer data among different types of frames. You can copy the contents of a Database or Spreadsheet frame into a Word frame, and sometimes you can copy the text from a Word frame into a Database or Spreadsheet frame. How successfully you can do so depends on the format of the data in the original frame.

When moving columnar text from a Word frame to a Spreadsheet or Database frame, the important point to remember is that commas between text items, and single-character spaces between numeric fields, behave as delimiters between fields. Also, if you have some tabular data in which some items are blank, the data will not fall into the proper columns when you move it to a columnar frame.

Suppose, for example, that you were beginning a project schedule, or importing one from another program, and the data appeared in the following form:

Date	Task	Person
6 July87	Make initial contacts	George
	Send Purchase orders	Francine
	Write ad copy	Sue
12July87	Pick up Merchandise	Marie
14July87	Place ads	Sue
	Follow up on purchase orders	George
	Call Deliveries, Inc.	Harold

This seems like a natural format for a database frame. However, there are some hazards you must watch out for:

- Spaces between numbers act as field separators

- A single space between text items does *not* act as a field separator

- A comma within a text field acts as a field separator

If you copy this text to a database frame, the result will appear as in Figure 8.17. The space between 6 and July will result in the 6 being treated as numeric data and placed in a separate field. Similarly, the comma in Deliveries, Inc. will result in this text field being spread across two columns. As a result, the third field in these rows will be placed in a fourth column. Finally, the fact that

Follow up on purchase orders

is separated by only a single space from the responsible person's name will result in the name being included in the Task field, and the Person field will be blank.

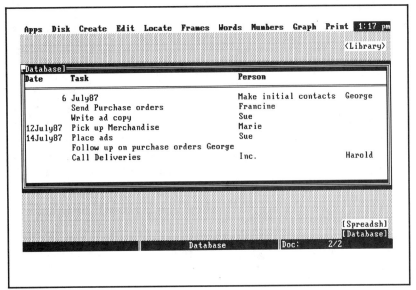

Figure 8.17: *A Database from Columnar Data in a Word Frame*

Moreover, sometimes the leading spaces in some rows will be ignored, so that the tasks in column 2 of this text will end up in column 1. Clearly, some editing of the text form of the data—such as replacing " July" with "July", adding more space between columns 2 and 3, and replacing commas with nothing, will improve the results.

SPECIAL TECHNIQUES FOR COMMA-DELIMITED FILES

Comma-delimited files can be imported with relatively little difficulty. Again, the technique is to bring the file to the desktop as an ASCII text file in a Word frame and then copy the contents to a Database frame. The same things can go wrong as in a transfer in the opposite direction, however. That is, you must be sure that the imported file has no quotation marks embedded within text fields, and no commas within numeric fields. Again, a bit of editing of the data while it's in the Word frame can help to ensure a smooth transfer with the results you desire. To see the results of such an import, you might take the comma-delimited version of the Sales People database, bring it to the desktop, and copy it to a Database frame of appropriate size. The result should be a reasonable duplication of the original database, as shown in Figure 8.18, provided that you converted all the numeric cells from currency to general format before you created the comma-delimited file.

```
 Apps  Disk  Create  Edit   Locate  Frames  Words  Numbers  Graph  Print  1:55 pm
 EmpNo     Last      First   Reg     SixMoSaleAvgPerMo Pbn        Hired

 82M1     Waterman  Pearl   MW      85977.83 14329.64 #NO        Sep 29, 1
 84M3     Brooke    Donny   MW      58439.33  9739.89 #YES       Dec 1, 19
 85M2     Olsen     Oscar   MW      1.15E+5 19089.46 #NO         Jun 20, 1
 66N3     Rizzo     Anne    NE      1.10E+5 19605.41 #NO         May 21, 1
 79N6     Herrera   Fred    NE      87654.32 14609.05 #NO        Nov 20, 1
 86N2     Sapolsky  Stan    NE      48675.30  8112.55 #YES       Jul 13, 1
 74N4     TakahashiBruce    NW      1.03E+5 17110.00 #NO         Mar 23, 1
 82N8     Woo       Eva     NW      93254.10 15542.35 #NO        Feb 25, 1
 85N5     Smith     Joe     NW      56733.45  9455.58 #YES       Oct 23, 1
 69S3     WashingtoEd       S       1.02E+5 17062.52 #NO         Aug 29, 1
 78S4     Curtis    Amy     S       47256.70  7876.12 #YES       Apr 12, 1
 82S6     HernandezEsther   S       83241.20 13873.53 #NO        May 5, 19
 72S6     SchroederArt      SE      94243.22 15707.20 #NO        Jan 24, 1
 81S5     Petrakis  Bill    SE      1.12E+5 18710.72 #NO         Aug 24, 1
 84S1     Smyth     Gloria  SE      87732.41 14622.07 #NO        May 17, 1
 78S1     SmithfielFrank    SW      51623.62  8603.94 #YES       Jul 22, 1
 83S9     Goldberg  Jack    SW      1.03E+5 17209.11 #NO         Oct 29, 1
 86S2     Smith     Ashleigh SW     67132.45 11188.74 #NO        Mar 4, 19

                       Comma-Delimited File].EmpNo  Recs:    25/25
```

Figure 8.18: *A Database from a Comma-Delimited File*

Comma-delimited files can also be used for importing and exporting spreadsheets, but you run into additional difficulties. Figure 8.19 shows a comma-delimited file created from the Activity Comparisons spreadsheet. Figure 8.20 shows the result after the file has been brought to the desktop in a Word frame and copied to a Spreadsheet frame. As you can see, while the numeric data has survived the transfer, the commas between the text fields have been treated as separate items of data, and given their own cells.

To transfer data to a spreadsheet by way of a comma-delimited file, then, you must edit the comma-delimited file. Specifically, you must remove all the double quotation marks. You can do this by replacing them globally with nothing. There is one other error that can result from this process, however: a *null string,* which is a string containing no characters. This is how an empty field is treated in a comma-delimited

```
"","Jan","Feb","Mar","Apr","May","Jun","Jul","Aug","Sep","Oct","Nov","Dec","Totals"
"Catering",83251,75495,68379,71658,76987,86174,84231,79243,75621,77821,84260,87402,950522
"Whsl Imp.",65732,64981,59875,62186,61864,62842,62436,61732,61482,59709,64821,65201,752861
"Whsl Prep",45681,38216,40102,43424,43841,42106,45234,45443,42879,43826,47365,47888,526005
"","_____","_____","_____","_____","_____","_____","_____"
,"_____","_____","_____","_____","_____","_____","_____"
"Total",194664,178692,168356,177268,182692,191122,191901,186418,179982,181356,196446,200491,2229388
```

Figure 8.19: A Comma-Delimited File from a Spreadsheet.

> Note: The series of underscore characters enclosed in quotes appears on two lines in the figure because of space restrictions. It is actually one long line in the file.

```
     Apps  Disk  Create  Edit  Locate  Frames  Words  Numbers  Graph  Print  1 20 pm
            A      B      C      D       E       F      G       H
  1                      Jan      ,          Feb    ,          Mar    ,          Apr
  2    Catering    83251  75495   68379   71658   76987   86174   84231    7
  3    Whsl Imp.   65732  64981   59875   62186   61864   62842   62436    6
  4    Whsl Prep   45681  38216   40102   43424   43841   42106   45234    4
  5               ,      _____ ,       _____ ,       _____ ,       ____
  6    Total      194664 178692  168356  177268  182692  191122  191901   18

                              om Comma-delimited file1.B1   SS:        2/1
```

Figure 8.20: A Spreadsheet from a Comma-Delimited File

file. It will be represented as

                    ""

As you may remember, cell A1 of the original spreadsheet was blank, and was therefore represented as a null string in Figure 8.19. After you delete all the quotation marks, the comma-delimited file will begin with a comma, and the first cell will disappear, causing misalignment of the column labels in row 1. You can prevent this error by adding a single space to the beginning of the file. With the comma-delimited file revised as shown in Figure 8.21, it is possible to recreate the spreadsheet correctly.

```
 ,Jan,Feb,Mar,Apr,May,Jun,Jul,Aug,Sep,Oct,Nov,Dec,Totals
Catering,83251,75495,68379,71658,76987,86174,84231,79243,75621,77821,84260,87402,950522
Whsl Imp.,65732,64981,59875,62186,61864,62842,62436,61732,61482,59709,64821,65201,752861
Whsl Prep,45681,38216,40102,43424,43841,42106,45234,45443,42879,43826,47365,47888,526005
 ,---------,---------,---------,---------,---------,---------,---------,---------
 ,---------,---------,---------,---------,-----------
Total,194664,178692,168356,177268,182692,191122,191901,186418,179982,181356,196446,200491,2229388
```

Figure 8.21: A *Comma-Delimited File for Export to a Spreadsheet.*
Note: The series of underscore characters enclosed in quotes appears on two lines in the figure because of space restrictions. It is actually one long line in the file.

EXPORTING COLUMNAR DATA TO A WORD PROCESSING PROGRAM

As mentioned earlier, you will get an error message if you try to export a Spreadsheet or Database frame to WordStar or MultiMate. One way around this is to export the frame to an ASCII text file, and then read the text file into the word processing program. However, when you export a frame to an ASCII text file, you will lose any styling and formatting information the frame may contain. If you want to preserve such information, first copy the Spreadsheet or Database frame into a Word frame, and then export the Word frame directly to the word processing program's format. Since formulas residing behind cells or column heads are not converted in any of the import or export formats, you will lose nothing by taking this extra step.

SPECIAL CONSIDERATIONS IN EXPORTING TO WORD PROCESSORS

The export programs for word processing programs are not as clean as they might be. Not everything is translated entirely accurately. There are three aspects of frames that you need to be particularly careful about:

□ Tabs

□ Page breaks

□ Frame labels and frames that are not Word frames

No matter what size tabs and paragraph indentations you use in your Word frames, the translation programs automatically convert all tabs to eight spaces. This is because the conversion is done by means of the Tab character (ASCII 9). While a typewriter's tabulator can be set at any point you want, in the world of computers the Tab character has traditionally been converted to eight spaces when a file is converted to text.

Framework II's hard page breaks are not translated into hard page breaks in WordStar files. If you know you will be converting to WordStar, you might simply insert WordStar's page-break code

.pa

whenever you want a hard page break, instead of using Framework II's hard page break.

Finally, you will have best results if you export Word frames, rather than Outline frames. If you have been creating text in an outline and you want to preserve your subheadings, you will probably have to copy the text from each of the subframes into a single Word frame, and use the Cut and Paste macros (Alt-F7 and Alt-F8) to paste the frame labels into the Word frame at appropriate points. If you export an Outline frame directly, you will lose all the frame labels.

SUMMARY

Framework II includes several different types of tools to help you work with other programs. It can convert Framework II frames into six different types of files:

- □ ASCII text files
- □ dBASE comma-delimited files
- □ Lotus 1-2-3 worksheet files
- □ DCA files
- □ WordStar word processing files
- □ MultiMate word processing files

It can also convert seven other types of files into Framework II frames:

- dBASE files
- ASCII text files
- Row-order DIF files
- Lotus 1-2-3 worksheet files
- DCA files
- WordStar word processing files
- MultiMate word processing files

In addition to its file-translating capabilities, Framework II allows you to run other programs without actually unloading Framework II from memory. You can run other programs using three different methods:

- In a DOS Access frame
- By means of a FRED program on the desktop
- By installing a FRED program on the Apps menu

These capabilities make Framework II an extremely flexible tool for working in a variety of environments. They allow you to customize Framework II so that you can use other types of software conveniently, and to share files with other programs that you may use. They also simplify considerably the task of sharing data with people who use software other than Framework II to accomplish the tasks that you usually perform using Framework II.

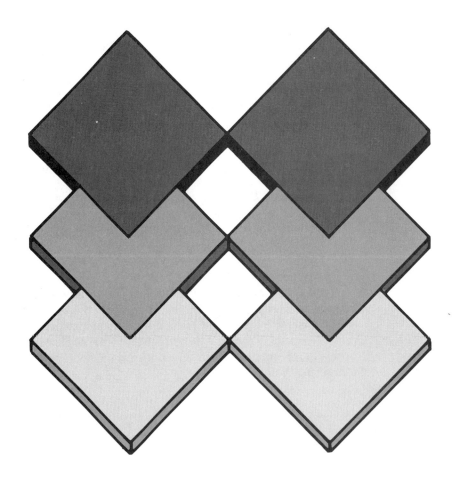

INSTALLING AND

CUSTOMIZING FRAMEWORK II

In this appendix, we will examine the Setup program and some of the most important options it provides for making Framework II conform to your hardware and your work habits.

The Setup program is extremely easy to use. You make all your choices by selecting items from menus, using the number keys at the top of the keyboard. You are prompted whenever you need to enter any text. If the instructions are not clear enough, context-sensitive help is available at any point via the Help key (F1). Since the program is so easy to use, we will not direct you keystroke by keystroke. Rather, we will point out some of the most useful options, or the most useful settings for the options that are available to you.

You must run the Setup program at a DOS prompt, not from the Framework II desktop. It is also best not to have any RAM-resident programs active while you are using Setup. When you are finished using the program, you have the choice of either saving the settings you have changed, or leaving the program without saving the settings. Therefore, you can feel free to experiment, knowing that you can cancel any changes you have made. You can use the Setup program to change Framework II's default settings as often as you like.

INSTALLING FRAMEWORK II FOR THE FIRST TIME

If you have never used Framework II before, you must take two steps to install it. First, you must *personalize* your copy, and then you must configure the program for your hardware.

To personalize your copy, place System Disk 1 in drive A, and at an A prompt, type

    id

You will be prompted to enter your name, the name of your company (which is optional), and the serial number of your disk, which you can read either from the label or from the warranty card. Once you have completed these steps, you can make working copies of all the progam disks, or install Framework II to a hard disk.

To proceed, place the Setup disk in drive A and type

    setup

In a short time, you will see the screen shown in Figure A.1. Press 1, and follow the directions that appear on the screen for floppy or hard disk systems, as appropriate. You will need to tell Framework II the name of your video card, your monitor, and your printer. Choose the appropriate models from the lists provided.

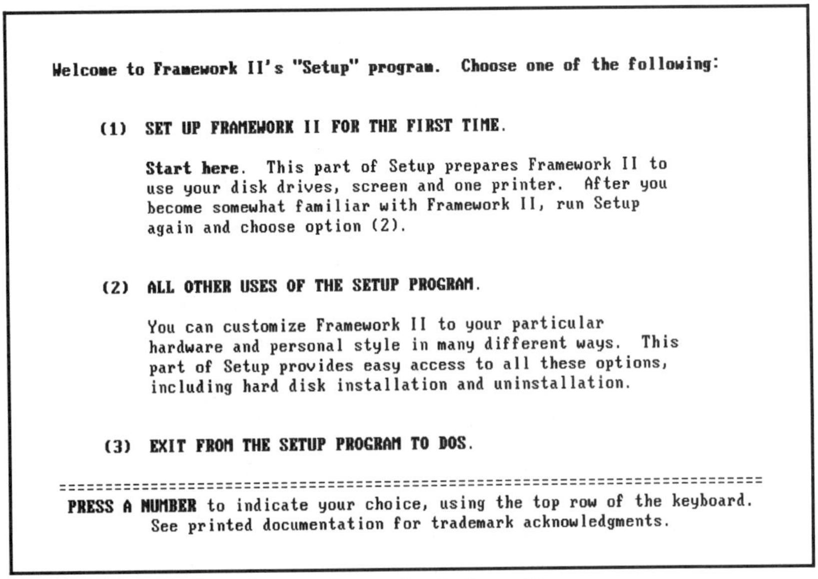

```
Welcome to Framework II's "Setup" program.  Choose one of the following:

    (1)  SET UP FRAMEWORK II FOR THE FIRST TIME.

         Start here.  This part of Setup prepares Framework II to
         use your disk drives, screen and one printer.  After you
         become somewhat familiar with Framework II, run Setup
         again and choose option (2).


    (2)  ALL OTHER USES OF THE SETUP PROGRAM.

         You can customize Framework II to your particular
         hardware and personal style in many different ways.  This
         part of Setup provides easy access to all these options,
         including hard disk installation and uninstallation.


    (3)  EXIT FROM THE SETUP PROGRAM TO DOS.

===========================================================================
    PRESS A NUMBER to indicate your choice, using the top row of the keyboard.
         See printed documentation for trademark acknowledgments.
```

Figure A.1: The Introductory Screen for the Setup Program

The Setup program allows you to do a great deal more to tailor Framework II to your hardware and your working habits. Let's look now at some of the options it provides.

TAILORING FRAMEWORK II TO YOUR HARDWARE

If you have already installed Framework II and want to go further with the options provided by the Setup program, load the program as though you were going to install Framework II, but press 2 when the screen shown in Figure A.1 appears. You will be greeted by the Setup program's main menu, shown in Figure A.2. Press 2, and the screen shown in Figure A.3 will be displayed. To customize Framework II for your hardware, you will use options primarily from the Configuration menu. Let's look at some of the options it provides.

```
                              MAIN MENU

(1)  QUICK-REVIEW all settings

     CHANGE individual settings

       (2)  CONFIGURATION. . . . hardware, install/uninstall, use of memory

       (3)  PREFERENCES. . . . . default frame sizes and menu settings

       (4)  TELECOMMUNICATIONS . menu names and setups, terminal emulation

       (5)  OTHER SETTINGS . . . spelling check, sort order, miscellany

       (6)  ADD-INS. . . . . . . applications, import/export

(7)  SAVE ALL NEW SETTINGS and then exit to DOS

(8)  EXIT TO DOS without saving changes .
============================================================================
 PRESS A NUMBER to indicate your choice, using the top row of the keyboard.
                Or PRESS [F1] for HELP (more information).
```

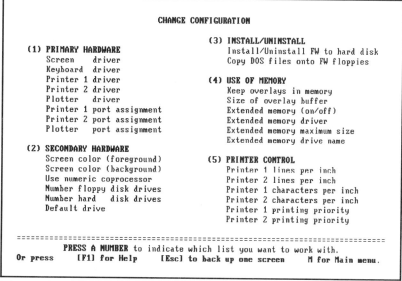

Figure A.2: *The Setup Program Main Menu*

```
                          CHANGE CONFIGURATION

                                       (3) INSTALL/UNINSTALL
(1) PRIMARY HARDWARE                       Install/Uninstall FW to hard disk
    Screen    driver                       Copy DOS files onto FW floppies
    Keyboard  driver
    Printer 1 driver                   (4) USE OF MEMORY
    Printer 2 driver                       Keep overlays in memory
    Plotter   driver                       Size of overlay buffer
    Printer 1 port assignment              Extended memory (on/off)
    Printer 2 port assignment              Extended memory driver
    Plotter   port assignment              Extended memory maximum size
                                           Extended memory drive name
(2) SECONDARY HARDWARE
    Screen color (foreground)          (5) PRINTER CONTROL
    Screen color (background)              Printer 1 lines per inch
    Use numeric coprocessor                Printer 2 lines per inch
    Number floppy disk drives              Printer 1 characters per inch
    Number hard   disk drives              Printer 2 characters per inch
    Default drive                          Printer 1 printing priority
                                           Printer 2 printing priority
============================================================================
        PRESS A NUMBER to indicate which list you want to work with.
Or press     [F1] for Help     [Esc] to back up one screen     M for Main menu.
```

Figure A.3: *The Configuration Menu*

INSTALLING DISK DRIVES

Framework II is extremely "well-behaved" with respect to disk drives and directories—it can navigate through subdirectories with ease. However, you should make sure that the program can access all the drives in your system, or all the drives that you want it to have access to.

In its default configuration, Framework II expects to find two floppy disk drives. Thus, if you have not installed disk drives, the disk drive cabinets on the desktop will be labeled A and B. If you have some other number or type of drives, press 2 on the Configuration menu to select Secondary Hardware.

If you have a hard disk, you probably do not have a drive B. You will want to change the number of floppy disk drives from 2 to 1 and the number of hard disk drives from 0 to 1.

If you use a RAM disk, things may be a bit trickier. If you have two floppy disk drives and no hard disk, your RAM disk will probably be drive C. If you have others, they will have letter designations after C. Set the number of floppy disk drives to the total number of drives—floppy disk drives and RAM disks—in your system.

If you have a hard disk and want to use one or more RAM disks, you will do better to ask Framework II to regard your RAM disk as an additional hard disk. Change the number of floppy disk drives to 1, and the number of hard disk drives to 1 plus the number of RAM disks you use. The next time you run Framework II, the changes you have made will be reflected in the disk drive cabinets.

INSTALLING TWO PRINTER CONFIGURATIONS

As you can see from Figure A.3, you can install two printers and a plotter. If your printer has two different modes of operation, one of which emulates another printer, you may want to install the driver for the emulated printer as the second printer. However, even if you have only one printer, you may still find it useful to install two printer configurations. To make the most of this possibility, you will need to use both the Primary Hardware and Printer Control submenus.

Notice that the Printer Control submenu allows you to determine the default number of lines per inch and characters per inch separately for two printers. You could, for example, have two default configurations for a single printer, one for 6 lines per inch and 12 characters per inch, and the other for 8 lines per inch and 10 characters per inch. Simply enter the appropriate values in the Printer Control submenu, and install your printer as both Printer 1 and Printer 2 in the Primary Hardware submenu.

CONTROLLING SCREEN COLORS

If you have a color card and a color monitor, you may want to have Framework II display its text screens in color. If your color card is, or emulates, an IBM color card, you have two quite different options. You can install Framework II to display its screen as *bit-mapped graphics*— that is, a representation of text that is painted dot-by-dot on your monitor. This has the advantage of displaying italics, bolface, and underlining exactly as they will appear in a printed document. To choose this type of display, use the IBM Color Graphics driver.

With this driver, the default colors are bright white on a black background. You cannot change the background color, but you can change the foreground to the color of your choice by selecting a color from Table A.1 and entering its color code in the Screen Color (foreground) option of the Secondary Hardware submenu.

Low Intensity	Code	High Intensity	Code
Black	0	Dark Gray	8
Blue	1	Light Blue	9
Green	2	Bright Green	10
Cyan	3	Bright Cyan	11
Red	4	Light Red	12
Magenta	5	Bright Magenta	13
Brown	6	Yellow	14
Light Gray	7	White	15

Table A.1: Color Codes

On the other hand, you may prefer a display that makes use of more than one color. To have this type of display, use the IBM Color (Text Color) driver. With this driver installed, italics and underlining will be represented by different colors (green for underlining, red for italics, and yellow for combined italics and underlining, unless you choose one of these colors as your foreground or background color), and boldface will be represented by the high-intensity shade of your foreground color. (If your foreground color *is* a high-intensity shade, boldface will be its low-intensity equivalent, which is somewhat confusing.) Text that is styled as both boldface and another styling option will appear in the high-intensity shade of the other option. Menu options that are available will be highlighted, and those that are not will be lowlighted.

The default colors with this driver are low-intensity white on a black background, with the main menu in bright green. You cannot choose the menu color, but you can set both foreground and background color in the Secondary Hardware menu, using the color codes from Table A.1. You cannot, however, use bright white as the foreground color.

Because both the low-intensity and high-intensity versions of your foreground color must be legible, the color combinations that are actually useful are limited. After extensive experimentation, we have found that a light gray foreground (7) on a blue background (1) is the most legible combination other than the default.

MANAGING MEMORY

Let's turn our attention now to the Use of Memory submenu. It includes some seductive options that generally do not have the desired effect.

Framework II is a large program. Ordinarily, it reads sections of code from an *overlay file* when you switch from one function to another, and only a small portion of the actual program code is in memory at any given time. You can increase the size of the overlay buffer, which theoretically should speed up performance by reducing the number of times code has to be read from disk. In fact, increasing the size of the overlay buffer will reduce severely the amount of memory available for your files, which may hamper your operations, and even slow the program down. We recommend *not* increasing the size of the overlay buffer.

You can use extended memory (above 640K) with Framework II if it is available in your system. To do so, you must make two entries in the Use of Memory submenu. First, you must install the name of the program that initializes your extended memory. Second, you must specify the maximum amount of extended memory that you want Framework II to use. You should be aware, however, that the largest file on the desktop is always kept in conventional memory, and conventional memory is also used to store *pointers* to the location of any files that are located in extended memory. Therefore, if you do not have enough conventional memory to store the pointers, you will not be able to use extended memory.

The Use of Memory submenu includes an option to use a disk drive as though it were extended memory. If you have a hard disk, this option may be tempting. However, since reading from and writing to disk is the slowest aspect of computer operations, using your hard disk as extended memory will slow down Framework II's performance markedly. Unless you need to work with immense databases, we strongly recommend that you do not use a hard disk as extended memory.

CUSTOMIZING THE DESKTOP

Let's turn now to the Preferences menu, which is shown in Figure A.4. To display this menu, press 3 at the main menu. As you can see, this menu allows you to determine a number of default settings for the options that appear on Framework II's menus. You can choose the size of various types of frames, the default dimensions of databases and spreadsheets on the Create menu, and some of the default settings for the Words and Print menus. If you would prefer larger disk drive cabinets, for example, or if you characteristically work with small spreadsheets, this is the easiest way to tailor these features to your style of working.

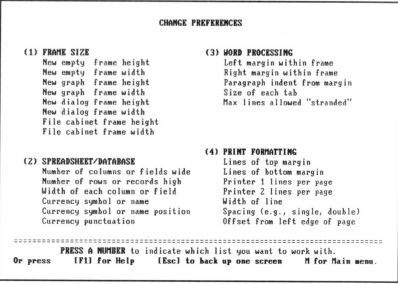

```
                        CHANGE PREFERENCES


  (1) FRAME SIZE                          (3) WORD PROCESSING
      New empty  frame height                 Left margin within frame
      New empty  frame width                  Right margin within frame
      New graph  frame height                 Paragraph indent from margin
      New graph  frame width                  Size of each tab
      New dialog frame height                 Max lines allowed "stranded"
      New dialog frame width
      File cabinet frame height
      File cabinet frame width

                                          (4) PRINT FORMATTING
  (2) SPREADSHEET/DATABASE                    Lines of top margin
      Number of columns or fields wide        Lines of bottom margin
      Number of rows or records high          Printer 1 lines per page
      Width of each column or field           Printer 2 lines per page
      Currency symbol or name                 Width of line
      Currency symbol or name position        Spacing (e.g., single, double)
      Currency punctuation                    Offset from left edge of page

  ===========================================================================
            PRESS A NUMBER to indicate which list you want to work with.
  Or press     [F1] for Help     [Esc] to back up one screen    M for Main menu.
```

Figure A.4: The Preferences Menu

When you select one of the items on the Preferences menu to modify, its minimum, maximum, and default settings are shown, along with its current setting. This makes it easy to determine what is available, and reminds you of the settings you are currently using.

Our only specific recommendation is that you leave the Paragraph Indent setting at 0. If you do not, the line after any carriage return in a Word frame will automatically be indented. This can be inconvenient if you want to place the inside address of a letter at the left margin.

INSTALLING TELECOMMUNICATIONS SETUPS

In Chapter 6, we noted that you can streamline your telecommunications work by saving the settings you need for remote computers you communicate with frequently in setup files. You can further streamline your work by installing your most frequently used setup files on the desktop Telecommunications menu.

To do so, press 4 at the main menu. As you will see, you can install up to nine setups. They appear in groups of three, with each group of three on a separate menu. For each setup, you will need to enter both the name to appear on the menu and the file name of the setup. The procedure for making these installations is the same as the one described in Chapter 8 for installing Applications Add-ins.

MISCELLANEOUS FEATURES

You should be aware of three options on the Other Settings menu, reached by pressing 5 at the main menu. When you use either of the Sort options on the Locate menu, Framework II normally arranges the items to be sorted in *ASCII* order. That is, the order is determined by the ASCII code of the characters in the field to be sorted. A glance at Table C.1 will reveal that the entire range of uppercase letters appears before any of the lowercase letters in the ASCII code.

If you prefer, you can use this menu to change the sorting order to Dictionary order. This will cause Framework II to place words in alphabetical order regardless of capitalization.

You can also change the default personal dictionary on this menu. If most of your work involves business correspondence, for example, you might prefer to have BUSINESS.DCT rather than PERSONAL.DCT as the default personal dictionary.

If your system allows you to capture text in a DOS Access frame, you can use this menu to change the number of characters that will be retained. Normally, after 32,000 characters have appeared in a DOS Access frame, any subsequent characters will replace characters at the beginning of the frame. You can increase or decrease the number of characters retained.

You may have noticed that the Disk menu includes room for three Import Add-ins and three Export Add-ins. In theory, you can add options to these sections of the Disk menu the same way you added the Applications Add-ins to the Apps menu. However, the format-translation files are extremely complex, involving many direct calls to machine language (the computer's native language), and are difficult to modify. Ashton-Tate was expected to make such translation files available for other file formats; however, as of this writing, none have been created.

USING RAM-RESIDENT SOFTWARE WITH FRAMEWORK II

Framework II is such a comprehensively designed software package that you should have little need for RAM-resident "background" programs such as macro processors, on-line dictionaries, and DOS access tools. However, if you are accustomed to using programs of this nature, you can still use them with Framework II. Most of them are quite compatible with it. The principal limitation is the amount of memory available in your computer. Remember that Framework II requires at least 480K, and unless you have extended memory, performs much more smoothly with at least 512K.

The only type of background software that does not generally work with Framework II is path-extension software. These programs allow you to use software that requires overlay or driver files without first logging onto the package's directory. When such a program is loaded, Framework II will look in drive A for many of its files, even if you are logged onto Framework II's directory on a hard disk. Even so, you can use this type of software successfully if neither your DOS search path nor your extended path includes the Framework II directory.

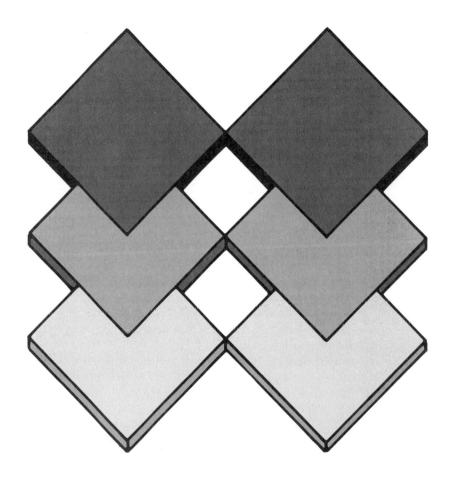

FRED FUNCTIONS

INTRODUCTION

This appendix presents a listing and brief explanation of all the FRED programming functions, with their syntax formats. The functions are listed alphabetically. By way of introduction, the following comments describe the major categories of FRED functions.

NUMERIC FUNCTIONS

The numeric functions all perform some operation on a numeric expression and return a numeric value. The parameters to these functions usually consist of a number, a numeric expression, or a reference to a number. This category includes rounding functions (@ROUND, @FLOOR, @CEILING); logarithmic and exponential functions (@LN, @EXP, @LOG); a random-number generator (@RAND); and trigonometric functions, among others. The parameters to the trigonometric functions @COS, @SIN, and @TAN must be angles expressed in radians.

STATISTICAL FUNCTIONS

FRED's statistical functions all return statistical information about a series of parameters. The parameters to these functions must be in the form of a range or list of numbers or numeric expressions. This category includes functions for finding sums, averages, minimum and maximum values, and the variance and standard deviation, as well as for counting the number of values in a range of values.

FINANCIAL FUNCTIONS

FRED's financial functions include the present and future value functions (@PV and @FV), the net present value function (@NPV), a function for calculating loan and mortgage payments (@PMT), and functions for finding the internal rate of return of a business investment (@IRR and @MIRR).

DATE AND TIME FUNCTIONS

FRED's date and time functions fall into two groups: those that return a date and time—and display the date; and those that convert the date-type value returned by the first group into a text string and format that string in various ways. The distinction is important: the first group returns date-type values, which can subsequently be sorted, used in the date arithmetic functions, or formatted. The results of the second group of functions can be used only as text strings—they cannot be sorted chronologically, used in the date arithmetic functions, or formatted in any other way. These are the functions that return date-type values:

> @date
>
> @datetime
>
> @diffdate
>
> @sumdate
>
> @time
>
> @today

All other date and time functions take one of these functions as a parameter and return text strings.

Of the functions that return date-type values, @DATE, @DATETIME, @TIME, and @TODAY all return both a date and a time and display the *date*. The times that @DATE (without parameters) and @TODAY return are always the current time on the system clock. When @DATE is used with parameters, the time it returns is Framework II's default time—12:00 AM. The dates that @TIME (without parameters) and @TODAY return are always the current date on the system clock. When @TIME is used with parameters, the date it returns is in the same format that the @DATE function displays. To get any of these functions to display the time, you must convert their results into a text string using one of the time formatting functions.

STRING FUNCTIONS

The string functions fall into two classes: those that perform some type of operation on a string, and those that convert numeric values to text values. The former include @LEN, @MID, @INT, and @VALUE. The rest of the string functions, with the exception of @TEXT-SELECTION, convert numeric values to text values in various formats.

NUMERIC DISPLAY (OR "TAILORING") FUNCTIONS

In this category are a number of functions that control the display of currency and other numeric values. The fundamental currency-formatting function is @NATIONALIZE. The functions that @NATIONALIZE takes as parameters are @DOLLAR, @POUND, and @YEN, to display currency values with their appropriate symbols and formatting. For other currencies, use @UNIT. Finally, the @THOUSANDS and @MILLI functions will control the display of decimal points and commas.

PRINTING FUNCTIONS

The printing functions determine the way printed output from a frame will appear on the page. The horizontal positioning of text on the page is determined by the two functions @PO (page offset) and @LL (line length). The functions that place headers and footers on the page determine left, right, and center relative to the printed line established by @PO and @LL, not the physical page edges. For example, if you set up your printed line so that it starts in column 15 and runs 50 characters, flush left will be at column 15 and flush right at column 65.

In those functions where the parameter appears in quotes, the parameter must be a text-type value. All other parameters represent numeric values.

MACRO-BUILDING FUNCTIONS

Macro-building functions are used to process the responses of a user to the macros you have created. They check the keyboard for responses, execute preprogrammed keystrokes in series, retrieve selected blocks of text, and select a particular frame or cell.

PROGRAMMING FUNCTIONS

FRED's programming functions handle all the standard programming operations. They fall into several classes:

Control functions
Logical functions

Input and output functions
Region-walking functions

The control functions include a loop controller (@WHILE), an assignment function (@SET), functions that pass values (@ITEM, @RESULT, and @RETURN), and a case structure (@SELECT). The logical functions include @IF, @AND, @OR, and @NOT, error-testing functions, and tests for alphabetic and numeric values. The input/output functions include @INPUTLINE, which prompts for user input; @PROMPT, which displays a prompt below the desktop; and @MENU, which processes a user-defined menu. FRED also includes the disk functions @WRITETEXTFILE and @WRITEFRAMEFILE, plus a number of other disk-related and directory-related functions.

The *region-walking* functions are a special class. They include the following functions:

@choose
@hlookup
@vlookup
@fill
@get
@next
@put
@reset

The first three are used for looking up items in tables. The rest are used to move a pointer within a specified range of frames or cells, and either retrieve values from or place values into them.

In addition, there are functions that fetch formulas from specified locations and place formulas in other locations and execute them, so FRED programs can modify themselves.

MISCELLANEOUS FUNCTIONS

In addition to all its other function categories, FRED includes graph-generating functions, sound and graphics sublanguages (which are only touched upon briefly in this appendix), and a function for reading records from a dBASE II or dBASE III file into Framework II.

THE FUNCTIONS

@ABS*(numeric expression)*
@ABS calculates the absolute value of its parameter.

@**ACOS**(numeric expression)

@ACOS returns the arccosine of its parameter, expressed in radians.

@**AND**(expression1, expression2, . . .)

@AND is a logical function that returns #TRUE if *all* of the logical statements among its parameters are true. Otherwise, it returns #FALSE. At least one of its parameters must be a logical statement, that is, a statement that can be evaluated as true or false. The @AND function is often used as part of the first parameter of the @IF function.

@**ASIN**(numeric expression)

@ASIN returns the arcsine of its parameter, expressed in radians.

@**ATAN**(numeric expression)

@ATAN returns the arctangent of its parameter, expressed in radians.

@**ATAN2**(expression1, expression2)

@ATAN2 returns the arctangent of the angle, expressed in radians, whose opposite and adjacent sides are represented by *expression1* and *expression2*, respectively. @ATAN2 allows you to calculate the arctangents of all four quadrants of an x-y axis system.

@**AVG**(expression1, expression2, . . .)
@**AVG**(range)

@AVG returns the average of all the numbers in its parameter list.

@**BEEP**
@**BEEP**(pitch, hundredths)

When used without parameters, @BEEP causes the computer to emit a standard beep. However, you can cause the computer's sound generator to produce any tone it is capable of producing, by specifying a particular pitch in cycles per second and the duration of the sound in hundredths of a second.

If you want to use @BEEP to play music, first set up a series of local variables assigning the various pitch frequencies to their letter names. Then you can use the letter names as parameters in a series of @BEEP expressions.

@**BM**(lines)

@BM sets the bottom margin for a page of printed output. Its parameter is the number of lines that will be left blank between the last line of text (not including the footer) and the bottom of the physical page. The default value is 6.

@BOP

@BOP*(indentation, format, left margin, right margin)*

@BOP starts a new paragraph of text, by inserting a hidden beginning-of-paragraph character. When used without parameters, it takes the default values of no indentation, flush right, a left margin of 0, and a right margin of 65. Choose a format by selecting its number from the following table:

0	Flush right
1	Align left
2	Justify
3	Center

The formula

"This is the end." & @bop(5,1,0,65) & "This is the beginning."

displays the text

This is the end.
    This is the beginning.

@BUSINESS*(numeric expression)*
@BUSINESS*(numeric expression, decimal places)*
@BUSINESS*(date)*

@BUSINESS rounds the numeric value in its parameter to two decimal places, formats the result with a comma between every three digits, and converts the result into a text value. If a positive number of decimal places is specified as the second parameter, @BUSINESS rounds its first parameter to the specified number of places. If the second parameter is a zero, @BUSINESS rounds its first parameter to an integer before converting it into a text value. If the second parameter is negative, the first parameter will be rounded to the nearest 10, 100, 1000, etc. For example, the expressions

@business(2654.7, −1)
@business(2654.7, −2)
@business(2654.7, −3)

will return the text strings 2,650, 2,700, and 3,000, respectively.

If the parameter to @BUSINESS is a date-type value, it will convert that value to a text string and display the result in the format

Month dd, yyyy

This result is identical to that returned by the @DATE4 function. For example, the function

@business(@date(1987, 8, 30))

will produce the text string

August 30, 1987

@CEILING*(numeric expression)*

@CEILING computes the smallest integer that is not less than its parameter. In other words, it rounds its parameter upwards. (Negative numbers are also rounded upwards, i.e., toward zero.)

@CHOOSE*(index, references)*

@CHOOSE retrieves a value from a specified position in a list or range of values. The first parameter, *index*, represents the position in the specified list or range where the desired value will be found. The subsequent parameter or parameters represent the list or range of values to be searched.

@CHR*(ASCII)*
@CHR*(ASCII, type style)*

@CHR is used to convert an ASCII code number into the character it represents. It can be used to display the graphics characters from the extended ASCII code, i.e., characters with codes from 128 to 255. It can also be used to supply special printing control characters to the @ST function.

You can specify a second parameter to assign a type style to the character returned by the first parameter. Choose a style by selecting its number from the following table:

1	Boldface
2	Italic
4	Underline

The effects are additive. For example, a value of 6 in the second parameter would indicate that the character returned by the first parameter should be italicized and underlined.

@COS*(numeric expression)*

@COS returns the cosine of the angle in its parameter, expressed in radians.

@COUNT*(expression1, expression2, . . .)*
@COUNT returns the number of numeric values in its list of parameters.

@CURRENCY*(numeric expression)*
The action of the @CURRENCY function is identical to that of the @BUSINESS function, except that @CURRENCY also includes a currency symbol in the resulting text value. Framework II's default currency symbol is $, which can be changed using the @NATIONAL-IZE function.

@CURRENCY is used to embed figures derived from other frames or cells in text. For example:

> "The tax on your order will be " &@currency(tax)

@DATE
@DATE*(yyyy, mm, dd)*
@DATE is usually used with three parameters, representing the year, month, and day, expressed as numbers. The result is a date-type value that can subsequently be sorted or used in the date arithmetic functions, @DIFFDATE and @SUMDATE. For example, the function

> @date(1987, 10, 12)

will return a date-type value that will be displayed as

> Oct 12, 1987

When used without parameters, @DATE returns the current date and time on the system clock and displays the date. The result of the @DATE function without parameters is identical to that of the @TODAY function.

@DATE1*(date)*
@DATE1 converts the date-type value in its parameter into a text string. Date arithmetic and chronological sorting cannot be performed on the result of @DATE1, because this result is a text value.
The parameter to this function must be another date function that produces a date-type value. For example:

> @date1(@date(1987, 8, 30))

will produce the text value

> Aug 30, 1987

Note that this resulting string is identical to the display format produced by @DATE and @TODAY. However, keep in mind the important difference: @DATE and @TODAY return date-type values, whereas @DATE1 (like @DATE2, @DATE3, and @DATE4) returns a string value.

@**DATE2***(date)*

@DATE2 converts the date-type value in its parameter to a text string and displays the result in the format

> Mmm yyyy

For example, the function

> @date2(@date(1987, 8, 30))

will produce the text value

> Aug 1987

The parameter to this function must be another date function that produces a date-type value.

@**DATE3***(date)*

@DATE3 converts the date-type value in its parameter to a text string and displays the result in the format

> Mmm dd

For example, the function

> @date3(@date(1987, 8, 30))

will produce the text string

> Aug 30

The parameter to this function must be another date function that produces a date-type value.

@**DATE4***(date)*

@DATE4 converts the date-type value in its parameter to a text string and displays the result in the format

> Month dd, yyyy

For example, the function

> @date4(@date(1987, 8, 30))

will produce the text string

> August 30, 1987

The parameter to this function must be another function that produces a date-type value.

@DATETIME*(date, time)*

@DATETIME takes two parameters, the date and the time. The @DATE, @TIME, or @TODAY functions can be used for either parameter. The @SUMDATE function can also be used for the date parameter. @DATETIME returns the date and time specified in its parameters and displays the date. For example, the function

 @datetime(@date(1987, 4, 18), (@time 14, 53, 10))

will display the date

 Apr 18, 1987

If the parameters are entered without their own parameters, this function, like @DATE, @TIME, and @TODAY, returns the current date and time from the system clock and displays the current date. To force the @DATETIME function to display the time, use @DATETIME as the parameter of @TIME1, @TIME2, @TIME3 or @TIME 4.

@DBASEFILTER*("Drive:filename.dbf", criteria, starting record, ending record)*

@DBASEFILTER is used to load selected records from a dBASE II or dBASE III file into Framework II. It has two required and two optional parameters. The first parameter gives the drive on which the file will be found and the name of the database file. The second specifies a criterion or criteria for selecting records from the database file. It may be a complex expression, choosing records on the basis of multiple criteria through the @AND, @OR, and @NOT functions.

The optional parameters tell Framework II at which record to begin searching for the selected criteria, and at which record to stop.

If you load a dBASE file onto the desktop from one of the disk drive cabinets, Framework II will automatically create a Database frame with a @DBASEFILTER formula behind it. Pressing the Recalc key (and then the Return key) causes Framework II to read as many of the records from the dBASE file as will fit in the memory of your computer. Alternatively, you can edit the @DBASEFILTER formula, expressing your own selection criteria, before Framework II begins reading records into the frame.

@**DECIMAL***(numeric expression)*
@**DECIMAL***(numeric expression, decimal places)*
@DECIMAL rounds its parameter to two decimal places and then converts the result into a text value. If a positive number of decimal places is specified as the second parameter, @DECIMAL will round to the number of places specified. If the second parameter is negative, @DECIMAL rounds the first parameter to the nearest 10, 100, 1000, etc., before converting it into a text value.

@**DIFFDATE***(date1, date2)*
@DIFFDATE calculates the number of days between *date1* and *date2*. If *date1* is earlier than *date2*, the result will be positive; if *date2* is earlier, the result will be negative. @DIFFDATE's parameters must be any of the following functions:

> @date
> @time
> @sumdate
> @today
> @datetime

@**DISPLAY***(frame name)*
@DISPLAY can be used within a program to display the contents of any frame that currently resides on the desktop or even on the "hidden" desktop. You can use this function to display specially prepared frames of information during a program's performance.

@**DOLLAR**
@DOLLAR can be used as a parameter to the @NATIONALIZE function. See the @NATIONALIZE entry for details of usage.

@**DRAW**
The @DRAW function puts at your disposal a complete graphics language for use in Framework II. Shapes can be drawn, lines plotted, and text placed anywhere within a frame. Areas can be filled with any of a number of patterns. Each of these commands is expressed as a number, followed by numbers representing various points within the frame as x and y coordinates.

@DRAWGRAPH*(source, #orientation, #type, "title", "x-axis title",*
"y-axis title", low value for x-axis, high value for x-axis,
increment for x-axis values)

The @DRAWGRAPH function draws graphs following the specific instructions selected from the Graphs menu. Framework II places a @DRAWGRAPH function behind every Graph frame that you create.

Selecting options from the Graphs submenu is by far the easiest way to draw graphs in Framework II. You can, however, change the graphs by editing the formula behind the resulting Graph frame. The easiest way to master the @DRAWGRAPH function is to create graphs from the menu and then study the formulas from which they are drawn.

@DRAWGRAPH has three required parameters:

@drawgraph(*source, #orientation, #type*)

Source is the section of a Database or Spreadsheet frame that will provide the data to be graphed. It may be referred to by row and column numbers or by their English-language labels.

#Orientation is the axis of the source frame indicating the source of x-axis titles for the graph. Either of two values is permissible:

#row
#column

#Type refers to the type of graph to be drawn. The following are the permissible values for this parameter:

#bar
#stackedbar
#line
#markedpoints
#xy
#pie

All types of graphs can have the following parameters included, in the following order:

"*Title*"	Graph title, in quotes
"*X-axis title*"	Title for horizontal axis, in quotes
"*Y-axis title*"	Title for vertical axis, in quotes

In addition, all types of graphs except pie graphs can have any of the following parameters included, after those mentioned above:

Low value for x-axis

High value for x-axis

Increment for x-axis values

In place of these parameters, pie graphs can have a parameter that tells which slice of the pie should be separated from the others. (Note that pie graphs must be drawn from only one row or column of figures.)

If you wish to use some, but not all, of the optional parameters, enter a comma in place of the skipped parameter. For example, to skip the titles but specify the numbers for the x-axis, your expression might read

@drawgraph(Income.A2:C5, #row, #bar, ,,, 200, 900, 50)

This expression would draw a bar graph from cells A2 through C5 of the Income spreadsheet, taking its x-axis orientation from the spreadsheet's rows. No titles would be included, but the x-axis would be numbered from 200 to 900 in increments of 50.

@ECHO(#OFF)
@ECHO(#ON)

@ECHO determines whether the effects of the keystrokes in a macro will be displayed. It can take either of two parameters, the constants #OFF and #ON. The expression

@echo(#OFF)

will execute the keystrokes specified in the macro without displaying any effects on the screen. The expression

@echo(#ON)

turns the display of keystroke activity back on again.

Care must be taken in using @ECHO(#OFF). If you use this function in a program and fail to turn the echo on again, no further keystrokes will be displayed. For an example of this function in use, see Chapter 7.

@ERASEPROMPT

@ERASEPROMPT erases a prompt displayed in the message area below the desktop.

@EXACT("string1", "string2")

@EXACT returns #TRUE if string1 and string2 are identical, #FALSE if they are not. Unlike comparisons of strings with the "=" operator, @EXACT compares every character in both strings. The result is #FALSE if one string is longer than the other, or if any character in one string is of a different case from the equivalent character in the other string. Wild-card characters may not be used.

@**EXECUTE***(frame reference, formula)*

@EXECUTE places a new formula behind a specified frame and then performs the formula. Any formula that previously resided behind the frame is replaced.

@**EXP***(exponent)*

@EXP returns a power of *e*, where *e* is 2.7182818. Therefore, the expression

@exp(x)

is the same as e^x.

@**FC***("footer text")*

@FC defines a string of text for the footer and specifies that the footer be centered below the last line of text.

@**FILL***(range, startvalue, increment)*

@FILL is used to fill a range in a database or spreadsheet with incrementing or decrementing values. It has three parameters. *Range* specifies the range that is to receive the values. *Startvalue* is the beginning value, and *increment* is the amount by which each subsequent value is to be increased. If the optional third parameter is not included, @FILL places the same value in every cell in the specified range. If the third value is negative, the values are decremented. The second parameter can also be a string parameter for filling columns or rows with text. Normally, @FILL should be deleted from the spreadsheet or database once the function has performed its task.

@**FL***("footer text")*

@FL defines a string of text for the footer and specifies that the footer be printed flush left below the last line of text.

@**FLOOR***(numeric expression)*

@FLOOR returns the largest integer that is not greater than its parameter. In other words, it rounds its parameter downward. (Negative numbers are also rounded downward, i.e., away from zero.)

@**FP***(line)*

@FP (footer position) determines the number of lines that will be left blank between the footer and the bottom of the paper. Its value must be less than that of the bottom margin, @BM. The default value for the footer position is 3.

@FR(*"footer text"*)

@FR defines a string of text for the footer and specifies that the footer be printed flush right below the last line of text.

@FRAMETYPE
@FRAMETYPE(*"frame reference"*)

@FRAMETYPE returns the type of frame currently selected or, if the cursor is not within a frame, the type of location of the cursor, as a number from the following table:

1	Cabinet
2	Library
3	Menu
4	Help screen
5	Outline frame
6	Spreadsheet frame
7	Database frame
8	Empty frame
9	Word frame
10	Graph frame
11	Cell
12	Field
13	Telecommunications frame
14	Inside a Word frame
15	Inside the formula area
16	On the edit line
17	Inside a Telecommunications frame
18	In a local variable

If a frame reference is given, @FRAMETYPE returns the frame type of the specified frame.

@FRAMEVIEW
@FRAMEVIEW(*"frame reference"*)

@FRAMEVIEW returns the type of frame currently selected as a number from the following table:

1	Database in Table view

2	Database in Forms view
3	Database in dBASE view
4	File cabinet showing file names only
5	File cabinet showing dates and times
6	Frames view of other types of frames
7	Outline view of other types of frames

If a frame reference is given, @FRAMEVIEW returns the frame type of the specified frame. This function can be used to test before issuing commands. For example, if you want to leave a frame called OUTLINE on the desktop in Outline view after executing a program it contains, you might use the formula

@if(@frametype("outline") = 6, @performkeys("{f10}"))

@**FV***(payment, rate, periods)*

@FV returns the compounded future value of a series of payments, given the following:

- □ A value representing an amount of money that is repeatedly added to the investment at regular intervals (*payment*)

- □ A value representing the periodic interest *rate*

- □ A value representing the number of payments (*periods*)

Be aware that the interest rate given must be the interest rate *per period*. Therefore, you must divide the annual interest rate by the number of periods per year.

@**GET***(range)*

@GET is a region-walking function that returns the value of the current position in a specified range. The @NEXT function is used along with @GET to select a subsequent value after the current value has been processed. Both @GET and @NEXT will normally appear within a @WHILE loop. See Chapter 7 for examples.

@**GETENV***("variable")*

@GETENV retrieves a DOS environment variable. For more details see the DOS manual.

@**GETFORMULA***(frame reference)*

@GETFORMULA retrieves a copy of the formula from behind the

specified frame. A program might subsequently place the retrieved formula behind another frame, using either the @SETFORMULA or @EXECUTE function.

@**HC**("header text")

@HC defines a string of text for the header and specifies that the header be centered above the first line of text.

@**HF**(pages)

@HF determines the number of pages after the current one at which headers and footers will begin to appear. If you are on page 1, for example, and you use the function

    @hf(9)

headers and footers will commence on page 10. You can use this form of the function to allow for a title page, table of contents, etc.

@**HIDE**(frame reference)

The @HIDE function hides the frame named in its parameter. In other words, @HIDE moves the frame from the normal desktop to a special "hidden" desktop, where the frame will still be available in memory but not visible on the screen. The @UNHIDE function makes the frame visible again.

@**HL**("header text")

@HL defines a string of text for the header and specifies that the header be printed flush left above the first line of text.

@**HLOOKUP**(n, range, offset)

@HLOOKUP retrieves a value from a horizontally oriented lookup table. The function has three parameters: a lookup value (n), the *range* that contains the lookup table, and an *offset* row location from which to retrieve the target value.

@HLOOKUP searches the first row of the lookup table for the value n of its first parameter. When it finds n, or the last value in the lookup row that is not larger than n, @HLOOKUP moves down by the specified number of offset rows and returns the value stored in that location.

@**HP**(lines)

@HP (header position) determines the number of lines that will be left blank between the top of the page and the header. Its value must be less than that of the top margin, @TM. The default value for the header position is 3.

@HR(*"header text"*)

@HR defines a string of text for the header and specifies that the header be printed flush right above the first line of text.

@IF(*logical statement, expression1, expression2*)

The @IF function evaluates the logical statement in its first parameter to either true or false. If the statement is true, the expression specified by the second parameter is evaluated. If the statement is false, the expression in the third parameter is evaluated. For example:

@if(a>b, a: = b, a: = 0)

In English this would read, "If *a* is greater than *b*, set *a* equal to *b*; otherwise set *a* equal to 0."

The third parameter is optional. Without a third parameter, @IF performs no action when the logical statement is false.

@INPUTLINE(*"prompt", "starting text", cursor-pointing, auto-delete, select all*)

@INPUTLINE allows a FRED program to make use of the edit line located below the desktop. The function takes five parameters, all of them optional. The parameters and their effects are described below:

"prompt"	A word or phrase, in quotes, that will appear in the message area, to tell the user what to do.
"starting text"	A word or phrase, in quotes, that will appear as the default value on the edit line. Pressing Return will enter this text as a response to the prompt.
cursor-pointing	This parameter determines whether pointing will be allowed as a technique for entering a value onto the edit line. If this parameter is #TRUE or #YES, pointing is allowed; if it is #FALSE or #NO, pointing is not allowed.
auto-delete	If this parameter is set to #TRUE or #YES, pressing a character key will automatically delete the default text on the edit line. However, the text can be edited if a navigation key is pressed before a character key. If

this parameter is set to #FALSE or #NO (the default), the starting text will not be deleted automatically.

select all   If this parameter is set to #TRUE or #YES, the highlight will appear on the entire starting phrase. If set to #FALSE or #NO (the default), only the first letter will be highlighted.

@INT*(numeric expression)*
@INT*("string")*

When the parameter of @INT is a numeric expression, @INT returns the integer part of its parameter; i.e., it strips off any fractional parts of its parameter.

When the parameter of @INT is a string value, @INT returns the ASCII value of the first character in the string, expressed as a decimal number.

@INTEGER*(numeric expression)*
@INTEGER*(numeric expression, decimal places)*
@INTEGER*(date)*

@INTEGER converts the numeric value in its parameter to an integer and then turns the result into a text value.

If the value of the second parameter is negative, @INTEGER rounds the first parameter to the nearest 10, 100, 1000, etc., before converting it to a text value. If the value of the second parameter is greater than or equal to zero, the second parameter has no effect.

If the parameter to @INTEGER is a date-type value, it will convert that value to a text string displayed as numerals not separated by any markings, in the form

yyyymmdd

For example, if today were January 1, 2000, @INTEGER(@TODAY) would return the string

20000101

@IRR*(estimate, cash flow1, cash flow2, . . .)*

@IRR computes the internal rate of return on an investment. An investment's internal rate of return is the discount rate at which the present value of the negative cash flows equals the present value of positive cash flows. The parameters to this function are (1) an *estimate* of the rate of return, and (2) a series of positive and negative *cash flows* reflecting net periodic revenues or outlays. The estimate must be between 0 and 1.

@ISABEND*(expression)*

@ISABEND detects whether a program ended abnormally. It returns #TRUE if it did, #FALSE if it did not. If a parameter is given, the parameter receives the value returned by the function.

@ISALPHA*(expression)*

@ISALPHA returns #TRUE if the value of its parameter is a string or text value, #FALSE if it is not.

@ISBOP*(string)*
@ISBOP*(string, number of characters)*

@ISBOP returns #TRUE if the first character of the specified *string* is a (hidden) beginning-of-paragraph character; otherwise it returns #FALSE. If a number of characters is specified, @ISBOP returns #TRUE if the character at the specified location is a beginning-of-paragraph character.

@ISCAPSLOCK

@ISCAPSLOCK returns #TRUE if the CapsLock key is on; otherwise it returns #FALSE.

@ISDOCUMENT
@ISDOCUMENT*("frame reference")*

@ISDOCUMENT returns #FALSE if the currently selected frame is contained within another frame; otherwise it returns #TRUE. If a frame reference is given, it returns #FALSE if the specified frame is contained within another frame.

@ISERR*(expression)*

@ISERR is used to detect error conditions. If the value of its parameter is one of FRED's error constants, @ISERR returns #TRUE; otherwise it returns #FALSE. This function can be used to filter values from databases and to prevent erroneous values from being copied to numerous spreadsheet cells by internal formulas. It is often used in @IF expressions; for example:

        @if(@not(@iserr(Column1)), @set(Column1, Column1 *.12))

This formula will multiply the values in Column1 by .12, skipping those that contain error constants.

@**ISNA***(expression)*

@ISNA is used to detect the constant #NA!, which means that the value is not available. If the value of its parameter is #NA!, @ISNA returns #TRUE; otherwise it returns #FALSE.

@**ISNUMERIC***(expression)*

@ISNUMERIC returns #TRUE if the value of its parameter is a numeric value, #FALSE if it is not.

@**ISNUMLOCK**

@ISNUMSLOCK returns #TRUE if the NumLock key is on; otherwise it returns #FALSE.

@**ITEM***(index)*

@ITEM is used in the construction of user-defined functions, to receive the parameters passed to the function. In the called function, the parameters that are to be received are represented by @ITEM1, @ITEM2, @ITEM3, etc., up to @ITEM16. The actual values to be used by the function are passed to the @ITEM functions.

You can also reference a series of @ITEM values by using a variable index, in the form

    @item(i)

In this case, the value of the variable *i* selects one of the series of parameter values.

The number of values passed to a subroutine need not match the number of parameters set up to receive them. The @ITEMCOUNT function can be used to determine how many values have actually been passed.

@**ITEMCOUNT**

@ITEMCOUNT returns the number of values passed to a user-defined function. It is used in the called function. It is especially useful when the calling formula may pass a variable number of parameters to the called function. For example, to index through the correct number of passed parameters, you could use a statement like

    @while(INDEX < = itemcount, . . .)

This @WHILE loop would contain references to @ITEM(INDEX). After each parameter is processed, the loop will increment the value of INDEX in a statement like this:

    INDEX : = INDEX + 1

@KEY

@KEY is used in macros to record the last key that has been pressed. It reads keys, not character values, so any expressions involving @KEY should refer to keys by name, in curly braces. For example:

@if(@key = {esc}. . .)

@if(@or(@key = {X}, @key = {x}). . .)

@if(@key = {scroll-lock}. . .)

Note that the @KEY function considers uppercase and lowercase letters as separate keys.

@KEYFILTER({keyname})
@KEYFILTER({keyname}, frame reference)

The @KEYFILTER function is used to control user input into a program by reinterpreting various keys, groups of keys, or the entire keyboard. You can reinterpret the following groups of keys by using these parameters:

{char}	All the white keys in the center of the keyboard
{ctrl-a}	All the Ctrl-letter key combinations
{ctrl-1}	All the Ctrl-number key combinations
{alt-a}	All macro commands
{all}	The entire keyboard

The remaining keys—the function keys, Framework II's cursor-movement keys, and the rest of the gray keys—are filtered individually. Note that with the Ctrl- and Alt-key combinations, you must specify an additional key, but it doesn't matter which one. Ctrl-A or Ctrl-X will filter all combinations of the Ctrl key and letter keys, but Ctrl by itself is illegal.

It takes two frames to set up a key filter, just as it does with a macro. The first frame must contain a formula that defines the key or group of keys that will invoke the formula behind the second frame. For example,

@keyfilter({End}, Frame2)

will execute the formula behind Frame2 any time the End key is pressed. If you want to control input by restricting a user to parts of the keyboard, you should begin by turning off the entire keyboard with the expression

@keyfilter({all})

and then activate the keys you want to have usable with succeeding @KEYFILTER expressions that invoke formulas to be executed by those keys.

To cancel an established filter, enter the @KEYFILTER function a second time, omitting the frame reference.

@**KEYNAME***(key)*

@KEYNAME returns the name of a key, expressed as a text string. Its parameter can be any key name enclosed in curly braces, or either of the functions @KEY or @NEXTKEY. One of this function's primary uses is in building macros. It receives the name of a key and returns a text string that can then be used as a parameter to the @PERFORMKEYS function.

@**KP**

@KP is a printing function that establishes a conditional page break. That is, if the current frame has the formula @KP behind it, the frame will begin a new page if the text in the frame cannot all fit on the current page.

@**LEN***("string expression")*

The @LEN function returns the number of characters in the string represented by the expression in its parameter.

@**LIST***(expression1, expression2, . . .)*

@LIST is used to group a number of functions or expressions together where only one is normally used. For example, use @LIST when you want several actions to be performed as the result of an @IF function:

```
@if(test = #TRUE,
    @list(
        expression1,
        expression2
        ),
    @list(
        expression3,
        expression4
        )
    )
```

In the performance of this statement, expressions 1 and 2 will be evaluated if TEST is #TRUE; otherwise expressions 3 and 4 will be performed.

*@**LL**(characters)*

@LL (line length) is a printing function that determines the maximum number of characters that can be printed on any line of text in a document. The parameters of @LL and @PO should not add up to more than the number of characters your printer can print on a line. You must coordinate this setting with the Words menu's margin settings.

*@**LN**(numeric expression)*

@LN returns the natural logarithm of the numeric expression that is its parameter. The base of the natural logarithm is e, where $e = 2.7182818$. (The parameter must be positive.)

*@**LOCAL**(variable1, variable2, . . .)*

@LOCAL defines variables that are created for use only within a given subroutine. Local variables can be used for the temporary storage of values within the subroutine in which they are defined.

*@**LOG**(numeric expression)*

@LOG returns the base-10 logarithm of the numeric expression that is its parameter. (The parameter must be positive.)

*@**MAX**(expression1, expression2, . . .)*
*@**MAX**(range)*

@MAX returns the largest numeric value in its parameter list.

*@**MEMAVAIL***

@MEMAVAIL has two effects: it clears the undo buffer, thus increasing the amount of available memory, and it returns as a numeric value the amount of memory available in the computer. It takes no parameter.

*@**MENU**(frame reference)*

@MENU turns the Outline frame named in its parameter into a user-defined menu. The frames within the frame named in the parameter become the items on the menu. If one of these frames contains additional frames, selecting that frame will cause the titles of the frames contained in it to be displayed as a submenu.

If the frame is set up with number labels turned off, the menu will be a full-screen menu. If the number labels are turned on, the menu options will be listed horizontally on the edit line. Text contained inside the frames that are part of a menu will be displayed in the message area when the menu option is highlighted. Each frame within the menu frame should contain a formula behind it, to be executed when the option is selected.

You can choose an item on a user menu by using the cursor keys and pressing Return when the selected item is highlighted, or by selecting the first letter of the menu option—just as with Framework II's own menus. The user can always return to the next highest level from a menu frame by pressing the Escape key; however, the programmer can also set up one item on the menu as an exit option. To do so, use the @QUITMENU function.

@**MID**(*"string expression", startpoint, characters*)

The @MID function extracts a group of characters from a string. Given a *string*, the point in the string at which to begin counting (*startpoint*), and the number of characters to extract (*characters*), this function will return a substring.

@**MILLI**

@MILLI is used as a parameter for the @NATIONALIZE function to control the form in which numbers are displayed. If @MILLI is used, numbers are formatted with periods between each group of three digits, and whole numbers are separated from decimal fractions by a comma, in the Continental style. The alternative format function is @THOU-SANDS. (See @NATIONALIZE.)

@**MIN**(*expression1, expression2, . . .*)
@**MIN**(*range*)

@MIN returns the smallest numeric value in its parameter list.

@**MIRR**(*risky rate, safe rate, cash flow1, cash flow2, . . .*)

@MIRR calculates the internal rate of return on an investment, using a modified method of calculation. It takes the following parameters:

- ☐ The interest rate on the money you borrow to make the investment (the *risky rate*)

- ☐ The interest rate at which you could invest the money you make (the *safe rate*)

- ☐ Positive and negative *cash flows*, representing revenues from the investment and outlays toward the investment

@**MOD**(*dividend, divisor*)

Given two parameters, the *dividend* and the *divisor*, the @MOD function calculates the modulus, or the remainder resulting from the division. The divisor cannot have the value of zero.

@**NATIONALIZE***(currency, format)*

The @NATIONALIZE function is used to control the way numbers are displayed. @NATIONALIZE takes either one or two parameters, allowing you to control the *type* of currency symbol used and the *format* in which numbers are displayed (Continental or English style). @NATIONALIZE can take any of the following parameters for the currency parameter:

> @dollar
> @pound
> @unit
> @yen

Either @MILLI or @THOUSANDS can be used as the format parameter. Framework II's default display parameters are @DOLLAR and @THOUSANDS.

@**NEXT***(region)*

@NEXT moves the selection from the current cell or frame of the region specified by its parameter to the following frame or cell, and it retrieves the value stored there. @NEXT is typically used in a @WHILE loop, along with the @GET and @PUT functions to walk through a range of values.

@**NEXTKEY**
@**NEXTKEY***(seconds)*

@NEXTKEY waits for a key to be pressed and then returns the value of the key. Its optional parameter tells how many seconds to wait before executing the next expression. If there is no parameter, @NEXTKEY waits indefinitely. The function can be used to create a delay, as in the following program segment:

> @prompt("Press any key to continue"),
> @nextkey,

@**NOT***(expression)*

@NOT returns #TRUE if its parameter is false and #FALSE if its parameter is true. @NOT can be used as a parameter of the @AND, @IF, and @OR functions. For example:

> @if(@and(A>B, @not(B=0)) . . .)

In English this would read, "If A is greater than B and B is not equal to 0, then . . .".

@**NP**
@**NP***(page number)*

@NP is a printing function that tells Framework II to begin printing the current frame on a new page. Its optional parameter tells Framework II to begin printing the current frame on a new page whose page number is determined by the parameter.

@**NPV***(discount rate, cash flow1, cash flow2, . . .)*

@NPV computes the net present value of a series of *cash flows* (positive and negative) at a given *discount rate*.

@**OR***(expression1, expression2, . . .)*

@OR is a logical function that returns #TRUE if at least one of the logical statements among its parameters is true. Otherwise it returns #FALSE. At least one of its parameters must be a logical statement, that is, a statement that can be evaluated as true or false. The @OR function is often used as part of the first parameter of the @IF function.

@**PANEL1**
@**PANEL1***("frame reference")*

@PANEL1 returns the left-hand number in the third status panel. If a parameter is given, it returns this number for the frame specifed as its parameter.

@**PANEL2**
@**PANEL2***("frame reference")*

@PANEL2 returns the right-hand number in the third status panel. If a parameter is given, it returns this number for the frame specified as its parameter.

@**PERFORMKEYS***("keystrokes")*

The @PERFORMKEYS function executes the keystrokes that comprise its parameter.Special key names should be placed in curly braces. The entire sequence must be enclosed in double quotes.

   The expression

        @performkeys("Hi. How are you? {Return}")

will enter the text

        Hi. How are you?

followed by a carriage return. The expression

        @performkeys("{ctrl-c}eTest{Return}{dnlevel}")

will create an Empty frame, label it "Test", and place the cursor within it. For more extensive examples, see Chapter 7.

@PI

@PI returns the value of pi calculated to 14 decimal places. For those trigonometric functions that require parameters expressed in radians, use the following formula to convert degrees to radians:

radians = angle * @pi/180

@PL*(lines)*

@PL (page length) is a printing function that specifies the length, in lines, of your physical page. All text, headings, and top and bottom margins must be planned within this line limit. The default value is 66, which is the normal number of lines on an 11-inch page.

Use this function if you are using longer or shorter paper, changing the vertical spacing on your printer to increments other than lines, or finding that your text isn't fitting properly on a page.

@PMT*(principal, rate, periods)*

@PMT computes the payment required to pay off a loan, assuming a constant periodic payment. To calculate this result, it must be given the following parameters:

  □ A value representing the *principal* of the loan

  □ A value representing the periodic interest *rate*

  □ A value representing the number of payments (*periods*)

The interest rate given must be the interest rate *per period*. Therefore, you must divide the annual interest rate by the number of periods per year.

@PN

@PN (page number) is used within header or footer functions to specify that the current page number should be printed as part of the header or footer. It can be used in conjunction with other text, for example:

@fc("Page "& @pn)

@PO*(spaces)*

@PO (page offset) is a printing function that determines the size, in spaces, of the left margin of your printed document. The default value is 10. Printing on a line will begin in the column after the number of spaces specified in the parameter of @PO. However, the text's actual left margin is determined by adding the @PO setting to the frame's Left

Margin setting, specified in the Words menu. The parameters of @PO and @LL should not add up to more than the number of characters your printer can print on a line.

@POUND

@POUND can be used as a parameter to the @NATIONALIZE function. See the @NATIONALIZE entry for details of use.

@PR(@printfunction1, @printfunction2, . . . , @printreturn)

@PR is used to group printing functions within a FRED program, to prevent the subsequent formulas from being recalculated during printing. It should appear before any other functions in the program. Its parameters consist of printing functions followed by the @PRINTRETURN function.

@PRINT(frame reference)

The @PRINT function issues the command to begin printing the document or frame referred to in its parameter. When the @PRINT function is encountered, the frame referred to will be printed automatically.

@PRINTRETURN

@PRINTRETURN should be used to close a list of printing functions that are parameters of the @PR function. For further details, see @PR. @PRINTRETURN can also be used by itself to separate a series of printing functions from subsequent formulas and thereby prevent the recalculation of the other formulas.

@PROMPT("message", position)

@PROMPT places the *message* specified in its first parameter on the message line. The second parameter, which is optional, specifies the *position* as a number of spaces from the left edge of the screen to the beginning of the message. To be sure that your message does not remain on the screen longer than you want it to, use the @ERASEPROMPT function to remove it after appropriate action has been taken.

@PUT(range, expression)

@PUT places the value of the expression that is its second parameter in the current cell or frame of the region specified by its first parameter. @PUT is used along with @NEXT, typically in an @WHILE loop, to place a set of values in a range.

@PV(payment, rate, periods)

@PV returns the present value of a constant stream of payments, given the following:

- ☐ A value representing an amount of money that is repeatedly withdrawn or paid at regular intervals (*payment*)

- ☐ A value representing the periodic interest *rate*

- ☐ A value representing the number of payments (*periods*)

This stream of payments can represent an investment from which regular withdrawals are made or a loan on which regular payments are made.

@QUITMENU

@QUITMENU should be placed in the formula area of a quit or exit option on a user menu. Pressing Return when the highlight is on a frame with the @QUITMENU function behind it causes exit from the menu to the next highest level of organization.

@RAND

@RAND is FRED's random number generator. It generates a random number from 0 to 1, inclusive, to 15 decimal places. It does not take a parameter.

@REPT*("string", count)*

The @REPT function produces a string value consisting of a repeated character or group of characters. The first parameter is the character or characters to be repeated, and the second specifies the number of repetitions.

To display a row of 60 asterisks, for example, you would use the formula

    @rept("*", 60)

@RESET*(range)*

@RESET selects the first cell, field, or frame in the range specified by its parameter and returns the value of that element. @RESET is used in conjunction with the @GET, @PUT, and @NEXT functions.

@RESULT*(expression)*

@RESULT causes a formula to stop executing; the function returns the value of its parameter at the time execution stops. It is usually used as part of an @IF or @WHILE expression.

@RETURN*(expression)*

@RETURN causes a formula to stop executing and returns the constant #FUNCTION as a value. It is usually used within an @IF or @WHILE expression.

@**ROUND***(numeric expression)*
@**ROUND***(numeric expression, decimal places)*
@ROUND can have one or two parameters. If it has one, it rounds the parameter to the nearest integer. If it has two, it rounds to the number of decimal places given in the second parameter.

@**RUN***(frame reference, "drive:progname.ext")*
@**RUN***(frame reference, "command line")*
The @RUN function can be used to run any .COM or .EXE program that resides on a disk in one of your drives, provided there is enough free memory to run the program. The first parameter names a frame in which whatever is written to the screen by the program will be captured. Any error messages will also be returned in this frame. The second parameter must contain the drive designation (and the path name where appropriate), the name of the program, and its extension. The frame referred to in the first parameter can also be the frame behind which the formula itself resides. For example, placing the formula

@run(WordStar, "c:ws.com")

behind a frame called WordStar will cause Framework II to look for the WordStar word processing program on drive C and run it, taking over the whole screen. Any error messages will appear in the frame called WordStar.

If you want to use this technique to run "internal" DOS commands or batch files, you must include the DOS COMMAND.COM file as one of the command line arguments. In addition, you must include the /c option to issue instructions to the command processor as though they were typed in at the DOS prompt. For example:

@run(DosFrame, "command.com /c copy a: ∗.fw2b:")

@**SCAN***("target string", "containing string")*
@**SCAN***("target string", "containing string", start location)*
@SCAN returns the number of the character in the containing string at which the target string is matched. The match must be exact. For example, if a local variable CONTAINING is assigned the value

"apes & grapes have similar shapes"

the function

@scan("apes", CONTAINING)

would return the value 1. If the variable CONTAINING were assigned the value

"Apes & grapes have similar shapes"

the value 10 would be returned, because the string "Apes", beginning with an uppercase A, would not match the target string.

The point in the containing string at which to start searching may be specified. If the formula read

@scan("apes", containing, 12)

then the value 30, the location of the a in "shapes", would be returned.

@**SCIENTIFIC**(numeric expression)
@**SCIENTIFIC**(numeric expression, decimal places)
@**SCIENTIFIC**(date)

@SCIENTIFIC rounds the numeric value in its parameter to two decimal places, converts its format to scientific notation, and then turns the result into a text value. If a number of decimal places is specified as the second parameter, @SCIENTIFIC rounds its first parameter to the specified number of places.

If the parameter to @SCIENTIFIC is a date-type value, it will convert that value to a text string and display the result in the format

mm/dd/yyyy

For example, the function

@scientific(@date(1987, 8, 30))

will produce the text string

08/30/1987

@**SELECT**(index, expression1, expression2, . . .)

@SELECT chooses and evaluates one expression from a list of expressions included among its parameters. The first parameter, *index*, must be a numeric value. If *index* = 1, *expression1* will be evaluated; if *index* = 2, *expression2* will be selected; and so on. If the value of *index* is greater than the number of expressions in the parameter list, an error message will be generated.

@**SENSE**(menu toggle)
@**SENSE**(menu toggle, "frame reference")

@SENSE returns #TRUE if a menu option that is a toggle is set to ON. If a frame reference is given, @SENSE returns #TRUE if the specified option is toggled to ON in the specifed frame. Otherwise, @SENSE returns #FALSE.

The menu toggles are given by the series of keystrokes necessary to access them, with the first character being the pound sign, "#", and the Ctrl-character combination that accesses the menu specified only by its letter. Thus,

> @sense(#ET)

would return #TRUE if the current frame were in Typeover mode on the Edit menu. Similarly,

> @sense(#PFPQ)

would return #TRUE if Quality Print were selected on the Page Layout portion of the Format Options submenu of the Print menu. Since the various subdivisions of the menus may have names in FRED that are not specified on the menus themselves, you should consult the Framework II Advanced Topics manual for the appropriate abbreviations before using this function.

@**SET***(reference, value)*

@SET is FRED's assignment function. It takes two parameters—the name of a reference or local variable and the value to be assigned to that reference or variable. The value may be either a literal value, a variable, or an expression. @SET behaves exactly the same as FRED's assignment operator, ":=". For example, the following two expressions perform identical operations:

> @set(TESTVALUE, – 1)
> TESTVALUE : = – 1

@**SETDIRECTORY**
@**SETDIRECTORY***("path name")*

@SETDIRECTORY, when used without a parameter, returns the name of the current default directory. For example, if the default directory is one called FRAMEWK on drive C, the following expression will assign the string "c:\framewk" to the variable DEFAULT:

> DEFAULT : = @setdirectory

When used with a parameter, @SETDIRECTORY sets the default directory to the directory specified in its parameter. The parameter must be a string representing a legitimate path name; for example:

> @setdirectory("c:\framewk\workfile")

@SETDIRECTORY can be used to change the current subdirectory of a directory simply by giving it the desired subdirectory name as a parameter. If the current directory is C:\FRAMEWK\WORKFILE, you can set the current directory to C:\FRAMEWK\DBASES with the following expression:

> @setdirectory("dbases")

@**SETDRIVE**
@**SETDRIVE***(drive)*

@SETDRIVE, when used without a parameter, returns the name of the current default drive. When used with a parameter, @SETDRIVE sets the default drive to the drive specified in its parameter. The parameter must be a drive name in quotes, for example:

> @setdrive("a:")

@**SETFORMULA***(frame reference, formula)*

@SETFORMULA places the specified formula behind the specified cell or frame. The second parameter may be the formula itself or the value returned by a @GETFORMULA expression. For example:

> @local(FORMULA),
>
> FORMULA : = @getformula(oldframe),
>
> @setformula(newframe, FORMULA)

@**SETMACRO***({alt-key}, frame reference)*

The @SETMACRO function is used to establish the command for a macro. It has two required parameters: the name of the Alt-key combination that invokes the macro, and the name of the frame behind which the macro resides. To cancel a macro you have set up, enter the @SETMACRO function again, omitting the frame reference.

@**SETSELECTION***("frame name")*
@**SETSELECTION**

The @SETSELECTION function moves the highlight to the frame named in its parameter. It is a more efficient means of navigation than a @PERFORMKEYS expression using a series of cursor-movement key names. See the Letters program in Chapter 7 for an example of @SET-SELECTION in a program.

When used without a parameter, @SETSELECTION returns the name of the currently selected frame.

*@**SIGN**(numeric expression)*

@SIGN returns a value of −1, 0, or +1, depending on whether its parameter evaluates to a negative value, zero, or a positive value, respectively.

*@**SIN**(numeric expression)*

@SIN returns the sine of the angle in its parameter, expressed in radians.

*@**SK**(lines)*

@SK is a printing function that tells Framework II to skip the number of lines specified in its parameter before printing the current frame.

*@**SP**(lines)*

@SP is a printing function that determines the line spacing of a printed document. @SP(1) will result in a single-spaced document, @SP(2) in a double-spaced document, @SP(3) in a triple-spaced document, and so on.

*@**SQRT**(numeric expression)*

@SQRT returns the square root of its parameter. Its parameter cannot be negative.

*@**ST**("printer codes")*

The @ST function is used to send printer codes to your printer. If the codes are sent as keys, they must be enclosed in quotation marks. Key names can be used if they are also enclosed in braces. To cause an Epson printer to print in "enhanced" mode, for example, the code is Escape E. To send this code to the printer, use the formula

    @st("{esc}e")

Alternatively, the printer codes can be sent by using the @CHR function as a parameter to the @ST function.

*@**STD**(expression1, expression2, . . .)*
*@**STD**(range)*

@STD returns the standard deviation of the numbers in its parameter list.

*@**SUM**(expression1, expression2, . . .)*
*@**SUM**(range)*

@SUM returns the sum of all the numbers in its parameter list.

@**SUMDATE***(date, days)*

@SUMDATE adds the specified number of *days* to *date* and yields the resulting date. The date specified in the first parameter must be a date-type value produced by one of the following functions:

> @date
> @time
> @sumdate
> @today

The second parameter specifies the number of days from the first parameter for which the date is to be calculated. If today is February 25, 1993, the expression

> @sumdate(@today, 10)

will return a date-type value displayed in the format

> Mar 7, 1993

If the second parameter is negative, the number of days specified will be subtracted from the first parameter.

@**TAN***(numeric expression)*

@TAN returns the tangent of the angle in its parameter, expressed in radians.

@**TEXTSELECTION**

@TEXTSELECTION makes available the currently highlighted text of a Word frame for internal use in a program.

@**THOUSANDS**

@THOUSANDS is used as a parameter for the @NATIONALIZE function, to control the form in which numbers are displayed. If @THOUSANDS is used, numbers are formatted with commas between each group of three digits, and whole numbers are separated from fractions by a period, in the Anglo-American style. The alternative format function is @MILLI.

@**TIME**
@**TIME***(hr, min, sec, hundredths)*

When used without parameters, @TIME displays the current date on the system clock. The result is a date-type value that can subsequently be sorted or used in the date arithmetic functions, @DIFFDATE and @SUMDATE. The result of the @TIME function is identical to that of the @DATE function when neither function takes a parameter.

@TIME can also be used with three or four parameters (hundredths of a second are optional). No matter what values you enter as parameters, @TIME will still display the date rather than the time, in the same format that the @DATE function displays the date. To display a time, you must use @TIME as the parameter of one of the time-formatting functions. If used as the parameter of one of these functions without any parameters of its own, it will display the time on the system clock. If used in this manner with parameters, the resulting display will be the time represented by its parameters.

@TIME1*(time)*

@TIME1 converts the date-type value in its parameter to a text string and displays the result in the time format

> hh:mm XM

For example, the function

> @time1(@time(15, 33, 57))

will return the text string

> 3:33 PM

@TIME2*(time)*

@TIME2 converts the date-type value in its parameter to a text string and displays the result in the time format

> hh:mm

For example, the function

> @time2(@time(15, 33, 57))

will return the text string

> 15:33

@TIME3*(time)*

@TIME3 converts the date-type value in its parameter to a text string and displays the result in the time format

> hh:mm:ss.hh

For example, if the system clock's time happens to be 15:33:57.12, the function

> @time3(@time)

will return the text string

> 15:33:57.12

@**TIME4***(time)*

@TIME4 converts the date-type value in its parameter to a text string and displays the result in the time format

> hh:mm:ss

thus if the time is 15:33:57, the function

> @time4(@time)

will return the text string

> 15:33:57

@**TM***(lines)*

@TM (top margin) is a printing function that determines the number of lines that will be left blank between the top of the paper and the first line of text, not including the header. The default value is 6.

@**TODAY**

@TODAY returns the current date and time on the system clock and displays the date. The result is a date-type value. The result of the @TODAY function is identical to that of the @DATE function used without parameters.

@**TRACE***(frame reference, #ON)*
@**TRACE***(#OFF)*

@TRACE turns the tracing function off and on. When used with a frame reference and #ON, it will trace each step in the execution of a program, and it will store the record of the performance in the specified frame. @TRACE(#OFF) turns the tracing function off again.

@**UNHIDE***(frame reference)*

@UNHIDE is used to make visible a frame that has been hidden via the @HIDE function.

@**UNIT***(symbol, #position)*

@UNIT is used as a parameter for the @NATIONALIZE function to format numbers using currency symbols other than those for pounds, dollars, and yen. It takes two parameters. The first is the characters representing the currency symbol to be used, enclosed in quotes. The second is a constant, either #BEFORE or #AFTER, which indicates the position of the symbol relative to the number to be formatted. For example, the formula:

@nationalize(@unit("DM", #BEFORE), @milli), 13846.44

would result in the display

DM   13.846,44

The same expression without the ensuing number or numeric expression would result in all subsequent numbers being displayed as deutsche marks in the illustrated form.

@**VALUE**("string expression")
The @VALUE function converts the string expression that is its parameter to a numeric value, provided there are numbers in the expression. This function will work with numbers enclosed in quotes, with numbers expressed as text, or with numbers that have been converted to a text format by the @CURRENCY, @DECIMAL, @INTEGER, or @SCIENTIFIC functions.

There are a few tricks to using this function without generating errors:

□ A numeric expression in quotes must not include parentheses.

□ A numeric expression in quotes cannot include letters.

□ Using this function with a numeric expression containing commas will generate an error unless the expression also includes a dollar sign.

Negative numbers, decimal points, and dollar signs cause no problems.

@**VAR**(expression1, expression2, . . .)
@**VAR**(range)
@VAR returns the statistical variance of the numbers in its parameter list.

@**VLOOKUP**(n, range, offset)
@VLOOKUP retrieves a value from a vertically oriented lookup table. The table can be a spreadsheet or a database. The function has three parameters: a lookup value (n) to be located, the *range* that contains the lookup table, and an *offset* column location from which to retrieve the target value.

@VLOOKUP searches the first column of the lookup table for the value *n*. When it finds *n*, or the last value in the lookup column that is not larger than *n*, @VLOOKUP moves to the right by the specified number of offset columns and returns the value stored in that location.

@**WHILE***(condition, expression1, expression2, . . .)*
The @WHILE function is used to construct loops in FRED. The expressions that are its second through last parameters will be executed repeatedly until the first parameter becomes false. For example:

```
@local(count, total),
count : = 1,
total : = 1,
@while(count < = 10,
        total : = total * count,
        count : = count + 1
        ),
ResultFrame : = total
```

This program will find the value of 10! (1 * 2 * 3 * 4 * . . . * 10) and store the value in the frame called ResultFrame.

A @WHILE loop will normally execute 2048 times unless interrupted by a normal terminating condition or by a @RETURN or @RESULT expression. You can change this through the Setup program.

@**WORDCOUNT**
@**WORDCOUNT***("frame reference")*
@WORDCOUNT returns the number of words in the currently selected frame or cell. If a frame or cell reference is given, it returns the number of words in the specified frame or cell.

@**WRITEFRAMEFILE***(file name, frame reference)*
@WRITEFRAMEFILE writes the specified frame to disk as a standard Framework II file with the specified file name. The file name can include a drive identifier, a DOS path name, and an extension. The effect of this function is identical to choosing "Save and Continue" from the Disk menu.

@**WRITETEXTFILE***(file name, frame reference)*
@WRITETEXTFILE writes the specified frame to disk as a DOS text

file with the specified file name. The file name can include a drive identifier, a DOS path name, and an extension. The effect of this function is identical to choosing "Write DOS Text File" from the Disk menu.

@YEN

@YEN can be used as a parameter to the @NATIONALIZE function. See the @NATIONALIZE entry for details of its use.

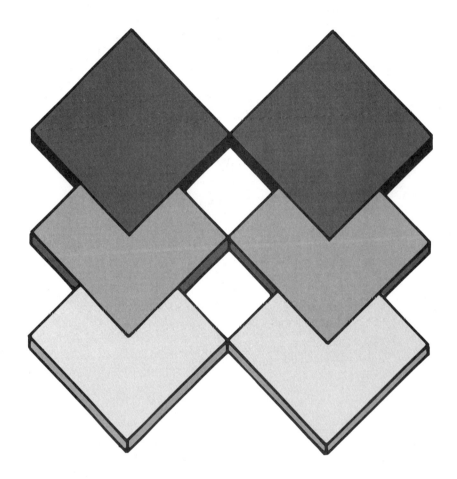

TABLE OF ASCII CHARACTERS

The following tables list the characters of the ASCII code for computers using the MS-DOS operating system. The codes are listed in decimal and hexadecimal notation.

Table C.1 shows the complete set of displayable characters available in Framework II. Table C.2 displays the standard ASCII control codes and their keyboard equivalents. These codes are used primarily in communication with other devices (including the screen), to control the flow and appearance of data. Most are not directly available in Framework II, which uses the key combinations for menu commands. You will, however, need to use some of the codes with the telecommunications component, as explained in Chapter 6.

Every ASCII code except 0 and 255 has a corresponding displayable character; however, the characters corresponding to ASCII codes 9 (Ctrl-I) and 13 (Ctrl-M) cannot be displayed in Framework II. Instead, these codes generate a Tab character and a carriage return, respectively. The characters that cannot be found on the keyboard can be displayed in a Framework II frame by holding down the Alt and Shift keys and pressing the keys corresponding to the decimal value of the code (reading from left to right) on the numeric keypad, letting up the Alt key after all the digits have been entered. Alternatively, you can display them by means of the FRED function @CHR(n), where n is the decimal value of the ASCII code. Whether the characters can be printed on paper depends on the capabilities of your printer.

The "standard" portion of the ASCII code consists of the 32 control codes shown in Table C.2 plus the printable characters numbered 32 through 127, and the Backspace character, ASCII 128. The additional displayable characters are part of the MS-DOS extended character set, and can be used to create various types of borders, or to display symbols and characters of non-English alphabets.

ASCII	PRINTS	HEX		ASCII	PRINTS	HEX
0 *		0		32 **		20
1	☺	1		33	!	21
2	☻	2		34	"	22
3	♥	3		35	#	23
4	♦	4		36	$	24
5	♣	5		37	%	25
6	♠	6		38	&	26
7	•	7		39	'	27
8	◘	8		40	(	28
9		9		41	)	29
10	◙	A		42	*	2A
11	♂	B		43	+	2B
12	♀	C		44	,	2C
13		D		45	–	2D
14	♬	E		46	.	2E
15	☼	F		47	/	2F
16	►	10		48	0	30
17	◄	11		49	1	31
18	↕	12		50	2	32
19	‼	13		51	3	33
20	¶	14		52	4	34
21	§	15		53	5	35
22	▬	16		54	6	36
23	↨	17		55	7	37
24	↑	18		56	8	38
25	↓	19		57	9	39
26	→	1A		58	:	3A
27	←	1B		59	;	3B
28	└	1C		60	<	3C
29	↔	1D		61	=	3D
30	▲	1E		62	>	3E
31	▼	1F		63	?	3F

* non-printable character   ** space

Table C.1: MS-DOS ASCII *Displayable Characters*

ASCII	PRINTS	HEX	ASCII	PRINTS	HEX
64	@	40	96	`	60
65	A	41	97	a	61
66	B	42	98	b	62
67	C	43	99	c	63
68	D	44	100	d	64
69	E	45	101	e	65
70	F	46	102	f	66
71	G	47	103	g	67
72	H	48	104	h	68
73	I	49	105	i	69
74	J	4A	106	j	6A
75	K	4B	107	k	6B
76	L	4C	108	l	6C
77	M	4D	109	m	6D
78	N	4E	110	n	6E
79	O	4F	111	o	6F
80	P	50	112	p	70
81	Q	51	113	q	71
82	R	52	114	r	72
83	S	53	115	s	73
84	T	54	116	t	74
85	U	55	117	u	75
86	V	56	118	v	76
87	W	57	119	w	77
88	X	58	120	x	78
89	Y	59	121	y	79
90	Z	5A	122	z	7A
91	[	5B	123	{	7B
92	\	5C	124	¦	7C
93	]	5D	125	}	7D
94	^	5E	126	~	7E
95	_	5F	127	⌂	7F

Table C.1 (continued): MS-DOS ASCII Displayable Characters

ASCII	PRINTS	HEX	ASCII	PRINTS	HEX
128	Ç	80	160	á	A0
129	ü	81	161	í	A1
130	é	82	162	ó	A2
131	â	83	163	ú	A3
132	ä	84	164	ñ	A4
133	à	85	165	Ñ	A5
134	å	86	166	ª	A6
135	ç	87	167	º	A7
136	ê	88	168	¿	A8
137	ë	89	169	⌐	A9
138	è	8A	170	¬	AA
139	ï	8B	171	½	AB
140	î	8C	172	¼	AC
141	ì	8D	173	¡	AD
142	Ä	8E	174	«	AE
143	Å	8F	175	»	AF
144	É	90	176	░	B0
145	æ	91	177	▒	B1
146	Æ	92	178	▓	B2
147	ô	93	179	│	B3
148	ö	94	180	┤	B4
149	ò	95	181	╡	B5
150	û	96	182	╢	B6
151	ù	97	183	╖	B7
152	ÿ	98	184	╕	B8
153	Ö	99	185	╣	B9
154	Ü	9A	186	║	BA
155	¢	9B	187	╗	BB
156	£	9C	188	╝	BC
157	¥	9D	189	╜	BD
158	₧	9E	190	╛	BE
159	ƒ	9F	191	┐	BF

Table C.1 (continued): MS-DOS ASCII Displayable Characters

ASCII	PRINTS	HEX
192	L	C0
193	⊥	C1
194	⊤	C2
195	⊦	C3
196	—	C4
197	+	C5
198	⊦	C6
199	‖	C7
200	⊔	C8
201	⎡	C9
202	⫤	CA
203	⫟	CB
204	⊩	CC
205	=	CD
206	⫟	CE
207	⊥	CF
208	⊥	D0
209	⊤	D1
210	⫟	D2
211	⊔	D3
212	⊦	D4
213	F	D5
214	⫟	D6
215	╫	D7
216	╪	D8
217	⌐	D9
218	⌐	DA
219	■	DB
220	▬	DC
221	▌	DD
222	▐	DE
223	▬	DF

ASCII	PRINTS	HEX
224	α	E0
225	β	E1
226	Γ	E2
227	π	E3
228	Σ	E4
229	σ	E5
230	μ	E6
231	τ	E7
232	⊽	E8
233	θ	E9
234	Ω	EA
235	δ	EB
236	∞	EC
237	⌀	ED
238	∈	EE
239	∩	EF
240	≡	F0
241	±	F1
242	≥	F2
243	≤	F3
244	⌠	F4
245	⌡	F5
246	÷	F6
247	≈	F7
248	°	F8
249	·	F9
250	·	FA
251	√	FB
252	ⁿ	FC
253	²	FD
254	■	FE
255 *		FF

* non-printable character

Table C.1 (continued): MS-DOS ASCII Displayable Characters

ASCII Value	Control Character	Hex Value	Keyboard Equivalent	Device Control Effect
00	NUL	00	Ctrl-@	Null
01	SOH	01	Ctrl-A	
02	STX	02	Ctrl-B	
03	ETX	03	Ctrl-C	
04	EOT	04	Ctrl-D	
05	ENQ	05	Ctrl-E	
06	ACK	06	Ctrl-F	
07	BEL	07	Ctrl-G	Beep
08	BS	08	Ctrl-H	Backspace
09	HT	09	Ctrl-I	Tab
10	LF	0A	Ctrl-J	Linefeed
11	VT	0B	Ctrl-K	Cursor home
12	FF	0C	Ctrl-L	Form feed
13	CR	0D	Ctrl-M	Carriage return
14	SO	0E	Ctrl-N	
15	SI	0F	Ctrl-O	
16	DLE	10	Ctrl-P	
17	DC1	11	Ctrl-Q	
18	DC2	12	Ctrl-R	
19	DC3	13	Ctrl-S	
20	DC4	14	Ctrl-T	
21	NAK	15	Ctrl-U	
22	SYN	16	Ctrl-V	
23	ETB	17	Ctrl-W	
24	CAN	18	Ctrl-X	
25	EM	19	Ctrl-Y	
26	SUB	1A	Ctrl-Z	
27	ESC	1B	Ctrl-[or Esc	Escape
28	FS	1C	Ctrl-\	Cursor right
29	GS	1D	Ctrl-]	Cursor left
30	RS	1E	Ctrl-^	Cursor up
31	US	1F	Ctrl-_	Cursor down

Table C.2: MS-DOS ASCII Control Codes and Their Effects

INDEX

#FALSE constant, 274–276, 282, 374
#N/A! constant, 158
#NO constant, 275–277
#NULL! constant, 374, 394
#OFF constant, 378–389, 391
#ON constant, 378–389
#TRUE constant, 274–276, 282, 374
#YES constant, 275, 276–277
&symbol, 390
:= symbol, 273–274
@symbol, 181–183, 375, 388
@ABS, 454
@ACOS, 455
@AND, 281–284, 373, 455
@ASIN, 455
@ATAN, 455
@ATAN2, 455
@AVG, 152–154, 157, 305, 455
@BEEP, 455
@BM, 455
@BOP, 455
@BUSINESS, 455
@CEILING, 457
@CHOOSE, 457
@CHR, 226, 457
@COS, 155, 457
@COUNT, 458
@DATE, 155, 184, 239–40, 261, 367, 458
@DATE1, 240, 458
@DATE2, 240, 459
@DATE3, 240, 459
@DATE4, 240, 364, 459
@DATETIME, 460
@DBASEFILTER, 460
@DECIMAL, 461
@DIFFDATE, 155, 239, 273–274, 400, 461
@DISPLAY, 423, 461
@DOLLAR, 461
@DRAW, 461
@DRAWGRAPH, 462
@ECHO, 389, 391, 463
@ERASEPROMPT, 371, 463
@EXACT, 463
@EXECUTE, 376, 395, 464
@EXP, 154, 464
@FC, 464

@FILL, 289, 464
@FL, 464
@FLOOR, 464
@FP, 464
@FR, 465
@FRAMETYPE, 465
@FRAMEVIEW, 465–466
@FV, 466
@GET, 372, 374, 393–394, 466
@GETENV, 466
@GETFORMULA, 466–467
@HC, 467
@HF, 467
@HIDE, 467
@HL, 225, 227, 228, 290, 467
@HLOOKUP, 372, 467
@HP, 468
@HR, 468
@IF, 372–373, 389, 424, 468
@INPUTLINE, 371, 468–469
@INT, 380, 402, 469
@INTEGER, 403, 469
@IRR, 155, 467, 470
@ISABEND, 389, 470
@ISALPHA, 470
@ISCAPSLOCK, 470
@ISDOCUMENT, 470
@ISERR, 470
@ISNA, 471
@ISNUMERIC, 471
@ISNUMLOCK, 471
@ITEM, 372, 375, 401, 471
@ITEMCOUNT, 471
@KEY, 472
@KEYNAME, 473
@KEYFILTER, 472–473
@KP, 473
@LEN, 403, 473
@LIST, 373, 473
@LL, 474
@LN, 154, 474
@LOCAL, 380, 474
@LOG, 154, 474
@MAX, 154, 157, 474
@MEMAVAIL, 365, 474
@MENU, 371, 395–397, 472, 475

@MID, 402, 475
@MILLI, 475
@MIN, 154, 157, 475
@MIRR, 475
@MOD, 155, 475
@NATIONALIZE, 476
@NEXT, 372, 393–394, 476
@NEXTKEY, 476
@NOT, 373, 476
@NP, 477
@NPV, 155, 477
@OR, 281, 282–283, 373, 477
@PANEL1, 477
@PANEL2, 477
@PERFORMKEYS, 361–365, 367–368, 376,
    389–393, 395, 400, 477–478
@PI, 155, 478
@PL, 478
@PMT, 155, 173–176, 478
@PN, 478
@PO, 478–479
@POUND, 479
@PR, 479
@PRINT, 376, 479
@PRINTRETURN, 228, 479
@PROMPT, 371, 389, 479
@PUT, 372, 374, 479
@PV, 155, 479–480
@QUITMENU, 399, 480
@RAND, 155, 480
@REPT, 480
@RESET, 394, 480
@RESULT, 375, 480
@RETURN, 375, 403, 424, 480
@ROUND, 155, 380, 481
@RUN, 421–422, 425, 481
@SCAN, 481–482
@SCIENTIFIC, 482
@SELECT, 482
@SENSE, 482–483
@SET, 271, 273, 372, 483
@SETDIRECTORY, 422, 425, 483–484
@SETDRIVE, 422, 425, 484
@SETFORMULA, 484
@SETMACRO, 484
@SETSELECTION, 367, 376, 389, 392, 395,
    484
@SIGN, 485
@SIN, 155, 485
@SK, 485
@SP, 485

@SQRT, 154, 485
@ST, 226, 228, 485
@STD, 154, 485
@SUM, 154, 156–157, 171, 178, 180, 231,
    304–305, 369, 485
@SUMDATE, 155, 231, 239, 486
@TAN, 155, 486
@TEXTSELECTION, 486
@THOUSANDS, 486
@TIME, 401, 486–487
@TIME1, 364, 367, 487
@TIME2, 401, 487
@TIME3, 487–488
@TIME4, 488
@TM, 488
@TODAY, 155, 231, 239, 273–274, 364, 367,
    488
@TRACE, 378, 488
@UNHIDE, 488
@UNIT, 488–489
@VALUE, 402, 403, 489
@VAR, 489
@VLOOKUP, 372, 489, 490
@WHILE, 374, 394–395, 490
@WORDCOUNT, 490
@WRITEFRAMEFILE, 490
@WRITETEXTFILE, 490–491
@YEN, 491

Abbreviations
    creating from macros, 359, 361
    creating from scratch, 361
    stored in Library cabinet, 52
    supplied with Framework II, 53
Addresses. *See* Cell addresses
Alarming results, 134
Alignment
    flush right, uses for, 242
    of labels in spreadsheets, 120, 137–139
    of numbers in spreadsheets, 120
    of text in databases, 258–259
    of text in Word frames, 199–200
Allow Editing option, 176
Allow Free Dragging option, 100–101
    and page layout, 241–242
ANSI.SYS device driver, 51
Apps menu, 23, 214, 217, 298–301, 312, 420
    adding programs to, 426–429
Arrays in FRED programming, 371–372
ASCII codes, 224, 262–263, 323–324, 327,
    493–498

ASCII text files, 328
  characteristics of, 415–416
  importing, 413
  writing, 414
Assumptions stored in Library, 369
Automatic log-on to remote computers, 333

Backspace key, 207
  to erase characters, 62, 118
BASIC language, compared to FRED, 372, 402
Batch XMODEM protocol, 310, 340
Baud rate, 315–316, 318
Begin Frame on New Page option, 234, 237
Blank All option, 236
Boldface text, 208
  in headers or footers, 226–227, 291
Brackets in cell references, 129–131
Branching in FRED programs, 372–373

Calculating values
  in databases, 268–275, 286, 289
  in spreadsheets, 121–126
Capture file, 325–327, 345
Cell addresses (in spreadsheets), 107–108, 121
Cell references
  establishing through cursor pointing, 123–125
  in spreadsheet formulas, 121–125
  using English names, 129–131, 180
Centering of text in Word frames, 199, 205
CLINK protocol, 310
Clock, Framework II, 8, 12
Color
  display of text styling, 38
  installing for screen, 445–446
Column width
  and number styling, 135–136
  and printed databases, 285
  changing globally in spreadsheets, 139–140
  changing in databases, 251, 256
  changing in spreadsheets, 131, 138, 140
Columnar data
  exporting to a word processing program, 437
  importing into a spreadsheet or database, 433–434
Columns
  adding to databases, 267–269, 296
  adding to spreadsheets, 114, 146–150
  hiding in spreadsheets, 182–183

Combining activities, 3–4
Comma-delimited files
  characteristics of, 416
  exporting, 414
  for exporting spreadsheet data, 436–437
  for importing spreadsheet data, 433–436
  importing into Framework II, 434–436
Comments, in FRED programs, 353
Communications networks, 321–325
Communications parameters, 310, 315–319
Communications protocols, 310–312, 336, 340
CompuServe, 41, 307, 318, 328, 341–342, 345
Computer bulletin boards, 41, 318, 338–340
Computer hardware
  and Framework II, 26
Contents area of frame, 14, 16
Control (Ctrl) key, 25
Control characters, entering, 224, 493
Copy (F8) key, 21, 209
  for saving to another drive, 91
  to make multiple copies, 95
Copying spreadsheet formulas, 140–142, 146, 158–159, 171, 175
  with absolute references, 142–146
Copying text, 209
Correcting errors, 34, 35, 118, 193, 206
CRC error-checking protocol, 310
Create menu, 23, 25–26, 58, 110, 112–114, 190, 253–254, 267–268, 296, 355–357
Crosstalk, 310
Ctrl key, 25
Ctrl-Break keys, to stop cursor movement, 116
Ctrl-Up Level keys, to exit an outline, 85
Cursor
  identifying current work area, 15
  in Word frames, 190, 194
  relationship to highlight, 62–63
Cursor keys, 17–19, 62
  and databases, 255–256
  and menu options, 22
  and spreadsheets, 115–116, 118–119
  in dBASE view of database, 304
  in Forms view of databases, 294
  in Word frames, 194–197
  moving through outlines with, 68
Customizing Framework II, xv
Cut-and-paste macros, 363, 365–366

Data bits, 310, 316, 318
Data types in database fields, 251–252, 257
Database frame, 40
Database management, 38–39, 46–47,
    248–305
Databases
    adding Word frames to, 296
    adding rows or columns to, 267–269, 296
    and computer memory, 252–253
    calculated values in, 40, 47
    capabilities of, in Framework II, 39–40
    changing column width in, 251, 256
    columns in, 250, 251, 257
    creating, 253–256
    data types in, 251–252, 257
    dBASE view of, 302–303
    entering data in, 259–261, 294–295
    field names in, 47, 251, 257
    filtering, 277–283, 291, 394–395, 399
    Forms view of, 293–294, 296–297
    Forms view of, for data entry, 294–295
    linking with spreadsheets, 302–305
    merging, 389–395
    rows in, 250
    searching and replacing in, 265–256
    size and dimensions of, 252–254
    structure chart for, 257, 269
    structure of, 38–39, 249–252, 257
    using filtered, 283–284
Date arithmetic, 239–240, 261
Date functions. *See* Functions, date and time
Date strings, 239
    in page headers or footers, 221, 240, 385
Date view of disk directories, 45
DB-25 connector, 308
dBASE programs, 3
    importing files from, 412
dBASE view of databases, 302–303
DCA files, importing, 412–413
Decimal places, setting in display, 137
Delete (Del) key, 19, 122, 207
    and outline headings, 73–75
    to erase characters, 62, 118
Deleting
    files from disk, 45
    frames from desktop, 44
    headings from outline, 73
    text in Word frames, 207
Desktop, 8–9
    customizing, 445

Dictionaries, editing, 217–218
Dictionary
    default, installing, 448
    personal, 215–217
DIF files, 337
    importing into Framework II, 413, 428, 430
    integrating into Framework II spreadsheets,
        431–432
    row vs. column order, 415–416
DIFFTIME function, creating 400–404
Direction of telecommunication, 319
Disk drive cabinets, 9, 11–12, 42, 90,
    103–104
    customizing, 445
Disk drives, installing, 444
Disk Export submenu, 411, 415–417
Disk Import submenu, 411
Disk menu, 23, 43, 88–89, 410, 414
Display Hidden Characters option, 203–204
Display Labels option, 423
Display screen
    and Framework II, 27, 38
    installing, 442, 445–446
DOS Access frames, 49, 51, 418–419
    capturing text in, 51
    establishing maximum size of, 447
    executing DOS commands in, 419
    running programs in, 418–419
DOS commands
    executing within a FRED program, 425
    executing within Framework II, 52
DOS files. *See* ASCII text files; Print files
Dow Jones News/Retrieval, 41, 328
Down Level (+) key, 19–20, 42, 90, 190, 296
    and spreadsheets, 115
    to add levels to outlines, 75, 96
Downloading files, 311, 341
Drag (F3) key, 21, 100–102, 296
Dragging (repositioning) frames, 9, 21, 101,
    296
    inside other frames, 100–102, 241–242
Duplex, 319

Edit (F2) key, 21, 226–227, 272, 276, 279,
    291, 352, 362
    for formulas, 127–128
Edit line, 13, 99, 122
    and frame labels, 60–61, 67
Edit menu, 23, 176
Editing spreadsheet data, 127–128

Empty frames
  for containing other frames, 32–33, 49, 76,
    230–231, 235
  for containing outlines, 65, 86
  for word processing, 190
Entering data in databases, 259–261,
    294–295
Escape (Esc) key, 22, 122
  for entering formulas without executing,
    353
Exit (DOS command), 52
Exporting files to word processing programs,
    437–438
Extend Select (F6) key, 21, 80–81, 90, 97,
    134, 138, 195, 258

Field names in databases, 47, 251, 256, 257
Fields
  as elements of databases, 39, 250–252, 257,
    271, 286
File cabinets. *See* Disk drive cabinets, Library
    cabinet
File names, 42–43
File transfers, 311–312
  binary, 336–338, 340
  by direct connection, 346
  protocol, 336–338, 340
  text, 327–328, 339
Files, importing and exporting, 411–418
Filtering databases, 277–283, 291, 394–395,
    399
Financial functions, 109, 155, 451
Flush-right alignment, uses for, 242
Footers. *See* Page headers and footers in
    printed documents
Form letters, 297, 299
  creating through a program, 381–400
Formatting for printing, 219–228, 232–234
Formatting text, 198–203
Forms view of databases, 293–297
Formula area. *See* Programming area behind
    frame
Formulas
  entering in databases, 261, 270, 272,
    278–279
  in spreadsheets, 34–35, 47, 107–108,
    121–126
  printing, 93
  revising in databases, 276
  shown in status panel, 123, 126

Formulas, (cont.)
  using cell references in, 121
Formulas Only option, 353–354
Frame labels, 14–15
  and file names, 16, 42–43, 61
  and outline headings, 60, 64, 67
  as elements in a menu program, 396
  editing, 63
  entering text in, 59–61
  entering via a program, 391
  in status panel, 16
  maximum size of, 42
  multi-line, 98–99
  printing, 232
Frames
  and trays, 10, 20, 61, 82
  as work areas in Framework II, 4–5
  border, 14
  changing size of, 100–102
  contents area, 14
  controlling through FRED programs,
    375–376
  deleting from desktop, 44
  dragging, 9, 21, 100–102, 241–242, 296
  naming, 16
  on the desktop, 10
  parts of, 14–17, 54
  printing, 45
  repositioning in outlines, 101, 241–242
  repositioning on desktop, 100, 102
  saving on disk, 42–44
  types of, 14
Frames menu, 24, 82–83, 236–237, 422–423
Frames view
  and printing, 232, 234
  of outlines, 85, 91, 94
Framework II
  and floppy disk systems, 11, 444
  and hard disk systems, 11, 444
  and keyboard, 17–18
  conceptual design of, 1, 4, 7, 12, 54
  conceptual design of, and spreadsheets,
    109–110
  loading, xvi–xvii
  parts of, 7–9, 11–16, 28, 54
  using for the first time, 439–440
FRED programming language, 17, 183–184,
    348–406
  features of, 351–352
  help with, 376–378

FRED programming language, (cont.)
  key names used in, 359–362
  operators for FRED formulas, 275, 390
FRED programs
  arrays in, 371–372
  branching in, 372–373
  creating menus in 395–398
  documenting, 353
  error trapping in, 389
  loops in, 373–374
  output for, 422
  subroutines in, 375, 398
  variables in, 371–372, 380, 385, 394, 397,
    399
Function keys, 17, 20–21
  and outlining, 57
Functions
  date and time, 109, 155, 183–184, 231,
    239, 401, 452
  financial, 109, 155, 451
  in spreadsheets, 108, 152
  logical, 281–283, 373
  macro-building, 453
  numeric, 109, 154–155, 451
  numeric display, 453
  output, 370–371
  printing, 224–228, 241, 453
  programming, 370–376, 453–454
  region-walking, 393–394
  statistical, 109, 154, 156–157, 451
  string, 452
  user-defined, 54, 369, 370, 400-405

Getting File by Name option, 43
GOTO command, 185–186
Graph menu, 24, 35, 162–165
Graph Options submenu, 167–168
Graphics characters, entering, 224, 493
Graphs, 2, 162–170
  adding to, 164, 166, 169
  bar, 167–169
  creating, 35
  from spreadsheet data, 35–37, 162–163
  marked points, 37
  on color monitors, 27, 163
  on monochrome monitors, 27, 163
  options for display, 35
  pie, 36, 164–166
  printing, 169
  recalculating, 168, 172

Graphs, (cont.)
  stacked bar, 36, 171–172
  types available in Framework II, 35–36

Hang up phone, 332–333
Hard disk, 11, 444
Hardwire transfers, 346
Headers. *See* Page headers and footers in
    printed documents
Headings, in Word frames, 205
Help (F1) key, 20–22, 376
Hidden characters, displaying in Word
    frames, 203–205
Hide Borders option, 237
Highlight
  extending, 80–81, 97, 138–139, 151
  extending in databases, 258
  extending under program control, 391
  identifying current work area, 15
  in spreadsheets, 115, 134
  in Word frames, 190
  relationship to cursor, 62–63
Hyphens, soft, 203

Indentation in Word frames, 200–201
  negative, 202
Input functions, 370–371
Ins key. *See* Instruct key
Insert Default option, 206
Installation
  of default dictionary, 448
  of disk drives, 444
  of monitors, 442, 445–446
  of printers, 444
  of screen colors, 445–446
  of sorting order, 448
  of Telecommunications Setup files, 448
  of video cards, 444
Instruct (Ins) key, 19–20, 22, 58
Interfacing with other programs, 410–439
Italic text, 209

Justification. *See* Alignment

Keep Frame on One Page option, 234, 237
Key names for FRED programming, 359–362
Keyboard, 17–18

Library cabinet, 9, 11, 52–55, 235–236,
    354–355, 358–359, 363, 365–370

Library cabinet, (cont.)
  displaying, 364
  phone directory in, 53–54, 365–368
  saving contents of, 364
Line spacing
  in printed documents, 220
  in Word frames, 191
Locate menu, 23, 184–185, 210, 263–267, 287
Lock First Column/Row option, 151–152
  and printing spreadsheets, 160
Logical expressions, 274–277, 281–283
Loops in FRED programs, 373–374
Lotus 1-2-3, 3
  exporting Framework II files to, 414
  importing files from, 412

Macros
  creating, 355–358
  cut-and-paste, 363, 365–366
  keys for, 355
  stored in Library cabinet, 52
  supplied with Framework II Library, 53, 363–368, 403
  using, 357–358
  writing as FRED programs, 366
Mailing labels, printing, 300–301
Mailmerge printing, 297, 299–301, 391, 398–400
Main menu, 8, 11, 22–23
Margins
  in printed documents, 219–220
  in Word frames, 199–200, 232
  setting globally, 201
  setting locally, 201
Memory
  and Framework II, 26–27
  configuring for Framework II, 444–445
Menu options
  currently available, 26
  selecting, 22–26
Menus, creating in FRED programs, 395–398
Message area, 8, 13, 60
Modem initialization string, 320
Modems, 309
  configuring Framework II for, 319–320
Move (F7) key, 21, 77–79, 81, 96–97, 209
  and free dragging, 242
  for saving to another drive, 90
Moving
  data within a spreadsheet, 148–150

Moving, (cont.)
  frames into outlines, 79–81, 96–97
  text in Word frames, 209
MultiMate, 3
  exporting Framework II files to, 414
  importing files from, 412

Null strings, 436
Number Labels option, 82–83
Numbers
  entered as text in databases, 260
  entered as text in spreadsheets, 129
Numbers menu, 24, 132, 134–138, 258–259
Numbers Options submenu, 176–177
Numeric functions, 109, 154–155, 451
Numeric values
  entering in databases, 261
  entering in spreadsheets, 120, 122
  in spreadsheets, 107
Numeric values and styling, 132
NumLock key, 18–19

On-line help, 20, 22
On-line information services, 41, 307, 318, 341–342, 345
Open All option, 391
Organizing activities, 3
Outline view, 85, 91, 94–95
Outlines
  adding levels to, 75–76, 96
  adding to, 30, 32, 69, 71–72, 75–76
  and frame labels, 60, 64, 97
  as tools for imposing order, 4–6, 28, 66, 169
  changing size and organization of, 30, 32, 69
  closing, 70–71
  creating, 6, 28–30, 58–59, 66
  creating in Empty frame, 86
  deleting headings from, 73–75
  entering, 84
  entering headings in, 64
  for organizing projects, 6, 28–30, 57, 60, 66, 95
  Frames view of, 85, 91, 94
  headings in, 59–60
  hierarchy as a principle of, 4, 66
  moving existing frames into, 32, 49, 79–81, 96–97
  moving parts of, 77–78
  numbering systems for, 64–65, 78, 101
  opening, 70–71, 73

Outlines, (cont.)
  Outline view of, 85, 91, 94–95
  printing, 91–93
  printing parts of, 93, 238
  reorganizing, 69, 77–78
  repositioning frames in, 101
  saving, 88–91
  symbols for identifying frame types in, 65, 78
Outlining, xii–xiv, 56–104
Output functions, 370–371

Page breaks, forced, 234, 236–238
Page headers and footers in printed
    documents, 221–227, 290–291
  alternating, 240–241
  multi-line, 240, 292
Page offset, 219–220
Parity, 310, 316, 318
Path-extension software and Framework II,
    447
Percent, displaying numbers as, 136
Phone, automatic dialing of, 343–344,
    365–368
Phone directory in Library cabinet, 53–54,
    365–368
Print Control Options submenu, 225,
    234–235, 237
Print Destination submenu, 243–244
Print files, 161, 242–244
Print Format Options submenu, 219–223,
    233–234
Print menu, 24, 45, 91–93, 160–161
Print Output Options submenu, 92–93,
    233–235, 238
Print quality, 223, 232
Print spooling, 92
Printers
  for printing graphics, 28
  installing, 444
  using with Framework II, 27–28
Printer escape sequences
  in documents, 223–224
  in headers or footers, 291
Printing databases, 284, 290–291
  and column width, 285
  filtered 284–285
  using Forms view, 297
Printing documents, 218–228, 232–235
Printing frames, 45
Printing FRED programs and formulas, 93,
    353–354

Printing graphs, 169
Printing outlines, 91
Printing parts of outlines, 93
Printing spreadsheets, 160–161
Printing parts of spreadsheets, 161
Printing templates, stored in Library cabinet,
    52–53
Printing to (disk) file, 161, 242–244
Programming. *See* FRED programming
    language; FRED programs
Programming area behind frame, 14, 16,
    226–228, 271, 291, 352–353, 362, 367,
    423
Programs
  running from Apps menu, 420
  running from desktop, 421
Protect from Editing option, 176
Protocol file transfers, 311–312, 336–338
Put into Column option, 101

RAM disks, 11, 425
RAM-resident software and Framework II,
    419, 447
Recalc (F5) key, 21, 168, 172, 181, 423
  to display Library cabinet, 364
  to execute FRED programs, 353, 388
Recalculation
  manual vs. automatic, 176–177
  of spreadsheet formulas, 126
  order, 182
Records
  as elements of databases, 39, 250
Restoring deleted material, 207
Return key, 19
  and menu options, 22
  and spreadsheets, 117–120, 125
  for opening and closing frames, 20
Reveal Type option, 65, 72, 82–83
Roman numerals, for outline sections,
    101–102
Rows
  adding to databases, 267
  adding to spreadsheets, 114, 146–150
RS-232 interface, 309, 313
RUNDBASE.FW2, 420
Running programs from within Framework II,
    52, 418–419

Save and Continue option, 43–44, 89, 159,
    218, 262, 277

Saving
  files to another drive, 425
  frames, 42–44
  outlines, 88–91
  parts of outlines, 90–91
Scrolling, 69, 116
Searching and replacing text, 210, 212
  as data entry shortcut, 287
  in Database frames, 265–266
Searching for text, 210–211
Secondary sort keys, 265
Selecting several items, 80–81, 97
Selecting text in Word frames, 191, 194–197,
    201–202, 205
Serial communication, 308
Serial port, 308
Setup program, 426–428, 441–449
  Configuration menu, 443
  main menu, 443
Shift-Tab key
  in databases, 256
  in spreadsheets, 117
Shuttle (Scroll Lock) key, 19–20, 42, 52,
    90–91, 235–236, 358
Size (F4) key, 21, 100, 182, 296
  in databases, 251, 256
  in spreadsheets, 135–136, 138
Size All option, 422
Size of frames, changing, 100–102
Smartcom protocol, 310
Soft hyphens, 203
Sorting, 235, 262–264, 292
  by more than one field, 264–265
  in spreadsheets, 184–185
Sorting order, installing, 448
Source, The, 41, 307, 318
Source of telecommunication, 318
Space bar, for editing text values in
    spreadsheets, 127–128
Spelling checking, 214–217
Spreadsheet programming, 2, 33, 47, 106–187
Spreadsheets, 106–187, 230–231
  adding rows and columns to, 146–150
  adding rows or columns to, 114
  calculating values in, 121–125
  changing column width globally in, 139–
    140
  changing column width in, 131, 138, 140
  changing formulas in, 127
  copying formulas in, 140–146, 158–159,
    171, 175

Spreadsheets, (cont.)
  correcting errors in, 34–35, 118
  creating, 33, 110, 112–113
  creating graphs from, 162–163
  editing data in, 127–128
  editing for creating graphs, 164–165
  entering data into, 116, 119–122
  labels in, 107, 112, 118–119, 150
  linking, 110, 178, 180–181, 431–432
  linking with databases, 302–305
  moving cursor within, 115–119
  moving data in, 148–150
  printing, 160–161
  printing parts of, 161
  size and dimensions of, 111–113
  structure of, 34–35
  text data in, 118
Statistical functions, 109, 154, 156–157, 451
Status panel, 8, 13, 16, 60, 193–194
  and filtered databases, 279–280
  and frame labels, 61
  and outline headings, 66–67
  and spreadsheet formulas, 123, 126
Stop bits, 310, 316, 318
String concatenation operator, 390
Styling and numeric value, 132
Styling of numbers
  in databases, 258–259, 270
  in spreadsheets, 132–134, 140
  in spreadsheets, global, 139–140
Styling of text, 38
  in databases, 258
  in spreadsheets, 131, 140, 150
  in spreadsheets, global, 139–140
  in Word frames, 207–208
  in Word frames, global, 209
Subdirectories
  treated as outlines, 103
  viewing contents of, 104
Subroutines in FRED programs, 375, 398
SuperKey, 51

Tab key
  in databases, 256
  in spreadsheets, 117, 119
  in Word frames, 202–203
Table of contents
  creating, 87–88
Telecommunications, 306–347
  as a background function, 41–42
  changing default settings, 330

Telecommunications Answer mode, 340
Telecommunications frames
    creating, 313
    leaving while active, 314
Telecommunications hardware, 307–309
Telecommunications macros, 330–332
Telecommunications Macros submenu, 330
Telecommunications menu, 312, 327
Telecommunications sessions
    conducting, 323–324, 336–340
    ending, 325
    initiating, 321–322
    recording, 325–326, 341
Telecommunications setup files, 328–332,
        334
    installing, 448
Telecommunications Setup Options submenu,
        315–320
Telecommunications Setup submenu, 329,
        333, 344
Templates
    creating, 94–95, 235–236
    for letters and memos, 365
    storing in Library, 235–236
Terminal communications, 311, 336, 338
Terminal emulation, 344–346
Time strings, 401
Transferring files, 311–312
    binary, 336–338, 340
    by direct connection, 346
    protocol, 336–338, 340
    text, 327–328, 339
Trays, 9–10, 20, 61, 82
Typeover option, 206

Underlined text, 208
Undoing a deletion, 44, 74, 207
Up Level (−) key, 19–20, 279
    and outlines, 69
    and spreadsheets, 115
Uploading files, 311, 328, 339
User-defined functions, 369–370, 400–405
    stored in Library cabinet, 53–54

Variables
    global, in FRED programming, 371–372,
        385, 394, 397, 399
    local, in FRED programming, 371–372, 380
View (F10) key, 21, 232, 234
    and databases, 293, 296
    and disk directories, 45

View (F10) key, (cont.)
    and frames, 30–31
    and outlines, 30–31, 85, 91, 94
View Pagination option, 237

Word Count option, 244

Word frames, 38, 84, 232
    adding to databases 296
    copying text in, 209
    correcting errors in, 206
    creating, 38, 190–191
    deleting text from, 207
    editing text in, 206
    entering text in, 191, 193
    inserting new text in, 206
    moving text in, 209
    printing parts of, 238
Word processing, xiv, 37–38, 188–218
Word wrap, in Word frames, 193
Words in a frame, counting, 244, 490
Words menu, 24, 198, 208
    used in spreadsheets, 138
WordStar, 3
    exporting Framework II files to, 414
    importing files from, 412
Write Setup File option, 329, 334

XMODEM protocol, 310, 336–337

Zoom (F9) key, 21, 69, 261–262, 294, 352
    and outlines, 30–31, 84–85
    and spreadsheets, 116
    for frame labels, 99
    for programming, 227–228

are different.

Here is why . . .

At SYBEX, each book is designed with you in mind. Every manuscript is carefully selected and supervised by our editors, who are themselves computer experts. We publish the best authors, whose technical expertise is matched by an ability to write clearly and to communicate effectively. Programs are thoroughly tested for accuracy by our technical staff. Our computerized production department goes to great lengths to make sure that each book is well-designed.

In the pursuit of timeliness, SYBEX has achieved many publishing firsts. SYBEX was among the first to integrate personal computers used by authors and staff into the publishing process. SYBEX was the first to publish books on the CP/M operating system, microprocessor interfacing techniques, word processing, and many more topics.

Expertise in computers and dedication to the highest quality product have made SYBEX a world leader in computer book publishing. Translated into fourteen languages, SYBEX books have helped millions of people around the world to get the most from their computers. We hope we have helped you, too.

For a complete catalog of our publications:

SYBEX, Inc. 2021 Challenger Drive, #100, Alameda, CA 94501
Tel: (415) 523-8233/(800) 227-2346   Telex: 336311